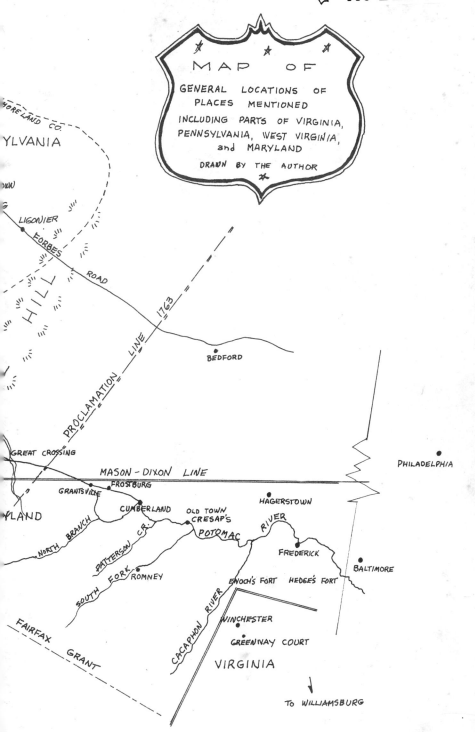

NING

MORELAND CO.

YLVANIA

MAP OF
GENERAL LOCATIONS OF PLACES MENTIONED
INCLUDING PARTS OF VIRGINIA, PENNSYLVANIA, WEST VIRGINIA, and MARYLAND
DRAWN BY THE AUTHOR

LIGONIER

FORBES

HILL

ROAD

PROCLAMATION LINE 1763

BEDFORD

GREAT CROSSING

MASON - DIXON LINE

PHILADELPHIA

FROSTBURG

GRANTSVILLE

YLAND

CUMBERLAND

OLD TOWN
CRESAP'S

HAGERSTOWN

NORTH BRANCH

PATTERSON CR.

POTOMAC RIVER

FREDERICK

BALTIMORE

SOUTH FORK

ROMNEY

ENOCH'S FORT

HEDGE'S FORT

CACAPHON RIVER

WINCHESTER

FAIRFAX

GRANT

GREENWAY COURT

VIRGINIA

TO WILLIAMSBURG

Westward of ye Laurall Hills

1750-1850

During the heat of the Pennsylvania-Virginia boundary dispute, Colonel George Wilson, born in Virginia
but ardently adherent to Pennsylvania, wrote to General Arthur St. Clair on August 4, 1771, about the
"resolves of ye inhabitants to ye westward of ye
laurall hills. . . ."

By Helen Vogt

Illustrated with facsimiles,
author's drawings and photographs

McCLAIN PRINTING COMPANY
PARSONS, WEST VIRGINIA 26287

1976

Standard Book Number 87012-226-6
Library of Congress Card Number 75-21087
Printed in the United States of America
Copyright © 1976 by Helen E. Vogt
Brownsville, Pennsylvania
All Rights Reserved

To

*Nelle Seaman Vogt, my mother, descendant
of pioneer Washington and Greene County
families whose spirit and steadfastness have
burned brightly for nearly one-half of the Bicentennial period (she was born in 1884);*

and

*Harald Philip Vogt, my brother, always equal
to any situation or emergency, including the
Index to this book.*

AUTHOR'S NOTE

PRINCIPAL MATERIAL used has been local primary data, including oral traditions, in the general area of the scope of the book; material either never consulted, forgotten, or not adequately digested or edited.

The form or style intended to be a dialogue between the writer and the reader and the contributor, with an intentional avoidance of footnotes, for this is a book for the general reader rather than the scholar. That is not to say that there has been a lack of scholarly selection and approach to material, or that sources are obscure.

Where material used is of a more modern or contemporary period than 1750-1850 there has usually been a definite link with the early or pioneer period. Also, it is felt that this use of more recent data adds perspective.

In the use of controversial Horn material, the writer has made an earnest attempt based on years of interviews and research, plus the unpublished Leckey-Swainson letters, to validate or refute statements made by Horn. This was a brittle limb on which to venture out, but in the intervening thirty years since publication of *The Horn Papers*, there have been few if any attempts by qualified local historians, based on a solid knowledge of history and tradition, to separate the truth from the fiction.

The main effort has been to present a cultural evaluation and interpretation of many, not all, of the aspects of a region and a period largely neglected by historians outside the general area of Penn's Southwest, west of Laurel Hill. The uniqueness of events, the accomplishments of its citizenry, the impressive roster of local names, its special contributions during the Revolutionary period, and the great natural beauty of the countryside have not been widely recognized. This so-called conversation between today and yesterday combines a retelling of basic history and familiar legends with facts and biographical fragments gathered from hundreds of rare manuscripts and court files, largely unpublished and unknown. The writer recreates the unrecorded history of towns in the migration corridor through which passed and paused the throngs of western-bound settlers, leaving behind stained, torn, wrinkled scraps of paper. The social fabric of the years is woven from these 'found' pieces of paper, carefully saved to 'prove' and to 'tell' their story to us in this Bicentennial year.

Chapter 1, "Getting Started," promises a story of "adventure and the daring approach. . . ." Perhaps the funding and publishing of her own book will turn out to be one of the major "adventures." When, after many years of research and many months of writing and drawing, the time before the Bicentennial year became too short to send the manuscript around to publishers, the writer decided to take the plunge, work with a regional printer and publish her own book. Hewing to the pioneer American tradition of standing on one's own two feet and listening to one's own counsel, without benefit of grants or outside funding, this book goes out with a hope and a prayer that it will be read and believed, and enjoyed, especially by the many who helped along the way.

ACKNOWLEDGMENTS

STAFFS of county offices in Washington, Greene, Fayette, and Westmoreland courthouses; staff of Waynesburg College Library and Miss Lois Westfall; staff of West Virginia University Library and Mrs. Pauline Kissler; staff of Washington and Jefferson College Library; Dr. Raymond M. Bell, retired professor of physics, Washington and Jefferson College; staff of California (Pennsylvania) State College Library; staff of Brownsville Public Library and town residents, J. W. Kisinger, Mrs. Virginia Campbell, Robert Whetzel, and David Gratz; George McMasters Jones of Darlington Memorial Library, University of Pittsburgh; Colonel Edwin MacBeth for loan of rare books from his collection; L. Myers Crayne for personal files; Voy Lacock for family files on Professor J. K. Lacock; and the many others who gave valued assistance in one way or another.

SCHEDULE OF CHAPTERS

1

GETTING STARTED

TO BORROW several phrases from Richard Bissell's *The Monongahela* published in 1952 for the Rivers of America Series:

> It's exciting and awful and dirty and beautiful up the Monongahela. . . .
>
> In order to have a river in your blood . . . you've got to eat it, sleep it, hate it and breathe it until you've got river in your shoe soles and in your pants pockets.

We've been doing just that: Eating, breathing, and sleeping Monongahela until we reached the point where it would flow out on paper as the exciting, awful, dirty, historic, and beautiful river it is and on whose banks we trace the Redstone, Tenmile, and Muddy Creek settlements, and so much early and important activity as traders, settlers, and soldiers followed the Indian warrior paths and pushed westward of Laurel Hill.

In his 1806 *Travels in America* the widely traveled English novelist and writer, Thomas Ashe, Esq. (1770-1835), wrote about the Monongahela and Ohio River valleys:

> . . . here we see the liberal English, the ostentatious Scotch, the warm-hearted Irish, the penurious Dutch, the proud German, the solemn Spaniard, the gaudy Italian, and the profligate French. What kind of character is hereafter to rise from an amalgamation of such discordant material, I am at a loss to conjecture.

* * *

1

The century with which this book is primarily concerned, 1750 to 1850, was one of *adventure* and the daring, hopeful, innovative approach to a new life in a new land and time. It will be "adventurers" who set the pace and the style as we find the term used over and over in historic records.

The merchant venturers of England made history when "gentlemen adventurers" fitted out a ship and all who shipped with it expected the voyages, called "adventures," to include chivalry and honor. In Philadelphia in 1754 when the Gratz brothers began their mercantile activities, an adventure was a business undertaking of special opportunity, outside of regular routine; it might be safe or it might involve great risk; groups of friends joined in adventures. In colonial parlance, the promoter of a settlement on the frontier was an "adventurer." No sharp line could be drawn between speculator and settler.

Frederick County was the truly *western* Maryland in colonial times, but compared with Virginia or Pennsylvania, it was more an area of land speculation and Indian fighting than of occupation and settlement. Maryland rent rolls reveal two conditions which have not always been clearly recognized: First, a considerable number of settlers of the same British nationality and type as on the tidewater took up land and established themselves in the *Maryland west;* second, a fairly large number of Germans became not *leaseholders* as on the Fairfax land, but *owners* of land, sometimes several hundred acres, in the fullest freehold title of the day.

The Maryland *adventurers* who settled the Redstone, Ten-mile, and Muddy Creek settlements, with which we are going to be most concerned, came from these two classes of people, and the Scotch-Irish.

In areas of Virginia which extended into Penn's Southwest and West Virginia, there was a marked bias against the Dutch in favor of English settlers. A county clerk, who was asked if there had been any Germans among the earliest settlers, said:

"This is an entirely English colony." When they looked into the earliest land register dating from 1742, the clerk had to admit that most of the names were German. Many Germans, or "Dutch" as they were commonly called, disowned their nationality and claimed English or Scotch parentage when they entered land, expecting to improve their social recognition. This custom prevailed as late as the 1870s.

* * *

The Six Nations were recognized as the real owners of the land along the upper Ohio, Allegheny and Monongahela rivers. The area between the Allegheny Mountains and the Ohio River was known as the hunting ground and considered the private preserve of the powerful northern Iroquois. Only by their permission were the Delaware and the southern Shawanee allowed to maintain hunting camps. To the Delaware it was a sanctuary as they were driven westward out of their lands. Through this country the "wandering" Indians traveled by well-established paths, according to Paul R. Stewart of Waynesburg College. They followed the streams and picked up all kinds of pebbles which accounts for the tremendous variety in material in their points and some implements. They traveled the Cherokee, the Catawba, the James River, which is now the Kanawha Turnpike, and the Great Warrior Path.

The Delaware Indian, Nemacolin, for whom the path from Wills Creek to the Youghiogheny was named, maintained a hunting camp on the headwaters of Dunlap, then called Nemacolin's Creek. Both Christopher Gist and the Cresaps stayed with him at this camp on their western journeys.

W. F. Horn related a story of a French-Indian, Jacques Poynton, who, according to "French Archives" married an Indian girl from the Monongahela in 1674. One of their sons married a Delaware Indian in 1714 and they were the parents of Nemacolin, who was first taken over the path across the mountains which was to bear his name by his grandfather in

1722. It has not been possible to prove whether there is any truth in the Horn story, but there are at least three other references to Nemacolin's father by name. In his *The Delaware Indians*, published in 1972, C. A. Weslager states Nemacolin is the son of the Brandywine Delaware Chief *Chicochinnican*.

C. Hale Sipe, in his 1927 *The Indian Chiefs of Pennsylvania*, wrote:

> How long Nemacolin resided at Dunlap's Creek is unknown. In 1785 General Richard Butler with Colonel James Munroe made an expedition down the Ohio to treat with the Miamis. In Butler's Journal of the expedition he speaks of an island called "Nemacolin's" between the mouth of Little Kenawha and Hocking, no doubt a subsequent dwelling place of Nemacolin who was the son of a Delaware Chief Chicochinican who dwelt on the Brandywine c. 1716.

In his book published in 1926, *Old Tom Fossit*, John S. Ritenour, using material from the Darlington *Christopher Gist's Journals*, quotes from a speech made by Nemacolin to Gist through an Indian trader named Charles Poke (December 8, 1751):

> My Friend:
>
> You were sent to us last year from the Great Men in Virginia to inform us of a present from the Great King over the water. If you can bring news from the King *to us* why can't you tell him something *from me?*
>
> The Proprietor from Pennsylvania granted my father a tract of land beginning eight miles below the forks of Brandywine Creek. The white people now live on these lands and will not let me have them or pay me anything for them.
>
> My father's name was Chickonnecon. I am his eldest son and my name is Nemicotten. I desire you will let the Governor and great men in Virginia know this. It may be they will tell the King of it and then he will make Mr. Penn or his people give me the land or pay me for it.

Speaking of this speech, Mr. Gist said: "I was obliged to insert this in my journal to please the Indian."

An inquiry as to more biographical data on both Delaware Chiefs Catfish and Nemacolin brought the following statement from National Archives:

Records of the Bureau of Indian Affairs in National Archives were created after 1800. They do not include items from the 18th century. The earliest files of the Bureau relating to an agency for the Delawares dates from 1824; at that time the agency was located in Ohio. There are no items concerning Catfish or Nemacolin.

As Massasoit was to the Plymouth Colony, so Nemacolin, the Delaware chief, was to the Redstone settlement. He was both intelligent and trustworthy and was the principal Indian employed by Gist and Cresap to guide, blaze, and clear the first road.

Some say the earliest trail, cleared sufficiently for the passage of the first settlers who came with their goods, or "house plunder" as they often called household items, was the southern route around the higher elevations of Laurel Hill. This easier trail led through *Wymp's Gap*, a low saddle in the blue range, little known today but easily located about four miles east of Route 857 in Springhill Township, Fayette County, near the West Virginia line.

Traveling northwest to the mouth of Whiteley Creek, the river was crossed into Monongahela and Dunkard townships in southern Greene County where the Eckerlins, conceded to have been the first settlers, were found in 1737 when Gist came through on one of his first trading and scouting journeys. The Gists knew the Eckerlins from having traded with them in Baltimore where they came to market their furs and skins. An early account of Eckerlin activity on the Cheat River:

Brother Gabriel Eckerlin was busy hunting and skinning . . . hides lay in such heaps that we slept on piles which could not have been purchased for one hundred pounds, or more. On one side behind the chimney were hanging so many dead bears that it horrified one to look at them.

Trader George Croghan made this entry in his diary in 1751:

A Dunkard from Virginia came to Logstown and asked leave of the Six Nations to settle on the Youghiogheny—he was Israel Eckerlin.

Neri Hart of Carmichaels in frontier dress kneeling by 1883 stone survey marker on the Mason and Dixon line, Greene County.

A local proponent of the more southern Wymp's Gap route as being earlier than the Nemacolin Path is Neri Hart of Carmichaels on Muddy Creek. A founding member of the Warrior Trail Association and descendant of Colonel William Crawford and many of the pioneer families of Greene County, Hart would have been entirely comfortable stalking game, catching snakes, or identifying edible greenery and herbs with Nemacolin, the Gists, or the Cresaps. Hart rambled over the countryside with Professor Andrew Waychoff and W. F. Horn in the 1930s locating the earliest routes over the mountains, as Wymp's Gap and other landmarks were mentioned in early documents. With so much factual information at hand, one wonders why Mr. Horn had to resort so often to flights of imagination.

* * *

The mainspring which kept the Indian trade in North America in operation during the eighteenth century was the demand for furs and skins in western Europe and to the east in China. The rivalry between Great Britain and France was chiefly due to trade competition. Enormous profits accrued to both countries from the traffic. Skins were a medium of exchange on the frontier for many years and it was not uncommon for estates to list furs among assets. In the estate papers of Indian trader and Ohio Company factor, Hugh Parker, probated in June 1751, his "truly beloved friend, Col. Cresap" as one of the executors, reported the following peltry:

> . . . summer skins, fox, fisher, otter, wolf, elk, bear and cub skins; 7 whole bears, also 3 pints of bear oil.

Indicative of the quality of "early Americana" still to be found in Penn's Southwest is a column by Waynesburg *Republican* feature writer, the legendary John L. O'Hara who, by his own admission and desire, has never been out of Greene County. His columns reprinted in the Washington *Observer* carry a special tang and flavor in both subject matter and treatment:

> Although many generations of trappers as well as the furbearing animals they trapped as a way of making a living have come and gone . . . some of their spiritual descendants still tramp the same streams in search of the same profit-paying pelts which their forbears sought.

> Focal point for much of this "action" which is scattered all over the county [in 1975 major creeks were posted with "No Beaver Hunting Allowed" signs] is at the old-fashioned Trading Post of Donovan Watters, who like his father before him, has been buying furs from Greene County trappers for over forty years.

Waynesburg Fur Trading Post with trapper Donovan Watters buying a pelt from Carl Rutan. Sketch from Waynesburg *Republican* photo.

Most publicized and maybe earliest hunter in southwestern Pennsylvania was Daniel Boone who spent a year or so trapping with the Harrods and others before going to Kentucky.

During the early 1920's and up to the 1929 crash fur trapping was a pretty profitable sideline for almost all farmers; some even trapped full time.

When the fur trade was just a little less important here than it was during the days of the Hudson Bay Company in Canada, New York dealers came to Waynesburg personally and bid competitively against each other for the pelts bought up from individual trappers; these included millionaire dealers such as Dave Brucestein, Charley Beechter, Martin Corenthall and others.

List of pelts as part of land transaction for Lot No. 51 in Washington, sold by John Hoge in 1784. Hoge Papers.

In the "good old days" prime muskrat brought $3-4, top skunk $4-5, good raccoons $10 and $20-25 for best minks. Now most of Greene County's catch of pelts is sold to New York dealers who ship them to European buyers. Prices range [1969] from 75¢ to $1 for muskrat, the most widely trapped animal, $3.50 to $4 for raccoons and the almost decimated skunk sell for only 75¢ and mink bring $10 for males and $5 for females.

* * *

As a result of the eagerness with which land was being sought along the Potomac in Virginia, the boundary of Lord Fairfax's "Northern Neck" grant was of interest very early. Many of the first settlers owned land and lived for a time within the manors of this large grant before emigrating to Penn's Southwest.

Fairfax forced those who had taken up land within the various surveys in his grant to take the property either by lease or purchase. In addition, he charged them with a fixed yearly rental and stipulated that no game was to be killed without his consent. The South Branch and Patterson Creek manors were surveyed with ninety-nine year leases and annual rent of twenty shillings per 100 acres. Those who did not approve of the English custom of no title moved on. The upper manor was reserved by Lord Fairfax for special use. When he died in 1782 his land was confiscated by Virginia and thrown open to settlement.

In the appendix of *Burnaby's Travels* in 1759 is an interesting history of the Fairfax family and their landholdings which figured rather largely in the lives of many who later came into the country west of Laurel Hill.

Thomas, Lord Fairfax, descended from a very ancient family in Yorkshire. Born c. 1691, he was the eldest son of Thomas, fifth Lord Fairfax of Cameron, and Catherine, only daughter and heiress of Lord Culpepper, from whom Thomas inherited the Northern Neck properties. Thomas lost his father when he was quite young and he and his brothers, Henry and Robert and their four sisters, came under the guardianship of their mother, Lady Fairfax and her mother, Lady Culpepper.

After some years, Thomas was placed in the position of having to sell Denton Hall and other ancestral Yorkshire estates of the Fairfax family which had been in their name for nearly six centuries, in order to redeem the deeply mortgaged Northern Neck lands of the late Lord Culpepper.

It later appeared that the estates had been disposed of for much less than their value through the treachery of a steward; for less even than the value of the timber which had been cut to discharge payments on the land. Thomas was very disgusted with the manner in which both his Mother and Grandmother had handled the affair and the cruelty they had both exhibited toward him; he never forgave them for what he considered was a grave injury to the Fairfax family.

After Thomas came into possession of the Virginia land, he began to inquire into the location and the value of the property. He

Greenway Court, from a painting of the original home of Thomas, Lord Fairfax in Clarke County, Virginia; erected ca. 1749 in the Northern Neck near Winchester. This old manor house replaced ca. 1830 by present brick structure. From a special collection at West Virginia University Library, Morgantown, West Virginia.

soon discovered it had been mismanaged and leased at too low a figure. He wrote to his cousin, William Fairfax who was in New England and asked him to go to Virginia and take the agency of managing the Northern Neck lands. William moved his family to Virginia and opened an office to grant land and collect quit rents which soon provided considerable income, although the rate was only two shillings for every 100 acres.

Thomas then decided to go to Virginia and visit his estates and left England in 1739. He spent the next year with his cousin in Westmoreland County, Virginia and liked it so well he returned to England to settle his affairs there so that he could permanently reside in Virginia.

In 1745 he returned to America and both he and William moved to Belvoir in Fairfax County. Several years later he decided to undertake the management of his own land and moved to a fine tract on the western slope of the Blue Ridge in Frederick (later Clarke County), where he built the small, neat house "Greenway Court" shown in the sketch made from a painting. This building stood until about 1830.

At Greenway Court Lord Fairfax lived the life of an English country gentleman, with many servants, both white and black, several hunters, a plentiful but plain table, and his mansion was one of hospitality . . . he dressed very plainly, was liberal almost to excess . . . distributed the produce above his own needs to poor planters and settlers in the neighborhood and frequently advanced money to help them clear land, etc.

He presided at the county courts held at Winchester, acted as surveyor and overseer of the highways and public roads. His sole amusement was hunting and he frequently took his hounds to distant parts of the country and entertained every gentleman of good character and decent appearance who attended him in the field, at the inn or where he took up residence for the hunting season.

In 1751 his sister's son, Thomas came to live with him. He died, a bachelor, in the first months of 1782 at the age of 92 and is supposedly buried at Winchester.

Shortly after Braddock's defeat in 1755 when Indian massacres were occuring in all the back settlements and his own life was threatened, Fairfax said to his nephew, Colonel Martin of the Virginia militia: "The danger we are exposed to which is undoubtedly great, may possibly excite in your mind apprehension and anxiety. If so, I am ready to take any step you may judge expedient for our common safety.

"I myself am an old man and it is of little importance whether I fall by the tomahawk of an Indian or by disease and old age, but you are young and it is hoped, may have many years before you. I will therefore, submit to your decision as to whether we shall remain and take every precaution, or abandon our habitations and retire within the mountains, sheltered from danger. . . . If we retire, the whole district will immediately break up and all the trouble and solicitude which I have undergone to settle this fine country will be frustrated and perhaps irrecoverably lost."

Lord Fairfax and his nephew remained, like the seasoned frontiersmen they had become. History has not been too kind to the memory of this man who may have had Tory leanings at some period of his life in America, but who, from the above statement, sounds like a patriot of the first order.

Fairfax petitioned the king to order a commission to run the boundaries of his land and the survey conducted in 1736-37 was notable for the first recorded marking of trees in the virgin wilderness blazed as boundary markers, or "line trees" as we know them today. A few such trees still stand in Pennsylvania fence lines.

A map of the survey was published, but there was still a doubt as to which was farther west, the headsprings of the North or the South Branch of the Potomac. In the fall of 1746, Thomas Lewis, first Augusta County surveyor, made an official survey with a party which included the very young George Washington. When the actual headsprings of the Potomac were located on the North Fork of the South Branch, the Fairfax Stone was planted. The 1957 replacement of the original marker reads:

FAIRFAX STONE   This monument at the headspring of the Potomac River, marks one of the historic spots of America. Its name is derived from Thomas Lord Fairfax who owned all the land lying between the Potomac and Rappahannock Rivers. The first Fairfax Stone marked "FX," was set in 1746 by Thomas Lewis, a surveyor employed by Lord Fairfax. This is the base point for the western dividing line between Maryland and West Virginia.

The wording of the early Fairfax deeds is both quaint and colorful. One of the earliest Romney, West Virginia, deeds concerns the Van Metre family who later migrated to the Tenmile settlement:

Indenture September 8, 1761 . . . Thomas Parsons, Executor of the Will of Daniel Richardson to Henry VanMetre of the South Branch of Potowmack, Parish and County of Hampshire, Virginia . . . in 1756 Fairfax by his deed granted land in Frederick County on Millbrook Creek, Manor of Wappacomo (South Branch) on the South Fork in the David Vance Survey . . . 465 acres for 5 shillings and rent of one ear of Indian corn to be paid on Christmas Day. . . .

A few years later, the ear of corn was still a part of the transaction but it was called "pepper corn."

In 1937 a little history prepared by the West Virginia Federal Writers' Project was published to commemorate the 175th anniversary of *Historic Romney, 1762-1937,* from which we quote:

> The history of Romney is the history of Hampshire County and the South Branch Valley. It dates back more than two centuries to 1725 when the first explorers, Indian traders and hunters traversed the area. It was their glowing reports . . . that encouraged the Cobin, Howard, Walker, Rutledge and Forman families to settle . . . before 1735.
>
> Besides being unclaimed by the Indians and off the direct path of the warrior tribes on the Ohio, the territory offered many natural advantages . . . by 1748 nearly 200 persons had moved into the area known as Pearsall's Flats.
>
> Reports of the advancing settlements soon reached Thomas Fairfax at Greenway Court, 46 miles away and recognizing an opportunity to recoup his depleted fortune and build a perpetual income, he began at once to arrange for laying off the lands into manors and lots.

The map in this history was drawn in 1790 with the "in" lots numbered identically with those on a map prepared in 1762 for Lord Fairfax. The early owners of the lots are copied here:

1. and 2. Greitzner
3. and 4. Maloney
5. and 6. Endler
7. and 8. Tabb
9. Fisher
10. and 11. Fowler
12. Fisher
13. and 14. Tabb
15. Gilkeson
16. Endler
17. Greitzner
18. Combs
19. Perry
20. Mullady
21. Fisher
22. Marshall
23. and 24. Methodist Parsonage
25. Snyder
26. Davis
27. Allen
28. Ridenour
29. and 30. Wendle
31. A. White
32. Marshall
33. Kuykendall
34. Presbyterian Church
35. Tabb
36. Taylor
37. Virginia House
38. Parker

39. and 40. Friddle
41. and 42. Marshall
43. C. Taylor
44. Mytinger
45. Myers Heirs
46. Snyder
47. Wendle
48. Mytinger [restored]
49. and 50. Barker
51. Friddle
52. Colored Church
53. Charles Taylor
54. Wirgman
55. Parrish
56. Literary Hall
57. George Brown
58. J. Sheets
59. Church lot
60. [obliterated]
61. and 62. Armstrong
63. C. Poling
64. White
65. Jail
66. Court House
67. Mullady
68. Harper

69. Lambert
70. [obliterated]
71. Busby
72. A. McDonald
73. Snyder
74. Armstrong
75. Brady
76. Wirgman
77. and 78. Heiskell
79. Pugh Heirs
80. Kercheval
81. and 82. Armstrong
83. A. Monroe
84. [obliterated]
85. and 86. Keller
87. Gilkeson
88. Wirgman
89. Mayhew
90. School House
91. and 92. Armstrong
93. A. Monroe
94. Parks
95. and 96. Mytinger
97. Kern
98. Smith
99. and 100. Jacob

It is of further interest to know that until 1932 on a corner of Lot No. 48 stood the old log house in which George Washington spent the night of October 9, 1770, on his last recorded visit to Romney.

The Fairfax land was sold on a lease and re-lease basis and for each transfer of land there were always two transactions: the first for five shillings whereby the land was sold and transferred, and the second for the actual amount of sale which was variable, but most often for fifty pounds which covered a release and this was signed by both husband and wife, whereas the five-shilling transactions were usually signed by the husband only. Legal ramifications concerning this land filled the courts for many years.

* * *

Historically neglected for a long period was the fact that from 1748 to 1776 no other group of men so influenced the history of the west as did those of the Ohio Company, headquartered at Williamsburg. Nearly all of the important Ohio Valley Indian traders from Pennsylvania, Maryland, and Virginia, worked for the company, and the region around the forks of the Ohio was the focal point of the westward movement.

The situation of land speculation and land grants in eighteenth-century America has been oversimplified to make it appear that huge tracts were doled out to royal favorites, colonial cliques, and scheming individuals. Of course, some were, and men in high places did spend many of their waking hours devising ways and means of acquiring staggering amounts of land for virtually no cash outlay. The common denominator was greed—vast profit at little risk. Local collections of courthouse and private papers clearly indicate the feverish pitch of land speculation.

However, the drive for western lands also involved vision, sacrifice, and determination. The anguish of litigation, clear titles, and double-dealing in the legislatures were the lot of most. In some of the communications between Britain and Virginia it was hinted that western land would require more than just walking over it to substantiate claims; settlement was the key factor.

The Ohio Company served as an intermediate step between the old proprietary rights in Pennsylvania, the king's rights in the crown colony of Virginia, and the new, more speculative right of the settler or individual landowner. It was the first important company organized in America for the purpose of *settlement* west of the Allegheny Mountains. Many companies had received grants, but their purposes were primarily speculative and not to stop the French and secure British authority or to stimulate settlement by land-hungry frontiersmen.

The first tract of 200,000 acres was granted to the Ohio Company in June 1749 and plans went forward immediately to survey, lay out roads, and build storehouses and forts. The bold Thomas Cresap and Hugh Parker had been assigned to make the first survey, but there were interferences in the fall of 1748 and the survey was not made. As one of the original partners in the Ohio Company, Thomas Cresap was also one of our first lobbyists. He was paid twelve pounds, five shillings for his services in presenting the case of the company in Williamsburg.

An extract from the will of Eli Flint, probated in 1805 in Greene County, makes a rare mention of the "Ohio Company purches" where his land was located but for which no deed had apparently been issued.

Item I do Will and bequeath all my Estate both Real and personal unto my Beloved Wife Mary Flint As Consaning the Sevrl Lots of Land leaving in the _Ohio Company purches_ Belonging to Mc I mpour My My Wife to Make Seat as Soon as Convenintcy Will admit and Execute a lofull Deet to the purchesers a Cond in to Law

Item My will is that My Son William and My Dauter Minerva be Given Scooling as far as Convence Will admit of

Item My Will is that William May Chuse to Go to a Treade at the year of Sixteen if He Sees proper

September 11, 1750, a committee of the new Ohio Company made an agreement with Christopher Gist, retired and living on his farm on the Yadkin River. Gist's instructions are well known, but very much a part of this story:

... for the greater Encouragement of the first Setlers upon the Company's Lands ... You are to go out as soon as possible to the westward of the Great Mountains ... when you find a large quantity of good level land such as you think will suit the Company, fix the boundaries of it in such a manner as they may be easily found again. The nearest the land lies the better but we had rather go down the Mississippi than take mean, broken land ... when you discover a large body of good level land you are not to stop but proceed further as low as the source of the Ohio. ...

Gist's reports back to the company are delightful reading:

... near Pickaway wild ry, blue grass and white clover—delightful country ... invited to a long house of the Twightees—held a warrior feather dance, swan feathers and others woven in the shape of a fowl's wing made like the flutter of birds ... the Indians asked for a smith to settle in their town to mend their guns ... horses wore bells. Near the Falls of the Ohio found a place where the stones shone like high-coloured brass ... arms of Indians are painted on trees at their encampments.

There were few derogatory remarks directed at Gist compared with those circulated about Thomas Cresap. The two men must have complemented each other and worked well together as their names are often linked. On July 16, 1751, the company issued further instructions to Gist for a second journey:

... as soon as you can conveniently, you are to apply to Col. Cresap for such of the Company's horses as you shall want for the use of yourself and such other person or persons you shall think necessary to carry with you. ...

The Ohio Company was so anxious to begin their trading and land "adventure" that they deliberately violated a ruling of the crown by issuing secret instructions in April 1752 when Christopher Gist was commissioned as agent for the company to treat directly with the Indians at Logstown on May 16, and make arrangements for settlement and trade:

You are to apply to Col. Cresap for what wampum you have occasion of and also apply to him for a horse on which to ride out to Logstown.

Gist was prepared to make a purchase of land if the proper agreement could not be reached in behalf of Virginia. Both the Pennsylvania traders and the French had been discrediting the Virginians up to this point and the sumptuous gifts distributed by Gist and his interpreter, Andrew Montour, at the signing of the treaty, were given in a gesture to regain Indian friendship.

To balance the scouting trips of Gist for Virginia, Pennsylvania sent Lewis Evans out on a "secret exploring expedition" in 1750 (map issued in 1755):

> ... get informed of the stock and scheme of the Virginia Company, trading to Ohio and what disadvantages, or advantages they labour under. ...

From the earliest times, there existed this competitive, almost petulant atmosphere of suspicion between the commonwealth and the colony. More aggressive than Pennsylvania, Virginia wished to establish a trading monopoly with the Indians until they could be persuaded to move on and then the lands would be taken over and sold in parcels to settlers.

Thomas Cresap was not one to lurk in the background or stay out of the action for long. As early as 1746 the Virginian, Thomas Bladen, realized something was afoot and had written:

> Mr. Cressap's schemes or views are quite unknown to me but I believe it possible he may have his own interest chiefly at heart; he shall have no encouragement from me to do any unfair or unreasonable thing.

Thomas Lee had spent twenty years on the western frontier before he became active in the organization of the Ohio Company in 1747-48. He had been Lord Fairfax's resident manager and had tried to stimulate land settlement by colonizing Pennsylvania Germans in the valley of the upper Potomac. He too was suspicious of Cresap:

> I am concerned with Col. Cresap in a Company to settle by grants from the King on some parts of Ohio with the consent of the Indians. . . .

On July 20, 1748, Richard Peters, secretary of the Pennsylvania Executive Council, had written to Thomas Penn:

> That vile fellow Crisop has proposed a scheme to Colonel Lee and some of the other Great Men of Virginia. I believe Colonel Lee has engaged Crisop to go out . . . Lee has a plotting head. . . .

No one seemed to be quite sure who had started the Ohio Company "scheme" as they expressed it, but there was much speculation.

George Washington's half brother, Lawrence, one of the prime backers of the company, in a May 1749 letter had described the lands on the Ohio and its numerous branches in somewhat the same terms as Gist:

> . . . described by all of the traders as vastly rich and the banks of the River expose coals. There are many large plains clear of trees and covered with white clover. The skin trade is very profitable.

> The scheme of the Ohio Company will help the traders who have found it impossible to send clear to Philadelphia for their goods. The Company proposes to keep a large quantity of goods at the joining of the Ohio and the Monongahela in a fortified store, which are to be sold to the Indians or traders at a moderate advance and can during any season of the year, be easily procured by the Out Traders who follow the Indians many hundreds of miles during the hunting season.

> The traders can be supplied from the Head of Potomac more easily than anywhere . . . the further we can extend our frontiers the safer Virginia will be from the Indians as the mountains do not secure us. It can never be better timed than now when the Indians are our friends. They deem those the honestest who sell the cheapest. The French can not supply the Indians in this way as the navigation up the St. Lawrence is very dangerous, with land portage also.

The traders took journeys twice a year or more to the Indian villages, taking their trade goods; they lived with the Indians, often taking a squaw, and chiefly because they sold rum and liquor to the Indians, were generally regarded as an unsavory lot. Among the better class of traders were John Fraser, who made and repaired guns at his cabin-camp at Turtle Creek; the notable Irishman, George Croghan; the speculator, William Trent; Alexander Lowry of the trading family; and the Gratz brothers.

In June 1749 the governor general of Canada dispatched 250 men under Captain Céloron de Blainville in canoes to bury lead plates (11 x 7 x 1/8 inches with lettering punched into the lead) proclaiming French title in the name of Louis XV, at the most important "rivieres" flowing into the Ohio. Céloron's map of 1750 shows the locations of the buried plates.

This act caused great uneasiness among the Indian chiefs who did not understand what the French had set forth in the inscriptions they could not read. They dug one up and sent it to Governor Clinton of New York; being an opportunist, Clinton sent the plate to the Lords of Trade in London, told the Indians that it was a very grave matter and that the French should be expelled.

In 1974, a 3,000-acre Roaring Run Natural Area along the west slope of Laurel Hill was dedicated. The ceremony included a lead plate dedicating the land to the people of Pennsylvania. Later the plate was buried along Roaring Run "in the tradition of the French explorers who once planted similar plates along western Pennsylvania streams to claim the land for France."

The park area dedicated is now forested with trees ranging to a foot or more in diameter but it is planned that the westward facing slopes will be covered once again with gigantic oaks rearing 70 to 100 feet in the air. On the northward slopes will be giant sugar maples, basswoods, oaks, yellow poplars, and hornbeams. In the bottomlands will tower huge walnuts with a scattering of white pine and hemlock. As of old, the forest will be open and cathedral-like with a dense, leafy canopy to shade out the underbrush. This is one of the beautiful qualities of eastern hardwood forests compared to the dense undergrowth usually found in western evergreen forests. Loggers will be forever barred from the area although it is supposed that some cutting will be necessary to properly maintain the life of the forest as trees ripen.

* * *

When the government at Williamsburg proposed sending someone out to check reports of French activity, young Major George Washington packed his surveyor's theodolite (an instrument used to measure both horizontal and vertical angles for a more accurate survey than with a compass, especially on hilly ground) and plumb line and went to Williamsburg to volunteer for the mission. He was accepted and in November 1753 set out to see the French Commandant Saint Pierre at Fort LeBoeuf, now Waterford, Pennsylvania.

Washington engaged his old fencing master, Jacob van Braam, purchased horses and tents at Winchester and pushed over the mountains to Wills Creek. There he engaged Christopher Gist as pilot, John Davidson as Indian interpreter, and four frontiersmen, Barney Currin, John McGuire, Henry Stewart, and William Jenkins. On November 15 they headed their horses west in miserable, chill weather. It was about seventy miles to Gist's new settlement at "Monongahela" and in his report, Washington remarked that they only saw one family settled there, but on the return trip they saw several going out. Locations of all of the encampments on the route to LeBoeuf taken by Washington on his first journey to the Ohio Country are described in the May 25, 1932, issue of the Connellsville *Daily Courier*.

The trip was completed and on his return to the Virginia capital, Washington found that the people in government there considered his report so important in its disclosures that they wished it to be made public. He only had one day in which to transcribe a presentable statement from his rough field notes made while traveling. Williamsburg printer William Hunter published the slim volume entitled: *The Journal* of *George Washington to the Commandant of the French Forces on Ohio.* . . . Restored Williamsburg has reprinted this 1753 journal in its original form.

It had now been discovered that the French intended to hold the head of the Ohio and the territory west and north under the alleged discovery of LaSalle eighty years earlier. While the French had been first in the area (they had settled in Canada in 1603), they were never interested in or able to make settlements.

Realizing matters were rapidly coming to a head, Britain sent General Braddock in 1755 and as we know, not until the arrival in 1758 of General John Forbes, did French Fort Duquesne become the British Fort Pitt. This was followed by what the Virginia historian Samuel Kercheval in 1850 called "The War of 1763" by which the Treaty of Paris ceded French possessions to Britain after the fall of Quebec.

* * *

Another name of importance in these years of "getting started" and the activities of the Ohio Company was that of George Mercer. Lois Mulkearn's monumental work, *The George Mercer Papers*, published in 1954 by the University of Pittsburgh Press is *must* reading for detail of this period.

Just out of William and Mary College in Williamsburg in 1753, George Mercer was greatly interested in architecture and surveying. He did not stay in colonial seaboard Virginia, but turned to the west where he engaged in surveying and soldiering; he was not officially appointed a surveyor by his college until December 1759.

The committee of the Ohio Company which met at the Mercer family home, Marlborough, on the Potomac February 6, 1753, issued instructions to Christopher Gist to be delivered to him by young George Mercer:

> ... if Col⁰ Cresap has not agreed with any person to clear a Road for the Company, You are, with the advice and assistance of Col⁰ Cresap to agree with the proper Indians who are best acquainted with the ways, Immediately to cut a Road from Wills Creek to the Fork of Mohangaly at the cheapest Rate you can for Goods, and this you may mention publickly to the Indians at Loggs Town or not as you can see Occasion. ...

Like his friend and neighbor, George Washington, Mercer rode on his first recorded trip to the trans-Allegheny west and its problems which dominated both his and Washington's lives for the next decade, and longer. The 1958 volume of Alfred Procter James and Charles Morse Stotz, *Drums in the Forest*, mentions an unpublished biography of George Mercer which described him as a "frustrated Virginia aristocrat."

He enlisted in the First Virginia Regiment the following year under surveyor and map-maker Colonel Joshua Fry and supervised work on the road to Redstone at intervals from May 1754 to August 1758. The route to be followed was so poorly defined that only Gist, Nemacolin, and a few hardy traders were able to follow it. Near Cumberland on the way out, Colonel Fry was thrown from his horse and so seriously injured that he died and was buried under a large oak near the Wills Creek storehouse on May 31.

George Washington, now in command, advanced from Fort Necessity on June 16, 1754, and George Mercer's company marched down Laurel Hill to the Gist plantation where the Indian Conference was held on June 19. The mouth of Redstone Creek was the immediate and primary objective of Washington and road work began on the twenty-seventh with a few officers, a drummer, and about sixty men under Captain Andrew Lewis, Virginia surveyor and frontiersman, who cleared to within three or four miles of Redstone Creek.

Captain Mercer commanded a company of fifty carpenters who acted as axemen.

George Mercer became paymaster, quartermaster and commissary. He had the responsibility of keeping the Braddock Road open from Winchester to the Monongahela Valley, a feature of which was to provide supplies for Colonel James Burd in his construction of the road in 1759 to the mouth of Redstone Creek. It was Lewis, Washington, and Mercer who started to make the Burd or Redstone Path a real road in 1754.

Gordon Donaldson in his 1973 *Battle for a Continent* paraphrased the remark of a number of earlier historians concerning the confrontation of the French and British forces at Jumonville:

This valley in the backwoods of America set the world on fire.

2

THE BUSINESS OF ACQUIRING LAND
AND SURVEYING

ON OCTOBER 17, 1681, William Penn constituted his
friend, Charles Ashcom, one of two assistants to the surveyor
general, to measure, divide, and lay out:

> . . . such shares and proportions of land as are bought or taken up
> of me by diverse *adventurers.*

The kings of England paid their debts to wealthy subjects
by grants of land in America; they also had a habit of founding new colonies within the boundaries of those already char-
tered and established. If Virginia, Connecticut, and Maryland,
to say nothing of Delaware, all founded before Pennsylvania,
had succeeded in maintaining their claims to lands they believed were within their charter limits, there would have been
very little left for Penn's Woods.

That Pennsylvania emerged as large as it did was a com-
mentary upon the colony's pugnacity, luck, and leadership.

The Pennsylvania Historical Association has commented:

> Perhaps no political entity in the Western Hemisphere has had
> such a complex, lengthy and fascinating history of boundaries as
> Pennsylvania.

In order to support her claim to that portion of southwestern Pennsylvania where many Virginia settlers had taken up
land, by a "strange and absurd construction of her charter,"
Virginia claimed a large part of Maryland along with three-

fourths of Pennsylvania. In 1609 a new charter was obtained for the colony which included all that part of America from Point Comfort two hundred miles north and two hundred miles south along the coast, and from sea to sea west and northwest.

As far as Maryland was concerned, Lord Baltimore's grant of June 20, 1632, also claimed land on the west side of the Delaware River. There were many controversies with the Pennsylvania proprietaries due chiefly to a general faulty knowledge of geography, and the common boundary was not really settled for one hundred thirty years.

* * *

On the general subject of land acquisition and surveys, a fine volume was published in 1887 by the chief justice of Pennsylvania, the Honorable Daniel Agnew, LL.D. The title is: *A History of the Region of Pennsylvania North of the Ohio and West of the Allegheny River: of the Indian Purchases, and of the Running of the Southern, Northern and Western State Boundaries and an Account of the Division of the Territory for the Public Purposes and of the Lands, Laws, Titles, Settlements, Controversies and Litigation within this Region.* A few quotes from this volume are pertinent to the area of this book:

> The legislation peculiar to the region [described in the Agnew title] was unfortunate, and gave rise to contests which retarded improvement and rendered titles uncertain for many years.

> It was my fortune to begin practice when lapse of time and the State of Limitations began to urge a final settlement of the disputes between the "warrantees" and the "settlers."

> In 1829 I read the second volume of Charles Smith's edition of "Laws of Pennsylvania" containing his exhaustive note (156 pages) on the Land Laws. Thus began my large practice in land titles. The number and variety of the original titles and their ramifications are so great they must be historically considered to understand them.

* * *

In the Northern Neck confusing and fluctuating ownership clouded land titles to such an extent that there was literally no legal way in which the first settlers could have gained title to their lands. A restless spirit was noted in the 1750s as a large segment of settlers chafed under the system of quitrents and insecure titles.

When the Fairfax claim was approved to be laid off in manors in March 1748, a survey crew, composed of the first Hampshire County certified surveyor, James Genn, with George Fairfax, George Washington, Henry Ashby, and Robert Taylor as chainmen, and William Lindsey as pilot, set out from the Land Office at Greenway Court near Winchester. The lower manor as laid out was granted to individuals among whom were Solomon Hedges and Henry Van Meter whose descendants settled in southwestern Pennsylvania.

The early Fairfax survey had no established triangulation stations, such as were so meticulously set up by Charles Mason and Jeremiah Dixon during their 1763-68 survey of the famous Mason and Dixon's line. However, it stands as a tribute to the courage, skill, and determination of the men of the Fairfax survey party who came within nine angular minutes of the results obtained by feeding the same data into a modern computer.

The Pennsylvania method of granting land was supposed to be superior to that followed in other colonies. In 1767 John Penn wrote from Philadelphia, describing *quitrents* in particular:

> Respecting the manner of imposing quit rents and granting lands in the colony, I beg leave to acquaint you with the fact that the Proprietary Quit-Rents are created by way of "reservation" in the grants of land to settlers and they are levied by way of distress (legal seizure) according to the laws of England. If there be no distress, an action of debt lies against the grantee of the land for the quit rents.

> In many parts of the province these rents on old grants were so trifling that they have been a good deal disregarded and scarcely thought worth the trouble and expense of collection and have

remained so long unpaid that the old rent rolls are in much disorder. There have been about 7,000 grants since 1700 and before that time there is no regular account of grants by patent. The usual mode before that time was by Lease and Release of unlocated quantities to be afterward surveyed. These deeds were not always recorded.

There was great excitement and confusion in the period just prior to the actual founding of the Ohio Company and the surveying of relatively small grants for settlement. The Indian traders, the hunters, and scouts who had been over the mountains and down Laurel Hill to the valley of the Monongahela, brought back stories of magnificent country abounding with timber, rich soil, myriad waterways, game, and fish.

Some of the first settlers took land "on examination" and often when they actually saw the land and compared it with what Mr. Gist and others had described after the early Ohio Company surveys, they "suffered their original grants to expire" and moved farther west. Many places were described but nothing was accurately located.

Surveyors followed quickly on the heels of the Indians and the traders. There were few who were qualified to run a complete survey but there were many neighbors and friends who worked with the certified surveyors as axemen, chain carriers, etc., in running lines; their names are often noted on survey draughts. The country was opened to the conflicting claims of innumerable "locators," who often worked counter to the certified surveyors.

Four years were allowed for a survey on the first Ohio Company lands and they were firm about wanting no *private adventurers* to go into these *choice* lands. They were first held by Col. Thomas Cresap, Lawrence, Augustine and George Washington, George Fairfax, and others. It was these great, propertied men who later stood with the *west* against the Crown.

* * *

Governor Fauquier of Virginia anticipated the king's action when he wrote to Colonel Henry Bouquet in March 1762:

> You may be assured that I shall give a certificate in writing to anyone who has a right by patent to any lands under consideration and shall not fail to inform you and his Majesty's Commander in Chief of my having done so. The persons who can make any Right appear will be found to claim lands a great deal to the southward of Fort Pitt, *it having never been ascertained whether the lands about that fort are in this Colony or in Pennsylvania,* though I imagine the instruction to all Governors from the King will adjust these affairs by absolute prohibition of all future settlements on lands not regularly ceded to the King's subjects by the Indians *which is to be by Treaty and not by private purchase.*

Henry Bouquet, Colonel of Foot and commanding at Fort Pitt, immediately after the Royal Proclamation of 1763, sent out this warning:

> I strictly forbid anyone settling out of sight of the Fort [Burd at Redstone] and no one is to hunt there. The Indians have only consented to our making a few settlements at Redstone Creek and nowhere else upon the Monongahela.... You may tell the people who have my leave to settle at Redstone that no-one is to plant corn or anything more than two miles from Fort Burd and no hunting anywhere along the Monongahela... they can buy wild meat from the Indians.

It was a matter of record that "for two years past these lands have been over-run by a number of *vagabonds* who, under pretense of hunting, make settlements."

George Washington had other ideas on the subject and made this comment in 1763:

> Any person therefore, who neglects the present *opportunity* of hunting out good lands and in some measure marking and distinguishing them for his own in order to keep others from settling them, will never regain it.

He said further that he had never looked upon the proclamation in any other light except as a *temporary* expedient to quiet the minds of the Indians until they gave their consent to occupation of their lands. But he was cautious when he wrote on the subject to his friend, Surveyor William Crawford, commissioned by William and Mary College to be a surveyor September 1773:

> I recommend that you keep this whole matter a secret . . . because I might be censored for the opinion I have given in respect to the King's proclamation . . . all this may be avoided by a silent management and the operation carried on under the guise of hunting game . . . at the same time you are in pursuit of land—I will have the lands immediately surveyed to keep others off.

The act of April 1784 confirmed the boundaries between Pennsylvania and Virginia, recognized private rights established under Virginia, and made good certain titles derived from Virginia to land within Pennsylvania. There was an Ohio Company ruling that made it necessary for Pennsylvanians to establish residence in Virginia for one year before they could get titles to their lands. Another confusing element was that some titles to land in Pennsylvania had been granted for military service to Virginia, such as officers under the 1763 royal proclamation. Previous to ratification of the boundary line, the Virginia Assembly, by law, directed commissioned officers to grant actual settlement certificates on a right to 400 acres including the settlement, and many of the titles to land in the southwestern part of Pennsylvania were taken under that law.

* * *

Following the activities of the Ohio Company of Virginia, many different land companies were organized. As early as June 1769, the Pennsylvania group around Thomas Walpole sent a petition to London asking for territory once settled by the Ohio Company. This group used many different names: the Suffering Traders (who had had their trade goods confiscated in 1763), the Walpole Company, the Indiana Company, the Vandalia, and Grand Ohio companies. Thoroughly frustrated by May of 1770, George Mercer came to terms with the Grand Ohio Company and surrendered to it the old Ohio Company claims.

In the summer of 1776 it was felt that the merchants in the Vandalia group were behind the plan to create a separate state to be called *Westsylvania.* Historian Howard L. Leckey found the signatures of some 2,000 persons who lived in Penn's Southwest who had signed these widely circulated petitions from 1776 to 1780. The petitions stated that since about 1768, 25,000 families had settled in the disputed area. The signers who lived in the area between the mountains and the Ohio, using the Indian boundary of 1768, were tired of the conflicting claims of Virginia and Pennsylvania, of the Croghan claims by private purchase, and those of the Indiana and Vandalia companies. The Revolutionary War ended the dispute and also the need for a new fourteenth state as Pennsylvania very shortly began to subdivide the large county of Westmoreland, setting off Washington County in 1781, Fayette in 1783, and Greene in 1796.

Freeman H. Hart makes the following statement in his *Valley of Virginia in the American Revolution:*

> One of the great ironies of the Allegheny area is that most of the land which had been won at such painful cost from the British and the Indians should fall into the clutches of speculators who had never set foot in the mountains.

It has not been possible to find out whether the great figure of the Revolutionary period, Robert Morris, was ever in Penn's Southwest, but there is a deed executed by him and his wife, Mary, recorded in Washington County by Recorder Samuel Clarke in 1795 which does not state it was signed in Philadelphia. Morris owned hundreds of separate tracts of land in the general area of southwestern Pennsylvania, many of them in Greene County. His involvement with the North American Land Company led to his financial ruin. There was a sheriff's sale in Allegheny County August 13, 1798, of the Robert Morris and John Nicholson land and it sold at very low figures, from seven to eleven *pence* per acre. In 1806 a James Everhart wrote from Lancaster by the "Great Western

Mail" that all of the business of the North American Land Company was now in his hands.

Washington and Jefferson College in Washington received a large box of the private and public papers of John Hoge in September 1968 from a descendant, Edward S. Claflin II. In response to the writer's query about the papers, Mr. Claflin wrote:

> I was so glad to learn that you were using the Hoge papers in your research. As I glanced over them in the process of clearing out the attic of my grandfather, John M. Henderson's home in East Cleveland, they seemed to my unhistorical eye to be of rather slight interest and I was tempted to consign them, with their accumulation of Cleveland grime and soot, to the flames.

> John Hoge was my great-grandmother's step-father; Ann Quail married first, John Moreland and second, John Hoge. The daughter of Ann Moreland Hoge married James Henderson a physician who came to Ohio c. 1830, as did quite a number of other western Pennsylvanians. It was his only son, John who built the "big

Robert and Mary Morris 1795 deed recorded in Washington and Greene counties. Washington County Courthouse.

house" in East Cleveland. I don't know why the papers ended up there instead of in the hands of a descendant of John Hoge. I believe Ann Hoge lived with James Henderson after John's death and this may partly account for it.

The Henderson and Quail cousins in and around Little Washington were great "savers" and seldom threw anything away, least of all, family letters and papers.

Most of the Hoge Papers were in bundles tied with linen tow thread, some were wrapped in newspapers dated 1818-34 and all appeared to have been undisturbed since shortly after the death of Hoge in 1824.

The correspondence and documents of the North American Land Company as found in the Hoge Papers shed light on activities of this company which had hitherto been largely unknown. Like the Pennsylvania Population Company, the North American Land Company issued warrants in many names to escape the Land Office ruling whereby they would issue only one warrant to one person. These persons later made the legal title over to the various companies by "deed poll," the same legal device employed by local sheriffs when taking land by reason of court order for unpaid debts, etc.

Land speculator John Nicholson took out many warrants in the name of the Pennsylvania Population Company in 1792, the largest year for warrants, following enactment of the new land law. Nicholson was involved in all the major land companies, but most particularly in the North American which was of vast proportions. The original plan of the company was for 250,000 acres, later modified to 120,000 acres in Allegheny County, north of the Ohio River. Another version reported original planning for the North American Land Company included six million acres in Pennsylvania, Virginia, North and South Carolina, Georgia, and Kentucky, with 647,000 acres in Pennsylvania, worth approximately $1 million.

Robert Morris established a partnership with two men: his friend, John Nicholson of Philadelphia, at one time comptroller general of Pennsylvania, and James Greenleaf of New York, former consul at Amsterdam who promised Dutch financing to buy the lands. After the Revolutionary War, the Dutch who had invested heavily in the colonies, decided to not remove their money but to make large purchases of land. The Holland Company was formed and they purchased three million acres in New York State and some acreage in Allegheny County in Pennsylvania from the Morris group.

Morris and Nicholson employed Daniel Leet and John Hoge as surveyors of the districts they controlled west of the Allegheny River. There is a contract dated June 13, 1794, between the Philadelphians, Robert Morris and John Nicholson on the one part and western surveyors Thomas Stokely and John Hoge on the other part. These men worked on the premise that "prevention of settlement by force of arms of enemies" did not annul the condition of actual settlement and residence. Correspondence reveals that if Hoge and Stokely were to receive 40,000 acres they would pay at the rate of ten shillings, for a total of 20,000 pounds. In 1797 in a final effort to save himself, Robert Morris organized the Pennsylvania Property Company for the holdings in Pennsylvania, but it was too late.

A May 3, 1800, letter from John Field & Son in Philadelphia to James Ross, Esq., was accompanied by an execution from the circuit court against the "property of R. Morris, Esq. at the suit of Parish & Company for $30,000." John Field was still writing to Hoge in 1806 about the North American Land Company, to which Hoge replied:

> As far as the 120,000 acres, the amount of the contract between Morris, Nicholson, Stokely and myself, I paid the purchase money and surveying fees and finally procured a separation of my interest before any judgment existed against Morris and Nicholson and before I knew anything of the North American Land Company.
>
> I would certainly not have taken the trouble without compensation had I not believed I was serving Mr. Morris individually. I

would go to great lengths to serve him for I believe he should be next to General Washington in the love of his country, but his disposition or mine cannot serve you if the company have a good title, or if there be prior judgments to yours against Morris and Nicholson.

The property claimed by the company northwest of the Ohio River at a low valuation, is worth $400,000 but in the present unsettled state of the title, cannot be sold for anything. I wish for the sake of those settlers who look up to me for their title, that there be a speedy adjustment of claims for unless the actual settlers are satisfied before the expiration of McKean's administration, then settlers will, in the event of the Irish faction being successful, which I anticipate with horror, assume another tone.

John Kibbe of the Receiver General's Office in Philadelphia wrote to John Hoge June 7, 1793, and included a list of patents with his comments on "the land jobbing business":

Sir: Your favor of 8 last m° was handed to me by Mr. Buchannon a few days ago, who left Town the next day. He promised to see me previous to his setting off in order to enable me to address you with a few lines, which I believe he forgot, by Mr. Atchison of your Town.

I now avail myself of the pleasure in forwarding to you 22 patents together with the Deeds and copies of the Drafts compleat, being the whole of the business you committed to my care when in this City. I fully expected to have this business (at least a part) compleated and forwarded to you previous to this date, but the great number of Individuals applying *personally* and *waiting* for their patents, besides the rapid continuance of the Land Jobbing business in applications for land warrants, unavoidably superseded my wishes, and which I am satisfied will be with you a sufficient apology.

Unsatisfied warrants continue about the price when you was in Town this City—18/ to 18/6 is the most current price tho' I have generally purchased at 18/ at which price I am willing to purchase at immediate payment, provided the unsatisfied warrants with the assignments etc. meet with no exception to their being receivably in the Surveyor-General's office as a credit to business which may be introduced.

Col. Johnston requests a return of his compliments to you. With sentiments of respect & esteem, I am Sir,

p.s. Pray make my respects   Your very obed^t & obliged
   to Mr. McFarland & son   Servt JOHN KIBBE
—a line from you of the rec^t of the patents etc. will be very agreeable.

On the following list of names included with the letter, we note three entries in the name of Daniel McFarland, surveyor:

James Clemons	401.75 a.	on a Va. Cert. warrant and draft
David White	400 a.	in right of David Whitman No. 6 draft
Bennett Zyenheart	234.17 a.	in right of Abel Carson No. 5 draft
Nathan Hughes	372.12 a.	in his own right draft
Jacob Rush	235.32 a.	in right of John Wright No. 15 draft
Geo. Packenbough	400 a.	in right of Geo. Brockman No. 10 draft
D. McFarland	300 a.	in right of R. Lookout No. 8 draft
		[probably a fictitious name]
H.T. & I. Smith	400 a.	in right of Z. Smith No. 9 draft
Shadrack Mitchell	201.80 a.	in right of Br. Virgin No. 1 draft
David Clark	377 a.	in his own right draft
David Ervin	264.92 a.	in his own right No. 2 draft
Jacob Hoosong	387 a.	in right of Luke Brown No. 3 draft
Jacob Rush	168 a.	in his own right draft
D. McFarland	314.14 a.	in right of David Barber No. 11 draft
Asa Dickinson	216.80 a.	in his own right draft
David Hayes	16.40 a.	in his own right draft
Abel Bell	357 a.	in right of Timothy Knight No. 13 draft
Heph. Stiles	254.80 a.	in right of Stephen Barber No. 4 draft
Samuel Clarke	330.78 a.	in his own right draft
D. McFarland	168.96 a.	in right of Samuel Moore No. 7 draft
Ch'r. Slucher	406 a.	in right of Joseph Work No. 14 draft
James Mustard	241.80 a.	in right of Jas. Dougherty No. 12 draft.

William Nichols, another of the Philadelphia speculators who overstepped in acquiring western lands, wrote to John Hoge February 18, 1803:

I expect to have the pleasure of paying you a visit in the spring when I go out as agent of my creditors to dispose of my western lands; the plan is for payment in from one to five years. We expect the people settled on them will be the purchasers. Please indicate the value and what you think the people will be willing to give if the county town is laid out—I hear it was fixed on your property near my lands. I now have the benefit of a commission of bankruptcy.

In August, Nichols wrote again to Hoge:

... four years' credit would be allowed on my land, maybe even seven years, depending on the credit. On these terms a fortune may be made out of the lands I hold even by giving a price for them which now does not seem great ($4 per acre).

I will join you in the purchase and before payments become due we may have them patented, the title complete and the whole of the purchase money with less than half of the net proceeds paid. If you think well of this, write and I will make the purchase in your name for our mutual benefit under the direction of an able counsel.

Benjamin Chew, lawyer and Pennsylvania chief justice ca. 1775, wrote from Philadelphia in 1805 relative to his lands on Beaver Creek and patents he had tried to secure from the Board of Property for land he had lost to people who "proved settlement."

I am extremely anxious to obtain by a private conveyance if possible, the general draft that has been prepared to show the lines contemplated for the settlers.

It is of serious consideration whether they are all to be put on the *same footing* and of still greater importance whether the value of each tract will be even with those who came forward in due season, that is to say, if the settler takes all his improvements whether he ought not to have so much, the smaller quantity of land will be left to me on an equal participation with him. . . .

I wrote long ago on the importance of *not leaving to me all the inferior land*. . . .

A local version of the large Philadelphia-based land companies had the following document recorded in Deed Book 1-C in Washington County:

Article of Agreement between Dorsey Penticost and John Canon, Andrew Robinson, Samuel McCullough, and Ebenezer Zane of

Ohio County, Virginia as Directors and co-partners of a company entitled the *Ohio Trading Company* . . . members and purchasers from Capt. Paul Froman a tract, plantation and Improvement on Saw Mill Run one mile from Pittsburgh . . . whereas Col. John Neville was a co-partner with Froman and with him in the Army of the United States, and Isaac Cox, Esq. and James McMahan, Esq. relinquished their right to Dorsey Penticost on April 15, 1778 and Penticost did get title to the 635 acres for 635 pounds . . . now he sells to John Canon and others for 317 pounds 10 shillings. . . .

Western land speculation was an international game. One Charles Cooke wrote from Salisbury Square in London, April 24, 1802, to his son William at Wheeling "on the Ohio about 10 miles from Fort Pitt in the U.S. of America—by the Packet *Amelia* via Halifax in Nova Scotia":

. . . having lent a sum of money to Colonel John Connolly now in London where he is soliciting compensation for a disappointment is not being permitted to take possession of the Place of Superintendent General of Indian Affairs given to him by the Duke of Kent when he was Comdr. in Chief of British North America. As security for the payment of this money he has given a mortgage on his lands adjacent the Town of Louisville near the Great Falls of the Ohio containing 1,000 acres which are very valuable.

These lands are conveyed by a lean and release to me with power to dispose of them. Therefore, go to Louisville without delay; I have given you credit with Mr. James Wilson of Alexandria, Virginia.

Be careful to *avoid the snares of the designing* and cultivate the friendship and protection of Mr. Brown and other virtuous characters at Louisville. Inform me of the geographical and commercial state of the country, particularly the distance and mode of communication between the principal towns, value of produce at Louisville, how conveyed to market from whence and by what route. I may establish you in the mercantile line in that country. . . .

By far the most revealing and also most amusing letters in the Hoge collection were written by Ben Stokely who assisted surveyor Thomas Stokely. On May 4, 1797, Stokely wrote to John Hoge from Coolspring in Mercer County:

> We are of the opinion that some method should be found to remove the intruders off the land in this neighborhood; they become more troublesome daily by their threats in addition to throwing down houses and consuming provisions left therein; they have commenced stealing of which we had an instance yesterday evening to the amount of some salt, some dried venison and a shoulder of bacon which was taken out of a house on my land while the men who lived there was working at a distance.

> They are frequently seen to sculk in the woods as if determining to do mischief. I am informed they intend to kill Thomas Stokely the first favorable opportunity. There is an absolute intention on the part of the improvers [settlers on "improvements"] to maintain their possessions at all events. . . . The Chenango intruders on Nichols' claim seem desirous to comply since the Supreme Court ruling.

June 3, 1800, Stokely wrote again from Coolspring to John Hoge; the letter was sent by bearer Thomas McClain with instructions to "bring out more bacon for the Millwrights." The letter:

> The Millwrights will be out in less than five days and I will buy or borrow if possible until the horse can return, and McClain has been hired to bring him back. Send the horse and bacon to John Gastons who lives on the road from Washington to Elizabeth Town in four days. I bought 47 pounds of bacon. . . . I also enclose a bill of goods which I wish Mrs. Hoge to chuse out of some store and put this in the saddle bags I have sent. The Millwrights want the irons immediately. I am anxious to hear from the Land Office and hope to see you here by the 13th.

> The great quantity of provision used and the small quantity of work done by the Millwrights in proportion to their number is a matter of serious concern to me. They have been here nearly 11 weeks, generally 4 men, always 3 and for some time past, 7 besides hired hands which they get occasionally, not to mention a great number of hands which are to meet this week to assist in raising the heavy timbers. I verily believe the Hunter and his 3 hands would not finish the Mill exclusive of the Dam, to which there is very little done yet, in less than 3 weeks or a month. Now

if to this we add the Dam which they must do or hire done, we may safely estimate the work at about 2 months from this date, for 4 men.

The most meat that has been used by the 4 steady hands was 27 lbs. in 2 days beside other victuals—how they used it I know not, for at other times they have done pretty well on 1 lb. each man per day of fat middlings without bone by having potatoes, tea, sugar, bread and the like. We give them some butter and all the milk we can possibly spare and as many potatoes as they want in order to extend the meat as far as possible . . . with all our economy we are closely pursued by 3 tall men with open Mouths and axes in their Hans and a smaller one with a bag on his shoulder and a jug in his hand. But we have plenty of ammunition such as Indian Meal for Powder and Potatoes for Balls, that we have as yet avoided being taken! But if you were not John Hoge and I were not Ben Stokely, the Mill and the Wrights might and should before this day, have been on the way to Philadelphia. As it is, I will not yet surrender, nor endeavor the less to bring things to an issue as favorable as may be expected.

I enclose the division of your and Tom's land and think you had best confirm with Tom immediately. Don't forget to bring about 40 or 50 dollars if there is any money in your hands to which I can lay the lawful claim, and I shall begin to take breath a little. Remember—come out soon for you are much wanted. I am too *cunning* to believe evasive answers. It will answer no purpose for you to make any artful shift with a view of satisfying me short of coming. I will press the matter no farther lest you might think me rash or altogether in fun.

One of John Hoge's agents in Mercer County wrote in February 1807 complaining about Ben Stokely:

He told the settlers that if he had laid off their land and found the side line to be longer than 260:5 he would allow that into them and if he found the line short, he would make up their complement out of the residue. He is so great a friend to the settler, by sume means he found out that I measured the line and found more short of the measure than long . . . if this be the case there will be no vacant land between yours and the donation.

* * *

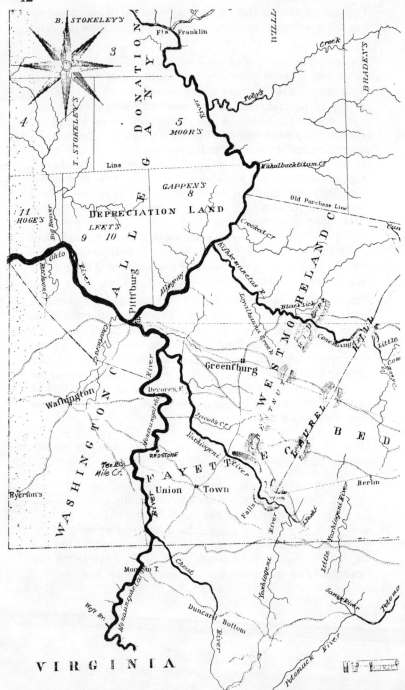

B. STOKELEY'S

3

Fort Franklin

4

5
MOOR'S

Line

GAPPEN'S
8

DEPRECIATION LAND

11
HOGE'S

LEET'S
9 10

Old Purchase Line

Muhulbucktitum Cr.

Crooked Cr

Big Beaver

Ohio

River

Raccoon Cr

Pittsburg

Allegeny

Kiskeminetas R.

Blacklick

Loyalhannah Creek

Conemaugh R.

Greensburg

Washington

Devore's F.

Jacob's Cr.

Youhiogeni River

RED STONE

Ten Mile Cr.

Ryerson's

Monungahela River

FAYET

Union Town

Morgan T.

Cheat

Duncard Bottom

River

West Br.

Monongahela Cr.

Berlin

Youhiogeni River

Little Youhiogeni River

Falls

Youhiogeni River

Yesh

Santi River

Potomac River

Potomack River

VIRGINIA

One of the last items of correspondence from Ben Stokely is dated 1813 from the town of Mercer and is written to John Hoge:

> ... saw your brother David in Steubenville. He is surely a gentleman of the first account as to integrity, natural abilities or genteel address among men.

The following document from the Hoge Papers is dated December 31, 1784, the year when Virginia titles in the area described, came under Pennsylvania jurisdiction:

> *Know* all men by these presents that we, *Benjamin* and *Amos White* are held and firmly bound unto David Redick and John Hoge, Esq., Surveyors of the County of Washington, State of Pennsylvania in the sum of five hundred pounds good and lawful money of the state aforesaid, to be paid unto the said David and John. . . .
>
> The condition of this obligation is such that if the above bound Benjamin and Amos White shall, will and truly execute all warrant orders of survey etc. also all rights acquired under, founded on or recognized by the Laws of Virginia, which may be directed to them by the said Redick or Hoge, upon receiving the fees, to make return of three-fourths of them, unto them or either of them, which is two pounds twelve shilling and six pence for every Survey on a Warrant granted under the late Land Office of Pennsylvania, and three pounds for all surveys made on Virginia titles, legal or illegal or old warrants or locations granted before the year 1775, and to make and deliver to the owner a Draught of the land and a fair Draught fit for the Land Office, as also a Transcript of field notes as soon as possible when demanded to them the said David or John or their clerk at their office.
>
> Above-mentioned surveys within the following District: beginning at the mouth of Ten Mile Creek and up the waters of same to William Hill's thence by a straight line touching at Thomas Crooks' and down Pigeon Creek from thence to the mouth and up the River Monongahela to the place of beginning. . . .
>
> Sealed and delivered in
> presents of: ISABELA COOK   BENJAMIN WHITE
> JOHN DOWNING   AMOS WHITE

In 1786 Surveyor General John Lukens noted on one of John Hoge's draughts that he wished he would be more particular in examining returns from his field notes before they were sent to the office; if there were errors, it was a detriment to those who were then unable to get their patents.

* * *

Joseph Doddridge's *Notes* first published in 1824 at the office of the Wellsburg, Virginia, *Gazette* contain much early information of interest, but they are also considered to be rather inaccurate in some respects. Doddridge wrote:

> The settlements on the west side of the mountains commenced along the Monongahela and between that river and the Laurel Ridge in 1772.

Perhaps he had in mind the first tax rolls of that year, but it is well established that they began to come and settle in the 1750s; and although there was some movement back and forth during Indian depredations and the French and Indian War, there appear to be few if any records to show that some families ever left their land during this period.

Pennsylvania *Colonial Records* state: Settlements in present Washington County began about 1756 with the first settlers coming by way of Braddock's Road from Virginia and Maryland.

James Dunlap, described as an old Indian trader, came forward on April 6, 1798, and "deposed" to prove a title:

> In the Spring of 1761 I saw a cabin which appeared to be up to the first story, no roof, and about 10 x 12 which 'improvement' was made on a piece of land called "Rinehart Wolfe and Philip Neifley" now claimed by George Wisecarver on the south side of Dunnings' Creek adjacent to Daniel Clark's survey on the south and my land on the southwest. I resided in the neighborhood to the present unless driven off from time to time by the Indians but do not recall any other improvement until some time after 1765.

In consequence of the Declaration in 1776 the title of the Penns became vested in the commonwealth in sovereignty; the Divesting Act of the assembly passed November 27,

1799, saved all titles granted by the Penns before July 4, 1776, and all private estates and lands of the Penns, including surveyed manors and certain quitrents.

* * *

In the original surveys of public land in Pennsylvania and other states east of Ohio, land was surveyed "hit or miss" or with no plan at all. It was Albert Gallatin of Fayette County who created the grid land system of the United States. The act applied only to lands northwest of the Ohio River and provided for townships to be six miles square with land to be sold in sections. The land system and the Cumberland Road are testimonials to the breadth and accuracy of Gallatin's views.

The meridian border of Pennsylvania served as a surveyor's base line for land grants and for states farther to the west. The author of the standard work on American boundaries of the U.S. Geological Survey said:

> The monument established in 1785 on the north bank of the Ohio in the west boundary of Pennsylvania is of considerable historic importance, for it marks the point from which the first surveys for dividing public land in the United States into ranges and townships, was commenced.

George Davison purchase money receipt showing various fees collected. Hoge Papers.

The primary features of the formation of townships, counties, and even states were the topography and direction and flow of streams and rivers. Nowhere is this more evident than in Penn's Southwest, laced with waterways and with ridges the dominant feature of the landscape.

Before surveyed lines, the settlers, guided by the tops of ridges and watercourses, arrived at their property lines chiefly by amicable settlement; where there was a conflict, fist fights in the presence of witnesses were often described and tales of prowess handed down from generation to generation.

The survey of a tract of land which had never been surveyed or on which the "Notes" had been lost is called an *Original Survey*. It was stated in October 1748 that every surveyor in Virginia must be able to see the land plainly bounded by natural bounds or marked trees. In case of failure, the fine was paid in tobacco with one-half going to the king. Notices for all entries of land were posted at the courthouse for two successive court days. Surveyors, required to be residents of the county where they worked, had to enter land for themselves before a justice of the peace, and were not to have more than one tract, but there were many ways to avoid that restriction.

In Pennsylvania, surveyors' fees were set during one of the early periods at three pounds for every 500-acre lot, two pounds for 300 acres, one pound ten shillings for 250- and 200-acre plots. This fee included all the expenses of chain bearers, markers, etc.

In Virginia, which had a tobacco economy, fees for many years were paid entirely in tobacco. As early as 1738, 500 pounds of tobacco for not over 1,000 acres; for a lot in town, 20 pounds; for running the dividing line between two pieces of property, 250 pounds, and for surveying one acre for a mill site, the fee was a surprising 100 pounds of tobacco. In later years a more or less standard fee was 30 pounds of tobacco for surveying 100 acres. If a person ordering the survey did not pay the proper fees, the sheriff could step in and with a writ from the appropriate court, attach his slaves, goods, and/or chattels.

* * *

It was recognized that the authorities wished to give all favor to the "poor settlers" who were injured by land jobbers (chiefly surveyors) who, when people discovered vacant land, pretended it was appropriated and then surveyed it for themselves. There were other mercenary practices concerning land acquisition. The *Western Telegraphe & Washington Advertiser* in May 1797:

> Christopher Slusher bought a large tract of land of James Caldwell of Ohio County who misrepresented. Inasmuch as Slusher and his associates were German and unlettered in the English language, they were easily imposed upon.

Also in May 1797, Robert McClean and Joseph Yard Provence published a notice that they had purchased military tracts of land of a certain Samuel Underwood for which they paid him $2,500 in cash and $3,011 in notes, only to discover the deeds were forged. They advertised a $100 reward for Underwood's capture.

There were four methods of acquiring title to land:

1. *Squatter's right* where the frontiersman simply lived on the land in a cave, the hollow of a large tree, or in some makeshift shelter.
2. *Tomahawk right* where a selected area was marked by blazing or deadening line trees with a tomahawk.
3. *Corn right* established by raising one crop of corn on a cleared plot of ground which gave the settler not only the planted corn plot but the privilege of a much larger adjacent acreage on a preemption right.
4. *Improvement right* where a settler could acquire land if he had made improvements to the value of twenty-four dollars or more; these were lands to which others had partial or complete titles. The differences between "im-

proved" and "unimproved" land was made in 1765 in Pennsylvania.

Among the hundreds of "depositions" at Washington and Jefferson College in the Historical Collection is a deposition of Alexander Boling stating that in the year 1770:

I noted various people going out to take up land not yet improved, and to gather their corn on a *Corn Right;* I also saw Indian Van Swearingen working with Henry Taylor surveying and marking a line on Chartiers Creek. Van Swearingen said he too was going out that way to see some land he had got of Baltzar Shilling, and would be glad of Taylor's company, that Shilling could show him land aplenty.

Later I saw the two men surveying and marking a line which Taylor said was on his land and they marked the white oak tree which stands about northwest of where Mr. Yeats now lives. . . . Taylor invited me to spend the night with him saying his "cabbin" was a little way from where we stood. The next summer I passed through and saw timber cut and a number of split rails in that part of the line. Shilling was expected at Taylor's camp that night. [Baltzar Shilling settled in Jefferson Township, Fayette County and appears to have been a land agent.]

Joseph Wills certificate from Virginia commissioners sitting at Redstone Old Fort showing preemption right to additional 1,000 acres. Hoge Papers.

A buyer applied to the state for the purchase of a certain number of acres in a given locality and a warrant was issued authorizing the survey. A deputy surveyor made a survey containing the area called for in the warrant, usually with an addition of 6 percent for roads. If the new farm lay along one side of a farm already taken, an effort was made to conform to the established line. Often there was an overlap or sometimes vacant strips were left where the surveys did not mesh (best noted in Vol. III of the *Horn Papers* township maps).

Many western Pennsylvania and West Virginia farms are shaped like amphitheaters, the buildings in a low situation near a spring and the tops of the surrounding hills the boundaries of the tract. Early farmers prided themselves in the arrangement which meant that everything from the hilltop, orchard fruit, hay for the stock, and wood for the fires, came to the house "down hill."

After the initial line was determined, the corners were selected arbitrarily by noting a large oak or dogwood, easily picked out in the woods; deviations were made to locate a bottom, a spring, or a good piece of timberland. By the time the complete circuit was made, many corners were established and often the number of acres did not approximate very closely the area called for in the warrant.

A patent on sheepskin (the earliest form) usually had a name; it noted the date of survey and in case of a line dispute, the old patent prevailed and was to be satisfied first.

Early survey books in county courthouses as well as the original draughts in special collections contain tastefully arranged and skillfully lettered drawings. One is constantly amazed at the classic style of lettering, as on the early gravestones, often of a quality which suggests the illuminated pages of medieval scribes. Others by less competent draftsmen lack both arrangement and description to the point that it is a wonder some of the tracts were ever located.

The names of the early grants are a study in themselves

Portion of masthead and group of three Pennsylvania seals
from early Washington County Courthouse deeds.

Thomas Ritchardson's "Folly," 389
acres . . . beginning at a corner dogwood. Surveyed September 15, 1784.
Washington County, Pennsylvania,
sheepskin deed.

Benjamin Anderson, Donegal
Township, fifty-three acres. Surveyed March 1, 1820. Washington County parchment deed.

Enoch Vanscoyoc, Morris
Township, twenty acres. Surveyed December 12, 1816. Washington County sheepskin deed.

Mr. Christopher Graybill's Survey (15)

A — a Sugar Tree Corner
" to John Hulls . . . . .
B — Sycamore Corn.r to Do.
C — White Oak Corner
" to Newkirks
D — White Hickory
" Corner to Do. - - - -
E — White Walnut Corn.r
" to Colvins
F — Three white Oaks. cor.s
" to John Cramer
G — W. Oak by a Branch
H — Beach Corn.r Graybill
I — the Mouth Sugar
" Camp Run
K — Mouth Still house Run

N. 28. W. 50. 6 E.
En. 48. W. 60.
N. 62. E. 154. 8 W.
Mine Road
1500 Acres.
Cave
Sugar Camp Run

Yohogania Cty.

By Virtue of a Certificate granted Christopher Graybill from Commissioners appointed to settle and adjust Claims to unpatented Lands in the Counties Yohog.a Monongalia and Ohio. I have Survey'd for the said Graybill, four hundred Acres Lands on the Waters of Pigeon Creek. all which is contained within agreable Lines. Certified

June 3.d 1780

Exam.d Copy Given
Aug. 1 1780.

W. Crawford D.S.C.

Jn.o Brock. D.S.C.
For
William Crawford
Sur.d

Christopher Graybill's survey from William Crawford's book of surveys. Special Collection, West Virginia University Library, Morgantown.

and reveal much of the activity and atmosphere of the location. A close grouping of tracts in Aleppo Township, Greene County, indicates a not very peaceful situation in the late 1780s:

St. Clair's Encampment	Magazine
Artillery	Ambush
Equipage	Alack ! ! !
Battery	Barrier
Bastion	Bomb-Proof

In order to encourage enlistment and to reward those who entered military service in the Pennsylvania Line and the U.S. Navy, and anticipating the purchase of the Indian title provided by an act of March 12, 1783, the state set aside two large sections:

1. Redemption of the certificates of depreciation given to the officers and soldiers of the Pennsylvania Line providing that the certificates be equal to gold or silver in payment of unlocated land.
2. To fulfill the promise of the state, March 7, 1780, officers and soldiers of the Pennsylvania Line were given donations in lands according to their rank in the service. By an act of March 12, 1783, land on the Allegheny above Kittanning to the west boundary of the state from seven to eight miles south of New Castle. All land south of this line was appropriated to the redemption of depreciation certificates and was known as *Depreciation Lands.* The land north of the line was appropriated to donations to the soldiers of the Pennsylvania Line for their Revolutionary service and was called *Donation Lands.*

When the royalists and neutrals flocked to Philadelphia, occupied by Lord Howe 1777-78, for protection, their estates and those of other traitors were confiscated. By an act of December 18, 1780, the state provided for the settlement of the depreciation from Continental currency and the certificates were made receivable in payment of such confiscated estates and unlocated lands.

Receiver-General's Office, Philadelphia.

Jabez Baldwin's receipt showing payment in Continental certificates. Hoge Papers.

Depreciation land was laid out in lots of not less than 200 acres and not more than 350 acres. Donation tracts were all to be for 200 acres. As soon as 100 lots were laid out and surveyed, the surveyor general of the Land Office was required to sell them in numerical order at certain times and places, and bids were to be in silver or gold or depreciation certificates. Due to Indian hostilities, the surveyor general was not able to survey these lands until June 10, 1783.

In order to survey the land, the territory was divided into five districts, later increased to ten. In November 1785 it was directed that depreciation lands be sold by the acre at the "Old Coffee-House in Philadelphia" and the price averaged only two shillings six and one-half pence per acre. It was too low, sales were suspended, and city auctions ceased in 1787. Western lands were not in demand due to Indian hostilities and sales by soldiers, especially privates, of their donation lots at very low figures.

Some of the persons on donation land lists did not appear but they were given a time extension of two years to claim before the land could be disposed of. The comptroller general reported a list of persons entitled to donation lands to the council on May 3, 1785, and deputy surveyors were appointed. John Hoge in Washington was appointed to handle these lands and submitted a list of tracts on January 24, 1800, to be chosen before the first of October. Every effort was made to locate those entitled to land, but in 1793, land officers had to draw lots for every person who had not received his donation.

A news item in the Pittsburgh *Gazette* indicated that financier Robert Morris had an interest in 311 tracts of depreciation land held by warrants under the act of 1792. In March 1797 the *Gazette* noted that some 53,000 acres of valuable depreciation lands had been sold for taxes by the commissioners, although there were no taxes legally set on them.

The depreciation and donation lands were the twin progeny of patriotism and necessity. The March 1, 1780, act exempted soldiers' lands from taxation during their lifetime unless transferred or alienated.

The true line of the western boundary was unknown and an agent was appointed to explore the country with instructions in much the same vein as those of the Ohio Company to Christopher Gist in 1750; they wished especially to know about land considered unfit for cultivation which became known as the "Struck District." Most surveys were completed in 1786 even though from 1780 to 1795 there was no safety from invasion and massacre.

The Commonwealth of Pennsylvania, ss.

[Seal]

Whereas Joseph Swearingen ———————— of the county of ———————— hath requested to take up One hundred ———————— acres of land

Including an Improvement on the waters of Chartos Forks of Wheeling Creek adjoining Lands of Robert Morris or surveyo made by Daniel McFarland & others

in the county of Washington ———————— (Provided the land is not within the last purchase made of the Indians) for which he agrees to pay immediately, into the office of the Receiver-General, for the use of this state, at the rate of fifty shillings ———————— per hundred acres, in gold, silver, paper-money of this state, or certificates, agreeably to an Act of Assembly, passed the first day of April, 1784; and to an Act, passed the third day of April, 1792, entitled "An Act for the sale of vacant lands within this commonwealth." Interest to commence from the first of January 1794. There are, therefore, to authorize and require you to survey, or cause to be surveyed unto the said Joseph Swearingen ———————— at the place aforesaid, according to the method of townships appointed, the said quantity of acres, if not already surveyed or appropriated, and to make return thereof into the Secretary's Office, in order for confirmation; for which this shall be your warrant.

In Witness whereof Thomas Mifflin ———————— Governor of the said commonwealth, hath hereunto set his hand, and caused the less seal of the said commonwealth to be affixed, the fifth ———————— day of March ———————— in the year 1790

To Daniel Brodhead, Esquire,}
Surveyor General

To John Hoge ———————— Deputy Surveyor.
Execute this warrant and make return thereof into the
Surveyor-General's office, according to law.

for Dan Brodhead Esq S.G.

Wm Parker

Typical land warrant in name of Joseph Swearingen. Hoge Papers.

In 1793 William Littell, Allegheny County justice told:

About 1792 I was on the Ohio and Charles Phillis had raised a
Blockhouse on his improvement on the west side of the Ohio.
Phillis lived in the Fort and had layd the worm of a fence joyned
to the cabin at both sides around the corn, six rails high. The first
story is built of square logs supposed to be eighteen feet square,
the second story with round logs supposed to be twenty feet
square. Phillis raised the house in January 1792 and moved his
family there in February.

James Carrothers also made a statement that he had commanded a detachment of militia stationed at the blockhouse
at the mouth of Little Beaver Creek April 18, 1792, and saw
some land he wanted. "When Phillis and his sons first came
they said they came in the name of the Commonwealth to
work with a view of leaving my bit of time on this ground.
They planted peach stones, potatoes and Indian corn." In
June the Indians had taken his horses and he followed them
till he made a discovery of the Indians' blankets, returned

Robert Forbes survey note regarding Indian activity in 1792,
Washington County. Hoge Papers.

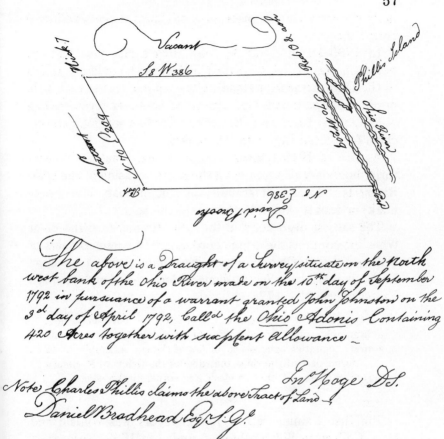

The above is a Draught of a Survey situate on the North west bank of the Ohio River made on the 10th day of September 1792 in pursuance of a warrant granted John Johnston on the 3d day of April 1792, Calld the Ohio Adonis Containing 420 Acres together with suspent allowance —

Note Charles Phillis claims the above tract of Land —
Jn° Hoge D.S.
Daniel Brodhead Esqr S.G.

Surveyor General Daniel Brodhead's copy of Washington County survey showing Phillis Island. Hoge Papers.

and swam the river, went after and killed one of the Indians; "sculped him and left his carcas for the crows." He then planted about a peck of potatoes and forty to fifty hills of corn, burned brush and deadened trees and Phillis made rails for the fence.

In the writer's family there is an amusing story about an early settler whose horse had been fed corn and in his wanderings over a certain piece of land "passed the title" on a corn right.

In 1795 David Reddick, John Hoge's surveying partner, billed Charles Phillis, who then owned the large Phillis Island in the Ohio River near Hoge's *Ohio Adonis* tract, for a little over fifteen pounds for provisions of bacon at seven cents a pound, some flour and the hire of Phillis's son for carrying chain for fifteen days with two horses.

As late as 1846 attorneys were asking: What is the territorial boundary of Virginia on the northwest side of the Ohio River? Is it lowest watermark, or is it ordinary low watermark, or does it extend to the top of the bank?

The earliest deed book in the Ohio County Courthouse at Wheeling contains the original order for the commissioners of Yohogania and Ohio counties in Virginia, signed by Isaac Leet, Jr., William Scott, James McMechen, and Richard Yeates, August 22, 1778:

> ... appointed as per order of the respective courts may most indisputably appear to ascertain the boundary line between the aforesaid counties agreeable to an Act of General Assembly ... to the nearest part of the ridge that divides the waters of Monongahela from those of Ohio to a blas'd and corner-marked stake.

* * *

The first training school for surveyors was William and Mary College in Williamsburg, founded in 1693. Records of the college have been burned several times so that significant background for the founding of the school of surveying is said by the college staff to be unavailable.

County surveyors had to be commissioned by the masters of the college and every person who wished to become a surveyor in October 1783 had to be certified by the college and commissioned by the governor with one-sixth of the surveying fee going to the college. Of course, commissions were granted much earlier; in 1753 the Ohio Company obtained commissions for both George Washington and Christopher Gist to be:

... appointed to officially survey lands upon the waters of the Monongaly and Youghgaine about the place now called the "Redstone Settlement."

The school was in part supported in the early years of the eighteenth century, in addition to survey fees, by duty on hides, skins and furs, which included both raw and tanned hides, dressed and undressed buckskin, doeskin, beaver, otter, wildcat, mink, fox, raccoon, muskrat, and elk furs and skins.

The quadrangular method of survey based on parallels of latitude and meridians was adopted in Ohio and to the west; by an act of Congress May 20, 1785, a method of survey based on lines determined astronomically, was established. The initial point was chosen so as to be prominent, as near the mouth or junction of two creeks or rivers.

It is to be remembered that Charles Mason and Jeremiah Dixon while acting as surveyors for the Penns, and the Calverts of Maryland, were hired because of their knowledge of mathematics and astronomy. Charles Mason was assistant observer at Greenwich Observatory in 1756. The best equipment for a surveyor is given as common sense, algebra, geometry, and trigonometry.

Specific performance on surveys demanded that the northwest corner of a lot be marked with its number. If a post, it or the nearest tree to the corner was to be marked. Often surveyors neglected to perform these directions due to hostile Indians or when the survey fee was not paid. The most important feature in the direction to survey was the northwest or numbered corner which became the earmark of the tract, the legal, original and true index of the ground occupied, superseding all other evidence.

The corner marking was achieved by cutting on the tree or post a broad, flat surface upon which the numbers were sunk with a tool such as was used by millers in marking the numbers on their barrels. These numbers were often seen fifty and sixty years afterward by removing the growths of the tree over them. Marks made in 1785 and 1786 were grown over annually with new wood made by the downward current of the sap in summer. The outward mark, when not detected by an ordinary surveyor after many years, would be noted by skillful surveyors by a discoloration of the bark. Then the tree was "blocked" or the growth cut away to prove the existence of the original cut.

In the case of the donation and depreciation lots, when a certain number had been surveyed, a connected draft with lot numbers was made and deposited with the master of the rolls as a public record to serve when the number was drawn and the name of the soldier noted on the lot, in lieu of recording the patents. In consequence of lapse of time, dying of timber, burning of woods and general loss of marks, the act of March 24, 1818, was passed, making the general drafts evidence of lot locations.

In running from the base or district line north or south, the surveyor would run the distance for each lot and mark its corner where he would set his compass, taking the course east or west. He would direct the axemen to mark a tree or two on the course and then instead of running the line through, he would go on in his first north or south direction. The end result was that the east and west lines were not marked through.

The usual way was to run the breadth of four tracts, marking the corners and a tree or two and then turning east or west to the opposite corner, repeating this for the district.

The uneven and woody surface of the country was well attested to by the diary of one Andrew Ellicott, a Pennsylvania commissioner on the western boundary in 1785:

> ... this part of the Country is not only a Wilderness at present but must ever continue so—the Vallies are too small for Cultivation and the Hills too steep and high. . . . I cannot see anything in this Wilderness that can make it tolerably agreeable.

Owing to the rough conditions and the mistakes of the chain carriers, chaining was often inaccurate and three out of four cross lines would not be taken. The carriers sometimes

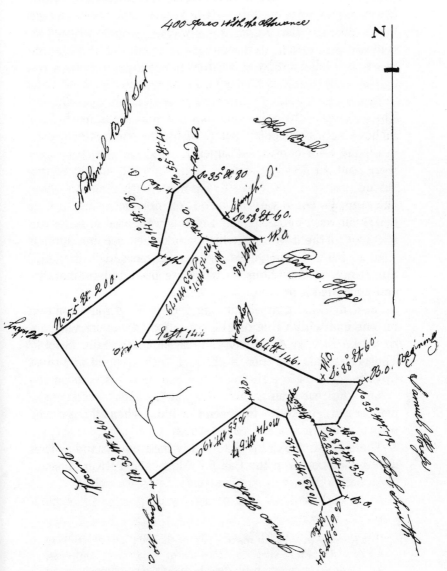

Nameless sketch showing the extremely irregular shape
of some surveys. Hoge Papers.

dropped pins by which they kept count. As a result of errors, the east and west corners of tracts were not opposite each other and irregular forms, not always the result of random tomahawk blazing, were assumed. Sometimes they would overrun or fall short by as much as fifty acres.

The chain used in surveying is made up of pairs of links united by three rings so that maximum flexibility is achieved. The Gunter's chain is composed of 100 links, each 7.92 inches long with an entire length of 66 feet, or 4 poles.

Chains were considered superior to steel tapes for rough work, but an 1818 newspaper article on the subject of surveying observed that two surveys made with the same chain and compass could vary by a foot or more according to how the chain was stretched. When chains were used in salt water it corroded the iron links which would then become thinner. The advice: "Chains must always be measured first...." Sometimes steel ribbons or wires are preferred as they are easily mended if broken.

Steel marking pins about one foot in length and pointed on one end with a ring on the other for ease in carrying, are thrust into the ground when the rear chainman calls "Stick!" The head chainman then sticks it into the ground and must call "Stuck!" before the rear man can relax his hold on the chain. The rear man gathers the pins as each new length is determined. An "out" has been measured when all ten or the total number of pins have been stuck.

There is a fine exhibit of the early instruments and articles used by surveyors in the Campus Martius and River Museum at Marietta, Ohio.

In an early college text on surveying practices it is mentioned in 1859:

> It is scarcely possible to make a survey these days in which there is not a disturbing attraction at some of its corners; iron pipes, wire fences, buildings with steel in their construction, railroad lines, etc. All of these affect the reading.

For instance, a needle set up at Washington, Pennsylvania, on July 4, 1776, pointed to astronomical north. Until 1808 the needle moved about three and three-fourths feet each year; until 1816 it almost stood still. From 1816 until 1849 it moved west at the three and three-fourths feet a year rate and in 1849 it again stood directly in the true meridian.

The degree of movement is recorded all over the world so that in order to make a survey good for all time, the date of the survey is most important. This date combined with the rate at which the direction of the needle changes, makes it possible to correct the bearing at any time.

* * *

Pennsylvania did not ratify the August 1779 agreement drawn at Baltimore to extend the Mason-Dixon line until September 1780 and she was not then satisfied with the ratification of Virginia.

On February 21, 1781, Alexander McClean and Joseph Neville of Yohogania County, Virginia, were appointed to run a temporary line. They met on the following May 10 and began to mark the line by clearing a strip through the woods fifteen feet in width with initials "P" and "V" carved or otherwise marked on large trees or rocks on the meridian. They received pay of twenty shillings per day exclusive of necessary expense.

Colonel James Marshel of Little Washington was directed to call out forty men of the militia to escort and guard the commissioners as there was so much controversy over the line. By Christmas Eve 1784 the boundary had been defined for the southwestern corner of Pennsylvania and by August of the following year, the meridian line from the southwest corner had been carried north to the Ohio.

Alexander McClean was the most famous surveyor in Penn's Southwest. He was born in 1746 in York County and immediately after the Treaty of Stanwix and the "new purchase" he began laying off tracts in Fayette County in 1769. He was associated with the running of the Mason-Dixon line and was officially appointed deputy surveyor of Fayette in 1772 and represented Westmoreland County in the first Pennsylvania Assembly in 1776. During the Revolutionary War when there were no land entries at the Land Office and little work for surveyors, McClean held numerous public offices in Fayette County: register and recorder and was clerk of court and prothonotary from 1772 to 1834, longer than any other person in western Pennsylvania. County records attest to his elegant penmanship. Alexander McClean died at Uniontown January 7, 1834.

In 1792 the assembly enacted a duplex and adverse system of acquiring title which placed Land Office rights and "Settlement" claims in direct opposition to each other. This act made it possible to purchase a warrant at the Land Office for a tract to be surveyed for not more than 400 acres with 6 percent for road allowance with purchase money and survey fees paid and actual settlement and improvement to come at a later date.

The other method was by actual settlement and improvement on not to exceed 400 acres by anyone desiring to settle, improve, and live on a tract. The difference between the warrant and the settlement right was this: The warrant gave the surveyor general the authority to survey a tract which had been applied and paid for; where actual settlement had been made, the settler had to make application to a surveyor to make a survey and then enter it in his books.

Local reaction to these various rulings is revealed in a notice which appeared in the Washington *Reporter* September 24, 1810:

> Jacob Tegarden, Chairman of the new branch of the Society in Greene County called the *Society of True Americans*. In the winter of 1809 a Philosophical School was held in this neighborhood and a Resolution brought forward by Mr. Thomas Craig, praying the western lands may be held by "Improvement"; a Resolution was also brought forward by Mr. Stephen Durbin requesting the Federalists and Democrats to unite on this question.

Jonathan Parkinson made a motion that a Committee be formed of Craig, Durbin, Parkinson, Martin and Tegarden to investigate the government and to remonstrate and show our representatives what we want or do not want that is contrary to the "Spirit of the Declaration of Independence."

Jacob Tegarden, Chairman
John Riley, Secretary

In the general area of land acquisition, deeds, and surveys is a term used in the transfer of land, and the word is *Indenture* (dictionary meaning: A deed or agreement of two or more copies with edges indented as a means of identification). There are many of these "scalloped" pages in regional collections. One of the earliest indentures is in Deed Book No. 1 in the Bedford County Courthouse:

George Croghan of Fort Pitt, Esquire, to John Campbell, Fort Pitt Merchant. . . . Chiefs of the six United Nations of Indians (named) did by their deed of August 2, 1749 sell to George Croghan a certain parcel of land on the south side of the Monongahela River beginning at a Run nearly opposite to Turtle Creek and down the Monongahela to its junction with the Ohio, computed to be ten miles, running down the East bank and sides of and unto the said River Ohio to where Raccoon Creek empties, thence up the Creek ten miles for 100,000 acres.

Whereas at Fort Stanwix the Indians did by their deed poll November 4, 1768 . . . now for 114.3.1 Croghan grants to Campbell three parcels on the east side of Chirtees Creek, late in the occupation of Barnard Wartner of 338 acres . . . then on the east side

Example of scalloped top of an indenture with original signature of Robert Morris on Washington County deed.

of the Creek, land in the names of Matthew Rodgers, Charles Lindsay and others, known as "The Clearfield" . . . the three parcels containing 1,161 acres. Done at Fort Pitt 1770 [with Indian signatures].

The capitalists near the Land Office in Philadelphia, having money, proceeded to procure warrants and lodge them with the deputy surveyor in a certain district, for execution. John Hoge was the most prominent of these early surveyors. In the collection of Hoge Papers at Washington and Jefferson College is his oath taken in Cumberland County:

> I do hereby certify that *John Hoge* hath voluntarily taken and subscribed the Oath of Alegeance and fidelity as directed by an Act of General Assembly of Pennsylvania passed the 13th day of June 1777 and supplements to said Act since passed. Witness my hand and seal the 29th day of October 1779.
>
> *Samuel Culbertson*

A few years later when Hoge was commissioned deputy surveyor he took a similar oath promising to act with fidelity and integrity. John Hoge (1760-1824) was a man of many parts and a complete biography of him could be written from the scores of receipts found in the Hoge Papers. He laid out and was proprietor of Little Washington, operated several stores in partnership, did a tremendous business in surveying, served in the Pennsylvania Assembly and the U.S. Congress from Washington County, operated mills, wrote a treatise in

Note for $2,070 from early Washington innkeeper Joseph Huston to John Hoge showing cancellation cut-out in upper right-hand corner. Hoge Papers.

1823 on how to handle sheep and supervised his large farm
known as Meadow Lands.

A few of the most colorful receipts are listed:

August 1783—Wm. Huston, bording and washing

Sept. 1789—Benj. Reed, stack of chimneys in new hous
and 2 harths in the room, set 2 stills and a chimney, 2
pirticions, plastring a rume and pointing the house

April 1786—Joshua Barnes, paling panels, hooping the
washtub and making a wheel barrow

March 1792—Nicholas Powell, to Mr. Hogan for one
month's dressing and 1 fals tail (hairdresser)

March 1792—Margaret Turbill, washed and mended silk
hose and cravat

Bill for billiard games at David Morris's famous Globe
Inn in Washington during 1800. Hoge Papers.

Dec. 1792 to April 1793—Miss E. Clinton, boarding at $4
week

Sept. 1791—Betsy Patterson, in Philadelphia, washed 5
dozen cloaths and 14 pair silk stockings

Aug. 1794—Job Gorby, setting 50 pannels post and rail
fence

Feb. 1790—John Clark, Philadelphia, hair riband, shaving
and dressing at 15 shillings per month

Oct. 1785—Thos. Harrison, breeches and clothes, 34 plated
Prince of Wales buttons

July 1795—James Gallagher, Philadelphia, misc. decanters,
caroffs, tumblers, wines, salts, sauce turreens, 2 fruit
baskets and stands

Aug. 1790—Jas. Smith, Jr., Philadelphia, colored Taffaty

Aug. 1790—Robert Crozier, 35# for Chaise and Harness

In February 1797 David Hoge in Washington wrote to
John in Philadelphia:

... the Philadelphia Merchants have their clerks out here in all
directions. Money is very scarce, no bills. I note that Brackenridge's 4th volume is out—please send it to me along with *Porcupine* & leave one end open like newspapers and they will cost but
a cent a sheet.

Other early deputy surveyors for Washington County,
Pennsylvania, and date of appointment:

July 15, 1769—James Henricks who turned in his first list
of surveys January 1770 for the following: Jacob and
Abraham Vanmetre, Thomas Thomas, Andrew McFar-

Porcupine Gazette receipt, 1800. Hoge Papers.

lan, Dr. Edward Hand, Clement and John Biddle, Silas and Ebenezer Zane, John, Moses and Jacob Decker, Paul and Jacob Froman, Peter Hanks, Henry Montour, William Peters.

April 17, 1776—Daniel Leet and Jonathan Leet (later).

March 27, 1780—Thomas Stokely.

December 7, 1784—David Redick.

August 12, 1785—Presley Neville and Joseph Neville.

August 1785—Matthew Ritchie.

August 1785—Alexander McClean; there were seven McClean brothers, six of whom were surveyors, chiefly in Fayette County.

1787-96—Isaac Jenkinson.

1795-97—Daniel McFarland, Jr.; Asa Stephenson; Andrew Swearingen; Stephen and John Gapen; Dorsey Penticost, Cumberland County surveyor 1770-74, also Augusta County surveyor.

February 2, 1810—William Hawkins.

3

THE REDSTONE SETTLEMENT

#1 Redstone Old Fort—the Indian Fort Ancient
#2 Nemacolin and Cresap's Trading Camp
#3 The Hanguard of William Trent—the Ohio Storehouse
#4 Fort Burd and the Settlers' Fort
#5 Brownsville

HISTORIC "Redstone Country" very nearly covers the area of present Fayette County, Pennsylvania, stretching from the Monongahela River on the west along the West Virginia border at roughly the Mason-Dixon line on the south, eastward to a north-and-south line from the Great Crossing of the National Road and the Youghiogheny River to the bounds of the county on the north, at Jacob's Creek.

The history of Redstone is as complicated as its intricate contours. The great "dividing ridge" that runs in almost a straight line from Uniontown north and slightly west to Brownsville, divides the watersheds of Dunlap Creek which flows to the west, and Redstone Creek flowing to the east. The ridge ends abruptly at the river at Brownsville; this crossing of the Monongahela has great significance both for its strategic position as a lookout and for the geological wonder of how the river ever pushed through the land mass of the ridge at this point. It picks up on the west side of the river in the wooded mound known both as "Indian Hill" and

"Krepp's Knob," one of the two highest points until the ridge reaches Little Washington, the other being Scenery Hill.

This dividing ridge was the route followed by the early Indian warriors and was chosen for the same reasons that they followed the succession of ridges slightly north of the Mason-Dixon line on what has been officially designated the "Warrior Trail of Greene County," established in 1965 on the route of the old trail. In 1970 trail member Burl Mackey wrote:

> ... the Warrior Trail is unique in that it does not cross a single stream; it is located at an approximate elevation of 1400 feet on a succession of ridges which provided the quickest route for warriors traveling between the Monongahela River near Greensboro and the Ohio River at Cresap, West Virginia.

The Cumberland Road commissioners chose the northern ridge for the route of the first National Road, now U.S. Route 40, begun in 1811. The roadbed of this highway atop the dividing ridge is so narrow in places that the deep valleys with their rolling farms and village clusters of buildings are visible on both sides of the road.

When the first white men crossed "the Laurall Hills" and followed the defile of buffalo traces and Indian paths to the place where Redstone Creek enters the Monongahela River, they saw, to quote from Franklin Ellis:

> A large, artificial mound so ancient that trees more than a hundred years old and five feet or more in diameter were growing on top of it.

Some of the trees had a ring pattern which showed they were from three hundred to five hundred years old, and these massive, living sentinel trees grew out of the decay of ancestor trees, chiefly oak, hickory, poplar, black walnut, wild cherry, and locust.

The *Fort Ancient* mound had been known for centuries as the "Old Fort" and when the white men came, more or less following the meander of Redstone Creek as it bisects *Red-*

stone Country, and saw the exposed red cliffs near the mouth, they dubbed it "Redstone." As a term, it gradually came to describe not only the ancient fortification, but the nearby 1759 Fort Burd which expanded into the more loosely defined "settlers' fort" until Thomas Brown arrived on the scene. Brown purchased the tract, and as proprietor, laid out the formal town plat about 1785 and officially named it Brownsville, although the old name clung and was used into the 1800s, just as residents were referred to as "Virginians" as late as 1820.

In the first volume of his *Monongalia Story* published in 1974, Earl L. Core describes "granite wash" as red beds of shales and sandstone (as exposed on Redstone Creek) which resulted from warm, dry periods as opposed to the popular or general concept of rock turned red from the heat of burning coal seams.

James L. Bowman, whose family had since 1788 occupied the sprawling brick and stone building known as Bowman's and more recently as Nemacolin Castle constructed on or very near the site of Fort Burd, wrote an article on "Redstone Old Fort" which appeared in 1842 in the *American Pioneer* magazine published at Marietta, Ohio:

> On an elevated and commanding bank on the east side of the Monongahela there was once an ancient fortification . . . on the Northwest the Monongahela washed its base, on the Northeast and the South deep ravines, and on the east, a flat to some extent.

> The burned coal exposed on the banks is red and sometimes used for Spanish Brown. These exposed red banks are now visible; the most prominent one is that near the junction of a creek with the river a short distance below the fortification which bears the name of Redstone. This was the most eastern of the "ancient works" and the only one known in the region.

> The military skill displayed in the laying out of the old forts and the remains of some "arts of mechanism" found have impressed on us the idea that they were built by a race very superior to the aborigines.

Although evidence of aboriginal occupation stretches back to the Upper Paleolithic caribou hunters or Paleo-Indians of 14,000 to 12,000 years ago, most of the comparatively recent archaeological activity in Penn's Southwest has been concerned with village sites of the Late Woodland Stage. These late aboriginal peoples of the Upper Ohio Valley have been subsumed under the name "Monongahela Culture" for the period A.D. 1000-1700, according to the Center for Prehistoric and Historic Site Archaeology at California State College, on the banks of the Monongahela.

One of the most exciting current "digs" in Penn's Southwest is at the Meadowcroft Rock Shelter at Albert Miller's Meadowcroft Village in Washington County which has become nationally known as the oldest carbon-dated site yet found in the Western Hemisphere and much older than any previous site in the eastern section, moving the occupancy date at this rock shelter back to 15,000 years ago.

It was the Adena or prehistoric Indians who lived near the mounds and ancient fortifications (1000 to 500 B.C. for early Adena and A.D. 1 for late Adena); the mounds are sometimes described as "cult of the dead." The characteristic location of upland Monongahela villages along historic Indian trails indicates a continuity between aboriginal and historic (1750-1850) Indian *paths* if not between Indian populations. In his 1882 history of Fayette County, Franklin Ellis stated:

> They were beyond the reach of the 1700-1800 Indians and their traditions; lost in antiquity. . . .

Lily Lee Nixon in her biography, *James Burd, Frontier Defender 1726-1793*, relates that "Cresap and Nemacolin had built a trading post at the mouth of Redstone." Here again we are faced with the confusion over the two creeks. It has been established from a number of sources that the Indian Nemacolin had a hunting camp on the bluff near the creek which bore his name but was later changed to Dunlaps Creek:

74

We also know that the terminus of Nemacolin's Path was at this camp on Dunlap, not Redstone Creek.

* * *

No one before or since has equaled the description of the "ancient fort" as recorded by the Englishman, Thomas Ashe, Esq., in his 1806 *Travels in America* (original edition printed for Richard Phillips in Bridge Street, Blackfriars, London, 1809):

> The neighborhood of Brownsville, or Redstone, abounds with monuments of Indian antiquity. A fortified camp (which is a fortification of a very complete nature) commands the town which undoubtedly was once an Indian settlement.

> This camp contains about thirteen acres, enclosed in a circle, the elevation of which is *seven* feet above the adjoining ground. Within the circle a pentagon is accurately described, having its sides *four* feet high, and its angles uniformly *three* feet from the circumference of the circle, thus leaving an unbroken communication all around.

> Each side of the pentagon has a postern (door or gate) opening into the passage between it and the circle; but the circle itself has only one grand gateway which directly faces the town. Exactly in the center stands a mound, about *thirty* feet high, hitherto considered as a repository of the dead . . . which any correct observer can perceive to have been a place of look-out.

> I confess that I examined these remains of the former power of man with much care and veneration; nor could I resist reproaching those writers who have ignorantly asserted: "We know of no such thing existing as an Indian monument of respectability, for we would not honor with that name arrow-points, stone hatchets, stone pipes, half-shapen images etc." I ask those writers what opinion they entertain of the object which I now describe; and I request them when they are again disposed to enlighten the world (!) to visit the countries which they profess to delineate, and diligently search for materials there, before they presume to tell us that such have no existence.

> At an inconsiderable distance from the fortification was a small rising ground; on the side of which I perceived a large, projecting stone, a portion of the upper surface of which was not entirely concealed in the bank. . . . I conceived that the surface had that

uniform and even character which exhibits the result of industry and art.

Animated by a variety of conjectures, I hastened to the town (Brownsville) to engage assistance; quickly returned to clear away the earth which bore strong indication of having fallen on the stone and not have primitively engendered it. My heart beat as I proceeded and my imagination traced various symbols which vanished before investigation.

The stone was finally cleared in a rough manner and represented to our view a polygon with a smooth surface of 8 x 5 feet. I persisted in the opinion that the hand of man had been busy in the formation of this object; nor was I diverted from this idea by the discouragement of the persons whom I employed, and the laughter of the multitude that followed me from the town [further proof that the ancient fort was quite separate from the site of Fort Burd which was in town] to gaze on my labour and delight in my disappointment. . . .

In cleaning the surface of the stone none of the indentations traversed the stone in right and parallel lines, but lay scattered without any apparent order. . . . With a pointed stick I followed the nearest indention and soon discovered that it described a circle which completed its revolution at the spot where I had commenced clearing it. A ray of triumph now shone on my countenance; the people no longer ridiculed me.

On continuing, I cleared a right line which made a segment on the circle though it did not touch the circumference at either end. I cleared in succession four other lines of this description, and the general view then presented a circle enclosing a regular pentagon whose angles were two inches from the circumference.

The multitude shouted applause; some even entered into the spirit of my design and returned to their homes for water and brushes to scrub the stone. When this was effected, there appeared a figure of the head of an Indian warrior etched in the centre. Each side of the pentagon was intersected by a small bar and the circle was also cut by one bar immediately opposite to a right line drawn from the head of the man. Near each line were an equal number of little dots and the circle was surrounded by many more, all uniform in size and in distance from the circle and from each other.

The deductions from this very interesting spectacle did not give me the pride and delight that I ought to have felt, for in reality they destroyed my favorite conceptions, that the predecessors of the Indians were not only enlightened by the arts and sciences, but were a different sort of men from the present race, superior both in body structure and mental endowment, and equal in the latter respect to inhabitants of polished Europe.

. . . the representation on the stone was nothing more than a rude sketch of the adjoining fort—the bars designating the posterns and gateway, the dots denoting the length of the lines . . . the warrior's head justified the opinion I had that the mound in the centre of the fort was a place for a sentinel of observation. The etching is deep and executed with considerable accuracy, yet the whole has an "Indian air" marked with savage features, resembling what modern tribes carve on their pipes and tomahawks.

Two burial places lie contiguous to the fort which I perforated in many places to discover the position of the bones. I was influenced by a tradition among the Indians that when their ancestors settled in a town, the first person who died was placed erect and earth put around him, and when another died, a narrow passage was dug to the first against whom he was reclined, the earth heaped, and so on. [One is constantly amazed at Ashe's grasp of history and archaeology at this early date.] The barrow which I opened might have been originally a parallelogram 60 x 20 feet and 30 feet high . . . the form of ancient works is not exactly similar to that which they first possessed. Such as are built of stone do not experience any material change, but those composed of earth afford a very scanty evidence of their original dimensions or purpose.

Perhaps the irregularities in the barrows of this place may arise from the bones deposited in them having been those of persons killed in battle and buried in one great mound. [This observation may be the answer to the perplexing question of why the Monongahela people abandoned the lower valley and surrounding areas in the late sixteenth century and withdrew to the upper reaches of the Monongahela drainage.]

I found a few carved stone pipes and hatchets, flints for arrows and pieces of stoneware . . . the workmanship of these articles did not surpass the efforts of some of the present race of Indians but it certainly destroys an opinion which prevailed, that the inhabitants in the most remote times had the use of arms, utensils and instruments made of copper, iron and steel. The discovery however, of these objects mixed with the bones of the dead, proves the high antiquity of the custom of burying with deceased persons such things as were of the most utility and comfort to them in life.

* * *

Of all the writers on the subject, Andrew Waychoff of Greene County is probably the most accurate as to the separate locations numbered in the heading of this chapter, and all included in the term "Redstone Old Fort." Waychoff must have read Ashe on Redstone as some of his comments are identical. The interesting difference is that while Ashe describes a thirty-foot mound in 1806, Waychoff, first exploring about 1900, states:

> The shape of the ancient fortifications as round, square ... to suit the natural structure of the land. They chose uplands on bluffs or high hills and water access was essential. Generally there was a large *depression* in the enclosure where no natural barrier existed, possibly for women and children out of danger; this center depression is plainly visible east or northeast of the town on a hill and I do not mean Old Fort Hanguard [#3] built by the colonists. It was in the low land beyond and across Redstone Creek.

> Neither do I mean Fort Bird [#4] built in 1759 nor Redstone Old Fort, the home of Nemacolin [#2], Chief of the Delawares. The last two now lie within the City of Brownsville [#5]. Nor do I mean one and one-half miles west of the reservoir where there is an ancient village site [near present Hiller where residents reported Indian artifacts found ca. 1930-40].

Except for Waychoff, the contradictions are legion; historian Lois Mulkearn of the Darlington Library, University of Pittsburgh, stated Fort Burd was built on the site of the Indian fortification; the notable historians, Alfred P. James and Charles Morse Stotz, in their 1958 *Drums in the Forest* stated:

> Fort Burd as it was called, stood near the site of Trent's storehouse. [Actually one and one-half to two miles distant.]

* * *

On the writer's first trip to Brownsville in 1951 from the West Coast, we first read the bronze tablet in the stone wall below the castle and then stopped in front of the stone Brashear Tavern on the Market Street hill. This was before the high bridge and grading of "New Forty" had destroyed so much of the original quality of the street. Careful not to say "Old Fort Redstone" but the more subtle "Redstone Old Fort" as we had been coached by our Greene County cousins, we inquired as to the location and asked if any part of it was still standing? Back home in Seattle, the name had conjured an image of a deteriorated log building on an ancient foundation, high on a hilltop overlooking the Monongahela, with a section of palisade still standing.

In retrospect, although we did not know the name of our informant, it seems that the somewhat shabby, slender gentleman might have been the well-informed Fayette County history professor, Jesse Coldren, who lived nearby. He pointed over his shoulder in the direction of the green spire of St. Peter's and said it was up there on top of the hill in a cornfield and that nothing of the original structure remained. It was late evening, rather dark, and we were on our way west. So, rather than attempt another exploration by flashlight as we had on the Boston Commons several weeks earlier, we decided to leave the cornfield for another trip.

In April 1974 the writer moved to Brownsville, her head still spinning with the criss-cross of contradictory statements by published historians and local 'experts' who for years, had been pondering the locations of the various forts.

Early in 1975, charter member of the Brownsville Historical Society, J. W. (Bill) Kisinger, met with the writer in his Brownsville office to chart (once and for all, we hoped) the fort locations and the route taken by Colonel James Burd and his engineer and brother-in-law, Major Joseph Shippen, to the special place called "Redstone." Bill describes himself not only as "Professor Coldren's favorite history pupil" but a

World War II military intelligence officer with training in aerial photo reconnaissance, navigation, and map reading; after the war he was an instructor in these subjects in the military reserves for ten years.

We read aloud excerpts from the various diaries and journals of the time and place, checked early maps and above all, we read Thomas Ashe. Bill had just received an excellent blowup from a small, early photograph of the hilltop where Ashe reported the ancient fortification was located. Photographer Pratt had stood at about the middle of the covered bridge across the river at Brownsville. There, on the horizon in the photograph, exactly where it should have been, was the clear shape of a symmetrical mound!

Next we drove across the present lower iron bridge which replaced the covered wooden one, and sighted from the point where the 1895 photograph was taken; clue to the exact date being identification of the riverboat *Venice* at dockside. The hilltop site was now entirely flat, the ancient mound replaced by a modern ranch house, small stable, and fenced field.

Aware of Ellis's statement in 1882 that "neither the central mound nor the parapet have been visible for many years" but confronted with the 1895 photograph that plainly showed the mound, we continued to wonder when it had been removed and Bill thought the date would coincide with the years when the game of baseball came into prominence. As a lad of about ten, Bill had played baseball, as had many much older residents of the town, at the diamond on the hill called "Old Fort." Some of these early ballplayers had also been present when the Carnegie Museum had conducted a dig at the site in the early 1930s.

A call to Dr. Don Dragoo at the Department of Man, Carnegie Museum, brought the statement that there had been no major excavations or finds but that after the large mound at Moundsville, West Virginia, had been penetrated in the 1870s, the few other mounds in the area had been unscientifically excavated and plundered ca. 1895-1900.

We now had three factors besides the 1895 photograph that fairly well placed the time of leveling the mound at around 1895-1900: Professor Waychoff did not report it in 1900 so it must have been gone; the collection of historic photographs of the Greene County Historical Society includes an 1890 "Fat and Lean Baseball Club" bearing out the baseball theory; and Dr. Dragoo's statement about mound destruction 1870-1900.

The only other known archaeological excavations for Indian occupation in southwestern Pennsylvania, and Fayette County in particular, were done by Frank C. Cresson and Edgar E. Augustine ca. 1941 as reported by the American Philosophical Society. Current excavations by California State College at the Campbell farm site near Brownsville and work done by members of the Paul R. Stewart Chapter of the Society for Pennsylvania Archaeology do not relate directly to the Redstone mound.

* * *

In the initial planning of the Ohio Company, was the need for building proper storehouses at convenient stages and to provide corn and hay for the great number of horses necessary to carry on their trade and make their settlements. Shortly after the death of the company's factor in the Ohio Valley, Hugh Parker, William Trent, then a trader and partner in the Pennsylvania Indian trade with his brother-in-law, George Croghan, was contacted by the Virginians as a replacement for Parker. It was Trent who set in motion the Ohio Company's first broad-scale expansion in January 1754.

On January 6, George Washington returning from his mission to the French on the Allegheny, met Trent and his entourage one day from Cresap's storehouse at Wills Creek, on the road to Redstone. Accompanied by settlers going out to take up Ohio Company land, Trent had as his first objective the building of an Ohio storehouse on the Monongahela at the mouth of Redstone Creek. Because of the great danger on the frontier from both Indians and French at this time, Trent was able to gather only thirty guards who traveled with him to a flat plot of ground near the mouth of Redstone, presently occupied by the Assad Iron and Metal Company as a yard. The site was confirmed when William D. Pratt, the Brownsville photographer, many years ago unearthed some old half-burned logs buried in the ground. The "Hanguard," as it was called, is described as:

> A large shed, 49 feet long by 20 feet wide made of timbers laid upon each other and roofed with bark.

To avenge the death of his half brother, Jumonville, Captain M. Coulon de Villiers sought and received command of an army of French and Indians. Setting out in large canoes, part of the army traveled up the Monongahela and disembarked at the mouth of Redstone Creek where they burned the Hanguard as described in de Villiers's Journal:

> Came to the Hangard on June 30, which was a sort of fort built with logs, one upon another, well notched in, about 30 feet in length and 20 in breadth.

On July 1, 1754, a French chaplain "offered the first mass to be celebrated within the western shadows of the Alleghenies, beneath the site of the present Saint Peter's Church . . . the first religious service of any kind recorded as being offered in Brownsville" according to the 1936 restoration booklet, *The Historic Church of St. Peter.*

The Trent forces spent only a month on the Hanguard when Thomas Cresap brought a captain's commission from Williamsburg for William Trent with instructions for him to go downriver to the Point with his work force and construct a fort there. Croghan's Diary noted in February 1754 that:

> Mr. Trent has just come out with ye Verginia goods and a quantity of toules and workmen to begin a fort and as he cant talk ye Indian languidge, I had to stay and assist him.

There were other comments relative to the fact that although the free consent of the Indians had been given at the

Treaty of Logstown in 1751, "no other forces were sent but about thirty half-starved men under a very improper commander, Captain Trent, who went about building a small, ill-constructed house at the mouth of the Monongahela." This was the lamented Fort Prince George which the French occupied almost immediately and on the site of which they built Fort Duquesne. An entry in the Calendar of Virginia State Papers for April 8, 1754, is for a bill from William Trent to the governor of Virginia for "carriage of 14 horses loaded with powder, lead and flints from Colonel Cresap's to the Ohio River." This was the material to be stored in the Hanguard.

Captain Trent received much criticism from his peers, chiefly because, unlike most of them, he was not a military man. He is also credited with making one of the first comments about coal in the area. He wrote in his ledger in April 1754:

> ... the hills abound with bituminous coal ... the inflammability of this mineral must have been known to the inhabitants at a very early period where it was exposed and ignited ... these fires came

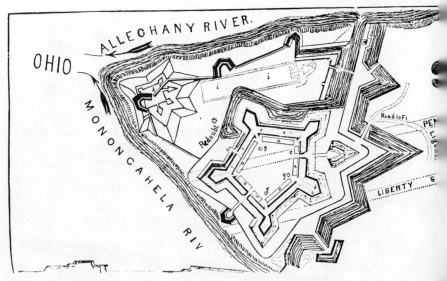

Drawing of Forts Duquesne on the Point and Pitt back of it. Drawn by R. Rat in 1761, copied from London records by Isaac Craig of Pittsburgh. From *Amer Pioneer* magazine, 1842.

in contact with the earth and stone and gave them a red appearance. The most prominent perhaps is that near a junction of a creek with the Monongahela River a short distance below the fortification which bears the name Redstone ... from the red banks near its mouth.

On May 11, 1754, George Washington sent out twenty-five men with orders to go and find some place about the mouth of Redstone which he considered "the first convenient place on the river Monongahela" where they could build a fort. The story of the next events of these fateful years is well known: the encounter with Jumonville and the French, the hasty building of Fort Necessity, followed by the burning of the Hanguard and the defeat of Braddock.

* * *

Colonel James Burd, known as the "Scotch road builder," had been constructing wilderness roads through untouched forests for years. With a party of 1,500 men, Burd left Bedford on August 23, 1758, and arrived at Loyalhanna (now Ligonier) on September 3. He began to consider the best location for Fort Ligonier in much the same way he would check out locations at Redstone the following year. Both Major Joseph Shippen and Captain Harry Gordon, as engineers, worked with Colonel Burd building Ligonier.

The Washington Bicentennial book, *Fort Necessity and Historic Shrines of the Redstone Country*, published in Uniontown in 1932, describes activities at this time, using extracts from the Burd Journals, said to be written in a minute, very legible hand, and now in the archives at Harrisburg:

At dawn of September 11, 1759 Colonel Burd's men rolled out of their blankets and stirred the ashes of last night's camp fire. Each waggoner had caught his team of horses and brought them down to drink from a little run of water close by the stockade of Washington's abandoned Fort Necessity, from which the hungry provincials had marched in a pouring rain five years before.

Wisps of vapor still showed white against the blue ridges when Burd's men broke camp for the last day's journey toward Red-

stone. They passed Braddock's grave and from the top of the next
ridge, the Western Country spread out before them in its limitless
extent, like the sea on a day when waves run low and the horizon
melts into mist.

Leaving the Nemacolin Path at Necessity and bearing right,
past Braddock's grave they did not follow present Route 40
with the dip and steep grade to the Summit, but took the
more gradual grade down the mountain to Gist's camp at
Mount Braddock, near Dunbar's. Knowing the early people
followed the creeks for water for their men and horses, from
Gist's they moved due west, crossing Big Redstone and cross-
country at Vance's Mills to follow the creek northwesterly to
Waltersburg on present Route 51. Then more nearly due west
through Smock and Tippecanoe, turning west with the creek
to the town of Grindstone and thence to the bottomland
below Coal Hill on the outskirts of Brownsville and on to the
Hanguard site, following the French and Indian trail along
Redstone to its mouth. Burd's Journal reads:

> (began) to open the road along some old blazes we took to be
> Colonel Washington's. At noon [September 13] began to cut the
> road to Redstone; began a quarter of a mile from camp [Gist's at
> Mt. Braddock], the course N.N.W. The course of General Brad-
> dock's road N.N.E. and turns much to ye eastward . . . marked
> two trees at the place of beginning thus: "The Road to Redstone,
> Col. J. Burd 1759" and "The Road to Pittsburg."

Burd's comments in his Journal indicate his powers of observation. Following Trent's remarks, he noted that Redstone
Creek ran on a solid bed of stone coal at the point now called
Coal Hill, near the old Lynn Mine. He left his men at the
bottom of Coal Hill across the creek where there is a fine
camping place on flat land. With a few others on horseback,
they rode on to the site of the Hanguard and on September-
ber 22, Burd wrote:

> Concluded upon the place for the Post being on a Hill in the Fork
> of the Monongahela and Nemacolin's Creek. Had contemplated

building the fort at the mouth of Redstone where Captain Trent
had erected the Hanguard.

On checking it out, Burd considered it a very poor location, too low to defend and susceptible to flooding. They
rode on up the shoulder of the bluff on the south side of the
creek which then rose in a gradual incline from the river, so
clearly described by Ashe. After the railroad bed was graded
at this point in 1902, the gentle slope was cut back to a steep
cliff.

In his 1758 reconnoiter, Harry Gordon had blazed the
large trees, which research indicates would be near the First
Methodist Church, as a possible location for the fort. Burd
considered it too far inland to sight up and down the river
and rode down through what has locally been called the
"Gully Tract" visible today from the east end of the high
bridge. Then the Journal records that he went up the second
hill and could see that this bluff which extended out above
the river would make an ideal fort location. The slash in the
bluff for present Market Street, graded down in 1815-17 during construction of the National Road, extended from the
"Neck" up the hill and past the great stone wall below Nemacolin Castle and hides the fact that the bluff originally extended out and over the old Municipal Building. All vestiges
of Fort Burd were removed during this grading.

On September 25, Colonel Burd described in some detail
the building of the fort: "I think this will be a very fine post.
It stands upon a hill with a regular drop on three sides, about
50 yards from the river and commanded by nothing—a very
pleasant situation." He mentioned materials used, shingles,
rafters and clapboards for the roof and the need for hinges
for the main gate.

On September 30, J. Burd wrote two letters from the
"Camp at the mouth of Nemocallings Creek on the Monongahela, one mile above the Mouth of Redstone Creek." Colonel
Bouquet observed the name was too long and also had
"rather too much of the Indian" so it was changed to Fort

Burd. The letter addressed to General Stanwix was located in the British Museum by Reid W. Stewart while pastor of the Fort Burd United Presbyterian Church in Brownsville; the second letter to Captain Harry Gordon is very similar and often quoted:

> I arrived here the 23rd current with a Detachment of 200 men of my Battalion to erect the post Colonel Bouquet advised you of from Bedford. I have a very good road from Gist's. . . .
>
> You may remember last winter you blazed the trees on the point of a hill and then you went up another which Colonel Shippen informs me you called the "Rich Hill" and on which you saw an old Indian Fort. [This name would derive from the rich coal deposits noted at the back of the hill.] At the point of this Hill I am building next the river.
>
> I determined upon this last place for two reasons, one was that just by the other place you blazed, there was a very deep gully which I could not command by so small a works, another was that Colonel Shippen told me the place where we now are you preferred, and indeed it is a very fine place, being in the fork of the river and creek, commands both and is commanded by nothing.

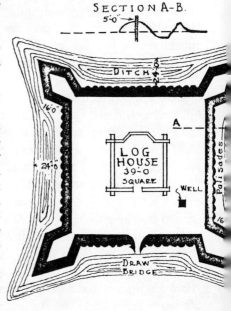

FORT BURD OR REDST
BROWNSVILLE, P.

Built by Colonel James Burd 1759
Drawn by — Joseph Shippen

Colonel Joseph Shippen's
plan of Fort Burd.

Colonel Shippen made a draught of the fort, described as being about 150 feet square with an outer defense of logs stuck upright in the ground, the faces of the bastions thirty feet, the ditch between the bastions twenty-four feet wide and opposite the faces, twelve feet; the log house thirty-nine feet square for a magazine and to contain the women and children when necessary, a gate six feet wide and eight feet high and a drawbridge over the dry ditch.

The fort was not designated to be a place of great strength for danger. When it was almost completed by the end of October, Burd garrisoned it with one officer, probably Captain James Paull, and twenty-five Virginia troops. On November 4, Burd left by canoe for Pittsburgh where he had a small house near the Point.

Fort Burd was under military occupation during Dunmore's War in 1774 and was a rendezvous point for George Rogers Clark, David Rogers, and Michael Cresap. During the Revolution many families sought shelter within the stockade of the pioneer fort which grew up and around the original Fort Burd. The writer's great-great-grandfather was born in the fort during an Indian raid in 1775. During the Indian uprisings it was used both as a storehouse and meeting place because of its strategic location; it served as a point of observation for settlers and adventurers who set out from the landing below, on the slow-moving Monongahela downriver to Pittsburgh and the Ohio.

A most unusual and little-known volume, edited by A. Margaretta Archaumbault, entitled *Guide Book of Art, Architecture and Historic Interests in Pennsylvania* was assembled for publication in 1917 by the State Federation of Pennsylvania Women, but due to World War I, it was not published until 1924. We quote from an opening statement in this book:

> During the French and Indian War, Fayette County was the scene of some of the most thrilling events in American history. There were sixteen frontier or settlers' forts in the county; only Fort Gaddis still stands [and still stands in 1975].

The Virginian, Thomas Gaddis migrated to Fayette County some time after 1755 and settled on a tract called Hundred

Acre Spring on the Catawba Indian Path, today's U.S. Route
119 in South Union Township. As Captain of the Monongalia
County, Virginia, militia in 1776 he constructed "Fort Liberty," which historians consider is the first name given to Fort
Gaddis.

In 1777 Governor Patrick Henry promoted Gaddis to lieutenant colonel in his role as Revolutionary War leader and
patriot. In August of that year, John Mason, a blacksmith
living in the area of Masontown, warned Gaddis of a planned
Tory and Indian attack on the fort at Redstone where all the
powder and lead west of the mountains were stored. Gaddis
immediately notified Lt. Colonel Thomas Brown and 100
militiamen quickly assembled and marched from Redstone
against the Tories. It was a successful rout and twelve of the
foe were captured, put in chains, and marched to Williamsburg. The squelching of the Tory uprising was one of the first
important backup actions of the Revolutionary War on the
western frontier, after the march of Captain Michael Cresap
and his sharpshooting frontiersmen from Redstone Old Fort
in 1775.

Brownsville

When Colonel Henry Bouquet directed operations at Redstone from his headquarters at Fort Pitt, he was very sensitive
about allowing any "adventurers" to settle on land around
the fort. His orders were to allow no one to cultivate gardens
or take up land more than two miles distant from the stockaded Fort Burd. The exceptions were the men who had
served at the fort 1760-65 to whom Bouquet had dispensed
military permits called "Deeds of Preference." These deeds
were recognized by the Penns as valid even before some of
the land was purchased from the Indians.

The Ellis *History of Fayette County* states that Michael
Cresap first took refuge in Fort Burd when he was in Redstone Country as a trader, when only about twenty years of
age. Realizing its importance as a location, "he bought several

hundred acres on a Virginia Certificate and based his operations there at the mouth of Dunlap Creek." Cresap was thoroughly familiar with the area having accompanied his father on many trips over Nemacolin's Path.

William Crawford's *Entry Book of Surveys for Yohogania County* shows Claim No. 38:

> ... entries in right of settlement considered by the Virginia Commissioners for Adjusting Claims as they sat at Redstone Old Fort December 16, 1779: Thomas Brown, assignee of Michael Cresap produced a certificate for his [Cresap's] settlements in the Year 1763 known by the name of "Redstone." ...

About 1770 or a little earlier, Michael built what histories describe as the "first shingled house west of the Alleghenies." As the sketch shows, he used the identical plan his builder-father, Thomas Cresap, used for his small, hewed log house at Old Town, Maryland, in 1740 as in Kenneth P. Bailey's

Michael Cresap's house at Redstone Old Fort. From drawing in *American Pioneer*, 1842.

Thomas Cresap published in 1944. After purchasing Cresap's tract, Thomas Brown occupied the log house, using it for the "first hotel in Brownsville," tavern license issued in 1783. William H. Lowdermilk's *History of Cumberland, Maryland*, has a sketch of "Cresap's Fort" showing a stockade fence; in an early photograph of the gravestones of Thomas Brown and John Washington in their original location in the public graveyard adjacent to Fort Burd, a section of old picket or paling fence is visible. It could be that a picket fence had replaced the stockade line originally constructed around the fort area. Tying it all together, and working from early draughts and maps, it seems quite clear that all of the first developments, the Public Square, Cresap's log house, the graveyard, and Fort Burd, centered in the area where the abandoned high school building now stands on the site of the old "Jeffries' Row" of red brick buildings and extended across the present Castle grounds to the river.

The earliest surveys and deeds for Brownsville include the names of Robert Thorn, Wendell Brown, and Luke Collins, all names which appear in the earliest Hampshire County, Virginia, court records, showing that the military personnel stationed at Fort Burd after 1759 were mainly recruited from that area. Hampshire County estate settlement of Peter Reed shows a payment to Michael Thorn in 1763 and payments made at Harpers Ferry to John Lemley, Wendell Brown, and Luke Collins. John Reed had "Reed's Lot" near Redstone surveyed in April 1769. Another Hampshire entry for 1769 shows George Parker's widow, Anne, administering his estate and paying out sums to Samuel Eckerlin of the Dunkard Settlement.

There is an intriguing reference in the following Fayette County deed:

> To Luke Collins, Sr. of Hampshire County, Colony of Virginia for 50 pounds Virginia Money, a certain improvement made by me in the bottom adjacent to the mouth of Dunlap Creek on the Monongahela River where I now live, bounded on one side by John

Martin above and on the other side by "Point Look Out." ...
April 9, 1770

                    —ROBERT THORN

The "bottom" through which Dunlap Creek flows was once part of Bridgeport which was absorbed by South Brownsville in 1908 and incorporated into Brownsville in 1933. Above this flat land is the knoll on which are built Nemacolin Castle and the old Jeffries home (now Crawford) which certainly answers to "Point Look Out."

The Martin plantation is where the first settlers were wont to meet for purposes of defying first the king, and then the Pennsylvania authorities, who for various reasons tried to keep them from making settlements. The Calendar of Virginia State Papers shows that 220 of the people "westward of Laurel Hill" presented a petition July 15, 1772, to the court asking that the sheriff serve no more processes as they were *not* in Pennsylvania. Always in the forefront when there was a conflict, the comment was made that "Colonel Cresap seemed to be the prime mover in this matter." Arthur St. Clair had been down in the Redstone area where the rioters took their stand on the Martin plantation, and wrote to a friend:

> The Sheriff knew several of them, particularly Abraham Tee-Garden and William TeeGarden the Younger who was the ringleaders of this gang of villains, also John Death, Andrew Gudgell and Michael Cock [Cox]. They were all armed with guns, tomahawks, pistols and clubs and the Sheriff is of the opinion that only for a pocket pistol which he produced, he would certainly have met with ill usage if he could have escaped with his life.

The "villains" and "rioters" of record became leading settlers and as an amusing aftermath of the years of conflict, Andrew Gudgell called his tract in Luzerne Township, "Peacable."

First Fayette County Survey Books show the following tracts in the Brownsville area:

Maunus Brown June 14, 1769, 306 acres on the waters of Dunlap Creek in the "New Purchase" surveyed by Alexander McClean, adjacent to Richard Crooks, Adam Brown and William Downard.

Adam Brown, land on the west side of Laurel Hill on the waters of Redstone Creek in the "New Purchase" surveyed September 28, 1769.

Maunus and Adam Brown were sons of Wendell Brown, who perhaps, was the first settler in the Redstone area. Mrs. Raoul Vajk of Uniontown lent the writer some of her detailed 1974-75 research into the family of Wendell Brown. It seems to have been determined that there were no close family ties between Thomas Brown, founder of Brownsville, and his predecessor, Wendell Brown. Research discloses the following information from the Virginia State Library:

> Wendell Brown presented two petitions for relief to the House of Burgesses; the first in 1754 which stated he lost all his horses, cattle and possessions in the Battle of Great Meadows, and the second in 1758 which stated that he and his eldest daughter were taken captive by the Indians after he returned with his wife and five children to their home on the Monongahela in 1756. He was taken to Fort Pitt, then to Quebec and from there to England and back to Virginia.

Alexander McClean who was the first surveyor to lay off the Redstone area tracts in 1769, marked land for both Luke Collins, Sr. and Jr., which they called "Fort Limerick" leading one to believe that these first cabins were constructed and fortified to the degree that each was a small "fort."

Virginia historian Kercheval in 1833 mentions that the "late Colonel Angus McDonald of near Winchester went out in the spring of 1774 with several others to survey the military bounty lands on the Ohio and Kenawha Rivers, allowed to officers." McDonald must have been out with the earliest Virginia soldiers stationed at Redstone, for there is a letter from Colonel Bouquet in his "Papers" written in 1762 asking McDonald to send his horse down to Fort Pitt by Indian Peter. Governor Dunmore commissioned Colonel McDonald to take command of 400 men from western Virginia to rendezvous at Wheeling in June 1774. They went in boats and canoes from Brownsville to the mouth of Captina Creek, piloted by Jonathan Zane, Thomas Nicholson, and Tady Kelly. It also appears that Captain Michael Cresap was under the command of Colonel McDonald 1770-75. George Rogers Clark wrote in 1786 that "Colonel Angus McDonald assigned a Military Warrant for 200 acres to me which I had located on the spot. . . ." While he took up parcels of land with the others in 1763, McDonald did not remain as a settler in the Monongahela Valley as an indenture filed in Romney March 3, 1774, shows:

> Adam Stephens, Esq. of Frederick County, Virginia sells 542 acres taken out in the name of Thomas Tobin, to Angus McDonald, land located in the Northern Neck, for 100 pounds.

The deed was witnessed by Philip Pendleton who was one of the commissioners appointed to settle Virginia land claims and who also owned many thousands of acres in Hampshire County. Among West Virginia documents in the West Virginia University Library at Morgantown is the following deed:

> Angus McDonald of Frederick County, Virginia for 25 pounds Pennsylvania currency sells to Captain Luke Collins all my right to land held westward of the Allegheny Mountains at a place called "Fort Burd" by a warrant now held by the surveyor. . . . I have disposed of my warrant of survey to be laid near Fort Burd to Captain Luke Collins which you will survey and return to Captain Collins as he directs, to include the field cleared by me where the Saw Pitt was, above the mouth of Dunlaps Creek, March 14, 1770
>
> —ANGUS McDONALD

It is of interest to note that there was an attempt to set up a sawmill operation on Dunlap Creek many years before the Cadwallader Mill was erected on their tract "Peace" next to Collins's "Fort Limerick," surveyed in 1784.

When Nicholas Cresswell came through the country in

94

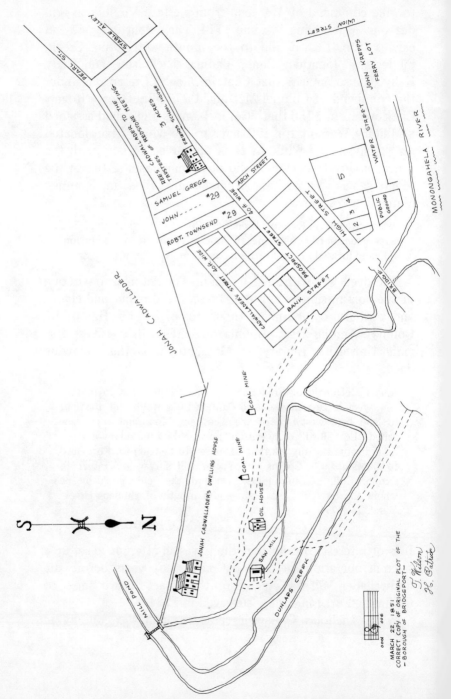

STABLE ALLEY

PEARL ST.

REES CADWALLADER TO THE
TRUSTEES OF REDSTONE MEETING
3 ACRES

FRIENDS SCHOOL HOUSE

SAMUEL GREGG

JOHN _____ #29

40 FT WIDE

ROBT. TOWNSEND #29

ARCH STREET

HIGH STREET

PROSPECT STREET

40 FT WIDE

BANK STREET

CADWALLADER'S STREET 40 FT WIDE

JONAH CADWALLADER

UNION STREET

WATER STREET

JOHN KREPPS
FERRY LOT

PUBLIC
GROUND

5

1 2 3 4

BRIDGE

MONONGAHELA RIVER

COAL MINE

COAL MINE

OIL HOUSE

SAW MILL

DUNLAPS CREEK

JONAH CADWALLADER'S DWELLING HOUSE

MILL POND

S N

MARCH 22, 1851
CORRECT COPY OF ORIGINAL PLOT OF THE
— BOROUGH OF BRIDGEPORT—

J. Wilson
H.G. Bellew

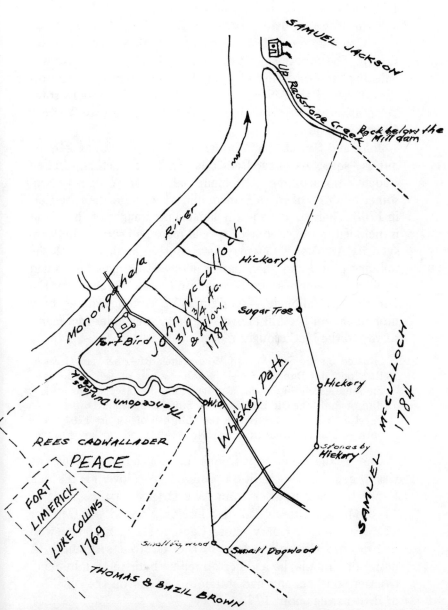

John and Samuel McCullough grant. Original Plans and Warrants, No. 1,
J. B. Hogg, Fayette County Courthouse.

1775 he noted in his Journal that he left *Catfish Camp* in July and traveled over very fine land, thinly inhabited to the river which he crossed at Redstone and stayed with Thomas Brown. This was the exact moment when Michael Cresap was enlisting the best riflemen around to march with him to Boston to the relief of Washington. Englishman Cresswell wrote: "Confusion to the scoundrels!" With that he left for Thomas Gist's plantation.

John and Samuel McCullough are described not as settlers, but as "squatters" near Redstone. They were actually Indian traders who acquired settlement rights with William Colvin, sometimes described as Brownsville's first permanent settler, in 1763. Their survey and the handsome draught of their land is included in the volume of special maps and surveys in Pennsylvania Archives. They may have come in originally with the military group and then moved west with Angus McDonald to Wheeling where Major Samuel, on horseback, executed the famous "McCullough's Leap" in 1777, commemorated by a monument on the hill above Wheeling. Alexander McClean's survey to the McCulloughs reads:

> Situated on the East Side of Monongahela River between Great Redstone and Dunlap's Creek including a part of each so far as the same extend up them, also including the place where Fort Bird or Redstone Old Fort formerly Stood in Menallin Township, Fayette County and Surveyed the 15th day of August 1784—In pursuance of an Order of Survey No. 3583 Dated 3rd July 1769.

One of the many expeditions that started from Redstone was the second expedition ordered by Governor Patrick Henry to bring powder from New Orleans in the spring of 1778. Michael Cresap had died in New York City in October 1775, so Patrick Henry chose Captain David Rodgers (who had married Cresap's widow) of the Redstone settlement. A native of Virginia, he had performed with distinction in many frontier conflicts and had settled on a farm on the outskirts of Brownsville about 1773.

Rodgers chose a group of about forty hardy frontiersmen

who were mainly farmers and not too experienced in military service. They traveled in two large flatboats built in Pittsburgh, one of which was taken up the *Mon* to Redstone where they were provisioned and the Redstone men boarded. One of the party was Bazil Brown, younger son of Brownsville's founder, Thomas Brown. The thrilling account of this voyage and the return trip is told by Edgar Hassler in his *Old Westmoreland* published in 1900. Captain Rodgers was killed during an Indian ambush on the return trip and Basil Brown with both arms hanging useless at his sides, managed with the aid of a companion to reach home at Brownsville. He lived to age seventy-five and died March 24, 1837, and is buried in Christ Church Graveyard.

* * *

There was quite a migration from Maryland, and Hagerstown in particular, when Brownsville was first laid out. The Browns and the Brashears were already there when Colonel Robert Elliott and Jacob Bowman came. Colonel Elliott purchased land in 1786 and set up a log trading post on or very near the location of Fort Burd and placed his young clerk, Jacob Bowman, in charge. In June 1788 Jacob purchased a portion of the original "Whiskey Path" tract from town founder Thomas Brown for twenty-three pounds. It is not known how long Jacob and his family lived in the log section of the present "Castle" but in 1818 the borough assessment roll lists his property as follows:

Jacob Bowman	Merchant	$7,000.
Jacob Bowman	Post Master on the Hill	3,334.
Jacob Bowman	President, Water Street	3,888.
Jacob Bowman	1 "phrame" house	900.
Jacob Bowman	log house on the hill	1,555.

After Colonel Elliott was ambushed and killed by Indians shortly after he had left his home to join General Wayne in 1794, Bowman took over the Elliott enterprises and was appointed postmaster in 1795, a position he held for many years.

The Washington *Telegraphe* and *Advertiser* ran an ad from "Redstone Old Fort" on January 15, 1796, placed by Adam Anthony and Philip Shafner who had removed their copper and tin business from Hagerstown:

> ... to this place on the bank of the river next to Mr. William Hogg's store where they will sell stills, brew, wash and tea kettles of all kinds and also give highest prices for old brass, pewter, copper and lead.

By spring of 1797 Adam Anthony was still advertising but with a new partner, Jacob Bowman:

> ... carrying on as coppersmiths in a house on the bank of the river near the bridge over Dunlap Creek; whiskey and flour will be taken in exchange for stills in the spring.

In 1796 two Quakers who were ingenious mechanics, Samuel Jackson and Jonathan Sharpless, raised in the neighborhood of paper mills on the Brandywine, planned and erected the *Redstone Paper Mill* four miles east of Brownsville. They also advertised, in May 1796, giving notice that they were making every exertion to complete their paper mill on Big Redstone and encouraged all people to save rags and bring them to the mill. Jackson, who was a millwright by trade, had built a large saw and flour mill in 1780 at the mouth of Redstone.

There is a lot of local detail in an action against Jackson taken by Robert Clarke and Neal Gillespie, Jr., in common pleas court, April term, 1812:

> ... to show that in July 1804 Samuel Savage purchased from Jackson a lot on Water Street on the Morgantown Road leading from Neal's ferry to Bridgeport, bounded on the southwest by a lot owned by Clarke and that Savage did not pay in full, but took immediate possession ... and continued there until 1810 when the property was sold by the sheriff to Clarke and Gillespie. In 1811 Clarke on behalf of himself and Gillespie took $300 in gold and silver in bags, to Jackson who refused to take the money or issue a deed.

Savage said he enclosed the lot with posts, rails and palings, walled the spring in back of the lot, planted a garden, hauled 100 odd wagon loads of stone for a dwelling house, and built a stable. Jackson furnished Savage iron which he paid for in smith work. Then when a road was about to be laid, Samuel Jackson said, "Why do thee suffer a road to be built through thy lots?"

This case continued in the courts until 1820 with several inquisitions held at Bazil Brashear's tavern on Market Street.

When the Friends migrated across the mountains to the Redstone settlement 1780-85, they came as part of the Baltimore Yearly Meeting. By 1793 the Redstone and Westland Quaker meetings had been established and were active until 1825 when they were abandoned. Robert Patterson correspondence in the Boyd Crumrine Papers includes this remark:

The Redstone and Westland Quaker Meetings are in many respects, the most interesting settlements ever made in America, of which there is very little known.

Every issue of the early newspapers contained lists of letters awaiting claim at the various post offices. In the years 1793 to 1797 some of the names listed were:

Henry Alexander	Redstone Settlement
Abraham Corbin	Redstone Settlement
Maurice Dunlevy	Redstone Settlement
Saml. and Wm. McConnell	Redstone Settlement
Rich., John and Wm. Morrow	Redstone Settlement
Charles Scott	Redstone Settlement
William Taylor	Redstone Settlement
James Veech	Redstone Settlement
John and Chas. Elliott	Redstone Settlement
Alexander Leslie	Redstone Settlement
Joseph Galbraith	near Redstone Settlement
William Guttery	near Redstone Settlement
Matthew Coulter	near Redstone Settlement
Chas. Armstrong c/o Mrs. Ferrin	Redstone Settlement
Keady McSherry	Redstone Old Fort

Nathan Chalfant   Redstone Old Fort
Patrick and Nehemiah Broderick   Monongahela River

In July 1797 the Washington papers carried the following ad:

> To be sold in Brownsville, two lots commonly called the "ferry lots" adjacent to the River Monongahela together with the right of that well-known and noted ferry on the east side of the Monongahela known as the "Redstone Ferry" late the property of Thomas Brown, deceased, by his executors, Samuel Jackson, Thomas Gregg and Basil Brown.

A great controversy arose over the erection of a market house on land formerly owned by Thomas Brown. The *Genius of Liberty* in Uniontown carried a notice in May 1807:

> It is hereby stated that Thomas Brown gave a piece of ground known as "public ground" on which it is intended to build a market house.

The second Market House built in 1832; later occupied as a town hall; notable for its fine cupola. From W. D. Pratt Collection in *Tableland Trails*, Summer 1955.

Almost immediately another notice appeared stating that "Basil and Wilkes Brown announce that *they* own the land on which it is planned to build a market house." Then Jonathan Miller, John Sheldon, and Henry Wise gave notice that they would erect a market house in Brownsville on the "public ground," stating that "in his lifetime, Thomas Brown did lay out and appropriate a certain piece of ground on the southwest side of Brownsville, known as Public Ground." Construction did not take place until 1814.

Another resident of the town who ran many large notices in area newspapers was "Lang, the Auctioneer," who advertised "land in Monongalia for sale to settlers only." James Lang also kept hemp which he sold to the many shipbuilders established on the waterfront. A list of some of the local boatbuilders in 1818 included:

Nathan Chalfant	John McCartney
John Chenny	William McFall
Cushing Church	Nathan Smith
James Carter	Robert Scott
Elijah Clark	Peter Elston

Reuben Thwaites in his *Afloat on the Ohio*, published in 1900, tells of his expedition from Brownsville:

The emigrant or trader on arrival in Pittsburgh or Redstone had generally to wait until he could either charter or build a boat although sometimes he found a chance "passenger flat" going down and in 1817 they paid $5 from Pittsburgh to Cincinnati without food. . . . There were floating shops or stores with a small flag out to indicate their character. Blacksmiths moored their floating shops to country beach or village levee; floating theatres with large barges built as play-houses were towed from town to town by gaudily painted tugs with calliopes. There were traveling sawyers with old steamboats made over into sawmills, employed by farmers to work up logs which had floated down river; chairmakers, photographers, mattress renovators, all landed at villages, scattering about their business cards and staying as long as patronage warranted.

The volume entitled *The National Road* published by the National Highways Association in 1916 was lent to the writer by Voy Lacock, nephew of John Kennedy Lacock, the historian of the Braddock Road. This history of the road is prefaced by a copy of Thomas Jefferson's authorization for the laying out of the first national road in America, and reports as follows:

> The strategic location of Brownsville appealed strongly to the commissioners who were appointed by Congress to lay out the National Road, being defined in their report of December 30, 1806 as a "point on the Monongahela best calculated to equalize the advantages of the shortest practicable portage between the Potomac and the Ohio." . . . equally distant from Beaver Creek (a tributary of the Ohio above Pittsburgh) and Fishing Creek (the first northward-flowing water west of Big Savage Mountain in Maryland) convenient to all crossing places of the Ohio between these extremes. As a port it is at least equal to any on the Monongahela, and holds superior advantages in furnishing supplies to emigrants, traders and other travelers by land and water.

After the National Road was built through Brownsville ca. 1817-20, the grading for the road prompted early merchant Robert Clarke to complain to Cumberland Road Commissioners Lacock, McGiffin, and Wilson in a letter dated 1820:

> My property between Front and Water Streets, once the best in Brownsville, has been greatly injured by the grading for the bed of the road at this point. The mud has come into my house, the grading is either too high or too low with steep banks . . . my rope house and rope walk which cost $250 are ruined with the fill. . . .

Robert Clarke then moved up the hill and built the mansion known locally as the "Snowden House" in which he lived until his death in 1840. The house stood on the Ramsey Chevrolet corner of Market Street.

There is an amusing story about boatbuilder Henry Shreve and his activities on the river. Known as a keelboat builder, Shreve had come from New Jersey to run Daniel French's famous Brownsville-built *Enterprise* on its run from Brownsville to New Orleans and return. Shreve also had novel ideas about steamboat construction and it was said that Robert Clarke and Neal Gillespie first went into partnership to back him. They didn't want to be "laughingstocks" so they told him he would have to build his boat elsewhere, in case it was a failure. So, Shreve went to Wheeling but returned to Brownsville in 1815 to work on a new type engine. A few years later, Clarke and Gillespie were co-owners of a large saw and grist mill on the Brownsville waterfront, operated by river water for which they obtained special permission by act of the assembly to throw a dam across the *Mon* with a chute in the dam for passage of boats. This was a number of years before the lock system was built.

* * *

It is not the purpose of the writer to repeat what has already been well documented, but rather to bring together many obscure fragments from scattered sources. Certainly the history of Brownsville has been documented in great and fascinating detail in readily available sources, more so than almost any other town in the area.

In 1859, James Veech (b. 1808), the able attorney and historian of Uniontown who early in his life began collecting data firsthand from Gallatin and other prominent citizens, launched a drive to revive the historic and appropriate name of pioneer days, "Redstone Old Fort," which delighted the historian Bancroft and many others. However, residents of the town preferred Brownsville and rejected a change to the old name.

In the manuscript files of Boyd Crumrine's history of Washington County at Washington and Jefferson College is an interesting bit of Brownsville history written by Crumrine. In 1887 when he became disabled from hard work in his office at night, he amused himself writing weekly columns for the Washington *Reporter* as "Uncle Enoch."

In the winter of 1854-55 I was allowed to leave our old homestead in East Bethlehem Township to attend High School at

Washington County Roads and Bridges Docket, September 1784, drawn by the well-known surveyor James Knight, showing chiefly West Brownsville.

Bridgeport, then called "Hardscrabble." Principal L. F. Parker's house was small and two-story and the three-story brick school on Scrabbletown Hill is where we received the impulse toward a sturdy life. I remember the effect on me when on frosty mornings in October I walked to the building and heard coming up to me from all directions below, the sound of hammering on metal and wood and the rapid puffing of steam from the engines and from the boiler and machine shops of Snowden and Mason across the Neck; of Herbertson & Co. near the east end of the Monongahela Bridge, from the planing mills of Carver, Wood & Co. on the river bank in Bridgeport and the boat-yard of John S. Pringle over in West Brownsville, first put in operation by James G. Blaine's father and mine in 1831.

Brownsville with its sister towns made a busy place, and the noise of its industries a startling wonder to a country youth. Two of my most intimate school mates were Henry S. Bennett and Elisha Gray, all of us about sixteen to seventeen. Bennett was the son of Capt. Elisha W. Bennett who owned and/or commanded one of the Brownsville-Pittsburgh steamboats.

There were a number of Quakers in our school. Gray's mother after his father's death in Belmont County, Ohio married a Quaker farmer in East Bethlehem, Cozens Smith. Gray apprenticed himself as a carpenter in the Carver & Wood Planing Mill. We spent our evenings in the grocery store of Seaburn Crawford near the Neck bridge. Mr. Crawford put the three boys' names down in the back of his ledger saying he would see if any of them ever amounted to anything. Elisha Gray became the real inventor of the "Bell" Telephone and was awarded the Grand Cross of the Legion of Honor of France.

The Crumrine Papers contain the original agreement between Blaine and Crumrine referred to in the above column:

Ephraim L. Blaine, Esq. and Daniel Crumrine agree to build a sawmill in West Brownsville in partnership as Crumrine & Blaine with power to drive two saws; building and property to be equal to both parties and to go into production before March 1832. Crumrine to supervise the property for two years when Blaine is to give him one-half of the right and title to the mill lot and also a 30-foot lot on the southeast side of the National Road adjacent to the mill and one-half of a coal bank on the west side of the Monongahela, late of Jonathan Morris. The mill lot lately owned by Parker Campbell, Esq., dec'd. fronts on the National Road and back toward the river; Blaine secures to Crumrine use of the stone quarry and of getting sand for building of the mill . . . as Crumrine is considered a mechanic it is left to him to plan the whole establishment, making the engine, boiler and mason work. . . . Witnesses: John and Charles Bower

In 1820 Pennsylvania was divided into two districts, Eastern and Western, for the purpose of a "Census of Manufacturing" with William B. Irish as marshal for the Western District and assistant marshals William Coulter and Jesse Townsend. Categories of the census were:

Baskets	Iron	Musical Instruments
Brass	Houses	Pewter
Cabinetware	Jewelry	Stone cutting
Earthenware & Pottery	Lace	Stoves
Gunpowder	Lead	Whiskey

The remark made by the assessors in all areas was "most industries reported they were in bad shape due to the great influx of British goods." Compared to adjacent counties, Fayette was outstanding for diversification.

The *New Boston Green Glass Factory* in Washington Township reported:

Materials used:	stone coal, wood, salt, sand and potash at an annual cost of $7,000
Employees:	30 men and 10 boys, annual wages $25,000
Products:	window glass and holloware, market value annually $20,000

But for the enormous importation of glass from Europe this business would be flourishing. The white glass works languishes and is idle for want of sales.

The *Bridgeport Cotton and Woolen Mill*, reported by Jesse Townsend:

Materials used:	cotton, wool and rolled iron, 8,000 lbs. of cotton, 52 tons rolled iron goods, extra costs $4,400

Employees: 8 men, 2 women, 20 boys or girls, annual wages $32,000; market value of products $19,000 annually

Equipment: 1 steam engine, 1 cotton picker, 6 drawing heads, 2 mules, 480 spindles, 1 nail cutting machine

Prices to and during the late war and demand for cotton yarn was equal to all that could be prepared for market at prices exceeding above, but business not good for two years.

The *Connellsville Cotton Factory* employed two men, seven women, twelve boys and six girls. "Business has not compensated owners for their time and trouble. Until a radical change is made in the resources of the country, the business will languish."

The *Yough Paper Mill* in Bullskin Township employed five men, four girls and two boys but had "little business because of the great quantity of paper coming by way of New Orleans distributed through Tennessee and Kentucky."

In Dunbar Township the *Maria Forge* employed thirty-two men, their machinery was driven by waterpower; regular price for their iron before 1819-20 was $180 per ton but in 1820 only $100 per ton "because of the importation of Russian, Swedish and English iron and unless Congress lays a protective duty the industry is doomed."

In Redstone Township a fulling mill which produced 3,000 yards of woolen material in a year with one man and one boy reported an increasing demand but no cash and decreasing pay. The *Redstone Distillery* also reported very dull business with no sales.

The *Redstone Paper Mill* of Sharpless and Jackson reported:

Materials used: 35 tons of rags, 3 tons of tanners' scraps, 300 lbs. allum, 500 lbs. 'sope' and indigo Cost of materials $4,700 per year

Employees: 8 men, 16 women, 3 boys with annual wages of $8,500 and extra costs $500

Equipment: 2 engines and 2 vats

Produced paper of various kinds and "particle board" for a market value of $9,000 but no sales of consequence. Attached grist and saw mill for use of the concern.

The *New Albany Glassworks* founded by Samuel Jackson reported:

Materials used:	27 tons of sand, 1,440 baskets of ash, 45 bbls. salt, 225 cords of wood and 27,000 bushels of coal annually
Employees:	18 men and 8 boys with wages of $4,870
Equipment:	Air furnace for the glass works and 8 pots; $9,400 invested, extra costs $1,800
Products:	Window glass, usual yearly sales $10,800 No new sales for cash.

The *Bridgeport Smithery* in Luzerne Township reported:

Materials used:	3 tons of iron, 300 weight, 900 bushels of stone coal at a cost of $690
Employees:	5 men and 1 boy
Products:	mill irons, screws, cutlery, screw augers, blow pipes for glass blowing, irons for keel boat makers, shears, etc., market value $3,000

Demand considerable but no cash sales; with good pay could do twice the business.

The *Redstone Furnace* near Uniontown reported:

Materials used:	4 tons iron, 300 lbs. steel, 150 bushels of charcoal, 800 bu. stone coal, cost $1,050
Employees:	5 men
Products:	scythes, sickles, shovels, spades, fuller and printer crews, edged tools, mill irons with annual business $8,000; $12,000 capital investment; considerable demand but no sales at any price for cash
Equipment:	Tilt hammer, grinding works and smithery

The *Springhill Furnace*, which produced the first coked iron in the United States, reported:

Materials used:	3,000 cords of wood, 1,000 tons of "oar" at an annual cost of $6,200

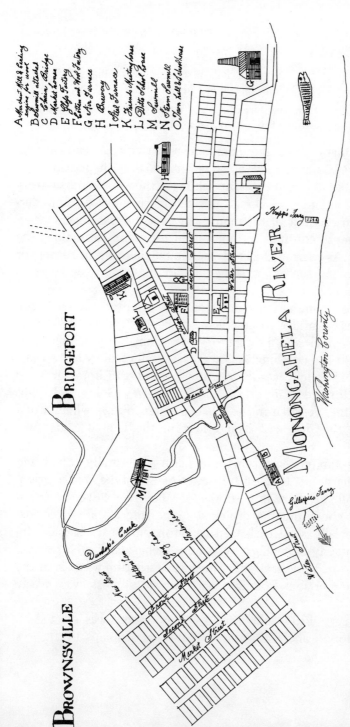

Diagram representing the relative situations of the boroughs of Brownsville and Bridgeport connected by actual survey of the intermediate space between the western end of Market Street in Brownsville and the northern edge of Bank Street in Bridgeport. Drawn by William Griffith, mathematician, in 1830. From Brownsville Public Library.

Employees:	50 men, annual wages $30,000
Machinery:	water-powered blast furnace, $50,000 investment
Products:	pigs and hollow ware; sales nominally $17,500 but none at any price for cash

Cannot sell iron because of the vast quantity of iron brought into the Western market by way of New Orleans.

Supplementing the commercial activity at Brownsville, Fayette County road dockets are filled with petitions for roads. In 1784 inhabitants showed the "intercourse from Redstone Old Fort along the river-side is now very considerable on account of the number of boats for passengers which are almost continually building in different parts along the river." As soon as the roads were built there was a clamor for bridges and there were some outstanding spans in and around Brownsville.

Judge James Finley invented and patented the first iron suspension bridge to be erected in Pennsylvania in 1801 over Jacobs Creek and a similar one over Dunlaps near the mouth. In 1820 the combination of a heavy fall of snow and a heavily laden freight wagon drawn by a number of horses was too much for the chain bridge and it gave way. Solomon Krepps drew the design for the next wooden bridge which stood until "the first cast iron bridge in the United States was erected in 1836."

The famous cast-iron bridge, still structurally sound and carrying a full load of traffic, is of arch-type construction, with all members in compression. The five cast-iron arches which constitute the principal supporting members, consist of specially shaped flanged cast-iron pipe, each section approximately seven feet by twenty inches; each arch consists of nine of these sections. The entire structure was cast at the old Herbertson Foundry and the total cost was nearly $40,000.

January 1794 John Krepp's "new ferry" was erected on the Monongahela above the mouth of Dunlaps Creek at a point viewed by old Henry Enoch, Andrew Blair, and Michael Clark. Downriver at the Brownsville riverfront the much earlier Gillespie Ferry ran across to West Brownsville. When the building of the Cumberland or National Road was begun in 1810, the Pennsylvania Assembly on March 20 authorized a bridge over the river to connect with the road to Washington, but there was much controversy and delay over actual construction.

The crossing at Brownsville is notable as the only place where the federal government did not build its own bridge to carry the National Road across; in March 1830 about the time when control of the Pike lapsed back to the states through which it passed, the Monongahela Bridge Company was incorporated with a capital stock of $44,000.

In the March term of 1831, the Washington County Common Pleas Court issued an order to value the lands on which the *Monongahela Bridge Company* was about to erect a bridge:

> Upon the petition of George Hogg, President and Robert Clarke, Peter Humrickhouse, Caleb Huntz, James L. Bowman and Daniel Moore (stage owner), managers of the company for the erection of a bridge over the river at Brownsville . . . agreeable to an Act passed at the last session of the Legislature to authorize the Governor to incorporate a company . . . they find it impossible to agree with the owners of the lands whereon said site has been fixed with regard to the valuation thereof.

The "seven disinterested men" appointed by the court, James Wilson, Alexander Clear, J. W. Nicholson, Colonel James Paull, James Gordon, Robert McClelland, and Joshua Dickerson, met at the house of John Kirkpatrick in Brownsville on February 22, 1831, and after due consideration and "mature deliberation" reported in favor of the owners of the land on the west side of the river for the sum of five thousand dollars.

The contract price for the old double covered toll bridge was $32,000 with an additional $5,000 for the approaches. It

112

was a wooden structure 630 feet long, had three spans, and was formally opened October 14, 1833. It carried traffic until September 1910 when it was condemned by the War Department and a steam cable ferry took its place. An early photograph of the wooden span shows the steamboat *Elizabeth* with its hinged smokestacks which made it possible for it to pass under the bridge. On October 8, 1914, the new steel bridge was opened for traffic and the ferry again disappeared.

* * *

In 1967 an historical restoration project was launched by the Brownsville community in alliance with the historical society. A survey of "Brownsville's rich legacy of tradition and landmarks" included the Black Horse Tavern of Whiskey Insurrection fame where the first and last meetings of the rebels were held, the Philander Knox residence, St. Peter's, the first Roman Catholic Church in western Pennsylvania, the lore-laden Episcopal Christ Church, and famed Nemacolin Castle. Brownsville's history intersects seven epochs from the American past: Prehistorical (Indian lore), French and early English Colonial period, Revolution

Nemacolin Castle built on the ground 1759 Fort Burd; a log trading post es lished in 1787 was absorbed into the c as a room. Opened in 1962 to the public twenty-two rooms furnished with anti and memorabilia.

and early Federal, Westward Movement, Preindustrial Revolution, Civil War and the Underground Railroad movement of slaves, and post Civil War Industrial Revolution.

As in the case of so many plans for restoration, sufficient funds and people to work were not forthcoming, and nothing more than the survey of landmarks was accomplished. Now in the glow of the national Bicentennial Year of 1976, plans are again underway. Under the supervision of Virginia Wright Campbell and the historical society, Nemacolin Castle has been entered on the National Register of Historic Places and is about to be completely restored. There are plans to expand and improve the old riverboat landing on Bank Street, and restoration of some of the fine old homes on Front Street by new and former residents, is well along.

In 1883 it was written:

> The situation of Brownsville is delightful with the broad and placid river dotted with steamers, tugs, flats and row boats and the town with its dark, massive buildings and the gray stone walls of the Gothic Cathedral Church, the tower of "Nemacolin," the spires of the churches . . . a creek, a tunnel, and three towns with green fields and country homes.

In 1975 the situation is still "delightful" but the steamers, flats and row boats have been replaced by the powerful towboats that tow the oil and coal barges up and down the river. To the many moods and colors of the *Mon* the chemical charge in the water adds periods of green when the river flows like a band of jade past the "green fields and country homes."

THE GREAT *HORN*SWAGGLE

WHEN WILLIAM F. HORN wrote to southwestern Pennsylvania newspapers before he emerged from Kansas in the 1930s and began to pour forth his considerable material, first in newspaper articles and then in book form, there was immediate and widespread interest and acceptance. Horn was like a "voice from the dead" explaining what was vaguely known but had never been documented.

In the introduction to *The Horn Papers* it is stated:

> The source material upon which this work is based consists of various diaries and Virginia Court records, maps and other records handed down through the Horn family, descendants of Jacob Horn, Judge of the first Virginia Court at Catfish, when this region was part of Virginia.

W. F. Horn's explanation of why these presumably official records were not on file with other papers of the period, and earlier, is:

> After the territory west of the Monongahela became part of Pennsylvania in 1781, Jacob Horn's diaries and other family papers and records of the Virginia Courts were boxed. . . .

The records apparently moved around in the family until the Horns went to Kansas from Pennsylvania in 1882, with the records stored in an old trunk. In 1891 when family records were needed the trunk was opened. The interval from 1891 to ca. 1930 seems to be unexplained; no doubt the WPA national surveys of historical records triggered Mr. Horn's activities as he emerged from the wings and occupied center stage for more than a decade in Penn's Southwest.

In 1947 the Institute of Early American History and Culture in Williamsburg published a report on its "Case Against the Horn Papers." This was reviewed in *Time* magazine with the heading "The Great *Hornswaggle* of 1945."

Residents of the Waynesburg and Clarksville areas who had met with and been interviewed by W. F. Horn in the early 1930s when he returned from his home in Kansas to the land of his ancestors, warmly defended the historical material he later published under the auspices and financing of local people. It is too late to separate what area residents told Mr. Horn from their family data and legends and what Mr. Horn either imagined or took from his family papers (some of them proven to be "faked" documents); the blend of fact and fiction after forty years has been largely accepted.

The director of the William and Mary College Institute replied to an inquiry from the writer in 1968:

> You understand, I assume, that the Report on the Horn Papers was not made to point out all the errors in the documents, but rather to show conclusively why the documents are suspect and thus to emphasize that these questionable elements (lacking ring of 18th century phraseology, geographic expressions most unusual, anachronistic words and phrases, doubtful for time and place) make the entire corpus of material unreliable . . . insofar as they are derived from the purported documents. The researcher, therefore, is skating on thin ice in using any information from Volumes I and II although they may include statements that can be authenticated in other sources.

In citing Horn material we have operated according to the last statement, attempting to authenticate, add to, or amend. In the case of official Virginia records which reach back of the period claimed by Mr. Horn, the writer has been unable to locate the Horn name in any documentation.

Perhaps the most accurate appraisal of Horn and his material is in a series of letters written 1940-50 from Howard L. Leckey of Waynesburg to his co-worker, the late Mrs. Otis Swainson of Washington, D.C., and Piedmont, California. Historian Leckey wrote from the position of chief researcher into the genealogy of some two hundred families who settled in the Tenmile Country, findings of which resulted in establishment of the Waynesburg Fort Jackson Chapter of Sons of the American Revolution with lines certified by the national society. Persons who resented the "outside" criticism from Williamsburg could accept the "educated" appraisal of Howard Leckey, who was digging out local history at the very time Mr. Horn and his "bottomless old trunk" arrived from Kansas.

The lively letters which follow were loaned to the writer for Xeroxing in 1966, by Bernice Swainson in the hope they would do some good in exposing what she considered a "hoax." The first letter in the group was written from Waynesburg May 29, 1940:

> I have hesitated to tell you of a History or rather a set of old records of Augusta County, Virginia that deal with this section that are at present being made ready for print by Mr. W. F. Horn of Wichita, Kansas. His early ancestor was a clerk for Christopher Gist and the records of Catfish Court were kept by this ancestor.

> Mr. Horn has the original papers; I have had many conversations with Mr. Horn and seen the original books but have had no chance to examine them fully for individual families.

> These documents will upset many things that have been told of the original settlers in this section. Until they have been thoroughly examined, I am holding back my own comments. Mr. Horn is an old man who was raised within sight of Tenmile and has been a student of early history all of his life. I have collaborated with him in carrying down many of the names found in these old papers.

July 17, 1945, Howard Leckey wrote:

> There will be a meeting here this week of the Historical Society and the subject of the Horn Papers will be the main topic. Mr.

Horn is here to say his work has been completed and that he leaves it now to his critics. I have spoken to him about the fact there will be just criticism in the genealogy as some of it was collected from outside the original records. He understands that part and will welcome any exposure of errors.

As for the real meat of the books, the publication of the old records . . . I am sure they will fill a part of history that you and many others have failed to find in Richmond and other sources. We shall wait and see what the reaction is. The old company rolls and tax lists will be very interesting reading, especially to Kentucky folks who never heard of Tenmile Creek.

By October of 1945 Leckey had seen the completed Vol. I and wrote:

I too am red mad about this Horn business. . . . I hope someone burns them plenty if they don't make some remedy of their mistakes. The book as it stands is ridiculous if it were not serious.

As for the original records, no matter how exact and truthful they may be, the other errors would ruin it. Honest errors can be excused, but fiction paraded as history is almost criminal.

December 11, 1945:

Now get set for this: the Horn papers are being mailed soon . . . they are worse in the second volume than they were in the first. Such a thing stands close to being criminal because so much of the record (genealogical) was available. Any person can make a mistake in using a tradition once in a while in writing history, especially where the facts are missing, but to constantly make false statements without any endeavor to ascertain the truths, borders on the criminal. [Leckey makes the point in this letter that military lists for early Washington County are found in Pennsylvania Archives under Westmoreland.]

January 4, 1946:

By this time you have received the Horn Papers and maybe have had time to cool off. I am still biting my nails. If the rest of the books are no more reliable than the biographical section then the world has a new and interesting work of fiction. I have been watching the daily papers for comments and plenty of blasting, but unfortunately when these things enter print they are accepted. All I can say is I have a fine book of maps (Volume III).

As for the old records, I don't know what to think. I know some of the names are wrong, but how to prove that is another matter. There is much that blows the Horn bugle, but *there are other things that could hardly be the fertile workings of a man's own imagination, and Horn didn't have the ability to concoct such a thing,* even were it a colossal hoax.

The tax lists pretty well follow the Bedford tax list of 1772 except for first names. How true the Clark land grants are, you may be able to find out in Washington. If they are true then we have a valuable addition.

What of Michael Cresap's Company? Is there another source to prove it? I never saw one. I do know the Virginia Militia was with General Greene, as found in Maryland records. [It seems strange that as careful a researcher as Howard Leckey would have been unaware of the list of Michael Cresap's Company in Kercheval's *History.*]

Here is an instance of important activity before and during the American Revolution by inhabitants of the Tenmile settlement that was lost and unrecorded until well into the present century when contemporary writers seized upon the colorful body of western riflemen who marched to Boston under the command of Captain Cresap.

January 10, 1946:

If the Horn Papers are phony, I mean the original stuff, then the Historical Society were taken in with the rest. You saw as much of the original as I did. You saw the old book at the time I examined it. I did suspect that some of the record had been tampered with, but not criminally. Only to bring out illegible records.

Something of this record is certainly authentic, but I do suspect doctoring . . . someone chose first names to fit initials, thus J. Seals became John Seals instead of James as it should be, and numerous other names like that. I know for sure some of the surnames are those of men of record, but the given names are wrong.

I could prove a thing or two that neither Horn or any of the ones who brought out the book could have any knowledge of, but which are in the book! Were it not for this, I would choose to treat the whole work as the figment of someone's imagination. I am informed by persons who have seen Gist's Journal that there is no mention of the Horns in that work.

February 15, 1947:

Now for the Horn raspberries again. There have been two committees here in the last few weeks to look over the originals for frauds. One is from William and Mary College and if you know Dr. Douglas Adair, you might write him a blast for safety. I have my own doubts as to the thing being other than a fraud, but some uncanny deductions must have been made by someone to have given the work any semblance of truth. . . .

June 4, 1947:

Had Horn kept to the old Journal, few could have jumped on his books. Evidence is piling up that all this land was taken up by the Traders that lost out in Pontiac's War in 1763 [The Suffering Traders] and that many of them were here 1751-58 . . . only need some verification of grants from Virginia and will try to get them at Richmond.

Looks like the Harrods may have bought their land from Thomas Gist, who reported the receipt of 2,000 acres for his services under Bouquet. He was guide for the Swan-Vanmetre party in 1769 and it looks like he was bringing them in to take over land he had owned or had bought from John Owens or another Indian Trader.

Recorded deed in Washington County shows John Owens selling the land in 1757 to Abraham Teagarden and the tract covered the Swan-Van Metre-Harrod settlement. I just lately found that the land on which the Swans settled was bought by Teagarden from Owens in 1757 at Fort Pitt. Teagarden lived in Frederick County, Maryland at the time but shortly came to Fort Redstone where he operated a ferry, close to the Gist settlement.

There is a possibility that Swan bought the right to settle from Teagarden before leaving Maryland. My theory is that he did, or else he bought it from Gist who had gotten it from Teagarden. I wish I could check the land sales at Richmond to find when this land was first recorded there and who got the *first grant*—it must have been a large one.

May 23, 1949:

I think I told you I had read the complete set of Bouquet Papers 1755-65 . . . there develops a picture of how so many of our Tenmile settlers came into a knowledge of the Monongahela Country . . . so many of them came here and settled. With my knowledge of the pioneers of this section, I get an almost definite picture, indicating that the Tenmile saw most of them during the 1751-60 period.

They seem to have been here selecting sites, then were in and out of it, depending on the attitude of the Indians, until the Stanwix Treaty was signed, then all these first pioneers flocked to pre-chosen lands. Horn guessed so near right about some of these things that if he had had any real knowledge of the first settlers, he could have put out a book that would have stood up. . . .

December 26, 1949:

Mr. Delf Norona of Wheeling [president of the Historical Society of West Virginia] was one of the most enthusiastic of Horn's collaborators and worked in West Virginia to help him in every way he could . . . we were all hoping for records we felt *should* exist, *but have so far escaped historians.* Norona turned it down as a fraud when shown the evidence.

5

MORE THAN JUST NAMES
Christopher Gist
Thomas and Michael Cresap

CHRISTOPHER AND NATHANIEL Gist were in Southwestern Pennsylvania and Kentucky some eighteen years before Boone but not until recent years were the Gists accorded credit for their part in western expansion.

The Reverend William Hanna of Greene County was one of the few early writers besides James Veech who gave firsthand geographical knowledge of Gist's itineraries and landmarks long before the time of highway improvement, when visible traces yet remained as guideposts on the original trails. Sherman Day's *Historical Recollections of the State of Pennsylvania*, published in 1843, mentions Gist's Journals fifty years before William M. Darlington edited and published *Christopher Gist's Journals* in 1893. There seems little reason for the mystery that has surrounded the name, or for as able an historian as the late Sylvester K. Stevens, director of the Pennsylvania Historical and Museum Commission, in a prefatory note to the recent edition of Gist's Journals, to state:

... the legendary figure of Christopher Gist truly appeared out of nowhere to become a strangely remote figure determining the course of empire in the mid-18th century.

Of English descent, Christopher (1705-1759) was the namesake of his grandfather who died in 1691; Maryland

121

newspapers carried notices of the sale of family holdings in Baltimore, the seat of the Gist family. Richard, father of Christopher II was surveyor of the Western Shore of Maryland, member of a commission to lay off the town of Baltimore, a large plantation owner, a justice, and member of the Maryland Assembly.

With the background of an educated and cultivated family, coupled with his understanding of the wilderness west of his native state, there was little wonder that Christopher Gist was chosen by the great landowners of America and England to explore, locate, and survey their holdings. He was not only mathematically exact, but was a precise draftsman in his early mapping of western lands.

Douglas Southall Freeman described Gist as a "very paragon of a frontiersman who could perforate a squirrel at one-quarter mile range and construct a woodland shelter at a moment's notice."

His character became his varied roles as explorer-trader-diplomat. Adversity never seemed to depress him; in writing in his Journal of sickness or delay on account of weather he was always optimistic, saying he had been sick "but was recovered" and although held in camp by rain had an opportunity to "kill a bear." He was never robust, but had vast endurance. His daily life was solitary and he was known to have left an Indian town to sleep in the forest rather than keep company with those he denounced as "reprobate traders." He could make himself comfortable anywhere in the wilderness or in caves, particularly in the one known as "Gist's Cave" described by Pittsburgh writer, George Swetnam, in the *Press* in 1956:

... identification was first made in 1951 by Lois Mulkearn, head of the University of Pittsburgh Darlington Library, on Wallace's Run in Fayette County, which Gist himself described as a large cavity in a rock about 30 x 20 feet, 7 feet high with an even floor and a large entrance. This cave was reported as six miles from Nemacolin's Camp at Dunbar Creek.

The Indians were devoted to Gist and called him "Anno-sanah," meaning a good man who had lived among them. No frontiersman understood them better or had greater patience in dealing with them, even though his knowledge of Indian languages was said to be scanty compared to Andrew Montour or his antecedent, Conrad Weiser. The fact that no one of his period left a physical description of Gist fortifies the impression we have of a reserved, modest person compared to the 1742 flamboyant description of Montour, the man Gist hired as interpreter:

... half French from his father and half Indian from his mother who had been very fluent in Indian dialects. His cast of counte-

Sketch of mural at West Overton, Pennsylvania, entitled "Washington and Gist Stop at Frazier's Cabin," painted ca. 1928 by Mrs. Joseph B. Platt of New York. A rare attempt to portray Christopher Gist as he and Washington watched the raising of the Rattlesnake Flag.

nance decidedly European, but his face circled with a broad band of paint applied with bear's fat. He wore a brown broadcloth coat with scarlet damask lapel waistcoat, shirt out over his breeches, black Cordovan handkerchief decked with silver bugles, shoes, stockings and hat. His ears were hung with pendants of brass and wires plaited like the handles of a basket.

Washington described Gist as indefatigable, patient, honest, and zealous. He was equally capable of handling a gun, a compass, or a canoe; conscientious in the performance of duty but not inclined to give counsel unless asked. More than any other man, Christopher Gist was George Washington's teacher in the art of the frontiersman who had to deal with both the wilderness and the uncertain savages.

One of Gist's first agreements made in 1750, with the Ohio Company, dealt with the removal of 150 or more families to the western land of the company. Within two years of their settlement on "contiguous grants" they were to have fee simple land of not to exceed fifty acres for every person more than four, and for every person with less than four, the settler was to pay the company four pounds for every one hundred acres within three years of seating. All settlers were given five years free of quitrent. Gist established his first families at his plantation Monongahela now known as Mount Braddock located between Uniontown and Connellsville and extending to the slopes of Laurel Hill. Gist's own dwelling shows on early maps only a few paces from the 1802 elegant stone Meason mansion.

There are such varying reports as to the actual number of families who first settled with Gist that it is impossible to be exact. Not even Mr. Horn attempted a list of names of the few families who first settled before the later migrations led by Christopher's son, Thomas. The most reliable clues are found in the Hoge collection, the William Crawford *Book of Surveys*, and comments by Howard Leckey.

In June 1754 Washington had been at Gist's throwing up breastworks around his buildings against the French. When they realized they could not defend their position, they abandoned the plantation for the retreat to Wills Creek. The Virginia House of Burgesses published Gist's plea for assistance:

> Petition of Christopher Gist saying he had used his utmost endeavors for some years to promote settlement on His Majesty's lands on the River Ohio, had engaged a number of families to remove there from adjoining Provinces.
>
> Gist had settled there with his family and Colonel Washington with his troops had camped on his Plantation and his horses and carriage being used in His Majesty's service, he could not remove his effects, worth about 200 pounds; they were taken by the French who set fire to his fences and all his houses. The fences had been used for palisades for Washington's troops. He was ready to risk his life and small fortune but wished to be recompensed for his losses.

On May 7, 1755, the petition was introduced again, referred to the next session and on May 9 it was rejected.

In one of his last reports, Christopher Gist warned John Forbes that there were 129 Catawbas, Tuscaroras, and Nottaways newly arrived at Winchester and that his "Intelligence" had warned of a large party of Indians with some white men who had been discovered in western Augusta County. After an investigation, General Forbes wrote to Bouquet that, "Byrd found no Catawbas at Winchester and Mr. Gist was too premature (as he generally is) in his Intelligence. . . ."

Bouquet then wrote back to Forbes that the Catawbas and Cherokees "exist only in Mr. Gist's imagination."

In July 1759 Captain James Gunn wrote to Colonel Henry Bouquet from Winchester that he considered it "proper to advise you that Captain Gist, Deputy Agent for Indian Affairs, died on the road from Williamsburg on July 25, with smallpox."

There is a final ironic and rather sad twist to the affairs of the Gists in Penn's Southwest in certain Fayette County land transfers after the death in 1787 of Christopher's son, Thomas Gist. In order to pay a debt of *nine pounds* owed by

Thomas, the Westmoreland sheriff seized the 400 acres where he had lived and sold it at public auction November 20, 1788, to the highest bidder, and Isaac Meason for a bid of thirty pounds began his acquisition of Gist land on which he founded his iron empire. In the spring of 1789 the Fayette County sheriff recovered against Anne Gist for 120 pounds by selling another Gist tract of 620 acres to Meason for thirty-one pounds. Five years later the Gists sued Meason and were able to make him pay a total of 1,200 pounds for 1,000 acres.

Meason was frequently in court over his land and he stated that "Gist hath surveys made on Virginia rights which are more agreeable to me than those made on Pennsylvania applications."

* * *

Yorkshireman Thomas Cresap was born in 1694 and emigrated to America when about fifteen years of age. Unlike his more reserved and mysterious counterpart, Christopher Gist, Thomas Cresap, almost from the moment he landed in this country, was identified as the "game cock of the Maryland mountains." As agent for the Marylanders Lord Calvert and Daniel Dulaney, Cresap was considered to be both "bright and tricky" and the only non-aristocrat in the original group of founders of the Ohio Company of Virginia.

In the Abraham Johnson scrapbook material in the West Virginia University Library is the statement that Patterson Creek in the Fairfax Northern Neck grant was named for a scout who "explored with Thomas Cresap 1730-40." That Thomas Cresap, the exceptional rather than typical frontiersman, was out unofficially surveying and locating land as early or earlier than any of the other frontier figures, is not widely known. Kenneth P. Bailey's 1944 *Thomas Cresap—Maryland Frontiersman* states:

> It was Cresap's life work to push the Maryland and Virginia frontiers across the Alleghenies and on into the Ohio Valley . . . he

was the outstanding American colonial frontiersman of his period.

The Gist Journals describe Colonel Cresap as the earliest permanent settler in western Maryland at Old Town, having obtained a Maryland warrant for 500 acres and moving there in 1731 some time after his first marriage to a Miss Johnson; the house was marked on Lewis Evans's 1749 map of Pennsylvania, as it stood in the disputed area between Pennsylvania and Maryland.

Trained as a carpenter, Thomas had ample opportunity to construct a number of substantial log and stone houses as the need arose to move from one location to another. As a leader of Maryland's western settlers he seemed to always be in the thick of any controversy. Both Pennsylvania and Maryland archives devote pages to the Cresap border conflict at "Peach Bottom" which resulted in the burning of his house and Cresap himself being taken to jail in Philadelphia which he cockily described as a "nice Maryland town." While he was imprisoned, friendly Indians who always got along well with Thomas, took his wife and children and cared for them in a town near Little York. After this experience there was another move to "Long Meadows" near Antietam, Maryland, where, after borrowing 500 pounds from Daniel Dulaney, Cresap settled down to become an Indian trader and to build a handsome stone house.

Seemingly dogged by adversity, the furs and skins he had accumulated and shipped to Europe were captured by the French. Again, in order to discharge a debt, he turned his fine house and farm over to Dulaney and moved to the plantation he called "Skipton" after his birthplace in England. Here on the banks of the Potomac near its fork at the place called Old Town he spent the remainder of his life.

There was a temporary move to the Conococheague settlement during the French and Indian War when Thomas Cresap, commissioned a colonel, lead a company against the Indians. His formal education was scanty but by industry and application he became surveyor of Prince Georges County and also represented the county in the Maryland Legislature. After he became associated with the Ohio Company, in 1750 Thomas with Factor Hugh Parker purchased a piece of Fairfax land and built the first company building, a timber two-story double storehouse which stood on the south bank of the Potomac, facing and directly opposite present Cumberland. This building was a well-known and official tobacco warehouse or "factory" for many years after its use by the Ohio Company. In October 1785 an act of the legislature established the inspection of tobacco in Virginia and designated the lands of Thomas Cresap "in Hampshire County in the forks of the North and South branches of the Potowmack" with tobacco transported by both boat and wagon. Tobacco was received there in payment of taxes with credit at the rate of eighteen shillings per hundred. The official warehouses were required to be sound with good locks, one brick stack either square or funnel-shaped six feet high and four feet in diameter with a proper arch at the bottom for burning tobacco that was refused at the warehouse. Of the sixty-seven cents collected on each hogshead, seven cents went for warehouse rent.

When the Wills Creek warehouse was first built in the early days of Ohio Company activity, along with every kind of trading goods, Cresap kept a supply of wampum and horses for Indians, scouts, or anyone who needed a mount. He maintained considerable pasture for there are notes concerning the "green guard" of various companies being sent to Colonel Cresap's.

Hampshire County records on file at Romney indicate numerous parcels of land held by Cresap:

> Indenture August 8, 1760 Hugh Murphew to Thomas Cresap for 30 pounds Lot 62 which Murphew holds by virtue of his wife Martha, late widow of John French, by dower which contains the dwelling and plantation of the late John French on the South Branch. . . .

Indenture February 15, 1763 Thomas Cresap of Frederick County, Maryland sells to William Haggard of Hampshire County, Virginia 100 acres laying on Wapecomo River or Great South Branch of Potomach for 10 pounds Virginia money or 1500 pounds good merchantable tobacco every year as rent.

Evidence of Thomas's sharp attention to business is clear in the agreement:

... Haggard agrees to plant an orchard of 100 aple trees on the most convenient part of the premises and within two years to build at his own expense and trouble, a good framed barn 50 x 20 underpinned with stone one foot high from the earth, and to clear and cultivate one acre as meadow. ...

In December 1763 Job and Bethia Pearsall granted Lot 64 of 310 acres in the Northern Neck to Thomas Cresap of Frederick County, Maryland. It is said that Thomas married a second time when he was over eighty. Margaret and Thomas Cresap sold a 400-acre piece to Michael Cresap of Hampshire County "on the North Branch where he now lives" in December 1779. Thomas had five children, three sons, Daniel, Thomas, and Michael, and two daughters, Sarah and Elizabeth. At a very advanced age he is said to have made a trip to England to see his old home. Death came to the tough spirited Marylander early in 1787 when he was ninety-three. Rather than a will, Hampshire County, West Virginia, Will Book No. 2 contains this entry:

Inventory of the Estate of Coll. Thomas Cresap deceased taken by us the subscribers, Robert Parker, Jacob Slagle, and Job Pearsall, appointed Appraisers by the Hampshire Court ... this 30th day of April 1787.

Items included many dishes, pewter, silver, old bedsteads and bedding, many pots and pans, hair and leather trunks, a most unusual item of a "pewter chamber pot" (In the beautifully restored 1799 Compass Inn at Laughlintown, near Ligonier, one of the bedrooms has an early wooden cabinet toilet with a pewter chamber pot.) and a Negro wench valued at fifty pounds. The personal property totaled a little over seventy-two pounds and was accepted for recording by the court on October 11, 1787.

* * *

Michael, son of Colonel Thomas Cresap and his first wife, was born June 29, 1742, in Frederick County, Maryland. In an effort to vindicate Michael's alleged involvement in the murder of members of the Indian Chief Logan's family, John Jeremiah Jacob wrote *A Biographical Sketch of the Life of the Late Captain Michael Cresap*, which was first printed in 1826.

John J. Jacob started life as Cresap's clerk and was placed in charge of Michael's trading post at Redstone Old Fort. When the Virginia commissioners to settle claims sat at the fort, they gave a table and chair to young Jacob so that when any of the captains or officers appeared on whom he had claims for Captain Cresap, the commissioners first deducted Jacob's claims for Cresap's accounts out of their pay. Thus, during the absence of Michael, Jacob obtained large drafts on the treasury of Virginia with the prospect of delighting him on his return from Boston with the sum. But Michael Cresap became very ill during the march to Boston and died in New York City on October 5, 1775. Jacob took charge of Cresap's affairs and remained with his widow and children until July 1776. He marched to General Washington's camp and remained in service until 1781, when he returned to Maryland and married Cresap's widow. They lived together for forty years, moving to Ohio where Jacob became chief justice in 1801 and was a Methodist preacher until his death at Chillicothe in the late 1850s.

Michael is described by the man who knew him and his family so intimately, as having "great energy, enterprise and decision and moved quickly to do things." He was naturally cheerful, full of vivacity, and very communicative; he was treated with marked and respectful attention by all who listened to his counsel. Out on the frontier with his father from his earliest youth, Michael was noted as a sharpshooter and a leader of men.

Married quite young to Miss Mary Whitehead of Philadelphia, Michael Cresap had his first business experience as a merchant near his father's establishment. Romney court records reveal a 1766 deed for fifty-four acres to Michael on the Potomac "below ye mouth of the South Branch and Col. Thomas Cresap's." With most of his creditors on the move westward, Michael had difficulty collecting for his goods. Deciding that he could make money in the rich bottoms of the Ohio if he could secure title to the land, he hired six or seven young men at two pounds ten shillings per month and went into the wilderness of the Ohio Valley in the early spring of 1774. They worked clearing land, splitting rails, and started a number of cabins. Michael's timing was unfortunate due to the hostility of the western Indians over the recent white settlements in Kentucky and Virginia Governor Dunmore's move to embroil the new settlers in a war with the Indians in order to keep British authority over the American colonies.

In June Michael had been given a Captain's commission in the Hampshire County Militia, and wishing to aid the settlers on the frontier, he had raised a company of 400 men from "Western Virginia" under the command of then Major Angus McDonald and marched with them to attack the Indians on the Muskingum. Major John Connolly, mouthpiece for Governor Dunmore, was largely responsible for the accusation of Cresap for the Logan murders during Dunmore's War. The many affidavits in Michael's behalf included one from George Rogers Clark who was also on Fish Creek near Wheeling at the time.

We know from Fayette County deeds that Michael had purchased land near Fort Burd in 1763 and had built a neat log house so that he might claim title by reason of settlement. Known for his endurance and boldness, he became the chief officer at Redstone, and during his command, rallies or musters were held at stated periods to exchange views and adopt plans, or to just spend evenings around a huge log fire recounting adventures or holding a stag dance:

> ... yeomanry, or men in the middle and lower walks of life, especially on or near our frontiers, were the best marksmen in the world. ... I remember when the company commanded by Captain Cresap lay at Redstone Old Fort, in the time of Dunmore's war, a buzzard came sailing over us at some considerable hight, when three men—Daniel Cresap, Joseph Cresap and William Ogle—all raising their rifles, fired at the same instant. The buzzard fell, ... all three of their balls had pierced it. [From Jacob.]

The affairs of Michael Cresap as revealed in Romney records seem to indicate he might have had a premonition of his early death, or in addition to being a fearless and daring frontiersman, he was also a cautious husband and father. The following sale of land took place March 13, 1775: "Indenture of Michael Cresap, Sr. and wife Mary who sell land on the South Branch. . . ."

Hampshire County (Romney) Will Book No. 2 contains the will of Michael Cresap:

> I, Michael Cresap of Frederick County in the Province of Maryland being in good health and of sound mind and memory but calling to mind the certainty of death and precarious causes . . . my executors to sell the following tracts of land:

> A tract in Maryland of 70 acres known by the name of "Betty's Blessing", also lands laying in the Colony of Virginia which I purchased of Isaac and Gabriel Cox and in Hampshire County.

> ... to my son James Cresap that tract of land laying in Frederick County, Maryland called the "Seven Springs" when he arrives at the age of twenty . . . the rents of my estate to my loving wife Mary Cresap during her natural life . . . the remainder both real and personal to be sold and equally divided between my daughters, Mary, Elizabeth and Sarah. Made this 28th day of June 1774

> NB—A certain Negro wench named Bett is not intended to be included in the personal estate but to be the immediate property of my wife, Mary as a gift . . . my executors to dispose of the vacant or unconveyed lotts in the Town of Skipton as laid off by the Plan of said Town and the money to be applied to the education of my son James Cresap . . . to my loving wife Mary all the plate etc. not before mentioned.

His father, Thomas Cresap, and Thomas Warring, two of the witnesses to the will, testified on the 24th day of November 1775 as to the execution of the document. The marked individuality of members of the Cresap family is apparent in most of the events in which they participated. On the third page of Michael's will is a note:

> Sir: I do hereby refuse to abide by my husband Mr. Michael Cresap's Will but take my third of his Estate as the Law Directs. As Witness my hand this 24th day of November 1775
>
> MARY CRESAP
>
> Wit: David Mitchell
> Thomas French

Considering the name of witness Thomas French and the fact that the will is recorded in Hampshire County, it is possible that Mary and her children were living on the plantation that her father-in-law had purchased from Hugh and Martha French Murphew. The mobile quality of the Cresap households seems to be confirmed by the fact that Michael Cresap did not refer

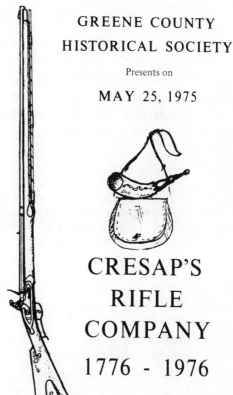

GREENE COUNTY
HISTORICAL SOCIETY

Presents on

MAY 25, 1975

CRESAP'S RIFLE COMPANY

1776 - 1976

Program of Waynesburg's Revolutionary War memorial *Cresap's Rifle Company* commanded by Captain Robert Faddis. Members of the company carry detailed and accurate copies of the muzzle-loading Pennsylvania long rifle, crafted by these modern-day riflemen. The frontier clothing worn by the men and their wives at local celebrations are as authentic as possible. Whether raising a "Liberty Pole" or engaged in a mock battle with red-coated Tories, the rifle company is a fitting memorial to Captain Michael Cresap.

134

to any of his holdings as "the place where I now live" which
was such a part of most early wills.

Washington and Fayette County records of court actions
are filled with suits brought by Mary and John J. Jacob as
Michael's executors over land titles and various debts. In the
spring of 1775 before the march to Boston, Michael had
returned to the Ohio with another group of young men to
complete the cabins and fencing they had started the year
before near Wheeling. His efforts were apparently rewarded
according to the following:

> Michael Cresap, deceased, is entitled to 400 acres in Monongalia
> County on the Ohio River adjacent to the mouth of Bull Creek in
> right of having settled tenant on the land to include his settle-
> ment made in 1775 with pre-emption rights of 1,000 acres. The
> heir-at-law of Cresap is entitled to 400 acres at the mouth of Fish
> Creek in right of having settled with a tenant in 1775, also 400
> acres more above the mouth of Bull Creek.

In June of 1775 Michael Cresap was asked to raise two
companies of riflemen to go to the defense of the Continental Army near Boston. Michael was unwell at this time and
did not think he could perform this tour of duty; he left his
hired hands in the west and with the help of Jacob, recruited
a group of men equipped with rifles. Michael had a talent for
recruiting men and it was said had he been in better health,
he could have raised a regiment. The description of this group
of 130 men "painted like Indians," who traveled 800 miles
from the banks of the Ohio, has become famous. Michael
marched at their head in the last brave and colorful episode
of his life.

6

THE HUPP CABIN

HOWARD L. LECKEY in his *The Tenmile Country and Its Pioneer Families,* published in 1950, stated:

Some time between 1766 and 1769 Everhardt Hupp chose a place for his cabin, later known as Black Dog Hollow, about opposite where the first bridge spans Tenmile Creek. Here he built a sizeable cabin which became a place of entertainment and shelter for the immigrants.

Field notes and original surveys of John Hoge, deputy surveyor, in the Washington and Jefferson Historical Collection show draughts for the 452-acre "Hops Regard" and "Hops Fragments" issued out of the Pennsylvania Land Office, Bedford County, in 1769 to Everhardt and John Hop.

January 1792 Quarter Sessions Court Docket in the Washington County Courthouse shows a petition for a road from Muddy Creek and Whiteley Road to:

Everhard Hupp's Mill to intersect the Pittsburgh Road, viewed by Everhard Hupp, George Teegarden, Abijah McClain and Frederick Wise [founder of Fredericktown].

The Hupp mill and dam near the mouth of Tenmile Creek were the subject of numerous agreements on file between the Hupp and Teegarden families over control of the dam. Prosperous George Teegarden was continually on guard to keep the Hupps out of his valuable bottomland.

Clarence Nyswaner, of the village of Clarksville, described

136

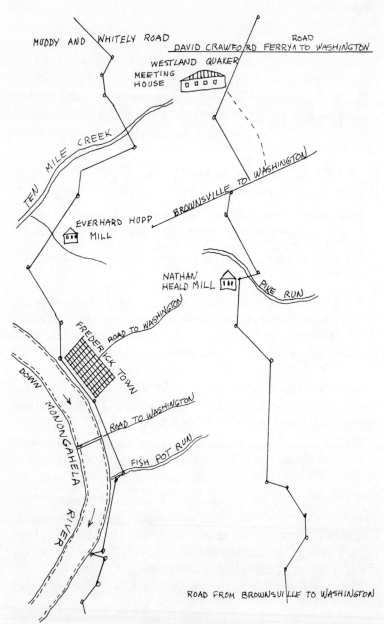

Washington County Roads and Bridges Docket No. 1. Road from the Muddy and Whiteley Road to the Pittsburgh and Brownsville Road, 1790, showing Everhard Hupp mill.

the early road from Black Dog Hollow up Hog Hill (so named for the "drove road" with its bands of hogs) as very muddy in winter and very dusty in summer; they used to build runs called "breakers" to carry the water off across the road and then rested their horses at these points with the wagon wheels in the troughs.

Abandoned shafts into the coal banks of old along the hollow weakened the bank as it slopes up from the small run and collapsed some of the road edge. Now another onslaught of coal activity is in progress, this time a strip-mining operation to reach the eighteen-inch vein of Waynesburg coal lying some forty-five feet below the surface.

It made me sick recently to drive the Sandy Plains Road in East Bethlehem Township, Washington County, through the hollow and watch and hear the snarling earthmover shove the chunks and slabs of sandstone and yellow clay down over the precipice to fill in a slide, widening the precarious road so that the huge forty-five ton coal trucks could make it down the hill to Tenmile Creek from historic Hupp Point.

During the 1920s the Besco or Vesta Coal Company dismantled the pre-Revolutionary log house and dragged the still solid, sound logs down the hill for foundations of miners' houses. However, ownership of the surface remained in the Hupp name until purchased in 1972 by the present strip-mining operator.

In 1970 a trip was made with Hobart and Ann Jennings, who live on part of the original Hupp grants, to the top of the ridge where the ancient cabin had stood. The entire flat area on the point, surrounding the foundation, had been somewhat desecrated by earlier deep mining so that it was difficult to distinguish the coal seam cracks from the defile of the original wagon road past the cabin.

Where we had traced the early path with its mounting block to the stoned-in spring, almost undisturbed for two hundred years, it was now a ruined jumble of rock, yellow clay, and brush which had destroyed the contour of the

138

ridge, the reputed Indian mound, the spring itself and almost every vestige of the place where the first settlers west of the Monongahela River had stopped with the Hupp family while they reconnoitered, built their own cabins, or sought safety from Indian attack.

A poignant reminder of the Hupp cabin as a welcome stopping place is the nuncupative will in Washington County Will Book No. 3, page 34:

Hezekiah Wright in the latter part of the month of December 1814 at the house of Everhart Hupp of East Bethlehem, being sick of the sickness whereof he died on the first day of January following, in the same house, did make and declare his Last Will which was witnessed by Rachel Perkins who said on December 27 Hezekiah called her and Philip Hupp to the bedside where he lay and there told the said Philip that he would will to him his riding horse, saddle and bridle, his watch and his gun, as he thought he would die, that he had enough in the house to bury him decently and anything that remained after the funeral charges were paid he gave to the family as there were no persons he respected more.

As to his people, they should have none of it. The black boy he had with him had rendered such service that if he, Hezekiah died, he was free from further bondage to anyone and was to have the black horse he rode when he came to the premises.

The will was witnessed by George Teegarden and Everhart Hupp. On May 24, 1815, letters of administration were issued to the witnesses "for Hezekiah Wright (A Traveller) who died on January 1, 1815."

Andrew J. Waychoff, Waynesburg College professor and historian, wrote a series of "Local History" columns for a Greene County newspaper in the 1930s and in one described the Hupp cabin:

Two radiating points for the pioneer settlers were Swearingen's Fort, later Crow's Fort near the Cross Roads in Fayette County, and the home of Everhard and Margaret Hupp about one mile west of Millsboro on the bluff west of Black Dog Hollow on the north side of Tenmile Creek.

The first road entered Greene County across the Monongahela River near Fredericktown; the crossing was located by the Westmoreland County Court (during its jurisdiction) as the road from Redstone Old Fort ten miles from the mouth of Tenmile Creek. In 1750 the Delaware Indians helped Michael Cresap clear the road for his pack animals and it became known as the Cresap Road. The Hughes, Neils, Hillers and Swans with others from Virginia came by way of the Hupp's, by the rudely cut road and camped near the log house.

Mrs. Margaret (Thomas) Hupp was the first white woman known to have lived west of the Monongahela. The Hupps bought a large acreage of the Indians who after the Rofoelty Massacre, came to the Hupp home, got something to eat, and were friendly.

Margaret Hupp's frugal repast consisted of johnny or journey cake shortened with bear fat, dried venison, and Adam's ale from the hillside spring, still running clear in 1970. The Hupp cabin became the Sunday morning rendezvous for all the men in the settlement who were tired of their own bad cooking. They brought their game to Margaret to prepare. For many years, this cabin was the most useful in the settlement of the western wilderness and was a rallying point in times of danger.

There are few pen portraits of early southwestern Pennsylvania settlers. One can conjure a picture from entries in the tavern ledger of the early Hotel Milford in Waynesburg showing that Hupp, Bumgarner, and Teegarden men gathered in the tavern room on their trips to the county seat 1813-15 to exchange gossip and drink "cherry royal," apple brandy, and the famous river rye whiskey.

Washington County attorney and historian, Boyd Crumrine, who died at age seventy-eight in 1916, wrote in 1908 of early days in the Monongahela Valley:

Do you not remember old George Hupp, son of Everhard who with George Bumgarner and Abraham Tegarden settled at the mouth of Ten Mile Creek 1767-69 upon land, a part of which is now occupied by the Town of Millsboro?

You were a very little boy when this George Hupp, then 75 or 80 years old, an old man, but strong and sprightly would come to your father's house (built 1805 in West Bethlehem Township) in the dead of winter, in a coonskin cap, fringed hunting shirt, deerskin trousers and moccasins, his old-time tomahawk and long knife stuck in his belt, his powder-horn and bullet-pouch hanging at his side, and his long-barreled flint-lock rifle thrown over his shoulder.

Your father liked the generous old man with the loud voice, and the best in the house was put before him, especially the big, round-bellied black bottle from the corner cupboard [probably made by William McCully whose glass house in Columbia down the river turned out green glassware, black bottles and window glass]. You trembled as you listened with strained attention to the tales told by the old man of his stalking Indians as well as the panther and bear, when ranging with his father.

You will never forget that old rifle, tomahawk and scalping knife which did service in the days of blood.

John C. Hupp of Fairmont, West Virginia, historian of the Hupp family, told the writer in a recent interview:

William Penn asked the first settlers to pay the Indians for the land they took up. Hupp would not pay but instead gave a rifle and other items to the Indians who were always on good terms with him. The land has remained in the Hupp name to this day. At the death of Miss Sarah Hupp of Henry, Illinois, (b. 1882) it passed to her niece, Letha Fern Hupp.

Russell Bane of Fredericktown took me to the site of the old cabin a number of years ago. If living, he would be about ninety and in his youth must have known old people who knew the landmarks. The place was on top of the hill where you can see the mouth of Tenmile, and not below near the Hupp Graveyard as some have said.

Letters to Miss Letha Hupp brought the following response:

I did find the enclosed very faded photograph which I am sure was the large house which used to be located upon the point of Sandy Plains. The old gentleman sitting on the porch was my grandfather. The Library of Congress has a volume which tells of the bravery and heroism of Ann, wife of John Hupp who helped protect the women and children at Miller's Blockhouse, Washington County in 1783. I am the last descendant of my Grandfather Hupp.

The postcard photograph from which the sketch was made was mailed from Beallsville, Pennsylvania, August 13, 1909, and was addressed to Miss Sadie Hupp at Henry, Illinois:

Grandpap's birthday is August 28. We are going to have a post card shower for him. You people all send him cards. . . . Cousin Ethel

This is the only known photograph of the old log house which served as a temporary home to so many but was never licensed or called a "tavern"—only a "stopping place."

A few people still living in the Clarksville area recall the cabin as an ancient and scary place and an object of great interest locally. Clarence Nyswaner remembered stooping to enter when he was a boy, and Theo Johnson who lives at Sandy Plains on the way to the site, recalled stooping to pass through the low doorways in the days when his mother was postmaster at Sandy Plains, then known as Racine. He identified the photograph and could remember when the house was dismantled for when he and his wife were married in 1920

The Hupp cabin ca. 1900. From only known photograph owned by Letha Fern Hupp.

they came to live in their present home next to the Hupp
land and the cabin was still standing at that time and occupied by members of the family.

Now that the brush and timber have been cleared from the
ridge top it is clear why the first cabin in the wilderness west
of the Monongahela was located there, for the outlook to the
southwest carries over the bends of Tenmile Creek below to
the wider Monongahela and across the ridges to the faint and
larger blue of Laurel Hill.

7

THE TENMILE SETTLEMENT
Cusutha's (Forks of Tenmile)
Clarksville

AN EARLY Greene County deed describes a certain piece of land as located in:

The Town of Clarksvill in the forks of Tenmile known as Cusuths or Cusutee's. . . .

The Fry-Jefferson map published in Virginia in 1751 shows Tenmile as *Cusutha's Creek* and Surveyor General Nicholas Scull on his 1770 published map used the same terminology.

The word *Cusutha* has an intriguing sound but its use is beyond anything recalled by the oldest residents. Files in the Pennsylvania Room of Carnegie Library in Pittsburgh and indexes in area histories give no mention. In the absence of information, we propose that it seems highly plausible that a hunting and trading camp at the Forks of Tenmile may have taken the name of the Six Nations Chief *Guyasutha*, corrupted to *Cusutha's* in the same way as "Catfish Camp" (now Washington, Pennsylvania) took the name of the Delaware Chief Catfish.

Searching for a firm bit of ground on which to stand and consider the earliest events and land ownership at the Forks, one is constantly weighing evidence that will not hold its own with local tradition and certain official records. With his bizarre blend of truth and fiction, Horn often supplies the

143

missing link; in this case, the Horn index lists Cusuthas Creek in reference to a map location, but gives nothing more. The introduction to Volume I of *The Horn Papers* gives a plausible and partial explanation:

> Source material relating directly to the early history of that part of Southwestern Pennsylvania which now comprises Greene and Washington counties has always been rare. As a result, there have been many unexplained and little understood details connected with the history and settlement of this region.

The *Fifth Report* of the Pennsylvania Historical Commission in 1931 describes an effort under way to investigate and preserve information on the American Indian in Pennsylvania; in 1929 this effort had resulted in the formation of the Society for Pennsylvania Archaeology. As early as 1924 it was reported that:

> ... no systematic effort to locate and preserve the evidence of Indian culture had been made in Pennsylvania and the National Museum in Washington reported less information about the Indian occupation in Pennsylvania than that of almost any other state in the Union, while its aboriginal history is more important than that in many states where surveys were undertaken.

In spite of the research into Indian activity during the past fifty years, there is still a paucity of material on the Indians Nemacolin, Catfish, and Guyasutha, all of whom played prominent roles in Penn's Southwest.

Statements in *The Horn Papers* indicate much of their Indian information was collected from members of the tribe living in Oklahoma in the late 1800s. Horn's Indian informants told of the cairns for signaling; one at Jefferson, the second on the ridge road on the old Jacob Rush farm, and the third on Hupp Hill overlooking the mouth of Tenmile. The fire-stone, described by Horn in such detail, stood in the center of Clarksville "until it was removed by Christopher Cox . . ."; the setbacks of the present town square were laid out to accommodate the circular stone.

To support the fact of an Indian council stone in the center of town, and use of the stones later in a milldam as reported by Mr. Horn, we have the original ledger of Christopher Horn for the years 1831-63 now in the library of the Greene County Historical Society:

> August—work at an oven. . . . September topped corn and dug coal; 1831-32 paid Christopher Cox for hauling council stone and McCullough's logs to Walton Dam. . . .

And to support the building of the Walton mill and dam we have the actual date stone "Walton—1832" from the gable of the stone mill.

As to the first land ownership, Horn made his usual nebulous references to an agreement between the Tegardens and the Enochs whereby Henry Enoch took over land the Tegar-

The age of George Teegarden the son of Abraham Teegarden and Mary his wife who made an improvement on the mononga hela River in Fayatt County in 1753 ofuis it the mouth of ten mile Creek he George was Born on the 29 day of June in the Year of our Lord AD 1744 his wife Rachel Daughter of Thomas Pribble and Mary his wife was Born on the 15th day of June 1751.

In his eightieth year, Thomas Teegarden (born 1782) made copies of "The Age of George Teegarden" for younger members of the family. Handed down in the family of Georgia Rita Teegarden of Lake Forest, Illinois.

dens could not hold under the Virginia law which specified "nothing over 400 acres on entries made before the Proclamation of 1763." The manuscript files of Darlington Library at the University of Pittsburgh contain an original *Note* dated 1751 for eight pounds Pennsylvania money which Abraham Tegarden owed to George Mason of Fairfax County, Virginia, during the early days of the Ohio Company when Abraham traveled back and forth across the mountains with his string of packhorses carrying company supplies to Redstone Old Fort, Gist's, and later to Fort Pitt. During these many trips, he had ample opportunity to assess western land and choose some of the choicest tracts. While his grandson, Thomas, born in 1782 on Tenmile, wrote that Abraham settled opposite the mouth of Tenmile in Fayette County in 1753, the first land purchase of record is 1757 west of the river. Boyd Crumrine in his *History of Washington County* gave credit to Abraham Tegarden for holding the first deed of record in present confines of the county, purchased from the Indian trader John Owen at Fort Pitt in December 1757 for twenty-five pounds. The land described in this deed bordered the west bank of the Monongahela from Enochs (present Pumpkin) Run to Muddy Creek.

Howard Leckey commented on the puzzling fact that this land from Rice's Landing to Carmichaels was where the later Swan, Hughes, Hiller party settled and for which there appeared to be no deed transfer. Perhaps the key transaction is to be found in Washington County Deed Book I-C:

> George Tegarden, yeoman of Monnongahela to Philomen Asken (who assigned to George Church in 1772 and to James Dailey in 1775) land on the south side of Tenmile Crik March 16, 1770 . . . by the name of James Brenton's Improvement.

Henry Enoch was in court over suits with George Church and James Dailey as early as 1783, so this could be land first held by Abraham and transferred in some manner to his son, George, about the time of his marriage to Rachel Pribble.

Horn maps show James Brenton in East Bethlehem Township so the land description as south of Tenmile may not have been entirely accurate.

When John Hormall sold Abraham an "improvement" on the north side of the North Fork, it was described as "twelve miles above the Great Fork (Clarksville)" and such a description would include not only the Breckenridge "Sugar Tree" granted to Henry Enoch in 1792 but possibly the Bumgarner tract also, if measurement began at the fork. It may also be that because of all the controversy over the Bumgarner tract, it came into the hands of the prominent attorney and land speculator, Hugh Henry Breckenridge, who almost immediately transferred to Enoch.

Completing the strange saga of deeds to Abraham Tegarden, the 1771 James Campbell deed for eighty-seven pounds covered land already taken up by a few 1769 settlers: "an improvement from the mouth of Dunkard Creek up the Monongahela north as far as the bottom holds good or will make two surveys." If a single survey was 400 acres, then this tract would have been for 800 acres, and would mean that at an early date Abraham Tegarden actually purchased and claimed almost the entire strip of land on the western bank of the Monongahela River from Dunkard on the south up to Tenmile Creek and north for twelve miles. Deed Book I-C shows that George and William, sons of Abraham Tegarden, after his death, sold the Campbell land in 1785 to Thomas Ramsey for 200 pounds.

"In a manner not known," stated historian Leckey in 1950, "George Bumgarner got possession of land where Clarksville was later built, and received a title to warrant it on June 3, 1769 from the Pennsylvania authorities." Then, in a somewhat contradictory statement, he said the town was built on "part of the uncertain tract sold by Richard Ashcraft to George Teegarden, although heirs of George Bumgarner made the first deed to Henry Enochs in 1787." References located since publication of the Leckey books reveal other

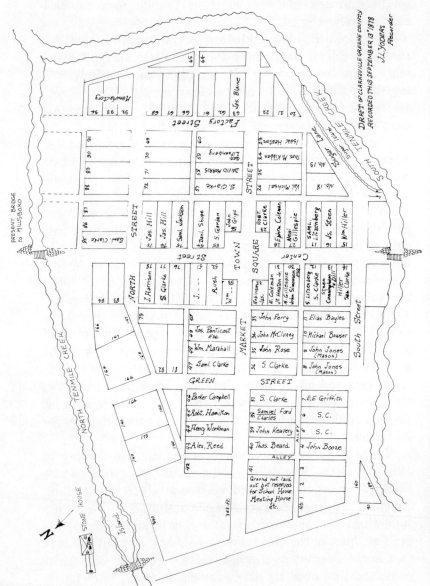

Map of Clarksville, earliest of record, ca. 1815; copied and recorded 1878 in Greene County

possibilities but also add to the confusion. A heavy cloud of ambiguity still obscures the first land transactions.

Described as a western Pennsylvania "coal mining town" in its recent publicity, the unique beginnings of Clarksville have been largely forgotten or discounted because of Horn misinformation. Market Square first contained the huge thirty-two by three-foot circular monument of the Delaware Indians known as the "Council Stone"; the two iron works may have predated the more famous furnaces of Fayette County; they built the first woolen manufactory around and had a try at making lead pipe from local lead deposits, and the slab of raw green glass that lay in a meadow for a century or more was mute evidence of an effort to make glass from local sand; several cooperages turned out tubs and barrels for flour and for the large distilleries which produced Monongahela Rye Whiskey, famous up and down the river for its superior quality.

The borough of Clarksville does not recall its colonial heritage as do the immaculate villages of New England. In 1975 it is a rather drab, commonplace town with very few of its earliest structures still standing or recognizable, most of them having acquired 'modern' store fronts or the large enclosed porches so popular about 1900 as a cover-up on the fronts of fine old buildings.

The earliest and most imposing building in the forks area is the two and one-half story stone mansion known by many as the "Taylor Place" as well as by the names of the many other families who lived in it over the years. If Mr. Horn was right about the Revolutionary iron foundry starting operations in 1779 on the North Fork where cannon balls were found in the creek bed, perhaps there was a neat tie-up with the building date for the house? Was the low kitchen wing built in 1778 as Jock Yablonsky told me, sitting in his pajamas and robe in that kitchen wing, on a Sunday morning early in the year in which he and his wife and daughter were murdered in that same bleak stone house? Or, did the Walton family build it, as some Walton descendants claim? With its colorful and sordid history as much a part of the structure as the mortar that holds it together, the story of this building will be told according to the writer's thesis, that it was begun by the Henry Enoch family in the late 1700s, was completed by Samuel Clarke before 1814, and was purchased in 1824 by John Walton.

* * *

Enter first the colorful and controversial Enochs whose prominence in the early annals of America is well known and yet, for some strange reason, area writers have been reluctant to mention the Enoch family. The story of this family, if not the first then the second at the Forks of Tenmile, much like the exciting and significant history of Clarksville, has been lost in time. The town is disposed of by Washington County historians, Earle Forrest in particular, by stating it is in Greene County; most Greene County historians, except for Leckey, overlooked its early history entirely.

The home of Henry I and Elizabeth Enoch in Hampshire County, Virginia, was mentioned in the journals of Gist, and George Washington wrote several times of staying "at Henry Enoch's at the Forks of Cacaphon." A military family, the Enochs were foremost in constructing the chain of neighborhood frontier forts suggested in the mid-1750s by Washington and other leaders. This chain commenced at the fortified cabin in northern Virginia where Henry II was born May 12, 1732; when only fifteen years of age he married his cousin, Sarah Enoch, also fifteen, and their first child was born the following year in 1748. One of Henry's first jobs (according to Leckey) was as a chain bearer on the Fairfax Survey in 1748; in 1750 Washington surveyed land for the senior Enochs, who operated an iron works, gristmill, and weaving shop on the Cacapon just as their son and his family did later in the Tenmile Settlement. Henry II was commissioned a lieutenant colonel and commanded the First Battalion of Washington County Militia, and yet his name is not included in the list of Revolutionary soldiers buried in the county. His sons, William and Isaac, were famous as Indian scouts and frontier rangers, and captains of their own companies before they migrated from the Tenmile shortly after 1800.

Among the John Hoge warrant and survey papers acquired by the Library of Washington and Jefferson College is the following statement by Hoge:

> ... along about 1784 application was made by Henry Enoch to execute a survey on an order in Frederick Bumgarner's name, who then claimed. I made this survey May 3, 1784 and returned it to Mr. Luken's office.
>
> Some time ago Frederick Bumgarner, who lives on the James River, sent his brother-in-law Mr. Livingle with a Power of Attorney to settle his claims in this county. He disclaims the land as located and demanded it be surveyed in the manner laid down on the enclosed draught [missing]. William Enoch also disclaimed title to the location and described his land, said he might bring a survey on a Virginia Certificate, and Mr. Forbes [surveyor] brought Mr. Hupp to prove to me that the location was laid on land for which it was never intended, in consequence of which the enclosed draft ... has prevented all settling on the location.
>
> Now the desires of the parties and myself are that the return in Frederick Bumgarners name may be withdrawn and the enclosed return in said name be accepted in its place, and further that William Enoch's return be excepted and made in pursuance of an alternate certificate as will appear on record.

The above piece of paper rescued from a Cleveland attic clears some of the mystery concerning the 300-acre tract that Henry Enoch purchased from Frederick Bumgarner, officially dated October 25, 1786. It also shows why Samuel Clarke, with a long background of courthouse activities in Washington County as recorder of deeds, was so apprehensive about the title to Enoch land he purchased at sheriff's sale in the early spring of 1799. Gathering an impressive number of witnesses, Samuel entered a *"Petition in perpetuum rei memoriam,"* which is actually a capsule history of Enoch activities at the Forks:

To the Honorable Court of Common Pleas—November 5, 1799:

That about the year 1771-72 Colonel Henry Enoch purchased an improvement and settled thereon in the forks of Ten Mile Creek, and continued his settlement and improvements thereon. That on the 3rd day of May in the year of our Lord 1784, the said Henry caused a survey to be made of said tract, including the forks of Ten Mile Creek and containing 395 acres.... That whilst the Commissioners appointed on the part of Virginia to settle the boundaries of said state were setting in this Country, he the said Henry procured a certificate for said land. That afterwards a survey was made and returned on the Virginia Certificate bearing date of May 13, 1785....

That he the said Henry continued his settlement and improvements thereon peacibly and without interruption until October 28, 1795 when he executed and delivered a bond for the conveyance of 101½ acres, part of said tract, to his son, William Enoch. That on January 18, 1794 he executed and delivered a bond to his son Henry for 178 acres, and on October 23, 1795 he executed . . . a bond to his son Isaac Enoch of the *Homestead* of the said Henry lying and being in the Forks of ten Mile Creek.

That on February 4, 1795 Colonel Henry Enoch executed another bond to Isaac of all that part of said tract between the North Fork of ten Mile Creek and William Enoch's land on which the *Enoch Mills* stand.... And whereas also Henry Enoch, son of Colonel Henry Enoch on January 18, 1794 granted by deed to his brother William 34 acres on the North Fork which was part of a tract granted by the State of Pennsylvania by Patent dated July 26, 1792 to Hugh Brackenridge. That by virtue of the respective bonds, they the said William, Isaac and Henry did proceed to the settlement and improvement of the proportions of said land. That on the part granted by the said Father to his sons, Isaac and William, they erected a *furnace*, saw mill and boring mill and made divers other valuable repairs and improvements without any adverse claims or hindrances from any one.

That Henry the brother was witness to the conveyances by his Father to William and Isaac, that when a survey and division was made, each of them were satisfied with the division. That at the time the Survey was made, Henry the Younger had made no claim to his Father's Survey but that he had frequently applied to one of your Petitioner's Witnesses, urging him to purchase from his brothers a share in the lands on which the *Iron Works* are erected, in order to relieve his Brothers from their entanglements. Also that Henry applied to his Father to purchase the said tract and to give him lands on the Kenawha in exchange, to which Colonel Enoch objected:

—SAMUEL CLARKE

Witness:	James Bristor	George Teegarden
	Jacob Morris	Everhart Hupp
	Isaac Jenkinson	Henry Coffman
	Enoch Gallaway	David Ruble, Sr.
	David Montgomery	Jesse Bumgardner
	Elias Bane	Ephraim Coleman
	Richard Sharpless	Humphrey Montgomery
	John Hoge	Lucy Wright
	Joseph Penticost	Alexander Reed

If we knew what was meant by William and Isaac Enoch's "entanglements" we might have the answer to the riddle of the stone house and who built it. The Clarke memorial found in miscellaneous papers of the common pleas jacket files in Washington County does not cover the details of the October 1795 agreement which may support the proposal that the family became involved in grandiose plans for a fine house, begun ca. 1796.

As early as January 17, 1794, Henry and Sarah Enoch deeded 120 acres of "Sugar Tree" to their son Henry for the good figure of 215 pounds; on the following day Henry, Sr., stood bound to Henry, Jr., for 600 pounds: "The condition of this obligation is such that if the above bounden Henry, Sr. or his heirs . . . do well and truly convey in fee simple unto Henry, Jr. all that tract on Tenmile by lands of Henry, Sr. and lands *in dispute* which Henry, Jr. and his wife Elizabeth (Tegarden) deeded to his brother William on the same day for 5 shillings, and appropriately called 'Hazard'."

By October 1795 Colonel Henry Enoch had become involved in numerous land transactions. It is difficult if not impossible to explain the various deeds between members of the family which seem to overlap known boundaries and acreage. One of the most significant documents which, in the absence of a will for Henry, Sr., appears to fulfill the requirements of a will, is the following deed to his son, Isaac:

> For divers good considerations, Henry Enoch grants to his son Isaac Enoch all his possessions bordering on Tenmile Creek; my *homestead* lying and being in the forks, also the Grist and Saw Mill with as much land as is necessary for a log yard and all other conveniences for said mills, and water courses, in consequence of which Isaac is to *build a good house* with one convenient room for my use and to support me and my wife until our decease; also to discharge all debts and demands with such legacies as is herein mentioned; to William Enoch pay 300 pounds to be paid in six equal payments, the first 50 pounds to be paid by October 23, 1798 and the other payments yearly; to Eliabeth Bell [his daughter, wife of Benjamin Bell who administered Henry's estate in 1797] 100 pounds to be paid in two years from this date. If the said Isaac shall well and truly comply, the above to stand in full force. If there is non-performance, then the said premises revert back to Henry Enoch, Sr. until his decease at which time Isaac is to inherit the above premises as the rightly heir.

With the seemingly overlapping deeds there is a recital of the many large sums borrowed on notes and mortgages, first by Colonel Henry himself, and later by his sons. In a perhaps parallel case, after construction of the elaborate stone building by the Canon family in Canonsburg after the death of Colonel John Canon in 1798, a situation of heavy debt led to eventual bankruptcy.

January court cases in 1797 reveal a number of actions of George Teegarden vs. Henry Enoch in matters of trespass and debt. John Hoge surveyed the tract "Hazard" again stating it was done "in pursuance of a warrant granted to George Teegarden in 1793 but the land is claimed by William Enoch and on his special request was surveyed for him on his warrant." In July 1798 William and his wife, Mary, conveyed seven acres of the tract to her father, George Teegarden. Early in 1798 Bartholomew Connolly's judgment for $2,900 was executed in Washington County:

...on a plantation in Bethlehem Township of 140 acres, land includes the iron works and grist mill on Tenmile sold to Samuel Clarke together with houses, mills, building, barns, stables. . . .

Indicative of the confused and complex ownership of land at the Forks, the above document was followed by a record in Greene County Common Pleas Court April Session 1799, quoted by Leckey:

The Sheriff of Greene County took over and proceeded to sell the assets available. These included the grist mill of Colonel Henry Enoch and the Iron Works Henry operated, as well as the land on which they stood, including the tracts of both Isaac and William; buyer at the sale was Samuel Clarke of Washington. . . .

At the suit of Robert Clarke & Company of Brownsville against Isaac and William Enoch for over 400 pounds worth of merchandise, and Ezekiel Hoover's suit for $1,200 against Isaac, legal actions against the Enochs began to pyramid. Several inquisitions were held at Joseph Huston's tavern in Wash-

From Greene County Common Pleas Court files, this rather amusing note regarding one Jones who held land claimed by Henry Enoch.

ington in attempts to handle the demands of debtors in numerous court actions.

Colonel Henry Enoch died ca. June 1797 and his personal property was inventoried at $684.78 in his Greene County estate file:

> Pewter ware, coffee and tea potts—at Henry, Jr's.
> Colonel Henry's Trap [2-wheeled spring carriage]—at Benjamin Bell's
> Henry's clothing in possession of son, William—"lost"
> Among small misc. items was a pair of "spoon molds"
> Corn worth $80—held by son, Isaac but "could not be recovered from him"
> Isaac Enoch by Agreement amongst the rest of the children— "considered to be the sole proprietor of a yoke of oxen as the former property of his father" valued at 25 pounds
> 2 cast iron potts and 1 dutch oven—to be "sent down the river to Amy Sergeant and Hannah Pribble"[Henry's daughter Hannah married Thomas Pribble and lived in Virginia (West)]
> Henry, Jr. provided whiskey in 1790 and submitted a bill
> Enoch Galloway [Henry's grandson]—"to receive a suit of clothes and a rifle gun worth six pounds in return for his labor"
> Jesse Rush submitted a bill for hauling a mill stone from Laurel Hill for Henry's Mill and was also to be paid for hauling 1,800 feet of plank from John Heaton's
> William Enoch had 5-3/4 yards of homemade cloth suitable for a great coat pattern and was willing to allow parts of it to Isaac and Henry at 6/6 a yard

The items in this estate are the most unusual the writer has found in scanning hundreds of early estate files; they reveal the vigorous, contentious style of the family and corroborate Claire Johnson's observation that the prosperous Enochs always had the best of everything for the period. From 1770 to 1800, in spite of contending ownership, there was very little land adjacent to the Forks, for some distance down the main creek and up the North and South branches, that was not claimed by Colonel Henry and his sons.

In the various Enoch transactions, Henry III seems to have stood somewhat aside from his brothers, William and Isaac. While William and Isaac are never listed individually with land on tax rolls, Henry paid the highest tax among 160 taxpayers in Morgan Township, Greene County, where he lived in a twenty-four by thirty-foot two-story log house with nine twelve-paned windows valued at $200 which was high for a log house. In February 1800 he was summoned to court to answer Henry Miller, supervisor of revenue, for duty of $42.79 owing on his still since 1798.

When Lyman Draper interviewed William Harrod, Jr., in Kentucky in 1845, Harrod mentioned the deaths at the hands of Indians during the Crow Massacre, 1793, in Greene County, of Abraham and John Enoch, sons of Colonel Henry. Also, in naming "principal stations" for defense, he mentioned Henry Enoch's at the forks of the Tenmile. At this period of frontier conflict, Lt. Henry Enoch was commissioned as a member of the Corps of Washington County Riflemen for immediate defense of the frontiers, and for some reason, declined the commission. In August 1793 Major Henry Enoch was a member of the Second Regiment of the Second Brigade of Militia; the military title for Henry III was never as clear as for his father who was always referred to as "Colonel Henry Enoch."

* * *

Samuel Clarke's entry into affairs at the Forks of Tenmile coincides with the departure of the Enochs who finally quit-claimed to Samuel on the last parcel of their land in 1804. As Enoch descendant Claire Brown Johnson has stated: "There was a regular Enoch exodus from Pennsylvania just as there was from Virginia earlier."

We pursued with no success, the possibility that Samuel may have been a member of the George Rogers Clark family and entered Tenmile country in the early 1770s with George and William Clark. A co-searcher, Ralph Johnson of Philadelphia, who did detailed Clark research for his 1974 *Johnson-McGinnis* history was also unable to connect the two families, except to propose that they may have been cousins. The twelve-volume *History of England* in the inventory of Sam-

158

uel's estate suggests an English background. When Myrtle Richey made a survey of the burial places of Revolutionary soldiers in 1932, she listed "Samuel Clarke, New Jersey troops 1775-78, buried with no marker in the Old Graveyard in Washington."

Samuel Clarke's name first appears in Washington County records ca. 1785 and this would coincide with the date of the migration from New Jersey to Tenmile. The lack of specific biographical data is as puzzling as for the Enochs, but with his early involvement in public life, Samuel emerges with more clarity. He comes through to us as an involved, conscientious, and able businessman with an above-average education.

When the first meeting was held in February 1789 to form the "Washington Society for the Relief of Free Negroes and Others Unlawfully Held in Bondage," eleven members signed the constitution including surveyors John Hoge and Andrew Swearingen, counselor David Bradford, and merchant Samuel Clarke. In November, Samuel Clarke, "Gentleman" was appointed coroner, followed by several terms as county commissioner and auditor. Subsequent appointments to county offices carried through the next decade at the same time "Captain Samuel Clarke" was a busy storekeeper on Market Street in a thirty-two by thirty-eight foot log and frame building next to an eighteen by thirty foot building, two kitchens, and a stable. Of the ten stores listed in Washington in 1798, Samuel Clarke and

General Henry Taylor's account Captain Samuel Clarke. From manus files at Washington and Jefferson College

Hugh Wilson had by far the highest valuations. Absalom Baird reported seeing "Clark's wagons with supplies" on the road between Washington and Philadelphia in 1795; after the *Reporter* announced the dissolution of the partnership of Samuel and David Cooke "by mutual consent" Samuel continued to advertise his merchandise which included saddlery, school books, many grocery and hardware items, good wines, and a "few skins of parchment for executing deeds." Samuel's wife, Dorcas Cooke, was probably a sister of David Cooke.

Samuel Clarke's flowing, modern handwriting on hundreds of courthouse documents during his years as register and recorder as well as his English and grammar indicate as well educated a person as his counterpart in Greene County, recorder and clerk John Boreman. When Greene County was laid off from Washington in 1796, Samuel bought one of the first lots in the new county seat of Waynesburg, No. 10. He also purchased lots in Carmichaels and upriver in Greensboro where Alexander Vance began to manufacture the famous stoneware. In 1797 he requested to take up 400 acres, including an "improvement" on the waters of the South Fork of Tenmile adjacent to land of Heaton & Company in Greene County, "provided the land is within the last purchase made of the Indians" and paid at the rate of 50 shillings per 100 acres with interest to commence March 1, 1797. This commonwealth deed was not recorded until coal activity in 1901.

We have reviewed Samuel Clarke's purchase of the Enoch land at the Forks and assume he took over operation of the Enoch gristmill as he applied for a flour brand in 1800. In 1803 he viewed a proposed road from "Clarke's Mills at the forks to the Monongahela River." In 1809 he was taxed as a "miller and distiller" with eight horses and the slave, probably his body servant, that had been with him since his Washington days. He continued his interests in Washington and became worshipful master of the Masonic Lodge organized there in 1802. Before he moved to Tenmile where he operated the large distillery on the North Fork, Samuel signed the Whiskey Insurrection Oath as circulated in the town of Washington by David Bradford and Dorsey Penticost [record from the Library of Congress]:

September 11, 1794—

I DO promise to submit to the Laws of the United States; that I will not directly nor indirectly oppose the execution of the Acts for raising a Revenue on Distilled Spirits and Stills, and that I will support as far as the Laws require, the civil authority in affording the protection due to all officers and other Citizens.

After purchasing all of the various parcels of distressed Enoch land and founding and laying out the town of Clarksville in 1809, coupled with his involvement with the woolen mill, Samuel must have grown weary of his many interests. The August 1, 1814, issue of the Washington *Reporter* carried this ad:

FOR SALE—A Valuable Plantation where I now reside in view of the woolen manufactory of Clarksville, containing 400 acres of excellent land, 100 of which are first quality creek bottom all clear and part in timothy meadow, several tenements, 2 bearing orchards of pippins, vandiveers etc. A *new large two-story stone house* finished to the roof in the newest and neatest manner, a large dairy, merchant grist and saw mills, fish aplenty in season, a large frame barn and out-buildings.

Copy of whiskey advertising on the back of an early small purse mirror from collection of Anne Jennings of Clarksville.

A stone distillery, two stories high 40 x 47 works three stills, a boiler tube and boiler, fixtures and stoves complete. Whiskey made here is *extremely superior* and I will give my skill to the purchaser.

This property in the first estimation at once invites the man of business and taste. The whole or in part may be examined by calling on your proprietor. Terms part cash and part property when it may suit me.

—SAMUEL CLARK, Washington County
11 miles above Brownsville

p.s. An inexhaustible mine of pit coal free from sulphur may be had with the above.

Samuel and Dorcas continued to sell off parcels of their land. In 1819 they deeded Lot No. 19 to trustees of the Christian Church, John Heaton, William and George Litzenbaugh, Adam Bottenfield, and James Rush; sale price was twenty dollars and the deed was witnessed by Janetta and Elizabeth B. Clarke. Known as the "Little Red Brick Church," the building constructed on Lot 19 is the oldest church in the borough and continues in use for holding serv-

"Little Red Brick Church" built in 1819 showing the outline of Furnace Hill in the background. From 1974 photograph.

ices by a loyal few who gather on Sunday afternoons with the Reverend Alec Kennedy and his wife.

In April 1824 Colonel Samuel Clarke and his wife, Dorcas, recorded two deeds to John Walton of East Bethlehem Township:

> ... for $1,800 land in the forks of Tenmile in Morgan Township, adjoining Clarksville, to the corner of a house of Samuel McGuire to a stake in the creek, land of Carothers [Green Iron Works] ... heirs of John Stull to Saw Mill Run, to a hop yard fence, of 120 acres granted to Henry Enock, Jr. called "Mount Pleasant" which was seized and sold January 2, 1799 as the property of William and Isaac Enoch at the suit of David Cooke and conveyed to Samuel Clarke by the High Sheriff of Green County June 4, 1800, but remains unrecorded. ...

The second deed was for the 435-acre tract on the North Fork where Samuel had lived in the stone house and which he had first advertised in 1814. The price for the valuable tract was $20,000.

From census records it appears that Samuel Clarke must have been about seventy-five when the Washington paper printed this simple notice:

> DIED—Samuel Clarke of East Bethlehem, September 15, 1824, early settler in the county.

Two days later, Sheriff Samuel Workman levied on the 400-acre tract with the "double stone house" and on into 1825 one suit followed another in a repeat of the Enochs' financial disasters. Tavern keeper David Morris sued for $4,000 on an 1821 conditional agreement; executors of Samuel Jackson had a judgment of $1,766; the Philadelphia Bank sued for varying sums, which indicated Samuel had been borrowing money from them since 1820. No will or estate papers were found but Item 63 of the 1824 November term of court along with a recap of Samuel's indebtedness, included an inventory of his personal property which was sold on November 11 for $481.47. On October 12 a sale of whiskey at the distillery had netted $582.71 on David Morris's judgment

1 Side Board
1 Secretary
1 doz chairs
½ " Ditto
1 Square wash stand
1 old Beauraou
1 Large Kitchen Table
3 Bed Steads
1 Pair Knife Cases
1 large chest with divisions
2 Big Spinning wheels
1 Smaller Ditto
1 Corner cupboard
1 Square Ditto Kitchen
1 Settee
1 cherry Tree Toilet Table
1 Looking Glass
1 History of England 12 vols.
besides others

1 windmill
1 Waggon
1 cart
1 Harrow Iron Teeth
1 Harrow Wooden teeth
2 Patent Ploughs
2 Shovel Ploughs
1 Common Gun
2 mens Saddles

1 Large Iron Kettle
1 Small Ditto Suppose 10 Gals.
1 Large Brass Kettle
1 Cross cut Saw
6 whisky Bls
Some old cider Barrels
1 Large meat Tub
1 Barrel Salt

2 Large dutch ovens new
2 Smaller Ditto Ditto
2 Small Skillets with Lids Ditto
1 Large Stewpot with Lid Ditto
(Still worm in cellar)

contents of the Distillery
vz
1 Singling Still and worm Suppos
to Hold 360 Galls cap or head 40
1 Doubling Still and worm Suppd
to hold 120 Galls cap or head 15 Gls.
2 flake stands not in good order
18 Still Tubs apparently good
4 Tops made of Straw
6 Singling Barrels
1 Doubling Keg

a number Hogs Larg & Small
I cannot ascertain the number
1 Steer
1 Heifer } 3 young
2 milk cows

Inventory of Samuel Clarke's personal property. From Washington
County Appearance Docket, 1824.

levied on seventy-one barrels of Samuel's "superior quality" Monongahela Rye.

"Mount Pleasant" was a deceptively simple name for land which generated so much legal maneuvering and heavy indebtedness for each new set of owners. In spite of the recorded indenture to John Walton from Samuel Clarke of the 400-plus-acre tract, an order issued from common pleas court on January 24, 1825, and again on June 26, 1826, for the sheriff of Washington County to sell the right and title of Clarke to the land in East Bethlehem Township at the suit of David Morris and the Bank of Philadelphia.

In April 1825, Samuel's daughter, Elizabeth Clarke, married Major Samuel Maguire, and during the next decade, Maguire, who was mayor of Clarksville and a leading citizen, became involved with the Waltons in the former Clarke prop-

Early drawing of David Morris's Globe Inn on Main Street, Washington, Pennsylvania.

erty. By 1840 at the suit of the Merchants and Mechanics
Bank of Wheeling, Greene County Sheriff R. H. Lindsey took
action for a debt of nearly $2,000 against Maguire's Lots 1,
2, and 3 in Clarksville with a frame dwelling house and tan-
yard, which were sold for $700 to Zenas Johnston.

* * *

Culture was taken quite seriously by certain groups of citi-
zens in the early towns, with all manner of societies formed.
In some way a quaint little booklet entitled *Rules for the
Government of the Select Grammar Society at Clarksville*
found its way into the recorder's vault in the Greene County
Courthouse:

> It being the desire of the members composing the select Grammar
> School late under the tuition of Mr. Samuel Colver to form them-
> selves into a Society for the purpose of improving themselves in
> the science of English Grammar, this Society shall be governed as
> follows:
>
> *First*—The officers shall consist of a President and Secretary who
> shall be chosen half yearly by the voice of the Society, or a
> majority of the members present. . . .
>
> *Second*—It shall be the duty of the President to keep order in all
> our meetings and to act as instructor or appoint some person in
> his place for that purpose.
>
> *Third*—It shall be the duty of the Secretary to receive all monies
> paid in for the use of the Society and to keep a correct account
> thereof and submit the same to the inspection of the Society
> when called upon. . . .
>
> *Fourth*—Any member nominated for President or Secretary shall
> be proposed by one member and seconded by another and two
> thirds of the members present voting in favor of the candidate he
> shall be declared elected.
>
> *Fifth*—Every Gentleman [lady members but not mentioned!]
> who now is or shall become a member shall pay to the Sec'y
> immediately 25 cents and such other sums as from time to time
> the necessities of the Society may require . . . and shall keep an
> account of expense and items paid for.
>
> *Sixth*—Any member behaving in a disorderly and indecorous man-
> ner shall be expelled from this Society by a motion, two thirds
> voting for such motion.

Seventh—Members agree to be punctual in their attendance at the hour appointed for meetings, and unless it shall appear that the attendance of any absent members was impracticable to a committee appointed for that purpose, they shall pay a fine of 12½ cents for use of the Society.

Eighth—All meetings and the hour shall be appointed by a majority when called upon by the President to decide.

We whose names are hereunto subscribed, members of the late Grammar School, having adopted the foregoing Rules, are to be considered members—January 16, 1824

Names of Gentlemen	*Names of Ladies*
Benjamin B. Woodruff	Jane Dill
James Walton	Mary Clarke
Alexander Lindsay	Sarah Bane
Jesse Stephenson	Em— Clarke
~~David Weaver~~	Mary Dill
Alexander Dill	Elizabeth Dill
	Dorcas Calhoun
Officers	Elizabeth Clarke
Saml. McGuire, President	Sophronia Walton
David Weaver, Secretary	

February 14—David Weaver resined the office of Secretary, Benjamin B. Woodruff is Secretary

* * *

Drawing from 1971 photograph of the old stone house in Clarksville after Joseph Yablonsky's renovation.

Walton family traditions point to early residence by John Walton in the stone house, with the implication that he built it. However, family records made available to the writer do not at any point state that the house was built by Walton. Mary Walton Martin of Waynesburg gave data from the Walton Bible, rescued from the Pittsburgh fire in 1845; entries show the first John Walton born on the Strand in London in 1785, married Sarah Huston Paul in 1805, and they were noted as the "owners of the Walton house."

Dr. John Walton of Johns Hopkins University, who has compiled and published data on various branches of the Walton family, sent the writer several pages of "personal recollections" of Martha Walton Hagerman as told to her by her father, John Walton, grandson of the founder:

My father's grandfather's homestead lay across Ten-Mile Creek from the Village of Clarksville, which as I understand, was in Greene County, but this home with its 1,200 acres was in Washington County.

The house was a large stone structure built on the hillside that is the east bank of Ten-Mile [North Fork]. It had two stories, a garret and basement. There was a small porch on the south and a porch on the east too. All the house was plastered, even the garret [as Samuel Clarke said in 1814 'finished to the top in the neatest manner']. There were dormer windows and my father remembered two of the large bedrooms, one painted red and called "The Red Room" and one painted blue, called "The Blue Room."

Father's grandfather had a large barn, a grist mill, saw mill and a still house. The estate was worth about $100,000 at his death in 1834. John Walton's brother, James was at St. Clair's defeat and came home without a hat or coat. They raised a great deal of wheat and rye, the latter for whiskey, cut it with sickles and "led the field" so father told me.

My father, John Walton was born December 16, 1831 at the upper or Garret Farm in Washington County near Clarksville, but Aunts Martha and Elizabeth and Uncle Amos were born across the creek at Clarksville in Greene County where Grandfather owned a house and lot and a store-room where he kept General Store for years. Grandmother was Eliza Hickman; some said she was the prettiest woman they ever saw, small and dainty with curly black hair. My father remembered seeing her dance—the Hickmans were all good dancers.

Father's Grandfather Hickman was German and Grandmother was a Yankee. They kept a hotel at Jefferson. Just before the Pittsburgh fire in 1845, Grandfather sold out his Southfield Hotel business and furniture to his brother, Dan. The old Bible and two or three feather beds were all that were saved by Uncle Billy Drake who was a lame Englishman and Dan Walton's father-in-law [Daniel married Mary Drake in 1834].

Father remembered being at his Uncle Jonathan Walton's and seeing him cook a turkey hanging up in the big fireplace on a hook and turning round and round. Jonathan had a dispute with the carpenter who had been putting a new roof on his house and wanted 75¢ a day. Jonathan said, "You worked in the boiling sun for Amos at 60¢ and now you want 75¢ for working in the shade!" One of his favorite sayings was: "I can buy and I can sell you, and buy you back again." In Clarksville it was said that John Walton's grandfather could chop six cords of wood in a day.

Grandfather went security for Mayor Samuel Maguire for about $2500; Maguire bought part of Grandfather's estate and then ran heavily in debt and debtors came from far and wide; everything was sold out of the house and cellar, even a fine bureau and other things. Grandfather moved to a smaller house with a stable and a garden with currant bushes on the lot.

Washington County Deed Book 2-Y contains the August 1837 agreement between Samuel Maguire and James Walton:

. . . mutually agree to dissolve the partnership of Maguire & Walton, and Samuel Maguire agrees to take the property in Washington County consisting of the Mansion House, Mill, Distillery etc. with 100 acres late the property of John Walton, at its original cost to be adjusted as follows: the mills, distillery etc. as taken by James Walton to be closed and paid for by the firm of Maguire & Walton as is now nearly done, also the payment yet due on the Stull farm and the payment that is to be made to Amos Walton on the part we purchased of him which is $1500. Each to get full possession of the property taken by them except the dwelling house which said Walton now occupies which he is to retain until April 1, 1838, also the privilege of stabling for the stock, grain on hand and Maguire to take at market price any stock of hogs on hand, the fat hogs will be ready for market and sold. Horses, waggons, gears, farming utensils, tools of every description to be divided. . . . The titles of the Greene County land to be made to James Walton and for the Washington County property to Samuel Maguire. (Dower settled on the property not to be taken into account.)

* * *

Returning to the writer's visit with Jock Yablonsky in 1969, it is part of the story to know how this powerful labor leader in the miners' union happened to be attracted to the old stone house.

Yablonsky reminisced that in 1927 while a mine worker in California on the Monongahela as his father had been before him, he had been jailed for some offense and treated miserably by a police officer named Nockton. The chagrin and bitterness of this period of his life stayed with him and many years later, in the 1940s, he had encountered Officer Nockton again at the stone house. At that time the building was used as a rooming house for single, retired, or incapacitated miners. One of these men was an Italian who had become deranged as a result of war experiences. Mrs. Christie, who ran the place, had a flock of special black and white chickens, and Annie Crayne of Clarksville, who also remembered the incident, said she had gone to the house for a setting of eggs and the Italian who was trimming the hedge and piling up the branches, told her the army was coming to get him. They became frightened and called the police to subdue him, not realizing he might have a gun. Officer Nockton answered the call and went after the man who had barricaded himself in his room. Tear gas was thrown in, and after he had shot and killed Nockton, the man had saved himself by tearing down a stove and putting his head in the chimney for air.

In the investigation which followed the sordid affair, Yablonsky had gone to the house, become fascinated with it, and finally bought it. Shortly after he started to clean it up and it became known he was going to renovate, someone brought a strange, punched brass picture to show him how it had once looked. The complete layout of the old mill and buildings in their prime, with an oxen team and wagon and whiskey barrels at the distillery, was punched in a design on the brass plate. With his Polish background, Yablonsky was not too interested at first in the historical aspects of restoration, but later he regretted having made certain changes, especially the sandblasting of the stone. He was never able to locate the person who had brought the picture. Another feature he regretted destroying were two cell-like wooden cages which Clarksville residents told him had been used in the early years for misbehaving slaves.

* * *

On June 7, 1909, the Court of Quarter Sessions in Greene County received an application for a charter of the "Freeholders" of Clarksville:

> . . . said town contains a collection of houses allocated after a regular plan in regard to streets, alleys or lanes; said petitioners do not exceed fifty-six and reside within the limits thereof. They are desirous of incorporating, beginning near the center of the creek on the upper side of the iron bridge over North Tenmile, said bridge being designated as the "Corbert Bridge", thence to a point near the center of South Tenmile and down South Tenmile to its junction with North Tenmile and back to the iron bridge, containing 66.74 acres.

8

EARLY IRON FURNACES

A CLUE to the undeniable existence of a furnace near the Greene-Washington County line, on Tenmile Creek, is the reference by Clarksville residents over the years to "Furnace Hill" opposite the town and down which Legislative Route 30133 winds to the second crossing bridge.

A few lines appear here and there, but no historical comment on early iron furnace activity at the Forks of Tenmile other than the questionable account in the *Horn Papers* and the statements by Sharp and Thomas in their 1966 study of "Old Stone Blast Furnaces" for the Historical Society of Western Pennsylvania.

Apparently there was little conjecture about the existence or operation of a furnace until the second decade of the 1900s after the Chartiers Southern Railroad proposed its line at the base of Furnace Hill.

Again in the 1930s the WPA investigators in company with W. F. Horn from Topeka, Kansas, located ancient iron cannon balls in the North Fork creek bed and identified certain iron ore banks along Tenmile. Local residents began to talk about the fact that there had indeed been iron manufacture in their town and the millrace for one of two furnaces was noted as plainly visible by persons investigating the remains in 1939.

In a recent interview with Clarence Nyswaner in Clarksville, he recalled during his employment by the railroad contractor that three large plates of old iron, about half the size of a modern car, had been removed from the site of the North Fork furnace and sold for scrap ca. 1920.

Intriguing statements concerning not the "Green Iron Works" of record, but the "McCullough Iron Works" on the South Fork and another unnamed furnace on the North Fork, both at Clarksville, were made by Mr. Horn. Prominent backers of the iron manufactory were, according to Horn, Colonel John Canon, Zackquill Morgan, and Patrick Henry, who about 1780 began operations to produce much needed cannon balls and ammunition for Revolutionary troops. It is well known that on April 24, 1777, Colonel Zackquill Morgan had issued a warrant for supplies for 100 men to go to Saint Louis for gunpowder and that Morgan and John Canon commanded militia companies and 1775-81 drafted soldiers for the Continental Army. Patrick Henry was much concerned with powder supplies and military activities in the Virginia sector of southwestern Pennsylvania.

Mr. Horn stated further:

> In 1781 John Canon directed that a second blast furnace be built on the east side of North Tingooqua Creek. A dam was built . . . and a mill race carried the water across the field and along the old road in front of the Walton home. This second furnace was larger than the McCullough furnace but not so well constructed.

> Eighty-four oxcart loads of iron ore from the hill were hauled over to this furnace. After several blasts had been run, the cupola burst. It was full of molten metal which flowed over the iron ore piled around the furnace. This mishap took place in October 1782 and ended the life of the iron smelter on what is now the Washington county side of Clarksville.

When as able a historian as Boyd Crumrine of Washington admitted in a 1905 letter to James Hadden, the historian of Uniontown, that

> . . . it has been almost impossible to find out anything about Colonel John Canon of Canonsburg. . . .

one can neither entirely agree nor disagree with Mr. Horn's statement about Canon participation in the Clarksville furnaces.

At the time *The Horn Papers* were assembled, there were numerous publications which described early iron manufacture, so again, one questions the Horn details of furnace activity as found in the Horn family records and diaries:

> ... thirty men dug the millrace and dam on the South Fork, the blast furnace was built of heavy stone, lined with clay and air was forced by a large fan through a hollow log pipe running from the mill to the furnace. An over-shot water wheel 20 feet in diameter furnished the power to run the fan, millstone and reducing ram.

> The smelter at Iron Point produced about 1400 tons of pig iron during its brief history, with 67 men employed in May 1779 taking raw ore from the hill near where the company log houses stood.

Horn said the foundry declined and after an ice flow in February 1800 took the center of the dam, the foundry town was deserted. In another reference, Horn said 1784 was the terminal date for operation and to round out his variations on closing dates, we quote again:

> The forge was used in 1790 for the last time, when the iron gudgeons were removed by John Horn to Zollarsville where they were still in use in 1856.

These statements constitute an excellent example of Horn data; there is always some truth mixed with half-truths and guesswork. The material is used best for clues which should be followed until they can be corroborated, or otherwise. Present research seems to indicate foundry and furnace activity into the 1800s for a few years on a limited scale, and residence in the company houses for many years after 1800.

Waynesburg attorney, A. L. Moredock, one of the sponsors of the *Horn Papers*, assembled a large file of land abstracts covering the Tenmile country. In 1949 in connection with some of his historical research, Mr. Moredock in a letter to Pierre du Pont in Wilmington, wrote:

(after) publishing the Horn Papers . . . a committee of savants sponsored by the Institute of Early American History and Culture at Williamsburg, Virginia vigorously attacked the publication . . . one glaring instance is their ridicule of the Horn claim for the first iron furnace west of the mountains at Clarksville 1779-1784. The abstract of title on the land on which this furnace was located proves the Horns correct.

* * *

One midsummer day in 1968 the writer drove out to Clarksville from Waynesburg for the first of many interviews with Clarence Nyswaner, descendant of John Nyswanger, Revolutionary soldier and woolen mill director. Clarence had been recommended as the "historian of Clarksville."

Waiting on the front porch, across the street the ancient tilting gravestones marked the tiny Walton Cemetery where the earliest Waltons and William Drake of the woolen mill were buried. Behind Clarence's house, in Washington County on the opposite side of the North Fork, stood the forbidding stone house of the Yablonsky family. Clarence came to the door and said, "Come back after lunch, I'll drive you around town and point things out."

A distant cousin had a store on the square so we headed "up street" as they say here, and parked at Denzil Young's Grocery. Denzil had been named for an evangelist who came through to preach, but unless you call him "Pete" people don't know who you mean. Lunch was a carton of cottage cheese and two big red peaches while watching Pete cutting at the meat counter, exchanging tidbits about Clarksville, the Tegardens, and "Old Man Horn," who had spent so many months prowling the town in the 1930s.

As we began our round of notable spots, the writer marked the locations on the Clarksville Geological Quad: The distillery location where they rolled the whiskey barrels down the hill to the flat where they lay until loaded for the trip down the creek to the Monongahela and transfer to flatboats for the trip to New Orleans. The spot on the

North Fork near the Walton stone house and mill where the Revolutionary iron foundry had stood until it blew up during the war and then never reopened, was noted.

Since that warm July day, the story of the early iron furnaces has developed from the fact and fiction of Mr. Horn, which had been introduced into local traditions, to many references in official records and other primary and secondary sources.

* * *

New towns sprang up all over Penn's Southwest during these years. September 26, 1794, Abijah MacClain had inserted a notice in the Pittsburgh *Gazette:*

> ... in Cumberland Township a quantity of compleat lots of ground for a town [Rice's Landing] on the Monongahela River on each side of a run known as "Enoch's Run" where at the mouth is a new saw mill nearly ready for sawing.

> In a circle of about three miles around there are six grist mills and an *iron works* building. These lots lie about three miles above the mouth of Tenmile where the road comes to the river from Jackson's Fort [Waynesburg].

When Thomas Hughes advertised the new town of Jefferson in Greene County, of which he was proprietor, he mentioned in his July 1796 ad:

> ... several houses already begun, saw mills and *iron works* nearby and convenient. ...

One of the first references to foundry activity was in the 1798 federal direct tax lists for Cumberland Township in Greene County:

> Jesse Bowell—1/6 furnace, val. $40, 105 acres 15 x 15 frame house
> Ephraim Coleman—1/6 furnace, 1/6 of two houses 15 x 15 val. $145
> Henry Heaton—Forge on two acres $34, Smith Shop, two houses 15 x 15, 4/6 of a Furnace val. $314, Grist and Saw Mills, Cole House and 4 Cabbins

Valuation for the furnace and forge would seem to indicate a very modest establishment. Names in the 1798 tax lists showing involvement with the furnace operation included the founders, Jesse Bowell, Ephraim Coleman, and Henry Heaton, and forgemen, Lock West, James Young, and Henry Gillock.

The Moredock sketch of "Green Iron Works" shows the two-acre furnace lot and across the main street, six house lots and this division must have been originally planned to give a house and lot and a one-sixth interest in the furnace to six persons, as owner-operators, with the cabins for workmen.

Deed records show earliest ownership of the Green Furnace land was by the Heaton family. In early 1798 Henry and

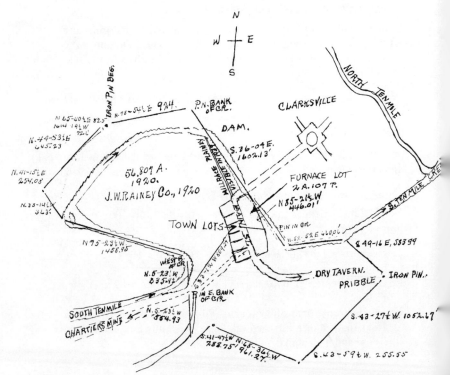

Map of town of Green Iron Works. Sketch shows exact surveyed location in rela: to Clarksville with the circular council stone indicated in Market Square; notatio "millrace plainly visible in 1939" and "Main St." connecting with Dry Tavern R Drawn by A. L. Moredock. From Greene County Historical Society Library files.

Martha Heaton sold to Jesse Bowell the one-sixth of the furnace and lot he was later taxed for:

> ... shown in the General Plan beginning at a post on Main Street, part of the 1791 Isaac Heaton grant ... free of all restrictions except the selling of liquor and if the assigns of Henry sell a lot nearby not under the liquor exception, the exception shall then be null and void. ...

By February of 1805 Jesse Bowell and his wife, Rebecca, had moved to Ohio and sold their part of the furnace to James Robinson for $1,000. It is difficult to equate this sum with the tax valuation placed on the property seven years earlier, if the furnace was not in operation.

On August 4, 1798, the Heatons also sold Lot No. 1 for ten dollars to Ephraim Coleman who, in addition to his holdings at Green Iron Works, had an eighteen by twenty-four foot frame house on 200 acres. In 1800 he was listed as a "Joyner" with a house, lot, and one-sixth of a furnace. In February 1803, Ephraim and his wife Hannah sold their one-sixth furnace and the two-acre lot "commonly called the Furnace Lot" to James Robinson.

When the Daniel Miller estate was settled in 1803 in Greene County, a list of debtors included the iron town residents, Ephraim Coleman and Job Pribble, who paid in bar iron. While there is very little historical information on the early Pribble family, the name seems to be linked with iron activity. In a March term 1782 court action, George Tegard of the Tenmile settlement whose wife was Rachel Pribble and Rubin Pribble of the Muddy Creek settlement had an agreement to pay 8/8/3 to Denton & Jacques Company, Iron Masters of Maryland.

Sharp and Thomas in their study quoted from the authority, James M. Swank, who wrote in 1892:

> ... the furnace was built before 1800 on Ten Mile Creek by James Robinson. The stack was visible after 1840.

In their own words, the authors wrote: "An old atlas shows James Robinson as the owner of the land and it seems he was the most logical man to build it." Well, with all credit to the trio of Swank, Sharp, and Thomas who tried to trace early iron manufacture, James Robinson did not build the South Fork furnace. Without specific reference, we consider that members of the large Heaton family, known as founders and masons, who sold the land to Robinson with a furnace and forge already built, constructed the stone furnace in the village that predated Clarksville by many years.

Washington County Roads and Bridges Docket No. 1, 1781-1816, lists the following road plans:

No. 7, 1796—Petition for a road from *Heaton's Forge* to Lindsley's Road at or near John Fulton's in Morgan Township.

No. 21, 1796—Petition for a road from *Heaton's Forge* to the mouth of Tenmile Creek

No. 10, 1807—Petition for road from Gantz Mill to Stephen Fulton's on road from Robeson's *Iron Works* to John Miller's.

Early assessment rolls often overlapped township lines and in 1800 the listing for adjacent Jefferson Township in Greene shows:

John Heaton—2-1/3 houses, 3 cabbins
Heaton & Robinson—100 acres, 5 houses, grist and saw mills, 5/6 of a furnace and forge

On a comparison basis with other taxpayers, John and Henry Heaton had large holdings: John's gristmill was valued at $1,000 and his sawmill at $600; in addition he had three horses, two cows, and a yoke of oxen. Henry had seven houses, two "cabbins," a $200 gristmill, and a $200 sawmill, $200 forge, two-thirds of a furnace, five horses, three cows, and four "yoaks" of steers. In the early years there were very few listings of steers or oxen and to own four yokes indicated a considerable operation, such as hauling fuel, ore, and bar iron and castings at the furnace.

Ownership of shares in the furnace went the rounds, year

by year. In December 1803 the Heaton deed to James Robinson was very involved:

> ... whereas Henry Heaton conveyed to Jesse Bowell a certain Lot #3 on the south side of the road adjacent to the furnace of which 2/6 of the furnace and lot have since been purchased by James Robinson. ... Henry also sold Lot #1 to Ephraim Coleman and a certain lot of about 3 acres to Job Pribble [the liquor restrictions must have been void at this stage as Pribble was licensed as a tavern keeper] ... all the rest of the tract of 101 acres, part of "Heaton's Cove" for $15,000, excepting only the said 2/6 part of the furnace and lot ... together with the forge, grist and saw mills, fulling mill and remaining 4/6 of the furnace, woods, waterways, dams, etc....

By the time the early deed provisions had been repeated three or four times in slightly different wording within a single document, it is easily anticipated that court calendars would be as crowded as they were with land and boundary controversies.

* * *

December term 1805 of common pleas court issued orders to Samuel Harper, high sheriff of Greene County, to recover for John and James Corruthers in the amount of $2,400 against James and Elizabeth Robinson. The sale of their personal property was insufficient so the sheriff levied on fifty acres of land with the forge and furnace. It was found by the common measure applied at this period that the profits, rents, etc., from the acreage were not of a yearly value sufficient within seven years to satisfy the debt and costs, so the property was sold on October 3, 1808, to the highest bidder at the courthouse in Waynesburg. The Baltimore merchant, John Corruthers, bought the piece for $1,600.

In the meantime, James Robinson had died and when his estate was inventoried April 18, 1807, the items revealed both store and furnace activities:

> 7 pieces of damaged castings, 4 bellows, quantity of charcoal, many household items made of iron, 2 forge hammers, 2 cast anvils. . . .

The July 23, 1810, issue of Uniontown's *Genius of Liberty* carried this ad:

> VALUABLE PROPERTY FOR SALE—At Public Auction Monday, August 27 at Waynesburg, the *Iron Works* situated on Ten Mile Creek late the property of Capt. James Robinson, adjacent to the Town of Clarksville and not distant three miles from the Monongahela River. The property possesses many advantages independent of seats for furnace and forge . . . there is water for nine months of the year sufficient for a merchant mill, also 100 acres on which is an ore bank and 30 acres of rich bottom.
>
> —SAMUEL HARPER, Agent for Proprietor

Although the land on which the village of Clarksville was laid out in 1809 by Samuel Clarke appears to have been included in the 1799 sheriff's deed to Samuel of the Henry Enoch tract "Mount Pleasant" (see also Clarksville data in chapter on the Tenmile Settlement), the fact remains that Tenmile Creek constituted the boundary between Morgan Township in Greene and East Bethlehem Township in Washington County. Therefore, the peninsula of Clarksville in Greene County since its formation in 1796, was thought to be within the "Heaton Cove" land of Isaac Heaton.

Confirmation of the Enoch claim is found in the Chartiers Southern Railroad files described in the Clarksville Woolen Mill chapter and which allude to the Mount Pleasant grant but do not mention Heaton's Cove. Claire Brown Johnson, many times great-granddaughter of William Enoch and his wife, Mary Teegarden, in her book, *From River to River*, traces what is truly a water journey as the complex, controversial Enoch family traveled from the Potomac, the Cacapon, the Monongahela, Tenmile Creek, the Ohio, the Kanawha, the Mad River in Illinois, and on. In correspondence with Claire Johnson, she writes:

> . . . back to the Iron Works. According to what I was told, this wasn't much of an operation to begin with—a sort of family affair not designed for profit, but for making items needed for the household and farm use.

The Enochs had operated iron works before they migrated to western Pennsylvania and did again later in Ohio. Henry the father operated the iron works before he deeded the place to his son Isaac. . . .

In November 1796 the newspaper *The Western Telegraphe and Washington Advertiser* ran this notice:

> . . . hides wanted and received at "Warwick Furnace" on North Tenmile by Isaac Enoch.

Before Hunter and Beaumont, publishers of the *Telegraphe*, moved to Kentucky "to establish a paper on a royal sheet in folio, larger than any other newspaper in Kentucky at $3 per year," they ran another notice for the Enochs in April 1797:

> Wood Cutters and Labourers wanted by William and Isaac Enoch at the "new furnace" on the North Fork of Ten Mile; cash will be

Exterior view of the restored Hammersmith Furnace probably very similar to the early Green Iron Furnace. Raw materials were brought to the charge hole at the top of the stone stack over the bridge; wooden wall served as windbreak; shed in foreground protected area in front of taphole from which molten iron was run from the furnace. From *The Making, Shaping and Treating of Steel*, U.S. Steel Corporation.

given—3 shillings 6 pence per cord to those who will cut 100 cords of wood.

* * *

While the 1798 federal direct tax lists are very specific as to materials used in construction of most structures, there is strangely, no detail or mention of foundry or furnace construction. The Tenmile furnaces must have approached in appearance the stone remains of a number of old furnaces still standing throughout Fayette County.

The syndicated writer, S. M. House of Centerville, on a recent reconnoiter in Washington County walked through the woods to a stone stack that he felt dated back 100 years or more, still standing straight and perfect in its isolation.

Earl Chapin May in his 1945 *Principio to Wheeling* book has described:

> . . . the remains of venerable furnaces where iron ore was smelted to shape the destiny of America. Stone on stone with little or no real engineering training, our forefathers painfully reared these picturesque, practical fire pots on strong foundations like conical altars with towering chimneys. Sometimes flying buttresses like on cathedrals and made of stone, skillfully laid, branched from their sides.

In her *Cloud by Day*, Muriel Sheppard wrote in 1947:

> . . . the little iron furnaces that painted the night sky red over the neighboring woods. In the 1790's when ironmasters could afford thousands of acres of woodlands . . . it took 840 bushels of charcoal every 24 hours for a furnace with a daily capacity of two tons. That meant wood from nearly an acre a day . . . often the furnace had to shut down while the whole crew helped the wood choppers and colliers make a supply of charcoal so they could go on running.

> The weird sounds of the blast tubes, the pacers and the ringer are no longer heard . . . the forgemen hammering the bars into shape—the clang of the hammers on the iron was a continuous sound.

Traditionally, the ironmasters loved to hunt and kept packs of hounds. Famous Alliance Furnace, claimed to be the first iron works west of the Alleghenies, blown in November 1789, has its "legend of the hounds."

> Peter Marmie, an avid hunter, after financial reverses, drove his faithful hounds into the fiery furnace and followed them. When the woods are lashed by midnight storms, it is said "Marmie, the mad Frenchman is out again with hounds and horn, and the ruins glow with the ancient fires."

Local tradition in Tenmile country tells of such national figures as Thomas Jefferson and George Rogers Clark attending fox hunts there, where many Virginia customs lingered long after the Mason-Dixon line was established. The fine breeding of their horses and hounds was indisputable.

The camaraderie established among a group of young men who served and fought together in the same militia or ranger companies often resulted in migrations together and business relationships. One such instance is revealed in a May 1793 deed involving William Harrod of Cumberland Township, Greene County:

> ... do sell part of the George Rogers Clark grant to the Illinois Regiment to Colonel Henry Heaton, Ephraim Coleman and Jesse Bowell.

The larger iron industries were organized on plantations of several thousand acres, like the small feudal manors of Europe, and included the mansion house of the ironmaster. Fayette County, where so many furnaces were established, has the prime example of an ironmaster's large acreage and mansion in the elegant house of ironmaster Isaac Meason built in 1802 on the site of the Gist Plantation at Mount Braddock; also in the skeleton of the Nathaniel Gibson stone house.

Of the three earliest furnaces in Fayette County, Union Furnace built by Isaac Meason, Sr., on the south side of Dunbar Creek and put in blast about 1791 was the only outstanding financial success. They turned out a large assortment of castings, stoves, dog irons, and sugar and salt kettles. Meason has been described "Seated as a feudal lord with complete control over Union and Mount Vernon furnaces, two forges, a grist and saw mill, two smith shops, a shoe and harness shop, and the many acres of former Gist land." The craftsman-architect for the post-Colonial Meason house, Adam Wilson was brought from England by Meason and as an expert carpenter, stonemason, and landscape gardener, created in the western wilderness this walled garden and stone mansion which in the words of Pittsburgh architect, Charles Morse Stotz:

... deserves a place in the first rank of early American architecture.

A. C. Bining in his 1938 history of Pennsylvania's iron manufacture in the eighteenth century, for the state historical commission, stated:

... the large stone house of Nathaniel Gibson on his iron plantation at Little Falls in Fayette County, one of the largest mansions constructed in the Monongahela Valley before 1800.

Although the furnace setups on Tenmile were obviously of a more modest nature, operations both large and small required homes for the workers, the furnace and forge, iron mines, charcoal house and dense woods, the office, store, grist and saw mills, blacksmith shop, etc. Bining describes workers' houses as log cabins of two rooms with a loft above the whitewashed walls and sanded floors. Mr. Horn described "log" workers' houses but the tax lists are definite as to "frame" construction.

The furnace, as described in various sources, was a truncated pyramid of stone built into the side of the hill in order that the ore could be put in at the top. The casting house or shed was directly in front of the furnace where the molten metal was poured into molds of sand. Wagons hauled the iron ore, described as carbonate ore, up the furnace road and from the bank. The fillers carried their baskets of ore, limestone, and charcoal across the bridge to the furnace. Henry Heaton's "vendue" listed a number of baskets and tax rolls carry the names of professional basket makers. Tenmile inhabitants dug and moved coal out of local coal banks by basket for years. Even today, estate auctions list baskets, and worn hickory and white oak splint models show up at country sales.

In 1804 a large order for sugar kettles came to a Fayette County furnace from Louisiana; they were cast, hauled to the mouth of Dunbar on the "Yough" where a boatyard was maintained, loaded on flatboats, and shipped downriver. There was great demand for sugar kettles locally also; one glance at the names of land grants in Tenmile country indicates the number of sugar camps.

Union Furnace in Fayette cast great salt kettles which were a source of pride. Like the Greensboro stone jugs, they were made in various sizes of twenty-two, fifty, and seventy gallons. The "chief backwoods artists and creators of the big kettles at the Meason casting house during 1801-02 were William McKelvy, Samuel Forsythe, John Hooper, John Templin, John Harbagar and Richard Jones. Moulder McKelvy was said to have moulded 638 pieces for one order." When the B&O Railroad came through, it destroyed the walls of the furnace that turned out the kettles used by Thomas Meason and William Pennock in their salt business on the Yough.

The market was "downriver" which meant anywhere between Brownsville on the Mon, Connellsville on the Yough, and the Gulf of Mexico. During the dry season, long ricks and piles of pig metal, kettles, and hollow ware from the furnaces and bar iron and "blooms" from the forges accumulated along the shore, awaiting the freshet rise, then were hastily loaded in flatboats and cast off on a "muddy tide" for a downriver port. Boats loaded with iron sometimes left in fleets of three boats at a time and furnace account books carried itemized lists of the boatmen involved in: "Adventure to Pittsburgh," "Adventure to Kentucky," or "Adventure to Limestone."

The first rolled iron in America was puddled and produced at the Plumsock Rolling Mill by Jeremiah Pears, founder of Redstone Furnace. The Plumsock Mill was constructed in 1800, twelve years before Christopher Cowan's mill in Pittsburgh.

While early iron furnaces in Fayette County have received detailed historical treatment, the earlier iron activity on Tenmile has been almost entirely overlooked, although Niles's *Weekly Register* reported in 1814:

> Clarkesville in Greene County manufactures wool and cotton extensively and makes many items of iron mongery. They are just getting under way at this place and will do handsomely in many things.

> Washington County, populous, wealthy and enlightened, has enormous salt works and *much iron* is manufactured [but no comment as to furnace or forge location].

By 1811 Ephraim Coleman had his turn with Greene County Sheriff Thomas Wood to whom common pleas court in April term had issued orders to recover $424 and damages against Coleman's goods and chattels for Thomas Fletcher & Company of Jefferson, including the "lot at Greene Iron Works where he now lives." John Corruthers also picked up this property which, for lack of buyers, did not sell until 1816 and then for only $291.

The name was still in use when Ralph and Experience Drake in 1837 recorded a sale of "Green Iron Furnace" to Robert Robinson for $2,600. As recently as 1867 Reuben Teegarden received a deed to the old furnace site described as the ninety-seven acre "Green Iron Works Farm with Dickinson Lodge" on Tenmile Creek, purchased for $3,050.

9

CLARKSVILLE WOOLEN MILL

IN JANUARY and February of 1811 notices of a stockholders' meeting to consider the new woolen manufactory at Clarksville appeared in the local papers. John Grayson's Washington *Examiner* carried the following on January 1:

> An election to be held at Clarksville to elect Directors to conduct the business of the Manufacturing Company for one year. . . .

It was apparent that there was an urgent need for domestic manufacture when Thomas and David Acheson advertised in 1811 that they had just opened a domestic warehouse in Washington where people could bring things to sell which they had made or grown:

> With the stupendous usurpation of the European powers, it behooves us to look for happiness and prosperity within the limits of our own Country. . . .

In spite of British restrictions, there was evidence even earlier of cloth making in the area. The Washington *Telegraphe* in August 1795:

> Joseph Blakely has set up the trade of coverlid and diamond weaving. . . .

> William Dunsmore carries on his fulling and dying business on Millers Run doing everything except scarlet and blue—will take in cloth every first Tuesday of the month in Washington.

In 1810 the Washington *Reporter* noted a survey conducted in Chartiers Township showed that there were 424 spinning wheels on which housewives turned out flax and tow linen, cotton linsey and flannel, and also fulled cloth.

The year when manufacturing of various types began in earnest in Pittsburgh and vicinity was 1810.

* * *

King George III was considered by many to have been a sincere and conscientious ruler during his long reign from 1760 to 1820. Except for periods of derangement, especially during crises with America, he worked for the common good of his subjects in England and also (he thought) for the refugees who had settled the English colonies.

George III has been called a model family man with such a strong concept of family that he looked on his colonies as extensions of his family and had no patience with "children" who did not show an equal reverence for the instutition; that is, with Papa presiding and holding the reins.

However, it was too much when after nearly two centuries of struggle, starvation, and sacrifice, the king asserted his control over the colonies by permitting them to raise flax and wool to ship to England, but not allowing them to weave at home.

Niles's *Weekly Register* for 1811:

> Quoting from Lord Sheffield in England, exportation of woolen goods is way up and exports of cloth to America very good in anticipation of the removal of the non-importation law. If the practice of non-intercourse with the American States should continue through a partiality for France, it will not be general.

> The people of America will not go naked through their affection for the French or enmity to this country. It does not appear that they can get cloth from any other country at present and it will not be possible for them to manufacture it for a long time.

The editor commented that Lord Sheffield was one of our worst enemies in Europe. Furthermore, in the matter of trying to procure homemade articles of military cloth for the United States, woolen offers were abundant:

... the best cloth is suitable for commissioned officers and very near European prices due to the introduction of Merino sheep. Our old native sheep wool will do for the non-commissioned officers and privates [!]. Farmers are urged to breed sheep with heavy fleeces and remember that Merino and other fine wool cannot be combed but must be carded.

In October 1812 Niles continued with the subject by reporting that small factories for coarse woolen cloth were getting into operation in all directions and manufacturing was growing by "leaps and bounds."

As to the French sentiment, pro-French feeling was strong in the post-Revolutionary period from 1785 into the early 1800s. The Englishman, Thomas Ashe, Esq., who came over in 1806 to explore "the western part of America . . . interesting in every point of view . . . little known, and misrepresented by the few writers on the subject . . ." included this comment:

> John Adams is the first statesman, followed by Mr. Jefferson who has more theoretical talent than sterling political ability, fluctuating between the interests of his country and his attachment to the French.

The University of Pittsburgh, founded in 1787, represented the hub of Francophile activity in southwestern Pennsylvania.

British trade policies were a bitter disappointment to the many Americans who had hoped that independence would bring rich commercial rewards. Seeking an outlet, they began to develop a thriving commerce with France and her possessions. The subsequent treaty entered into by Chief Justice John Jay and the British in 1794-95 was not popular in America. It produced a fury among the Republicans, particularly in Pennsylvania.

The Republican Party was formed from the early Democratic Society clubs, three of which were located in western Pennsylvania: Mingo Creek, the Republican Society of the

Yough' and the Democratic Society of Washington. Samuel
Clarke of the woolen mill was a member of the latter group.

In 1798 a Maypole was erected in Washington and the
French flag was raised. It was ordered cut down by the
town's authorities as some feared it might be changed into a
liberty tree. A town poet composed this doggerel verse:

> The pole stood firm with flying flag,
> And stripes sixteen in number,
> Columbia's boast and all her brag
> Red round with stripes of umber.
> But dignity whose eyes were foggy,
> Thought this the flag of France,
> Around which those who were so groggy
> Began to hop and dance.

In Pittsburgh the *Gazette* for April 24, 1794, carried this
ad:

D. McLain at the *Whale and Monkey* Tavern announces to the
Public and *All France* that he has taken the well-known and
beautiful house formerly occupied by J. Tannehill on the bank of
the Monongahela, for the purpose of entertaining travelers. . . .

The visit in 1824-25 of Monsieur Lafayette to southwestern Pennsylvania stimulated great interest and activity. The
Gazette advertised articles for the Lafayette receptions:

. . . badges, waist ribbons, gloves, elegant gilt coat and vest buttons, plates, tumblers, swords, epaulets, plumes, sashes, cock-
ades. . . .

The "leaps and bounds" being taken toward manufacturing were shown in the many ads and notices inserted in local
papers:

Daniel McFarland's Fulling Mill has been completely repaired
with two stocks for fine and coarse cloth. Home-coloured cloth
and linsey will be fulled and pressed for 6¢ per yard, black 20¢,
brown 30¢, bottle green 36¢, smoke 20¢ and drab 16¢—N. Fork
of Tenmile 1813

James Kelly's Fulling Mill on the North Fork of Tenmile will take cloth at William Carter's on the Waynesburg Road, Ephraim Sayer's in Waynesburg, Ephraim Cooper's Tannery in Morris Township, Henry Black's in Jefferson and Stephen Hill's in Brownsville. Mr. Kelly learned the art of colouring from Mr. Kelso in England, a Gentleman who was in the business for years in London. Rates as low as any of his neighboring fullers.

Abraham and Jacob Bane's new Fulling Mill built about 100 yards from their old one on the Middle Fork of Tenmile, October 1813

The dyes ordered for the early blue and red coverlets were "Imperial Red" and "Nicholson Blue" and in the 1880s they could be purchased from Lutz and Movius in Philadelphia.

The tailors of the area met in Washington in the fall of 1813 to decide on a scale of prices. Members present were Charles Hawkins, Patrick Moore, Archibald Kerr, Richard Ledwith, Samuel Robb, Joseph Teeters, and James Dunlap. The prices set were:

Fashionable full dress coat	$ 3.50
Pantaloons	1.25
Vest	1.25
Great Coat with Capes	4.00
Uniforms with Full Dress Coat	10.00

* * *

The land on which the proposed Clarksville Manufactory was to be built was part of the tract called Mount Pleasant which William and Isaac Enoch had inherited from their father, Colonel Henry Enoch, and which, to settle the complicated affairs and estate of Henry Enoch, the Elder, as he was known, in the latter years of the eighteenth century, was sold by order of the court, by the high sheriff of Greene County to Samuel Clarke on June 4, 1800.

When the Washington Mechanical Society was organized on May 12, 1792, Samuel Clarke was one of the members of a group whose object was to create a fund and loan money, not to exceed three months, for "charitable, political and generous purposes at six percent."

The following letter is from the manuscript collection of the Washington County Historical Society:

Connellsville April 14th 1812

We Abram Baldwin & Daniel S. Norton of Connellsville County, of Fayette State of Pennsylvania Agree with John Feith of Allegany County, State of Maryland to build for him a good Wool Carding Machine upon the construction we usually build at our Factory near this place & have ready for delivery on or before the fifteenth of June next — (Unless our Cards which are shiped from New York for Baltimore should be lost at sea)

And I John Feith do hereby agree to receive sd Machine at sd Factory, & at same time to pay sd Baldwin & Norton the sum of Two Hundred Dollars & at the same time to execute my obligation with such security, as sd Baldwin & Norton shall approve for the sum of Two Hundred & Fifty dollars now payable half in in six Months & half in one year spd interest from sd rect of sd Machine — Sd Baldwin & Norton are not to find Mill gearing Straps Jacks &c nor to set it up after transported. In Confirmation of the above we bind ourselves to each other in the Penal sum of eight Hundred dollars

Witness our hands & seals

Danl Norton for self

In presence of

Abram Baldwin

Solomon Spess

James Feith

Contract to build a wool carding machine by Abram Baldwin and Daniel Norton of Fayette County for John Feikk of Maryland in 1812. From Washington County Historical Society collection.

In 1794 the society resolved to get an accurate account of various machines in use in the western country, prices of labor in mechanical employment, money spent for public buildings, obstructions to navigation in creeks and rivers, ways of transporting produce to market, and noting the history of mechanics in building the early settlements.

They opened correspondence in 1795 with the society in Philadelphia in an effort to encourage foreign mechanics to come to southwestern Pennsylvania. A committee composed of Robert Hamilton, Samuel Clarke, and David Cooke was appointed to report on a method of procuring tin for a manufactory. A quantity was brought to Washington and placed with various citizens to be made up and Samuel Clarke was active in seeing that the tin was made up and the society repaid.

By August of 1809, Samuel had closed his store in Washington where, after the Revolutionary War, he had operated as a successful merchant for a number of years. He had also completed terms as coroner, recorder of deeds, register of wills, justice of the peace, and Washington County commissioner. On the flat land of Mount Pleasant, according to deed records, but within the Isaac Heaton grant called Heaton's Cove according to the township map, Samuel Clarke laid out a town which he advertised in local papers:

Proposed new town at the junction of the Forks of Tenmile Creek . . . this beautiful tract now laid out in the heart of a rich, populous and flourishing settlement. The streams of Tenmile are superior to any in the country, yielding plenty of fish in season and afford easy access to the Monongahela. . . . Stone and Coal are abundant, best quality for smiths and fuel, and water for every purpose.

—SAMUEL CLARKE, Proprietor

At the January 1811 meeting for the proposed woolen mill the directors elected were: Samuel Jackson, Quaker proprietor of the Redstone Paper Mill, John Nyswanger, Revolutionary soldier under George Washington, Parker Campbell the attorney, William Buckingham, David Cooke, Samuel's partner in the Washington store until 1796, John Sheldon, William Ross, Thomas Register, Adam and Henry Wise, sons of the founder of Fredericktown, Abijah McClain whose tract Pigeon Roost became the lower section of Rice's Landing, and Colonel Samuel Clarke.

The first meeting of the directors was held on February 4 in the new town of Clarksville. Samuel Jackson was elected president, James Hill, treasurer, and Samuel Clarke, secretary.

> The Company being now organized, the stockholders agreeable to the 8th Article . . . are now called on for $5 per share to be paid within 30 days to James Hill at his residence near Mr. Montgomery's Mill on the North Fork of Tenmile.

Minutes of the first directors' meeting have not been found, but it can be surmised that fairly well defined plans were laid for the operation as well as for the building itself. On March 18, 1811, the *Reporter* carried this notice:

> TO STONE MASONS—Proposals will be received in writing until the first meeting in April for building the manufactory in Clarksville. Two proposals can be made; one for finding every material for the walls, 85 ft. long by 37 ft. wide, 2 stories high of 10 ft. each, stone is free and in sight, and one for all except the stone—to the Manager for the building near the ground.
> —ELI PHILLIPS, Manager

Cumberland Township, Greene County, assessment rolls for 1789-99 list Eli Phillips as a miller and in conversation with a descendant in 1973 we learned that Eli belonged to the early Theophilus Phillips family in whose cabin the first Fayette County Court was held near New Geneva.

In a notice posted June 10, 1811, the name of the new company had been chosen and set forth in boldface type:

MONONGAHELA MANUFACTORY

> Stockholders in said company will please take notice that their first and second installments are due, money is much wanted; pay to John Auld in the vicinity of Germantown, Fayette County, Thomas Collins near Uniontown, Samuel Jackson at Brownsville

and in the vicinity of Clarksville where nearly all have paid, to Samuel Clarke or James Hill. The building will be ready for the roof by July. . . .

—JAMES HILL, Treasurer

In his locally famous *Notes*, Andrew J. Waychoff said Sherlock Negus erected the woolen fulling mill at Clarksville [the fulling mill was a separate building]. It has also been said that this was a name given in jest. However, Brownsville Postmaster Jacob Bowman in April 1797 listed a letter waiting at the post office for "Shadlock Nigus."

Fayette County records show Shaidlock Negus purchasing a 300-acre tract, Mount Royal, from Nathan Brown's widow, Margaret, in June 1796 and the following year he purchased part of Colonel Edward Cook's Whiskey Mount where he had a bark and curry (tanning) house; in 1820 Shadlock was named guardian of Zachariah Gapen's children in orphan's court records.

As to the stonemasons who may have answered the March 1811 notice, tax rolls for 1811-12 show the following masons living in East Bethlehem Township, Washington County:

John Nicholson	Aaron Yarnall
Aaron Baker	Benjamin Kinney
Barnet Johnson	

Thomas and William Williamson—Welsh stone masons who lived on Samuel Clarke's Greene Twp. land in 1798

Director Thomas Register and his three sons

Enoch Kees, whose stone coffin shed is still noted in the township

Nathan and Samuel Heacock

By the mysterious methods of research known only to himself, W. F. Horn reported that twelve masons worked to erect the mill and were paid six shillings for a ten-hour day.

No doubt the master stonemason in the whole area had been Isaac Heaton, Sr., whose name in all records is followed by the word "Mason"; in 1801 Isaac and his wife, Susannah, sold their sixty-five acre tract Ashley on Casteel Run to Samuel Clarke, Esq., for $400 and shortly thereafter, Isaac's estate was probated.

The Heatons were a large and influential family, noted as millers, founders, and stonemasons. Their land acquisitions were usually on waterways where there were good millsites.

Publicity continued and on December 30, 1811, Samuel Clarke concluded the first year of mill building activities with

the announcement of a stockholders' meeting in January to elect directors.

The only known photograph of the stone woolen mill building before the roof caved in, was sketched for this chapter and is from the Greene County Historical Society's collection. The photograph is undated but was taken before 1900 and someone had lettered in ink across the gable end:

1811 W. DRAKE FACTORY

Caldwell's 1876 Atlas shows the "Drake Factory" on the plat map of Clarksville.

When application was made to the quarter sessions court in March term 1788 to divide Bethlehem, one of the original Washington County townships, into East and West sections, the suggested line was run from Peter Drake's Drake's Choice in the northwest corner of the township to Wise's Mill on Tenmile above Clarksville. The Drakes came originally from New Jersey to Fort Pitt.

February 24, 1812, laborers were wanted immediately for the job or by the day, to undertake the digging of a race for the mill. Men were to report directly to Samuel Clarke.

In May 1812 Samuel Jackson advertised:

WANTED—fine wool at 40¢ washed and on the sheep. To be delivered to the factory on Tenmile, Greene County. Small quantities can be received at the paper mill on Redstone Creek in Fayette County.

Stockholders take note that the Monongahela Manufactory's 8th installment is due and wool to the amount of the unpaid balance is immediately wanted at the mill. The factory will be ready to go in a few days.

It must have been some time after the May notice before the mill actually began operation. In August, Samuel Clarke notified the stockholders that part of the machinery was in operation and that there would be a general meeting at the factory in October.

Journeyman woolen weavers of "sturdy habits" were needed and were to report to Manager Eli Phillips at the factory through the fall months of 1812 and into 1813.

Early assessment rolls for all of the southwestern Pennsylvania counties contain the names of many weavers. One of the first to come to Clarksville was Ami Moore (1767-1823) who bought Lots 20 and 21 at the corner of Sugar Lane and Factory Street from Samuel and Dorcas Clarke in 1814. Other weavers whose names appear:

Hamilton Fletcher	Joseph Slonacher	Joshua Hutchins
Hugh Gilroy	James Carroll	William Noble
John Hawthorn	Robert Dorris	Maylon Linton
Thomas Pollock	Adam Dell	Christopher Robinson
	Cheeseman Drake	

A number of the weavers were Quakers; Mahlon Linton belonged to the Westland Monthly Meeting and married Ann Hilles March 1803; he was a son of Joshua and Hannah Linton.

* * *

With national Bicentennial interest mounting, in the summer of 1974 Clarksville celebrated "U.S.A. Days," the first community effort to reach back to colonial days when the village was known for its manufacturing and not just as a mining town of the 1900s.

Cherished photographs and heirlooms were brought out and displayed in local store windows; coverlets and blankets made in the old woolen mill were taken out of their tissue paper to reveal their beautiful rose pattern and still-vivid scarlet and blue. The blankets were of cream-colored wool with narrow bands of pink and blue. Annie Crayne of Clarksville, whose blankets were displayed, said when local girls became engaged to be married they had their blankets woven to order at the mill with their initials monogrammed in the corner of the blanket.

Visitors came from other Pennsylvania counties and out of state to reminisce over early days and one of the most well-

Rose pattern, blue and white wool coverlet woven at Clarksville Woolen Mill
during the Ross operation. Owned by Fay Ross Antonio of Clarksville.

remembered features of mill operations was the long line strung the length of the mill property where cloth in all lengths and colors was hung out to dry.

When the Chartiers Southern Railroad Company proposed its new line extension from Champion in Jefferson Township in 1917, the route lay directly through the woolen mill property and the derelict stone factory. Deeds and abstracts on file in the office of the red brick Union Station Building on the Brownsville riverfront reveal much of the early history of Clarksville and its woolen mill.

One of the railroad blueprints shows the placement of the thirty-seven by eighty factory, the thirty-seven by sixty fulling mill and the twenty-five by thirty-seven dye house which comprised the establishment on Factory Street.

* * *

N

FACTORY STREET

ESTATE

NORTH ST.

ELIZABETH ROSS

SITE OF FACTORY
180 × 37

31 × 25 SITE OF DYE HOUSE

NORTH FORK

SITE OF FULLING MILL
60 × 37

R.R. BRIDGE   To Millsboro

To Waynesburg

92 93 94

SOUTH FORK

TENMILE

DEC. 12 1925
PLAN No. 25003

Map of factory location. From Monongahela Railroad Company files, Brownsville, courtesy of Mr. Whetzel and Mr. Gratz.

Samuel Clarke's former merchandising partner in the Washington store, David Cooke, believed to have been his brother-in-law, advertised his property for sale in 1812:

... 300 acres of first-rate limestone land with several sugar camps, an apple orchard, two square log houses, an 80 x 30 barn with stone stables underneath, shingled roof and 5 miles from the Monongahela Mfg. at Clarksville.

In November 1812 he ran another ad:

WANTED—10 to 12 men for two months to cut cord wood and boat timbers and 2 men who understand making broad rails for a post and rail fence; generous wages paid in cash at my residence on the Monongahela one mile above Rice's Landing, or if more convenient, applications may be taken at Thomas Fletcher's store in Jefferson.

Samuel Clarke advertised in the same month for a good farmer, well acquainted with merchant and gristmills to work at the forks of Tenmile, "a good, steady, single man preferred."

In Pennsylvania statutes for 1813 the yearly income for the new factory was computed as of March with a volume of not to exceed $2,000 for the first partial year of operation.

The Washington *Observer* carried this notice August 1, 1814:

Lots 92, 93 and 94 whereon the factory now stands, also adjacent parcel including the present fulling mill race, to stake in the island, to Factory Street, including streets and alleys and sufficient space on the creek to erect a dam. . . .

Reserving for Samuel Clarke the privilege of erecting a fence or gate across the premises for the use and enjoyment of the adjacent property owners. The Society shall from time to time at their own costs, erect, make and keep in good repair, good and sufficient bridges over every street and alley whereat the race or any water course may cross. . . .

The property so described was sold by Samuel and Dorcey Clarke to the Monongahela Manufacturing Society for $1,000.

Shortly after Samuel's name disappeared from newspaper notices for the mill, appearance dockets for April term 1817 in Washington County show an action of Alexander Caldwell against the society for $373 with Manager Matthew Dill as defendant. Judgment was levied on:

> ... the Monongahela Manufacturing House and 3 lots where it stands and an adjacent lot where the fulling mill and dye house stand ... inquisition held and rents, profits etc. would not pay the debt and interest in seven years. ...

Apparently the land and factory were put up for sale but were unsold for want of buyers according to Sheriff Adam Hays. No records are on file in the Greene County Courthouse, but railroad files reveal a sheriff's unrecorded deed to Parker Campbell and Samuel Jackson at the suit of A. Caldwell for $3,260 and the property was sold to them March 17, 1819.

Parker Campbell, whose name was so long associated with the mill's activities, died at his Washington home July 30, 1824, at age fifty-four.

In June 1819 there was an amicable action with a judgment for $4,900 by the *Philadelphia Bank* v. *Parker Campbell and Samuel Clarke* with a lien on the property as leased to Matthew Dill by Samuel. By September 1824 Samuel Clarke had died; the property was condemned during January 1825 term of common pleas court and sold at public outcry to the Philadelphia Bank for $2,000.

While court and abstract records appear to indicate dissolution of the mill, operations continued. The 1820 census of manufacturers in the western section of Pennsylvania includes a report of mill operation and equipment by Matthew Dill in his strong, flowing and legible hand.

Matthew Dill, like Samuel Clarke, operated a store in Washington under the trade name of *Cunningham & Dill*, opposite the courthouse. The first map of town lots in Clarksville shows *Cunningham & Dill* on Lot 13 facing on Center Street just down from the Square.

The 1820 report of the Clarksville Woolen Mill:

Use 3000 lbs. of wool a year which is made into broadcloth at a cost of about $1500. Employ 8 men, no women and 8 boys and girls.

Machinery: 4 carding machines
3 shearing machines
1 Nappy machine
5 broad looms
2 narrow looms
2 fulling stocks
1 Billy
4 Jennys
1 Picker
1200 gal. blue vat
2 common dye kettles

Three looms are in operation and all the other machinery. Capital investment: $20,000. Cannot say how much is used for wages as it varies annually according to business, as the factory is driven by water; some seasons are wet and more business done of course. Then in dry seasons about $3-4000 in wages.

The only goods manufactured here are woolen broadcloths and cassinettes. The broadcloth sells at $3-9 a yard and the satinets and cassinettes at $1-1.75 a yard. We card and full country work to the amount of about $1,200 a year.

This manufactory is seated in the forks of Tenmile Creek . . . the main building is stone . . . with an additional building of frame 37 x 38, one dye house and one fulling mill. It was erected in 1811 by a Company and sold in 1815 and is now owned by Parker Campbell and Samuel Jackson from whom it is rented by M. Dill and business continues by him for himself.

The machinery now in this establishment is capable of doing a much greater business than it at present does owing in part to dryness of the season past and the want of a cash market for our goods. At present our prospect is better than for several years past, the cloths are in demand but no cash for them.

—M. DILL

In 1817 John Hoge over on Chartiers Creek in Washington County wrote to a friend that his funds were so exhausted in rebuilding his mills that he could not make an advance in cash which someone had requested of him. He had wool on hand, one-half and three-quarter blooded which he would be willing to sell at sixty-two and one-half cents but there were no purchasers.

Those concerned with operation of the woolen mill persisted through the years in their efforts to make it a going and profitable business. Then, on Monday the fourth of February 1821 the Brownsville *Western Register* carried this ad:

CLARKSVILLE WOOLEN CLOTH MANUFACTORY—
FOR SALE

This extensive and excellent establishment is now offered, with all its machinery and other appurtenances. Situated . . . about 10 miles from Brownsville. A newspaper description of the advantages . . . is unnecessary as those who may have a desire to purchase will examine and judge for themselves, upon which it will be found equaled by none in the Western Country except Steubenville. For terms inquire of Samuel Jackson or Parker Campbell in Washington.

Alexander Reed, Washington merchant, advertised an assortment of Steubenville and Clarksville cloths and cassinettes in 1822. The new Steubenville mill offered strong competition; Matthew Dill placed another ad:

WANTED—WOOL—Subscriber will attend in Washington June 11 and on for the purpose of purchasing wool delivered to the factory in Clarksville . . . almost any kind of trade will be arranged and prices the same as given in Steubenville.

Not to be overlooked at this time was the trend to a depression. Stimulated by the War of 1812, with the coming of the peace in 1815, English goods again flooded the market and the increasing depression of woolen manufacturing was noted. It had been found that woolen goods could be manufactured cheaper here than to import them except when people in England were willing to work for a "pittance" and then the balance was in their favor.

It seemed like a strange time for the Steubenville Woolen

Mill to commence operations in 1819. Hazard's *Register* for 1828 and 1829 reported on the two mills:

> Steubenville Mill machinery valued at $50,000 and total valuation of real estate, machinery and buildings $100,000. Operation commenced in 1819 to manufacture flannel and broadcloth with 100 hands and losses of $8,000 in three years.

> [about Clarksville's mill] . . . a very large and extensive woolen factory at Clarksville near the mouth of Tenmile was in full operation during the last war and for some time afterward, but for some years has languished and declined; lately it has changed masters and seems to have started with fresh vigor and under the auspices of a judicious tariff is likely to prosper.

By 1833 Thomas Gordon's *Pennsylvania Gazetteer* did not even mention the mill in describing Clarksville:

> Post Town for Morgan Township, Greene County at the fork of Tenmile, 2 miles from the Monongahela. The town is beautifully situated and contains about 40 dwellings, several stores and taverns.

For the first time in mill records, the name of Drake appears in a May 1, 1824, ad:

> We propose to conduct this business for the ensuing season, manufactory of wool for the country from the fleece or otherwise into finished cloth. Less than 20 lbs. will not be received [followed by instructions on how to clean the fleece before it would be accepted]. Wool can be worked on shares or at Steubenville prices. On June 1 M. Dill or Wm. Drake will attend in Washington to pick up wool.

Observer columnist Marcia Biddle remarked the other day:

> Greene County is filled with great traditions and stories about the sheep and wool industry. It seems at one time, within the memory of some who took part, there was a premium paid on wool which had been washed. Some sheep raisers would drive their flocks to the Monongahela, then onto the ferry. When the ferry was halfway across, they'd drive the sheep off into the water and make them swim back to shore.

In official records there is a December 1831 deed from Joshua and Tryphena Secor to Ralph Drake of "the small parcel of land where the Dye House and the Fulling Mill stand." This small piece of land, separate to this day from the main mill property, was sold to Joshua by Samuel and Dorcas Clarke in April 1824:

> All that lot on the west side of the North Fork of Tenmile Creek, beginning at the bank of the race of the Monongahela Manufactory, south side of the bridge, down the race to the north side of the Dye House, containing 146 perches of ground . . . part of the tract of land sold by the Sheriff unto Samuel Clarke. . . .

The 1821 commerce census for Morgan Township lists William Drake with "4 persons in commerce" which might indicate the Drake family was even then involved at the woolen mill. William, related to the Clarksville Waltons and called by them "Uncle Billy Drake," was born October 4, 1770, in England and died at age ninety-four on April 6, 1865.

In 1838 there is a deed "without warranty" from the Philadelphia Bank to William Drake and Joseph Baily for $1,500 for the "Woolen Manufactory commonly known by the name of Clarksville or Monongahela Factory."

Greene County Orphans' Court March Term 1866 shows:

> Petition of Ralph Drake, Administrator of William Drake who died intestate . . . in 1863 he had an undivided half interest in the Clarksville Factory for $1,500 with $300 to be paid April 1, 1864 with possession at that date. . . . William Drake and William A. Stephenson entered into an agreement to sell Drake's entire half interest to Stephenson.

There is great confusion as to names and dates for owners at this period in the mill's history. There is a sale recorded to Stephenson and then to Thomas B. Ross for $1,121 in 1864. Joseph Baily's Greene County will shows:

> . . . 3 lots adjoining heirs of Thomas Clark on which there is a grist mill, saw mill and woolen manufactory . . . my interest in the Albany Glass Works . . . my daughter Elizabeth, wife of Thomas B. Ross all my interest in the river bottom opposite the

Albany Glass Works, in Washington County which I hold in partnership with the estate of John Krepps, deceased. . . .

In 1876 David and Eli Ross bought the factory for $4,000 and ownership continued in the Ross name until the property was condemned. In a February 1970 interview with Leslie Ross at his Clarksville home only a stone's throw from the tracks and the millsite, he said his family moved there when he was seven years old, about 1887, and the mill operated for another twelve to fifteen years, or until about 1900. He well remembered the wagonloads of wool that came in and at certain times the mill would be bulging with wool when farmers brought it in to be made up into cloth and yarn which they later picked up.

* * *

Just as there were two iron furnaces on Tenmile in the general area of the early Tenmile settlement, so there were two woolen mills. While William Buckingham was one of the first directors of the Clarksville mill, notices began to appear as early as 1813 over the name of Isaac Buckingham:

. . . a manufactory called the "Tenmile Factory" in West Bethlehem Township on the North Fork where I weave cloth from the finest Merino wool.

A Washington County history relates that Daniel Dunn became an apprentice carder at Buckingham's woolen factory and after marrying Sarah Baker in 1834, Dunn worked at his trade near Clarksville until 1840. Other names which appeared in Buckingham ads were Benjamin Spruance and Evan McCullough who stated that their manufactured articles sold at neighboring stores and taverns and included various kinds of cloth, flannel, and blankets.

In 1824 when the Society for the Promotion of Agriculture and Domestic Manufacturing held their spring fair in Washington, Isaac Buckingham took second prize for cloth; when the October fair was held, he took a first on his red flannel and fulled cloth.

Isaac Buckingham had an interestingly uneven tract of thirty-three acres running along the North Fork of Tenmile which he called Trousers with plenty of area on the creek for a dam and race.

By 1825 David Acheson and James McDowell had purchased patent rights for "steam" fulling whereby a process was carried on at small expense without the use of soap. It was advertised as working easier in the mill and especially good for indigo blues "which are now more even."

While Clarksville had the honor of sponsoring the pioneer woolen mill, the Washington group organized to promote domestic manufacturing seemed to be fulfilling its purpose when in January 1829 the following announcement appeared:

> Jonathan Pearson and Parks Walker to "Friends of American Manufacturing"—we have formed a partnership to make woolen machinery, carding, spinning and shearing rigs or napping machines, looms, etc. for the Western Country . . . located next to the Woolen Factory of L. and P. Prescott in Wheeling.

10

BILL BAILEY REMEMBERS
TENMILE CRIK

BORN AUGUST 10, 1877, at Clarksville, William Montgomery Bailey was the son of Aldorse Bailey who with his brother came to America from their native Spain in 1856. Bill Bailey had only one year of formal schooling and did not learn to read or write until after his marriage, the celebration of which lasted for three days. He worked as a coal miner until an event changed his life.

In 1909 he was baptized by immersion in a nearby creek and became an evangelist and ordained minister in the Church of Jesus Christ. The only book he read was the Bible; his daughter, Mary Bailey Anderson, has compiled a family history and from it she read the poem her father recited shortly before his death in September 1969. He had the memory and voice of a man young in years and in January 1969 the writer taped two interviews with this charming and lively old man, which are typical of the oral traditions and expressions of the neighborhood:

* * *

I must tell you about my mother at Tenmile Crik. She had a crane swung up with a chain on it and my father would roll in three logs on the log irons in the fall. She would rake the coals up and bake heavy bread—she didn't bake light bread— lots of corn bread. She would make cornmeal mush. She had this fire right down by the crik—we lived right by it, and me

209

and my sister would stand there with tin cups waitin' on that mush to get done.

We had a cow. We slept in a little trundle bed, pulled out from under the big bed. My family is all gone now.

There used to be an old lady by the name of Wittock who lived down below, next to Alec Teegarden, and she had geese. They had mustard plants and fennel and the yard was full of these plants. Me and Byron Greenlee would go down there with a piece of cord and tie a piece of paper and a grain of corn on the mustard. The old gander would pick at the corn with the old paper a-goin' it, you know [big laugh], so Ady said to me one day, "Willie, you musn't do that." Ady Wittock took me and nursed me—she loved me and had me on her lap pretty near all the time. I'd go there and Granny Wittock, the old lady, would rescue me when the old gander, squawking like the dickens, would come after me.

[Everybody raised geese in Clarksville—the alleys were full of them. Estate records show feathers sold at vendue and John Heaton's mill ledger showed customers made payments with sugar, linen, baskets, salmon, deerskins, buckwheat, hair, rags and *feathers*.]

Jesse Virgin played with us. Old Man Virgin married a Teagarden, maybe Sarah. They lived straight on through Clarksville to the bridge, on the right. Old John Rider [Horn mentioned George Rider helped move the council stone in 1832] lived across from them.

The Virgins farmed and Old Man Virgin worked for other farmers. He used to fish a terrible lot—we fished for trout, catfish, perch, and all such like that but they got mostly catfish and what they called a "white perch" at that time—it has little white stones on each side of its head. My father built a dam across Tenmile Crik and set a net in the center of it and he would catch these white suckers and we ate them a good bit.

The Virgin Bridge in Clarksville was covered; they laid on logs under the bridge with hooks on a line and fished—jerk up quick. Them white suckers laid there in great big pools and we'd snake 'em out of there.

There was a lower covered bridge where the iron bridge crossed Laurel Run and there was another covered bridge at the lower end of town. Up by Rice's Landing they were all covered bridges and what they called the old Newsome Bridge was way above Tenmile.

I mind one time P. M. Woods, an old man with a short beard, was a minister there. Right below the bridge on the left-hand side of the road in the crik there was a hole and they immersed them down there. The Campbellites always immerse, you know. That is now the Christian Church.

When P. M. Woods took my mother down to the crik to baptize her, I was with my father and wanted to jump in after my mother and save her—I thought he was going to drown her.

The Forwood Mill was operating when we lived there. The flour mill was Pollock's, above Clarksville and way up on Tenmile, but I never got over around there. They ground corn and it was coarse meal in those days.

My mother would take the corn up there and get it ground and then fetch it down and while it was warm sometimes. Me and my sister would take green corn and put it in a skillet and parch it and then we had a salt sack and we would put the corn in it and take it to school to eat. My pants pocket was all greasy from that old salt sack of corn.

The Old Man Pollock lived there—he was very cross-eyed. He had a Burson boy that worked for him and he said to the boy he was going to kill a calf—going to hit it in the head and he told the boy to hold it while he hit it. The boy took ahold of the calf and looked at the old man, and he was looking right at the boy—nearsighted he was. The boy said, "You hit where you look?" Pollock said, "Yes Sir!" The boy said, "Would you get somebody else to hold this calf?"

The old woolen mill? I used to go down there at the Drake Mill and I would watch them make cloth. They strung it out you know—they used water on it to stretch it. The house at the Forwood Mill when we lived there, stood right above the dam. It was a sawmill—the Forwoods were all gone—that's an old place you know. They come in there from England or Ireland. They died off, you know. That was an awful looking place, the stones were all hollowed out back there—right above the old sawmill. It was a kind of cave.

These are all things that happened right at the mill. The house was covered with white siding—part log and part frame. Balloon framing with boards right up through—shingled roof—no metal roofs in them days.

I've made many oak shingles with a frow—my father had one and it went off here and out that way—I'd take that and hit the pieces of log cut long enough for shingles and strip it down and then my father would put them in what they called a shaving horse and they would shave them down. They made hickory shingles but they curled up in the fall and in the summer they straightened out.

Stone chimneys? Pretty near everybody built them out of stone. In that old log cabin where we lived there was a big chimney with a broad fireplace. My father would roll in logs with a cant hook up on the log iron with three legs and a round place up there to put the logs on. Three logs would last pretty near all winter. It made a nice fire—we didn't burn any coal until we went to Brownsville.

The first cooking stove my mother ever got she got off a man by the name of Hiram Holly in Brownsville—that was something to see! My father built a bake oven and the first time she baked in it she burnt the bread.

Food? We didn't get much ham like today. We had white side meat—my mother would parboil it and then put it on with a little brown sugar on it. They mostly served pork and potatoes and cabbage in the hotels. They used a lot of sweet potatoes in them days—peeled them and put them in a pan in the stove and baked them, served with pork. No baked beans that I can remember. My mother baked prune pie and punkin

and sweet potato pie. No cranberries, but black and raspberries. My mother made jelly out of the fox grapes. My
father would go out and get them—they were about as big as
the end of my thumb. They grew out in the woods, and she
made jam out of that.

My father was a regular fox hunter—he kept three, four, or
five dogs. This was a sport and he was a fox hunter till he
died. They didn't hunt much with horses here. They just
gathered in the woods and let the dogs run; they could tell
what dog was ahead all the time—they knowed the voices of
them dogs. They called the dogs Old Drive and Old Truman—
They would argue as to which dog it was and would even
fight over this and say, "I'm goin' in to you!"

They used to get into these arguments pretty regular. A
man up here came over to my place one day—I lived on the
little crik. He said, "Neighbor, I come down to shoot your
dog." "Not my dog," I sez. "He's never been off the leash."
He said he had been attacking his sheep and just as we were
talking, there came a dog down the road and he looked in his
mouth and there was wool in it. He was the dog that was
running them sheep.

I knew the Pearsons and the Teegardens; they had smoke-
houses—would hang the meat and then cut sassafras green.
They would hang in the old meat house. It had no floor, just
dirt, and they built a fire in the center. The blacksmith done
pretty near all the wagon business.

Abner and Frank Miles had a dog churn. Abey used to say,
"Come on Bowser," and they would take him down to the
springhouse, had a long pole with a nail in each end and old
Bowser would peddle that churn. He would never look
around at you, he just kept peddling till the butter went
down and then he would bark.

All we had on Tenmile were skiffs we rowed and what
they called a "dog boat"—you rowed that.

The boys would go sled riding; they had a big plank on and
they would take seven on this plank and go down the hill and

the boys said, "Get on Mr. Degood, and we will take you down to church." So they fetched him down and Sol Pryer made shoes and suchlike. The shoe shop was a little bit of a place and had a big stick hanging out with a boot on it made out of some kind of stuff, I don't know what it was.

When Degood went down the hill he dug in his heel, like that you know—thought they were going on over the bank, but they wasn't—they had a big stick in front. Then when they went around on the other side, he dug in his heels again. He had just bought a new pair of boots off Sol, so when he got down he said to P. M. Woods, the minister, "P. M., there is something the matter with me." And the minister said, "Well, I don't know what is the matter with you, Mr. Degood—let's see your boots." And he had dug both heels off his boots—they was put on with wooden pegs and he said, "Well, I'll be doggoned, I kicked both heels off a my boots."

The next day he fetched them down to Sol Pryor and said, "Put bigger pegs in so I don't dig them off." Sol had a big beard and I used to go up to his shop and make penknives out of a bit of leather and a shoe peg. In them days they had what they called a rocker cutter like a half moon and you cut your leather with it. He used to say, "Willie, you're a bad boy, you make penknives out of my leather."

We went to Carmichaels a good bit. Just a few stores and a couple of 'stopping houses'. Frank Byers had a hotel in Clarksville, and they would give us a stem glass for a nickel. We would go up to Willie Pyles' place and the man stopped there and would sell that glassware out of there [the river glass boats peddled 'seconds']. Right above where Sam Teegard lived—the next place, and I must tell you what happened.

They were snowballing one day and Tom Pyles hit McCulley with a water-soaked snowball and killed him, he died right in the street.

Jim Sears was a lawyer up in Waynesburg and he would go down to Carmichaels and get his dinner. Every time he come they would have mutton. So, the lady at the place where he ett said, "Mr. Sears, you return thanks." And he looked over the table and said, "Mutton rough, mutton tough, thank God we've all had mutton enough." They didn't have no more mutton after that.

Yes, Old Man Luse used to ride a horse and I must tell you what happened to him. He was goin' home one day—he had been in to the shop and got his horse shoed and he was leading a horse. He had a bar scythe—a big thunderstorm come up and he rammed the bar scythe down in his boot. When he circled the bars he got off and let them down and got on again. The lightning struck the bar, tore the bottom of his boot off, killed the horse, and never hurt him. Can't remember which Luse this was.

Calvin Bowser was an old man and there was Charlie—I knowed them all. They were German and Old Man Bowser had a long beard—there were two girls, or maybe three. Them Bowsers just died off one after another. Charlie was the oldest and married my cousin—lived at Belle Vernon. Calvin used to come to our place when we lived on the crik—he was there more than he was home. Their place was up by the Virgins, on the other side above Robinsons and Seth Robinson lived across the crik and right above was the Bowser log house.

It's quite different over here in Fayette County. You see, the packets came in here—the old *Germania*, the *James G. Blaine*, they all came in here. They would go to Pittsburgh for a load of stuff and fetch it back here. Up there at Clarksville you had to go clean down to Millsboro to the wharf for your stuff. They fetched lots of stuff in at Rice's Landing and we would go down there and get a barrel of meat off the packet when I worked for George Baker.

I must tell you about the mail. Old Morgan Munnell had a one-cylinder Cadillac and his rubber tires give out. He never bought new ones, he had Chris Teagarden's wagon shop put iron rims on them wooden spoke wheels—the front ones—and he drove and delivered the mail in that car for years.

They had dances on the old *Germania*—they used to get on her, and on the *Hy Knox*, too, and dance all the way up to Morgantown and back—we used to do that. They had musicians—first and second violins and they traveled with the packet. They had calliopes on the boats to Morgantown. You'd hear that old calliope and go crazy almost. They had live shows on the boats.

There were lots of old cemeteries—there was a graveyard at the lower end of town and where the Campbellite Church stands, they buried a lot in there. We went up to the Presbyterian Church for big Christmas parties—the Campbellites weren't so much for that. No Quakers in Clarksville—I didn't know of any. All churches had bells.

11

THE MUDDY CREEK SETTLEMENT
New Lisbon
Carmichaels

WHAT IS referred to historically as the Muddy Creek Settlement embraces the tract of land warranted to James Seaton before the end of the Revolutionary War, where the town of New Lisbon, later Carmichaels, was laid out. When the Seatons arrived from Winchester, Virginia, they called the area "New Lisbon," but after James and Betty Seaton Carmichael took over the land, it became Carmichael's Town and finally just plain Carmichaels.

In his unpublished Volume 8 of "The Tenmile Country . . ." Howard Leckey reviews the history of this area in considerable detail and traces the interrelationships of the Seatons, Boremans, Greggs, Carmichaels, and others of the cluster of wellborn, chiefly English families who first settled on Muddy Creek. The Seatons traced to Mary Ball, mother of George Washington, and the locally famous "Muddy Creek Ledger 1793-96" kept by a member (probably William) of the Seaton family, was presented to the Library of Congress after Howard Leckey accidentally came upon it in Greene County on a pile of trash about to be burned.

After the death of Mr. Leckey when his papers and notes came into the possession of Robert Yoders, curator of the Greene County Historical Society, Dr. Yoders made a study of the old ledger and came forth with some interesting new

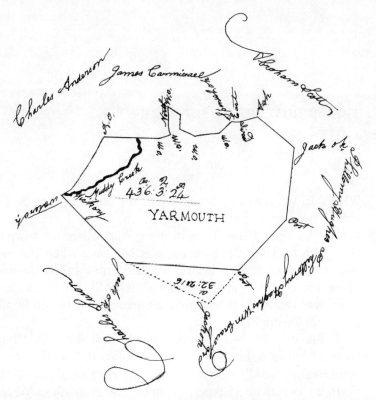

Draught of John Hoge's survey made April 15, 1785, for Francis
Seaton on Muddy Creek. Hoge Papers.

deductions. He concluded that the Pittsburgh-based firm of Turnbull & Marmie, iron founders and merchants, were the owners of the Muddy Creek store and mill operated by the Seatons and also by John Boreman. The partnership of Turnbull & Marmie was dissolved on August 22, 1793, with all bills owing the firm to be paid to William Turnbull in Pittsburgh or to Peter Marmie at the Alliance Iron Works on Jacobs Creek in Westmoreland County. Peter Marmie had come to America as General Lafayette's personal secretary. In 1789 Marmie and his partner, William Turnbull built the Alliance Furnace and Forge, so named for its "alliance" with other business holdings of the owners, such as the Muddy Creek Store. The Greggs, who were related to the Seatons, had a large mill on Muddy Creek in 1788; whether this was separate from the Seaton Mill is not known. Dr. Yoders's articles for the *Historical Society Quarterly* are quoted in part:

> The Mill was an important part of the Turnbull & Marmie enterprise on Muddy Creek; at the period covered by the ledger, they leased the mill to Miller John Antill. They provided 284 barrels of flour shipped on the first "Adventure" to New Orleans from the mouth of Muddy on the Monongahela; 213 barrels were sold for $1,278 and the remainder damaged in shipment, brought less.

> Turnbull and Marmie built and bought boats for their shipments down the Monongahela to Pittsburgh and on to New Orleans.

It is a rather amazing coincidence that Dr. Yoders arrived at his conclusion without having seen either of the following letters found by the writer. In the outstanding collection of historical documents in the library of the Washington County Historical Society at

Address on letter from Turnbull & Marmie folded to make an envelope; sent from Philadelphia in 1786.

LeMoyne House in Washington is the first of two Turnbull & Marmie letters to John Boreman at Muddy Creek:

Philadᵃ Decʳ 2ᵈ 1786

Mr. John Boreman
Dear Sir:

The present you will receive by Mr. John Copley's Waggons, agreeable to the enclosed List and his receipt for the same. The Invoice we expect you will receive some time before this will reach you by a young man we are getting ready to send you, and we expect will leave this the 4th Inst. as we shall write you particularly by him; shall only add our wish that we could have sent you these Goods sooner but hope they will still answer a good purpose, and reach you safe.

We remain Dʳ Sir
Your very hm. Servᵗs
TURNBULL, MARMIE & Co. (W.M.)

In a miscellaneous drawer in the Greene County Recorder of Deeds office, the second interesting letter addressed to John Boreman at Muddy Creek, was found:

Pittsburg 5th Janʸ 1789

Dear Sir:

It is the want of an opportunity only that has prevented me from writing you before this time, & in that obeying the most strict injunction of Mr. Turnbull at his departure.

The works have for these three weeks past been in compleat order & not a bushell of Grain to Distill—those on whom we had reason to depend for a supply have disappointed us entirely & your Batteau not arriving before this time when the River must be broke up is a greater cause of uneasiness as we can only suppose you have no grain to send. Our own team is starving for want of feed and that from the Saw Mill has been here above a week & the mill is stopped on the same account. There is no grain to be purchased here but for cash & that is not to be procured. Do send us as soon as possible all the corn, oats, Ry, wheat, Barley etc. you possibly can.

I am happy in having this opportunity of guarding you against a temptation you may be exposed to in a few days. Colonel Blanie had done all he can to prevail on me to let him have 50 bbls. flour & is now gone towards your place to try you on the same subject—he makes fair promises of Cash but I am afraid they cannot be altogether depended on. I have given him no reason to suppose he will get it as I conceive it would be altogether contrary to Mr. Turnbull's intention. I think you ought not to promise him any as all the wheat you can procure is wanted here for the Distillery. This however you may keep to yourself as you must have Mr. Turnbull's instructions to the same effect. I have some thoughts of paying you a visit one of these days. Meantime, I am Dear Sir, Yours Sincerely,

Wᵐ J. MILLER

John Boreman, born in England, came to America and settled at Havre de Grace, Maryland, before moving to Philadelphia where he was a merchant before the Revolutionary War. He joined the Continental Army and was commissioned a colonel. Early in 1777, Colonel George Morgan requested that "Mr. Anderson of Anderson's Ferry" come to Fort Pitt to build boats. At the same time he turned over the stores at the fort to John Boreman who became his chief assistant and secretary. After joining the Continental Army and being commissioned a colonel, Boreman was soon promoted to the rank of assistant paymaster general with headquarters at Fort Pitt. Boatbuilder Anderson was no doubt the Daniel Anderson who, with John Boreman and others who had been associated at Fort Pitt

Example of John Boreman's penmanship [an]d taste evident in the label on the first [qu]arter sessions docket covered with hand-[pri]nted early wallpaper, probably stocked by [Bo]reman at Muddy Creek. Greene County [Co]urthouse.

during the Revolutionary War, settled on Muddy Creek, where Anderson built the *Second Adventure* and other craft in his boatyard.

After he had established himself in the Muddy Creek settlement, on Christmas Day 1787, John Boreman married James Seaton's daughter, Sarah by whom he had eight children. Their son, Kener Seaton Boreman, was a saddler in Waynesburg and his son became the first governor of West Virginia.

When Greene was taken off of Washington County, the first item in Deed Book No. 1 dated July 13, 1796, granted the right to administer oaths, etc., to John Boreman and John Minor, Esqrs. In April, John Boreman had been appointed prothonotary of the court of common pleas, clerk of the court of quarter sessions, clerk of orphans court, clerk of the court of oyer and terminer and jail delivery, recorder of deeds and register of wills. He must have possessed outstanding ability to have been appointed to all of the "row offices" in the first Greene County (log) Courthouse on Greene Street in Waynesburg and his elegant and legible penmanship fills the earliest dockets in all offices. It is of interest to note that there may well have been a kinship between John Boreman and Samuel Clarke of Clarksville, who held similar positions in the early Washington County offices; James Seaton, brother of John Boreman's wife, Sarah, married Mary Clarke, and they had a brother, Samuel Clarke Seaton.

At April term of Harrisburg Court of Common Pleas in 1798 in an action of debt, Wilson Hunt recovered against John Boreman for 526 pounds. . . . High Sheriff Jacob Burley at Waynesburg issued an order to seize the goods and chattels of Boreman "who now lives at Lots 154, 155 and 156 at Morris and Greene and has two outlots." The vendue was held in June 1804 and Wilson Hunt was the highest bidder but the paper states "no deed was issued to him."

On the 25th of August 1814, Greene County Deed Book:

Manumission of Pendy Miles—Know all Men that I, John Boreman of Waynesburg, in consideration of the faithful services and tender care of Pendy Miles, a Mulato woman, to my children for above seventy years and also in pursuance of the request and wishes of Sarah Boreman, my late, beloved wife whose servant she was, have manumitted, discharged, liberated and acquitted . . . and renounce all title and claim to any services or obedience of the said Pendy to my heirs. . . .

There seems to be a pattern of puzzling estate settlements for many of the prominent and prosperous early people. Kenner Seaton Boreman, John's son, took out a bond for $600 with William Seals and John and William Ingraham November 3, 1827, in the matter of his father's estate. The appraised value of the estate as given was $42 and there was "one spy glass" mentioned which they could not sell but which Kenner was willing to retain and charge himself seven dollars for it.

* * *

Miscellaneous items from local newspapers fill in gaps in detail about the early days of Carmichaels:

Public Fair to be held for three days on Muddy Creek beginning October 20, 1795; principally for the disposal of cattle and to show off horses, etc.

In May 1796 William Seaton lost a horse and anyone who found it was to convey the animal to him at Carmichael's Town or to John Badollet at Greensboro.

Letters at the Washington Post Office awaiting John Boreman of the Muddy Creek settlement were advertised in 1797 in the *Western Telegraphe.*

April 4, 1797, Samuel McFarlane "secretary" wrote from Greene County that a "Nocturnal Society" of farmers was being formed in the Muddy Creek settlement for "mental improvement and graceful delivery, but that certain people doubted the utility of such a group and the voices of detraction arose with murmurs of envy and ill nature."

September 1814—Samuel Kennedy on Muddy Creek advertised for two or three journeymen "Winesor Chair" makers for constant employment at high wages.

Summer 1817, stockholders of the Lisbon Bank of Greene County published a notice that they had joined the bank "without realizing the mischief such an institution was to produce, witness the recent fall of the New Salem, Fayette County Bank known as the Mutton Town Bank." Signed by Paul Dowlin, Samuel Huston, several Lowrys and Bailys, the latter still prominent in Greene County banking.

* * *

Some of the earliest data about the families of the Carmichaels region was given by Ann Collins Lindsey, born 1805, descendant of both John Swan and Thomas Hughes who came from the South Branch of the Potomac, tomahawked claims, and built their first cabins in the Muddy Creek valley.

In 1797, Isaac Jenkinson, described both as an "artist" and as a "surveyor," was paid twenty-two dollars out of James Carmichael's estate for laying out the town lots and we assume he drew the map of New Lisbon found by the writer among forgotten deeds in the recorder's vault. The surveyor John Gapen laid off tracts on Muddy Creek and he is another possibility as the draftsman of the map.

In 1814 when William and wife Nancy Carmichael and Aleph and Margaret Carmichael Shepherd as heirs of the founder, James Carmichael, sold a lot adjacent to Carmichaels to Charles Swan, Jr., the deed revealed some interesting details about the town:

> . . . opposite the outlot of heirs of William Seaton on the continuation of Market Street and Washington Road at a post opposite on the corner of Samuel Harper's Blacksmith Shop by Strawberry Alley to the north corner of the tavern house in which Charles Swan now lives, to the corner of the old kitchen by Crooked Alley, granted in 1801 to William and Margaret Carmichael by the Commonwealth. . . .

In 1798 William Seaton lived in a three-story twenty-one by twenty-eight foot log building with eight windows of

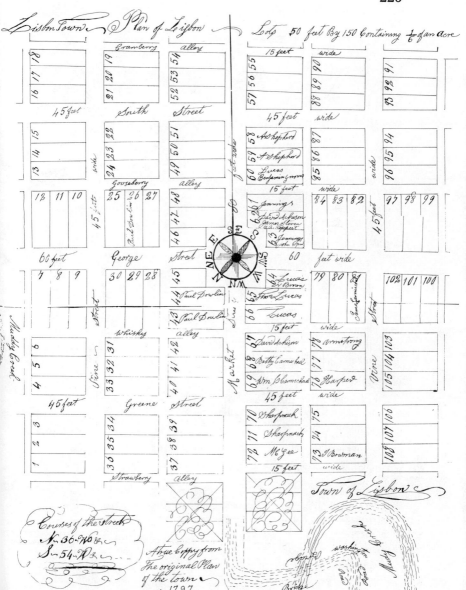

Map of New Lisbon, unrecorded and unpublished. Found by writer in Greene County recorder's vault.

Second map of Carmichaels recorded in Greene County Deed Book No. 16.

twelve panes each and a separate twelve by twelve-foot log kitchen. His brother, James Seaton lived nearby in a twenty-four by twenty-six foot frame two-story house that also had eight windows but one hundred four panes of glass and a separate twelve by fourteen-foot log kitchen—it would be many years before the kitchen would be a part of the main house.

The Pribbles were among the first families to settle west of the Monongahela, some of the sons in the Tenmile Settlement and others "of Muddy Creek." Howard Leckey was never quite certain where the Pribbles had come from. A recent discovery in September 1783 common pleas court jacket files covers a transaction between Stephen Pribel and James Moore of Muddy Creek with an endorsement made in Harford County, Maryland, October 31, 1774. The charges covered in the unpaid bill date back to April 1768 when Stephen Pribble still lived in Maryland. Henry Jamison's record of rations to Revolutionary militia from the Carmichaels area 1778-1782 as found in a ledger dating to 1790 shows Thomas and Henry Moore working at the Muddy Creek Mill, hooping hogsheads.

There were two ferries on the Monongahela in the vicinity of the mouth of Muddy Creek known as the Upper and Lower Davidson ferries. When Joseph Davidson, keeper of one of the ferries, died in 1845, his estate sale was held May 22:

> James Cree—bought many lots of shingles @ 77¢ cwt. for which he paid by making Davidson's coffin for $6, writing the Will and clerking at vendue.

A good description of shingles used at this period comes from a 1795 ad in the Pittsburgh *Gazette:* "WANTED— shingles of pine, chestnut or black walnut to be 2′ 9″ long, 6″ wide with a 5/8″ butt and well shaved [tapered]."

> William Armstrong of the boat-building family on Muddy Creek—Geographical History for 78¢, Sheridan's Dictionary

for 78¢, Pinkerton's Geography for 69¢, a lot of "old linnen" and a corner cupboard for $1 [which would probably bring $300 at a country sale today].

Daniel Moredock—Josephus' Works for $3, Guthrie's Grammar for 31½¢, 11 yards of blanketing @ 43¢ a yard and one "konk shell" for 25¢

William Miller [is this the same person who wrote to John Boreman for Turnbull & Marmie?]—Dialogue of Devils for 12½¢, American Museum for the same, an arm chair for 50¢, Umbrella for 09¢ and a Lantern for 06¢

Abraham Armstrong—a lot of books and some furniture; returned the furniture and did not pay 44¢ due on the books.

Isaac Biddle and others took "many picture frames"

Hamilton Smith—The Navel [!] Monument for 50¢ and a Map of the United States for $2.

Hiram Smith—paid $30 for two Stills, bought a lot of good horses and paid $137.12½ for one gold watch.

Alfred Frost—Views of Louisiana for 18¢ and Fox' Book of Martyrs for 95¢

Other volumes from the Davidson library listed in the inventory: *Dickenson's Geography, Goldsmith's Natural History, Burns' Works, Religious Ceremony, Book of Masonry, Declaration of Rights, Goldsmith's Life of Murry, The Temperance Book, The Register of Pennsylvania, American Biography*, and a "Map of Pensylvany" which brought $1.

When Andrew Kennedy died his large file contained an amazing assortment of tools and cabinet woods indicating that he must have been a partner of Samuel Kennedy, Windsor chair maker in a shop on Muddy Creek although he does not seem to be listed as a cabinetmaker or joiner in assessment rolls. At his vendue held June 19, 1812, the following were sold:

lott of bedstead stuff and bedstead screws several dozen planes, including Cornish planes quantities of cherry, walnut and poplar plank sandpaper, spunge, paint stuff and red sanders

One voucher read "Andrew Kennedy must have credit for one Bureau at $16 and a set of Winsor Chairs at $12"; both

1768   Stephen Fribel Dr To James Moore

Aprie ye 7 To one paire of Shoes for Feniks by ordr 0 9 2

To one paire of Shoes your Vamps 7 0

To thend one paire of Shoes 2 9

Augst ye 20 To one paire of Shoes for wig 7 6

To one paine of Shoes for Selt 9 0

To one paire of Shoes wil Watson had By ordr 9 0

ocktober 18 To one Pis of uppr Leather Pris 2
1768 To one Paine of half Soles 1 3

To Leather for Hope-ls 2 0

Errors Excepted 2 10 8

Harford County maryland ocktober 31. 1774
Then Came James Moores Before me one of
his Lord Ships Justices for The County aforsaid
And maid oath on the Holy Evangelis of
Almity God That The above Accot is Just
And True as it Stands Stetted and That
he hath not Received any part parcel
Securitis or Sodisfaction for ye Sam Moore
Then upon Credit Given To The Best
Of his knoledy

Sworn Befor Jn Love

And Likewis Did Deliver To William Flannah
one Not of hand on ocktober 27th 1773 Paibel from
Stephen Fribel To me James moore for The Sum of
for ten Pounds Seven Shilins and Three pence and
Henry Mc Bird Evedenie To & Not Exclewsiv of
the above Acct. certified Before me one of his Lordships Justies

very good prices for the times. The Kennedys may also have been involved with the Lincoln family in the Lincoln Pottery which predated that of Alexander Vance at Greensboro according to ledger entries at the Greene County Historical Society. Andrew's inventory included dozens of milk crocks and dishes and an item of travel expense listed covered a trip of "one day to Crooked Run for earthenware." Crooked Run was an early name for Casteel Run.

In 1792 boatbuilders John and David Armstrong who settled ca. 1767, built the first *Adventure* on the banks of Muddy Creek; the voyage to New Orleans was apparently a success as Daniel Anderson built a second *Adventure* the following year. There was much hardship and illness associated with these trading voyages. Estate No. 85 in the Greene County Courthouse is for Abraham McDowell who died during the voyage of an *Adventure*; the McDowells lived at Muddy Creek and were mentioned in the ledger in 1795.

> ... Abraham McDowell, deceased; inventory taken in New Feliciana, Florida December 7, 1803: 2 hats, suit of clothes, 2 stocks, 1 shirt, 1 pair "shillivalles" [?], 2 jackets, an Indian belt, 4 pair stockings, part of an Indian blanket, 1 gun, 1 falling ax, shoemaker tools, 1 apple mill, a blanket coat, silver watch, one gray horse with saddle and bridle. ...

There was a receipt from Gilbert Miller for "30 bbls." of "flower" and a list of notes due at Natchez March 8, 1803; Michael Loughman to pay $15.50 in three months, Speed and Kemper to pay $4 on demand January 26, 1803, Charles Forgett agreed to pay $29.50 at Natchez four months from February 28, 1803.

In addition to boatbuilding and saw and grist mills in and around Carmichaels, some years after the Clarksville Woolen Mill was erected in 1811, James Barnes opened his "Greene Woolen Mills" pictured in the Carmichaels bicentennial booklet. This mill built on the banks of Muddy Creek used waterpower when the streams were high but Barnes is said to have used the first steam engine in Greene County so the mill could run year 'round. It was later purchased by A. P. and W.

A. Stevenson and produced quality woolens of all kinds—
blankets, cassimeres, flannels, and yarn.

John Minor Esquire being sworn in open court saith that Philip Minor is sick and unable to attend court that he has at present & for some time past has had a boat prepared to descend the river Ohio, and that it is owing to the indisposition of the said Philip as this deponent believes that a commiss on to the Intendent of New Orleans is not forwarded—

John Minor

Sworn.

John Boreman

Affidavit of Col. John Minor. From Greene County
court files, 1797-1799.

East and West Bethlehem townships were created out of
Bethlehem in 1789; in an undated petition from "Bethlehem
Twp." to "The Honourable Court" of Washington County, an
objection was raised over a recent survey of a road laid out
from the Muddy and Whiteley Road to the Pittsburgh and
Brownsville Road:

> . . . which Road as now laid out is contrary to the true intent and
> meaning for which Roads are usually made.

> That said Petition was seen or signed by few if any of your
> Petitioners, nor any of them through whose lands, or living in the
> vicinity of it, were consulted with on the occasion, but on the
> contrary, said Petition was mostly signed by Persons living at a
> distance and not thoroughly acquainted with the Reasons of such
> a Road being wanting. That your Petitioners are desirous of hav-
> ing a Road opened from the said (Westland) Meeting House to the

mouth of the Run for the convenience of going to the Grist Mill on that Run, as well as to the Mouth of the Run, where as soon as a Road is opened, a Ferry is to be kept, which will prove of infinite service to the settlement and the Publick in general.

That your Petitioners conceive themselves greatly aggrieved by the manner the Road is laid out now, it being part through Rocky ground, and part through wet ground, which will be very expensive in making and keeping up, and are unwilling to spend their labour and substance to answer private ends, for which said Road has been laid out, as appears from all circumstances in the Case.

We your Petitioners wish that your honors would order a review to be had and your Petitioners humbly implore your Honours to appoint men of sound judgment and who may have the good of their Country and fellow Citizens more at heart, than private Interest, and your Petitioners as in Duty Bound shall Ever Pray—

Jas Powell

Zebulon Hefton
Eber Heeton
Aaron Baker
Isaac Morris
Henry Hormell
David Lewis
Joseph Lee
Joseph Lewis
George Peake
Daniel Stanton
Thomas Farquhar
Jacob Ringal
Henry Alexander
Moses Marshall

Aaron Newport
Robert Sweeny
Jesse Newport
John Acklin
Felty Kinder
John Robison
William Taylor
Samuel Smith
John Ekey
Nathan Baker
Jesse White
Henry Hughes

ROAD FROM OLIVER CRAWFORDS FERRY ON MONONGAHELA RIVER TO WASHINGTON.

PETITION:

To the Worshipful, the Court of Washington County.

The Petition of Oliver Crawford humbly Sheweth.

That your petitioner hath (from the time of the earliest settlement in this County) kept a ferry cross the Monongahalah River at the lower side of the mouth of Muddy Creek, and at a very Considerable expence supported the same as well for the purpose of transporting the Militia, as also Other's the Inhabitants of this Country, during the time of the late War, for which he hath received but little compensation. This burthen he cheerfully submitted to, in expectation, that when peace would be established his Country would inculre him with Opening such roads to his said ferry as the conveniency of the public would require, and indeed the Worshipful, the Court of Fayette hath Order'd a road from Union Town, to the said ferry, which road is already Open,notwithstanding your petitioner is inform'd that a Certain Jno. Armstrong hath Obtain'd and Order from your Worships at the last March Court to open a road from the Mononrahalah River, about a mile above where your petitioner now keeps ferry untill it intersects the road that leads from Washington, to the Mouth of Whitely Creek, this he the said Armstrong hath done without the Knowledge of the principal Inhabitants of the Township in which we live knowing that if they were made acquainted with this his design he the said Armstrong would be opposed in the matter.

Your petitioner begs leave to observe further that the Inhabitants of Jackson's Fort and the Settlements adjoining thereunto, hath laid off a road from that part of the County to your petitioners ferry afored. which road the said Armstrong hath had Alter'd by a late Order from your Worships, no doubt he the said Armstrong inform'd the Court that his measures would answer better for the conveniency of the people at large, which consequently wou'ld influence your Worships to adopt them, your petitioner therefore prays that your Worships will stop any further proceedings being had on the said Armstronge Order, and that you'll order a road to be Open'd from my ferry afored. (which will meet the afored. road, that leads from Union Town) that is already Open'd untill it intersects the road that is to be laid Off from Washington to the mouth of Whitely Creek afored. which will answer the Conveniency of the Inhabitants of the Township more generally, then any Other way a road Could be taken, and at the same time prevents the Inhabitants of Fayette County from being Obliged to Open an other road, there being one already open'd to the Spot, as will more fully appear by the annex'd Certificate and yr. Petitioner as in Duty bound will pray etc.

Oliver Crawford.

We whose names are hereunto Annex'd do hereby Certify that we beleave that the Spirit and meaning of the foregoing petition is true and that if the aforesd. Armstrongs measures is adopted by the Court the Inhabitants on both sides of the river will be saddled with many inconveniencies, as we must keep a road Open to Oliver Crawfords Landing, there being at that place a good foard across the river for the most part of the Summer, and therefore pray the Worshipful Court to reject the aforesd. Armstrongs Petition and comply with the prayer of that of Crawfords aforesaid.

Wm. McCleery	William Davis	James Seals
James Carmichael	Azariah Davis	Barnet Reinhart
Jacob Clyne	John Heaton	Alexander Dollison
Alex. Monroe	Ezekeal Morris	Joseph Reinhart
Kenner Seaton	Nathaniel Hughes	Thomas Reinhart
Thomas Roach	Elisha Stuart	John Tomes
Richard Swan	Richard Stuart	Jacob Smittler
William McEntire	John Ankrom	John Johns
Gabriel Eakins	William Wells	John Thrasher
Abraham Vanmatre	Thomas Wells Sr	John Carins
Henry Vanmatre	Thomas Wells Jr	James Davis
Joseph Vanmatre	Joseph Rish	Francis Tincens
Jesse Vanmatre	James Morrish	George Knote
Daniel Morecock	John Smith	Abraham Armstrong
Isaac Milner	Robert Gorrell	Alex. Cochrane
Isaac Miller Junur	William Cather	Alex. Finley
Thomas Prible	Jong Kary	Jas. Hurhes
Job Prible	John Karal	Michael Dougherty
George Teegarden	Gorg Karal	Mathew Hennen
Wm. Teegarden	William Karal	Paul Huston
Benjamin Wood	Jacob Karal	John Crawford
Thomas Wilson	Henry Kirk	William McDowell
William Whitchlatch	Roburt Cather	Alexander Crawford
Joeph Whitchlatch	William Inghrem	George Smith
Thomas Whitchlatch	John Durfell	Thomas Davidson
Thomas Blackledge	Arthur Inghram	Absalum Littell
Joseph Suner	Thomas Fee	Michal Jones
Nicholas Milner	John Fee	John Moore
Edmun Dunn	Jorge Fee	William Davidson
Isaac Dunn	Thomas Fee	William Conwell
Samuel Thomas	Jams Porter	John Reilly
Ruben Pribble	John Huston	Samuel Swindler
Jams Perry	Frances Forth	Amos Mills
Thos. Pribble	Joseph Archer	Thomas Wilson
George Newland	John Brien	L----- -------
Samuel Jackson	John Thresher	Joseph Hofsman
Patrick Cree	Jones Thresher	

Two road petitions from Bethlehem Township; undated one from an historical collection and one for 1785 from roads and bridges docket, Washington County Courthouse.

These petitions are included as examples of many similarly well thought out, worded, and written documents filed in official places in Penn's Southwest during the first years of the Republic.

The list of names following the Oliver Crawford 1785 road petition is one of the most complete groupings of early settlers' names in a given area the writer has ever found. It is fascinating to break down the list by locations, working with Volume III of *The Horn Papers'* township maps. The list commences in Cumberland Township in Greene County, with William McCleery, then progresses to Jefferson Township, starting with the Pribbles and Tegardens. Then the names change to Franklin Township, with Robert Gorrell and many Waynesburg names, until the return to a group of additional Cumberland names, with Abraham Armstrong. The list ends with a group of Luzerne Township, Fayette County, names, beginning with John and Alexander Crawford. With a few exceptions, the name groupings include adjacent neighbors.

12

BIOGRAPHICAL FRAGMENTS:
Famous Names
in Penn's Southwest

John James Audubon (1785-1851)—On Audubon's first trip
into Penn's Southwest, he floated down the Ohio with a
companion, Ferdinand Rozier in 1807-1808. After his marriage to Lucy Bakewell of Pittsburgh, the Audubons went to
live near the French colony in Louisville. By this time, John
Audubon had discovered that Kentucky was a favorite dwelling place for birds and he made some of his finest watercolors
there. Ever restless, he would sometimes sight an unusual
bird, or a flock, and would take off on a journey that might
take him through several states.

In 1810 Audubon went into business with his father-in-law
and operated the store of Audubon & Bakewell at Henderson
on the Ohio River where they commissioned pork, lard, and
flour. While essentially he ran the store, he also fished, hunted, and traded work. He spent some time with Boone in
Kentucky and about 1814 acted as a trader along the Mississippi, roaming the country with a gun, a dog, and his knap-
sack. A little later he returned to Pennsylvania, this time with
a chance companion said by some to have been a fellow
artist, Chester Harding. They hired a cart for their luggage
and traveled to Meadville where they ran out of money so
Audubon set up shop in a vacant room and did some sketches
and portraits for small sums until he had enough to get to

Pittsburgh. He remained in the French colony there for two or three months and it is believed that he did his fine watercolor of the American raven against a shellbark hickory at this time. There were numerous trips to Pittsburgh, one during the time of Lafayette's visit 1824-25 when he painted a portrait of the French general.

* * *

Daniel Boone (1734-1818)—Discounting all Horn comments regarding the activities of Boone in Penn's Southwest, it is reliably reported that he was related to the Galloways of Tenmile who married into the Enoch family; also that Boone spent some time hunting with the Harrods and others who later migrated to Kentucky. When the old hunter died, the October 12, 1818, issue of the Washington *Reporter* carried the notice:

> *Death of Col. Daniel Boone*—as he lived so he died with his gun in his hand. Told by a gentleman direct from Boone's Settlement where last month Col. Boone rode to a deer lick, seated himself within a blind raised to conceal him from the game. While sitting thus with his trusty old rifle pointing toward the lick, the muzzle resting on a log, his rifle cocked, his finger on the trigger, one eye shut, without pain he breathed his last and was found the next day, stiff and cold but as if alive, his hand in the act of firing.

* * *

Aaron Burr (1756-1836)—When the family of Absalom Baird of Washington published his *Letters and Papers* in 1909 they included a letter from an accomplice of Colonel Aaron Burr in his treasonable movement against the United States. This letter showed that Burr was in western Pennsylvania and Ohio 1805-06 trying to secure adherents for what some called Burr's "New Kingdom." He apparently contacted Dr. Baird before his death in October 1805. He visited with Colonel George Morgan at Morganza near Canonsburg and the William Enochs after leaving the Tenmile settlement reported meeting Burr when their friends, the Blennerhassetts, were his hosts for some time at their island mansion in the Ohio

River. Burr contacted people in Washington and Wheeling for support before he was arrested in Alabama in 1807.

* * *

George Rogers Clark (1752-1818)—In school, George Clark was more interested in geography and history than in English and math. As tales of the military and Indian skirmishes were told and retold to the Clark children, their imaginations were fired, and George began to consider entering military service and becoming a surveyor. His math improved as he decided to follow surveying, like his grandfather Rogers. With his chain, compass, and Jacob's staff, George first went out to explore when only nineteen. The following spring of 1772 with James Higgins as a companion, Clark set out for Laurel Hill. They followed Braddock's Road to the Monongahela, talking with Indians and frontiersmen as they roamed the wilderness. Lyman Draper, whose papers are now available on microfilm, spent fifteen years researching for a biography after becoming completely intrigued with Clark's character. The book was never written, but Draper's voluminous notes provide details of the years Clark spent in Penn's Southwest. Draper quotes from the journal of the Reverend David Jones, a missionary from New Jersey who was on his way to work with western Indians. George Rogers Clark and his companions met Jones in Pittsburgh and he helped them buy a canoe, as the journal relates:

I left Fort Pitt Tuesday June 9, 1772 in company with George Rogers Clark, a young gentleman from Virginia who with several other adventurers, is making a tour of the new world. We traveled by water in a canoe, noted the many creeks emptying into the Ohio . . . passed Mingo Town as quietly as possible as they have a reputation for plundering canoes.

Stopped at Grave Creek where we met the interpreter David Owens who had come cross country from the waters of the Monongahela. We slept on gravel by the side of the river instead of on feathers. This place of Zane's Settlement is at the mouth of Wheeling Creek; the Zanes explored the Wheeling country in 1769. . . . Kenawha land is not as rich as that near Fort Pitt. Left

238

our canoes on the return to Grave Creek and crossed country to
Ten Mile Creek and came to the house of David Owen. [Leckey
reported the group stayed with Owen some time in his Tenmile
cabin.]

On July 14, 1772 set out on horseback from Tenmile and followed a small path called "Catfish's Road" over very good land to
Catfish Camp.

There was great interest and excitement when Clark returned to his father's home in August as he was the first of
the family to go west. When he announced that he wished to
settle permanently in the west, his father decided to go out
with him and the two traveled by canoe as far as Fish Creek
where George had selected a farm that had been laid off and
held in the name of Michael Cresap. After his father returned
to his home, George Clark with several other young settlers
spent the fall and winter surveying to build up his cash fund;
he also cut rails, brushed land, and built a round-log twenty-
foot square cabin. Draper makes the claim that during this
second winter on his land near Wheeling and the Zanes',
George Washington visited him.

April term 1792 of Washington County Common Pleas
Court lists an action of *Clark* v. *John McIntire* and attached
to the letter is Ebenezer Zane's statement that he recognized
the handwriting of George Rogers Clark because "Clark re-
sided frequently at my house from the summer of the year
1774 til the spring of the year 1776, and by correspondence
at different periods since."

Clark raised a body of troops from the ridges and bottoms
of chiefly Greene County from his headquarters at Redstone
Old Fort in 1778 for his campaign against the western Indians; for his services he was raised from colonel to brigadier
general by the state of Virginia. In February 1781 after
spending some of that extremely cold winter of 1780-81 with
the Van Metres in their fort on Enoch's Run, Clark returned
to Fort Pitt where instructions from Washington awaited
him. His unbounded influence over inhabitants of the

Interrogatories to Ebenezer Zane

1 do you Know the hand writing of George Rogers Clark and how do you Know it —

2 A paper herewith annexed and in the following words viz:

Bear Grass July 17th 1786

Dr Col /

I have sold my place on Fish Creek Bottom to Mr. Jno. McIntire which he will Inform you of Coln. Angus McDonald asigned a Milatary Warrant of Two hundred acres to me which I had located on the spot done in the Office of Augusta I should thank you if you would be so Kind as to asign over that Warrant for me to Mr. McIntire as it is included in his Bargain of mine

You was so good as to tell me that you would try to get me paid for my Boat that Mesrs Smith & Colwell lost you would oblige me much if you would do it and Send me the Money as soon as possible or any thing you get for her. I gave just forty five pounds Virginia Money for her but if you think that these Gentn. did not loose the Boat thrugh neglect and ought to be abated something do it as this is a full power of Attorney for you to act for me in the cases mentioned in this Letter

I am Dr Col.
yr H. servt
G R Clark

Col. Zane

paper of which this is a copy is the signature to the above, in the hand writing of George Rogers Clark —

Letter written and signed by George Rogers Clark as part of Ebenezer Zane affidavit file. Washington County Courthouse court dockets.

western country as a result of his military skill and indomitable energy was well known, and he was chosen to raise another expeditionary force for his Illinois campaign.

* * *

Henry Clay (1777-1852)—A frequent visitor in Penn's Southwest, Henry Clay stopped frequently at Washington taverns, usually staying at Morris's "Globe Inn" on Main Street on his way to and from Congress. Clay was one of the prime backers of the first National Road early in 1800 and the town of Claysville, laid out on U.S. Route 40 was named for him.

Moses and Lydia Shepherd called their 1798 stone mansion at Elm Grove on the outskirts of Wheeling, Loring Place until the "once famous Henry Clay monument" was placed on the grounds and then it became known as Monument Place. John Kennedy Lacock photographed the monument in 1916 when the sandstone had already crumbled and it was stated in *The National Road:*

One can scarcely view the present condition of this monument without feeling that Henry Clay and his services to the old Pike at least deserves a better monument. Originally each of the four sides of the base column bore an elaborate inscription, none of them now wholly legible; one read: This monument was erected by Moses and Lydia Shepherd, as a testimony of respect to Henry Clay, the eloquent defender of National rights and National Independence.

Another panel read: Time will bring every amelioration and re-
finement most gratifying to rational man; and the humblest flower freely plucked under the shelter of the Tree of Liberty is more
to be desired than all the wrappings of royalty: 44th year of
American Independence, Anno Domini 1820.

The Clay memorial was carved by John Aery of Claysville
with the help of Alexander Ramsey who did the fine chisel-
ing. It was moved in dilapidated condition to the Wheeling
Frontier Museum some time after 1916 where it was destroyed by fire.

Henry Clay was a popular political figure with many ties to
Penn's Southwest. On March 7, 1832, he wrote to Thomas
McGiffin, Esq., in Washington:

> . . . as to the improved Cattle, I really have not had time to attend
> to them. If you can purchase three or four large mares for me at
> about the price you mention, and send them out to Ashland in all
> this month, I shall be greatly obliged. They ought to get there in
> time to put them to my Jack, which is the object with me in
> making the purchase. One man, whom you might employ, could
> take charge of them and reach Ashland in eight or ten days.

> The failure so far to produce cooperation between our friends
> and the Anti Masons in Penn. is to be regretted; but I think it
> would be better not to resort to any perceptible measure, and
> thereby entirely preclude the chance of any union between them
> hereafter . . . would it not be better for our friends to proceed in
> your State with their conventions, organizations etc. and thus
> prepare themselves for events? Public affairs are unquestionably
> tending to a crisis—the Bank—the Indian question—the
> Tariff . . . to adopt my resolution and stop with the repeal of the
> duties on unprotected articles, at this Session. . . . The proposi-
> tion of Mr. Clayton to inquire into the administration of the
> affairs of the Bank embarrasses the friends of that institution. . . .
> I am with constant regard, H. CLAY

February 10, 1844, the Washington *Reporter* inserted a
notice to the: "West Finley Boys to Wake Up! Citizens of
West Finley to meet at Windy Gap to form a Clay Club."

* * *

Thomas Edison, Harvey Firestone, and *Henry Ford—*

About 1935 when Lucille Carroll left Pittsburgh to return to the old Ackley Homestead of her great-grandmother, Sarah Price Parker Ackley, she found that the ancient covered "Ackley Bridge" that spanned Wheeling Creek between Washington and Greene counties, and stood almost in the Ackley front yard, was about to be removed by the county commissioners. During the next several years, Lucille launched a campaign to "save the bridge."

At this time, Henry Ford had commenced his Greenfield Village in Dearborn, Michigan, and was much interested in acquiring one of the McGuffey buildings in adjoining West Finley Township. Lucille marshalled her facts about the eighty-foot span, constructed of sound hand-hewn oak timbers, its abutments of dressed stone laid in the usual expert masonry of area inhabitants of Welsh background, and made a trip to Dearborn for a personal interview with Henry Ford. It took a lot of convincing and several years of letters before Mr. Ford agreed to take the bridge and move it to Dearborn. After stalling the Greene County commissioners until she had the Ford acceptance in hand, Lucille then found they were determined to take the bridge down and move it to another location. Weeks of daily trips to Waynesburg culminated the day she went in and said, "Look here, I don't want to see you any more than you want to see me, but how about the bridge?" Sick of the whole subject, the commissioner made a phone call and Lucille could hear a voice at the other end say, "Tell that woman to take her damned bridge out of there" and for a token sum, she had it! The rest of the story is known to anyone who has walked over the covered bridge that made the longest journey of any bridge in America to Greenfield Village where it is one of the favorite sights.

Also associated with the village and Penn's Southwest are the names of Ford's close friends, Harvey Firestone and Thomas Edison. They bought birdhouses from Waynesburg's

Jacobs Bird-House Company for their estates, and there is an amusing story told about one of their visits.

A man now living in the area tells of fishing in Wheeling Creek as a young lad in the 1930s, near Ackley Bridge when an older gentleman came by and stopped to chat with him. After a while the boy became curious and asked the stranger's name. When the man said, "I'm Henry Ford" his impulse was to answer back, "Well, I'm the King of England." Then two more men came by and started to talk; one of them looked very familiar and the shock was complete when they announced their names: Harvey Firestone and Thomas Edison! The trio of famous men had come from Michigan for the day to check out the covered bridge before Ford agreed to take it.

* * *

Stephen Foster (1826-1864)—In his 1934 published book about the *Minstrel of the Alleghenies,* Harvey Gaul describes the Pittsburgh of Stephen Collins Foster's years in the city:

> In 1826 Pittsburg was called the "Birmingham of America"; large lumber rafts idled down the Mon with their shanty crews from West Virginia. Primitive navigation abounded. Iron masters reaped the wealth of the district; there was steel and coal, but whiskey was part of the foundation of Pittsburgh and other river towns.

Stephen Foster was born on the Fourth of July during a Fourth celebration held by his father, William Foster, with an ox roast and picnic on the grounds of their home in the Lawrenceville section of the city which he owned and named. Stephen's grandfather, James Foster, had settled near Canonsburg in 1782 and his father, William, had attended the academy there. In the city of Foster's youth there were Negro stevedores, firemen, and bond servants. He heard many Negro songs as he grew up on the river. By 1850, the major diversion was horse racing with colorful crowds from the minstrel shows that came after the opening of the canal brought theatre and operettas to Pittsburgh. From his boyhood on, Foster was family and Pittsburgh oriented.

244

The music editor of the Pittsburgh *Press*, Carl Apone, in a recent feature on Stephen Foster wrote:

> One of the fascinating facets of his life is that this No. 1 publicizer of life in the *South* crossed the Mason-Dixon line on only a few occasions . . . his full-time pursuit of music was in Pittsburgh.

Among Foster's 200 compositions is a group of little-known hymns which Allan Gershwin (claiming to be the son of composer George Gershwin) was instrumental in locating and changing the complex, somewhat morbid lyrics without sacrificing their charm. Gershwin has also tried to change the picture of Foster as an unhappy, depressed man and bring out the fact that except for the final three or four sad years of his life, he was, to use today's term, "beautiful people." A fine portrait of his sensitive face painted by Malcolm Parcell hangs in the Citizens' Library in Washington.

* * *

Robert Fulton (1765-1845)—Early Washington historian Alfred Creigh wrote in 1870: "Few of the present generation are aware that the celebrated Robert Fulton of steamboat notoriety owned a farm in Hopewell Township." Washington County Deed Book 1-C records the sale of land on Cross Creek in Hopewell by Thomas and Margaret Pollock in 1785 to "Robert Fulton, miniature painter of Philadelphia for 85 pounds." When the *Caldwell Atlas* was published in 1876, the Robert Fulton cabin was noted in the township. Fulton was also an original lot holder in the town of Washington; in 1793 while in England, he deeded Lot No. 4 on Strawberry Alley to his sister, Mrs. David Morris, Lot No. 118 on Cherry Alley to another sister, Mrs. Isabella Cook, and a third sister received Lot No. 125 on Cherry.

In London, Fulton met James Rumsey of Virginia, who in 1783 had begun steamboat experiments on the Potomac; after Rumsey's death in 1792, Fulton carried on and proposed the idea of paddle wheels to the earl of Stanhope, who was not receptive to Fulton's ideas. His propelling apparatus increased the speed of early boats to five-six miles per hour and it was said the introduction of the steamboat was delayed by some twelve years because of the failure of Stanhope to recognize Fulton's ingenuity and to back him with capital.

After various experiments in France in 1803 and later in England, Robert Fulton returned to America in 1806 and began to plan double ferryboats for the East River in New York. The English-made engine for his *Clermont* did not arrive until late in 1806 and the boat was not ready for launching until the next year. Fulton invented the tubular boiler and in 1810-11 his steamboat, *New Orleans,* was built at Pittsburgh.

The Boyd Crumrine manuscript files contain a reference to an agreement between Robert Fulton, Edward P. and Robert L. Livingston to form a company to run steamboats between Louisville and New Orleans on the Ohio and to Saint Louis on the Mississippi, after Fulton's successful experiments in the Pittsburgh area. This agreement dated June 14, 1814, is referred to as the "keystone document relating to Mississippi River steamboat navigation."

* * *

Albert Gallatin (1761-1849)—A Huguenot of French and Swiss ancestry, Gallatin came to America in 1780 and went to Richmond, Virginia, where he was employed as an interpreter for a commercial house. In this position he became acquainted with many prominent Virginians including George Washington, who advised him to purchase land in the Monongahela Valley. After marrying charming, little Sophie Allegre of Richmond, Gallatin arranged to go into the western country. On a high bank above the Monongahela in a virtual wilderness of immense forest trees, he laid out his estate and built the brick and stone mansion Friendship Hill. This gracious house, very little changed since Gallatin's day, is still standing in somewhat shabby condition and is open to the public at intervals.

Albert Gallatin was known for his practical common sense and great ability as a financier and negotiator; especially did he call on the latter quality during the Whiskey Insurrection in western Pennsylvania in which he played a leading role. He enjoyed telling that he once lived for a whole year in Philadelphia on his limited congressional pay. It was said that neither Thomas Jefferson nor James Madison could have run the country without going broke if it had not been for the economical Albert Gallatin who was secretary of the treasury from 1801 to 1813. For many years, he rode horseback from his home near the town he named New Geneva on the Monongahela to Philadelphia and eastern cities where he was prominent in public life. His business activities on the river are covered in another chapter on the glassworks and potteries of New Geneva and Greensboro.

* * *

Marquis de Lafayette (1757-1834)—Southwestern Pennsylvania newspaper accounts in the spring of 1824 reported that General Lafayette had concluded to come to the United States. "The old gentleman says he is at a loss to express his feelings on the occasion and declines the honor of going in a national ship, but would take one of the Havre packets." Lafayette arrived July/August in the ship *Cadmus*, honored as the only surviving general of the American Revolution, as the steamship *Robert Fulton*, beautifully decorated, came down the East River. Many Americans had visited Lafayette in France after the close of the Revolution and had been most warmly received by him.

The first key to the Bastille had been presented to George Washington who displayed it at Mount Vernon; a second key was melted down into the sword presented by the American Congress to Lafayette which he always kept with him. During the time he was confined in a prison dungeon in France after the French Revolution, he had lost all of his hair, and on his American tour, wore what was called a "Washington Hat" over his wig.

In May 1825 Lafayette stayed at David Morris's *Globe Inn* in Washington where a colorful reception was held in the Long Room. When the party left for Brownsville the next morning at six o'clock, they must have made a gay and interesting procession as they traveled along the new National Road escorted by a large party on horseback as far as Hillsboro, where they had breakfast at the stone tavern, known today as the popular Century Inn, built in 1794. Along the way old Revolutionary comrades came out to hug and weep with him over memories of events of forty-seven years earlier. At the Monongahela for the crossing to Brownsville, a beautiful flower-decked barge and twenty-four girls representing the states, dressed in white gowns with ribbon sashes and carrying arm bouquets of garden flowers, greeted the party. It was a thrill for the writer to be shown one of these sashes worn by an ancestress as Miss Virginia, a length of pale blue "love ribbon" carefully packed away in a Washington attic.

* * *

William Holmes McGuffey (1800-1873)—Early educator and editor of the famous and collectible *McGuffey Eclectic Readers*, McGuffey was born in West Finley Township, near Claysville. His grandparents had immigrated to Washington County from Scotland in 1789 and during General Anthony Wayne's campaign in the Northwest, his father had acted as a scout. The small frame house where McGuffey was born was moved to Henry Ford's Greenfield Village but the early frame school he attended before entering Washington and Jefferson College is maintained as an historic place in the county. In 1839, McGuffey became president of Ohio University at Athens.

* * *

Robert Morris (1734-1806)—In a rare little book entitled *Robert Morris*, published in 1834 by David Gould, the author laments that Morris was not honored along with Washington and Franklin. When the writer was attending journalism classes at the University of Redlands in 1956, a member of the writer's colony there had just completed one of very few biographies of this famous American who has been somewhat resurrected in recent years.

Morris came to America in 1747 from Liverpool and settled in Maryland where his father, Robert, Sr., had established himself as a representative of an English trading company at Oxford, Maryland, in 1738. Before his father's death in 1750, he had apprenticed Robert to the mercantile firm of Charles Willig in Philadelphia. Morris became a member of the firm after the senior Willig's death and this company of Willig & Morris continued in business until it was dissolved in 1793. The ties of Philadelphia merchants with western Pennsylvania were early and strong. Howard Leckey wrote that, as in the case of so much of the history of this area, few realized the tremendous effect the private speculations of Robert Morris had on settlement in Greene County, where before the financial disaster of his vast purchases on borrowed money, he owned forty-one thousand acres of land. "These early men with Daniel McFarland [of Washington County] and others, held some 80,000 acres for speculation in western Greene County and held up settlement of it until after 1795." These tracts covered some of the rich lands reported by Gist on his early scouting trips.

A signer of the Declaration, Morris was superintendent of finance for the United States from 1781 to 1784 during which time he used his personal credit to get goods and funds for the early army and he was the only person who came to Washington's rescue with funds during the days at Trenton. In 1784, Robert Morris sent the first American trading vessel, a China clipper, to Canton with a large cargo of ginseng and other merchandise, but this venture was not profitable. The next big "adventure" for Morris was his speculation in western lands. One of the most well-known tracts was Valladolid, which had been patented on a Virginia preemption right in Richhill Township, and after the collapse of the North American Land Company, sold at auction to another Philadelphia merchant, Thomas Ryerson who lived on the land for several years, adjacent to the present town of Wind Ridge.

Because of his involvement in Greene County land, a copy of the will of Robert Morris is on file in Waynesburg. One of Morris's biographers made the comment that his will was lost until 1939 when workers found it yellowed with age and cracked by heat, near the furnaces beneath the Philadelphia City Hall. This will dated June 13, 1804, makes poignant references to various personal objects he had repurchased after his bankruptcy:

> . . . my Silver Vase or Punch Cup which I imported from London many years ago and have since purchased again.

> . . . my Silver Boiler which I also imported from London and have lately repurchased.

> I give to my friend Gouverneur Morris, Esq. my telescope Espying Glass, being the same I bought of a French refugee from Cape Francois then at Trenton, and which I since purchased again of Mr. Hall, officer of the Bankrupt Office.

> Here I have to express my regret at having lost a very large fortune acquired by honest industry, which I had long hoped and expected to enjoy with my family during my own life and then to distribute it amongst those of them that should outlive me. Fate has determined otherwise and we must submit to the decree, which I have done with patience and fortitude.

His wife, Mary Morris was sworn as his executrix May 29, 1806.

* * *

John Rockefeller—The Rockefeller name appears in Washington County records in the early 1800s and not having traced the genealogy of either the "rich" or the "poor" Rockefellers, we assume a relationship to the latter who early in the 1800s were active in the Pittsburgh area. *Caldwell's 1876 Atlas* shows John Rockefeller born in the county in 1821; farmer in East Finley Township with twenty sheep on thirty acres, a wool grower with a gristmill.

* * *

Arthur St. Clair (1734-1818)—In his biography of 1944, entitled *Arthur St. Clair, Rugged Ruler of the Old Northwest,* Frazer E. Wilson relates that St. Clair was born in a castle, of noble family near Thurso, Scotland. He first entered British service, but fought on the American side during the French and Indian War for which he received a large grant of land at Ligonier. In 1764 he was employed by the Penn family to survey and look after their interests in southwestern Pennsylvania. He married Phebe Bayard, whose great-grandfather was James Bowdoin of Boston, and from whom she inherited a legacy of 14,000 pounds.

St. Clair administered the counties of Westmoreland, Cumberland, and Bedford, and organized and equipped out of his own funds, the Frontier Rangers of 1774. He held most of the county offices of Westmoreland after it was organized in 1773; was admitted to the Bar of Washington County in 1794, and was governor of the Northwest Territory 1783-1803 with headquarters in Marietta on the Ohio River.

Like so many of the great patriots of our country's colonial period, St. Clair depleted his personal fortune and died in poverty. The Washington *Examiner* carried a feature in the May 18, 1818, issue on General St. Clair, furnished by "persons from the Western Country who stopped at his log house on Chestnut Ridge to warm themselves."

> The General was confined to bed with illness, but his wife, exhibited a striking figure of fallen greatness. A tall, majestic woman of 86 years with noble features and a ladylike deportment. . . . She wore a coarse country dress with ornaments of forty or fifty years ago and conversed with a Frenchman in the party in his language. Her manners were French but time and sorrow had weakened her mind which was surely originally very vigorous.

The same newspaper carried notices of the St. Clair deaths a few months later. The general died August 31, 1818, and his wife on September 16. They are buried side by side in a Greensburg cemetery. A fine memorial to the St. Clairs is a room from their first, fine home which is preserved in the main building at Fort Ligonier and stands on land once owned by Arthur St. Clair. George Washington is reported to have sent skilled carpenters from Mount Vernon to carve some of the woodwork and paneling in this room.

* * *

Peter Studebaker—The Studebakers came from western Maryland into Penn's Southwest and are found in Cumberland County Court records as early as 1756 when Henry Studebaker died and left an "orphan" son, Peter; the estate was administered by Clement Studebaker. After Westmoreland County was set off, Peter's estate is of record there in 1790 with 300 acres of land in Hempfield Township surveyed for him in 1784.

The Studebakers moved west to Indiana and started their wagon manufactory with the same names: John, the father was born in 1799 and died in 1877 and the "Studebaker Brothers" were Henry (1826-1895), Clement (1831-1901), and Peter (1836-1897).

* * *

George Washington (1732-1799)—Within the boundaries of Pennsylvania, especially in the southwest corner, young George Washington performed his first important public services in the French and Indian War when the Americans and the British fought side by side.

Citizens of Penn's Southwest do not subscribe to the sentiments of those who glibly ask "What ever happened to George Washington?" Or relate that his figure has been diminished and virtually emptied of substance. Neither have they "just discovered the intellectual dimensions of the American Revolution" as a recent Bicentennial booklet proclaimed. "Little Washington" was the third town in America to be named for Washington and grateful townspeople presented Lot No. 43 to him for his personal use. His great bronze figure watches over the city from the dome of the ornate courthouse. George Washington is very much with us as we review some of his ties with area counties.

Map with petition for a road from Canonsburg. Washington County Roads and Bridges Docket, No. 1, 1784.

One of the foremost owners of western land, Washington came into Mount Pleasant Township to check out his property there on September 19, 1784. He was the houseguest for three days of Colonel John Canon and his family on Chartiers Creek; later he expressed great respect for Canon as a sensible, sincere, and hospitable man. Local news items reported no ovation on his arrival to see about squatters on his land, and no tears shed at his going. Although the settlers had been encouraged to stay on the land by Judge Edward Ward of the old Augusta District Court, they were obliged to move after Washington's visit.

Although no proof has been found that Washington ever entered Greene County, one of the favorite local legends in the old river town of Rice's Landing is that Colonel George Washington and his small army crossed the Monongahela at that point in 1755 on the way to join General Braddock. Prior to the river dam at the landing and about where the later ferry crossed, the Monongahela was little more than a stream except during high water, and people rode back and forth freely on horseback.

In 1810 Thomas Meason advertised 234 acres of land including Great Meadows, formerly surveyed and owned by Washington, on the east side of Laurel Hill, ten miles out of Uniontown on the "Great Road to Fort Cumberland." Washington was constantly troubled by people who came in and settled on land he owned. Fayette County Continuance Docket No. 1 lists an amicable suit in March term 1788 of *General George Washington* v. *Uriah Springer and Joseph Torrence* for a debt of forty pounds on land in lower Tyrone Township. In June term, Washington brought another action for a debt of sixty-six pounds against Samuel Jackson of the Redstone Settlement.

During the most trying period of the American Revolution, Washington is said to have remarked: "Should it come to the worst, I will fall back into the mountain region of Pennsylvania and make my stand among the Scotch-Irish there."

Washington County ſsⁱ   May Term 1800

Bushrod Washington, Wm
Augustine Washington, George Steptoe
Washington Samuel Washington &
Lawrence Lewis, Exſ and Martha
Washington Exʳˣ of Genˡ George
Washington Deceased —   Am. act. Debt in the
                                                        Detinent $. 17640. —
ff
Alexander Addison, and John
Ritchie Exʳˢ of Matthew Ritchie
Deceased —   We the defendants do here
                                                        agree, that this action be entered
                                                        in the Court of Common pleas

Washington County court files, May term 1800, followed by an action November 1801 with the same principals in a suit against John Ritchie over a mortgage on 2,acres on Millers Run, formerly in Augusta County, Virginia, patented July 5, 1774 George Washington and from Washington by deed June 1, 1796, for $12,000 to thew Ritchie.

Fayette County ſs
General George Washington
    William Brooke
    James Coldwele &
    Obed Garwood

                          Issue Capias Dt £30 — Issued Nº 1

General George Washington
    John Emerson
    Thomas Johnston Jr
    Robert Rowan

                          Issue Capias Dt £58. 16 Issued —

To Ephraim Douglass Esqⁱ
Prothonotary
                                          Smith & Co
                                          21 Sept 1785

Fayette County court files, September term 1785.

13

THE PAW PAW STAND

OLD PAW PAW CHURCH near Davistown, Greene County, built by the Primitive Baptists of the Old School in 1805 was typical of the type of church erected throughout western Pennsylvania in pioneer times. It was the oldest building used for religious worship standing west of the Monongahela River and one of two log churches still standing west of the Allegheny Mountains and north (one mile) of the Mason-Dixon line until its collapse in the 1940s.

Because the log building stood in a grove of pawpaw bushes, it was called "The Paw Paw Stand" locally and by its members scattered through West Virginia adjacent to Penn's Southwest. The drab, deserted huddle of the defunct Pawpaw Fuel Company on Legislative Route 30071 marks the intersection of that road with a red-dog side road about two miles north of Bobtown and midway between Davistown and Bobtown; about 300 feet northwest on the red-dog is the log foundation of the old church.

In 1810 at Woodstock, Virginia, the *History of the Rise and Progress of the Baptists of Virginia* was published by Robert B. Semple, minister of the Gospel in King and Queen County. This rare book tells that the churches that were afterward formed into the Redstone Association belonged to the Union Baptist Association until 1804 when they separated. The original nine churches of 1804 are listed and Paw Paw, called "Meadow Run" in official records, is described as being founded in 1805 in Monongalia County, Virginia. The original membership was small, only seven persons. This grew to fourteen in 1810 and by 1877 had dropped to eleven. The last two members were sisters, Mrs. R. C. Keener and Nancy Sheets whose great-great-grandmother was Elizabeth Spicer of the well-known Spicer Massacre.

In 1828 Richard and Rebecca Brewer deeded the land for one dollar to church trustees Isaac Buckingham, William Furman, and Christopher Brewer. The tract had been patented in 1785 as Dunkard Neck by Leonard Everly and was first used for church purposes by the German Baptists who were akin to Dunkards. Members were variously called "Ironside," "Primitive," and "Seven Day" Baptists. The Primitive or "hard-shell" Baptists were called "Hard Heads" by some of the local residents who reported that they sang in long meter, a sort of monotone-like one-note Johnny song, quite unmusical, and a tuning fork was used for accompaniment. As in many of the backcountry areas, they sang according to the shape of the notes, some triangular and some circular.

The church stood almost untouched for a hundred and

Rear view of hewn log Paw Paw Church from postcard photograph, Dunkard Township, Greene County.

forty years before it was allowed to disintegrate. Numerous efforts were made by members of local patriotic groups to have the building removed intact to Waynesburg, but failed because of lack of funds and support. When Earle Forrest, late Washington County historian, visited the church in 1940 he took photographs and noted that a sign on the door stated mutilators would be prosecuted by the "Board of Trustees." Today the hewed logs of the foundation are still in place, forming a rectangle some four timbers high on the back wall, built on a ledge above the mine-polluted yellow-green water of Dunkard Creek where old-timers remember members were baptized. One of the neighbors reported to the writer in 1970 that fishermen, hunters, and bands of roving boys built fires in the church, breaking up the old hand-planed plank pews for firewood and threw rocks at the building until modern-day vandalism destroyed it completely.

The original hand-split oak shingle roof was replaced with a metal standing-seam "tin" roof, rusty remnants of which are at the site. The heavy, oak plank door hewn by the broad-

Interior view of Paw Paw Church with hand-hewn poplar plank pews and preacher's platform. From a photograph taken before 1940.

ax swung on large hinges of "ancient design," floors were of rough-hewn oak plank, and the walls were bare log. The ceiling was the under side of the roof with two huge oak "summer beams" crossing the room from side to side.

A center aisle with the poplar plank pews on each side ended at the preacher's platform, with three benches running the other way on each side of the raised platform. Originally a high pulpit stood with a circular stairway, but the elder in charge about 1900 had this interesting early feature torn out. Lighting was provided by seven windows cut in the logs and board shutters were provided. In the early years the church was unheated but later a large Burnside stove stood in one corner.

An Everly descendant told the writer that his great-grandfather helped build the church and reported it was also used during the first years as a schoolhouse. The Redstone Circuit met there for many years; services were kept up as a neighborhood tradition after regular church services ceased and were well attended by visitors from other areas. It is local tradition that the renowned preacher Alexander Campbell once preached at old Paw Paw.

When the home of T. B. Steele near Davistown burned in 1903, the church records, except for one drawer, were destroyed. In this way the last Minutes Book with fifty-six years of records has been preserved. The final entry in this book reads:

> 1933 Oct. the seckond sun met and after singing and prayer we had preaching by our pastor S. A. Clevenger, our preaching days are the seckond and fourth sun.

Pastor S. A. Clevenger came from his home in Grafton, West Virginia, to hold services two or three times a year until his death ca. 1935. Then Elder J. S. C. Henderson of Fairmont took charge and held the yearly memorial services first on the second and then on the third Sunday in June.

In 1953, Nat Youngblood of the Pittsburgh *Press*, working from photographs, created a Thanksgiving roto cover in watercolor, of the Paw Paw Stand for the November 22 issue.

14

THE JACOBS BIRD-HOUSE COMPANY

J. WARREN JACOBS, born near Waynesburg, Pennsylvania, December 5, 1868, in the tradition of Greene County ornithologists and archaeologists alike, began in his ninth year to fill cigar boxes with his growing assortment of birds, nests, eggs, and butterflies. The collection soon outgrew the special case in the Jacobs home on South Washington Street, next to his grandfather's carriage factory, and reached the impressive figure of 4,500 eggs of North American birds, one of the largest and finest collections in the country.

When the Columbian Exposition opened in 1893, Warren Jacobs exhibited his birds and eggs at the Pennsylvania section and with a similar exhibit at the 1904 Saint Louis Fair, won a gold medal. Not only did young Jacobs collect and stuff birds of all kinds, he made sketches and paintings of them. Almost from the beginning, his special interest was the type of swallow called a martin. Known as the first man to colonize the American purple martin, the Jacobs colony of the birds became famous.

Until Warren Jacobs came along with his ideas about bird-houses, gourds grown for their various and special shapes, were used by the Indians and first settlers to house birds. He began with sketches of rather simple designs, but soon, as the martin colony grew, the houses became larger and more elaborate. Warren had learned cabinetry in his grandfather's factory where he also painted and decorated the carriages and wagons. When the Baltimore and Ohio came through, Warren was hired to letter in gold leaf on its cars; he even decorated the gay Gypsy wagons when they came through the county every summer in the early years.

The Jacobs Bird-House Company was lodged in the combination carriage factory and blacksmith shop of the family where several men were employed, and there was a room upstairs for painting. With a flair for publicity and great faith in his unique approach to birdhouse construction, Warren placed an ad in the 1896 Greene County *Women's Centennial Magazine* for his publication *Among the Birds of S. W. Pennsylvania and N. W. Virginia*, fully illustrated. Soon arti-

The tradition of Warren Jacobs's popular little Bluebird Nest Box is carried on today by Ralph Bell of Jefferson in Greene County who has made and mounted hundreds of these boxes in connection with his Audubon activities.

cles about and by Jacobs began to appear in national magazines. *Gleanings* carried Jacobs articles from 1903 to 1912 and about 1920 an article about the business appeared in the *Saturday Evening Post*.

In the second volume of his own publication, the *American Bird-House Journal*, which had a nationwide circulation, Warren Jacobs published dozens of letters from satisfied and thrilled customers who wrote of the strange way in which purple martins had located their new Jacobs birdhouses only hours after erection. One 1914 letter from a town in Ontario, Canada, reported:

Our Style 1 house was occupied by a pair of martins the next morning after being put up—the first martins that were ever seen in town.

The No. 1 model was the largest house Jacobs built at that time and contained forty-five separate rooms.

Testimonials and photographs poured in over the years with varying reactions to martins, called the "Policemen of the Air" and the preeminent bird to colonize in large houses. People wrote that they no longer had worms on their currant bushes, in fact, had no insects of any kind, including mosquitoes. The darting flight of the martin is keyed to devouring insects in flight and occasionally during a very wet year when few insects are in the air, as occurred recently in Penn's Southwest, colonies have been almost wiped out as the martins literally starve to death. One reader sent an item about an Iowa Golf Club which had been so anxious to attract the birds to their grounds that they had spent $5,000 importing German "Von Berlepsch" type birdhouses. This reader had sent Jacobs literature to the club and anticipated a large order.

Everybody's No. 9 from a photograph showing martins perched all over the house shortly after erection.

As to the "mystique" of the Jacobs martin house, Mr. Jacobs commented editorially:

> I reasoned that a *new* bird-house could be made to appear as unsuspicious to the bird as one already in use, eliminating the timidity the martins show when approaching a new house. The secret is mine! Dearly bought with years of toil and struggle, it has been turned into use in connection with my bird-houses. Every bird-house going out from our factory is personally treated by me for the purpose here intimated.

In questioning Warren's son, Waynesburg architect, Harold Jacobs recently, he said there was no "magic" about his father's so-called treatment of the houses. They were all meticulously constructed of durable materials, with hinged panels so they could be cleaned annually, and they were all carefully painted. The inference is that the purple martin of America is an extremely discriminating bird.

Another amazing feature of Jacobs's product was that he not only priced them well within the range of modest incomes so that the simpler houses could be enjoyed by all bird lovers,

Style No. 5 with an added veranda on each side was very similar to No. 10.

but he paid the freight. Style No. 2 was so massive when crated for shipment that it weighed 225 pounds! The floors were all of three-fourth inch prime oak and other quality hardwoods were used for walls and roof. Style No. 5 came with a hinged pole for taking it down in winter. Since the advent of plastic, backyards far and wide in Greene County have their numerous Jacobs birdhouses carefully wrapped for the winter months.

Harold Jacobs recalled that Henry Ford, whose favorite was "Everybody's" No. 9, "hammered away at Father to make fewer models" but Mr. Jacobs enjoyed turning out the intricate balconies and porches on birdhouses which were really miniatures of the Victorian mansions of the gas and coal era in southwestern Pennsylvania. Warren Jacobs commented in his journal in 1913:

After a lifetime studying the requirements of house-nesting birds and publishing the results of studies and experiments, we ventured into the enterprise of manufacturing and offering a perfected bird-house to the public. Our venture was the first of the kind undertaken in America. We build bird-houses for birds rather than for money.

Style No. 5 with its twenty-eight rooms, handsomely painted and with angle-iron braces sold for eighteen dollars, freight prepaid, and was the preference of John D. Rockefeller. Also available and advertised in *The American Bird-House Journal* in 1915 was a sparrow trap which had been tested and approved by the Department of Agriculture for destroying the English sparrow. This retailed at $4.50.

The classical Parthenon
with sixty rooms.

Several models, including the elaborate and very large No. 4 called the "Capital" had painted clock faces on the sides of their domes or cupolas and the hands were always painted at exactly 8:22 which time marked the end of the Spanish-American War in which so many Greene County men had served. A new model built by Jacobs and stored in the old factory after his death, was presented by the Jacobs family to the Greene County Historical Society where it is on display. Another of these immense Capitals is mounted in the yard of the Loughman home, Bear Lakes, on Route 18 between Washington and Waynesburg.

The latest design in 1917 was the "new classical Parthenon" with 60 rooms with a doorway to every room to protect from both weather and heat; cost was $55 and shipping weight 550 pounds. "Jacobs pays the freight!"

Another product of the Jacobs factory was recalled by Furman Rinehart, native Waynesburger and retired New York patent attorney, who said Warren Jacobs also made sleds; one style more or less standard and small for young children and the other larger and more elaborately finished. They were made entirely of wood and while they didn't have the "Flexible Flyer" type steering device they were used by many Greene County youngsters who enjoyed their bright red color and their names lettered in gold across the top.

When the business was at its peak from 1912 on, with over forty Jacobs birdhouses in Long Island gardens, to name one location, the local paper reported two carloads of houses had left the Waynesburg freight yards for shipment to many points in the United States. In 1972 Waynesburg writer John O'Hara wrote a column on the old "Waynie" station in town where the train between Washington and Waynesburg ceased operations in 1929:

> There was a real "homey" sort of atmosphere about the entire area of the paved platform outside the station and the large lawn which extended east to Washington Street.
>
> Smack dab in the center of the rectangular lawn, close-cropped by a hand mower, was the traditional bed of red cannas from which one of the genuine Warren Jacobs martin houses arose on its lofty perch atop a tapered, wrought iron pipe.
>
> A traditional Waynesburg sidewalk of that period hand-quarried Cleveland flagstone shipped from Ohio, flanked the north side of the lawn.

15

SOME LAWS AND SOME COURTHOUSES

EVEN AFTER formal establishment of the first courts of law, "Congregations" in many localities acted as tribunal in matters of member conduct and in areas currently the province of the courts. "By the voice of the Church and our Brethren . . ." was the preamble used when certain persons were laid under censure for taking of hogs not belonging to them, misbehavior such as violent swearing, being in "licker," horse racing or stealing, adultery and fornication, and on and on. When charges could be proven, and this usually took more than one session, the person was excommunicated, and occasionally, reinstated at a later date.

Most complaints were directed against others, but there were some apparently voluntary confessions by persons who regretted having become "dangerously drunk at the raising of a house" with the result that they "fot, swor and did malishus mischief." As an example of mischief, one session's entry covered a long discussion of the fact that one man laughed at another when he fell. There was no quick judgment passed; they were very careful to *prove* that he *did* laugh. People were even reprimanded for walking in the street in a "lofty" manner.

Not only the raising of a house brought on sieges of drunkenness but one member was "intoxicated last fall at the Widow Hill's husking," and at a daubing frolic where they

266

spent all night in the still house where several members swore they had to drink to keep warm.

Another category often placed before the elders of various congregations was the endless testimony from men who had made trips over the mountains to Hagerstown for salt ca. 1790-1800 and had witnessed unkind treatment of horses, especially of mares. At the regular monthly meeting of the Reverend John McMillan's congregation important problems of the day were considered, but some early minutes reveal the kind of petty problems that still irritate and cause trouble today.

During one session, a member of the congregation asked for a hearing on the matter of a tablecloth stolen during the marriage of one of her relatives "thirty-six years ago." She was asked to describe the cloth after such a lapse of time and she did, saying it had raised figures wrought in the shape of a five-penny. When the tablecloth was produced it did not have any such marks and the woman was found guilty by the session for "speaking rashly on mere trifles."

Another charge was brought during the same session for calling a man a "papist son of a bitch" (a charge brought frequently) and his wife a "damned whore." In 1805 it was resolved that no self-murderer could be buried within the bounds of the congregational burial ground, and this too reveals some of the narrowness of the times. Later in the year the comment appeared that the "West Alexander pewter communion service has not yet been found."

In 1794 there was an act of the Pennsylvania Assembly to prevent all *worldly employment* on the Sabbath. Then shortly afterwards someone reported in the Pittsburgh *Gazette* that they had seen fires on the way to divine service and concluded that "someone was boiling sugar on the Sabbath!"

Aside from censure for what now seems to be frivolous or petty conduct, some very fair judgments were also handed down. In the 1790-1822 records of one congregation, the following advice was given to a member who opposed an elder's appointment on the grounds that the candidate had taken over land many years before that didn't belong to him:

> A Company of seven men came out to this country and entered into an agreement to improve land with a plan for the waters around which they built their cabins; when any two of the Company could not agree as to their lines, they would choose two more of the Company to decide the matter, and then they abided by the decision.

Concerning prospective church members, one session book ca. 1850, contained this remark: "People met with the Elders and gave satisfactory evidences of their *experimental* acquaintance with religion. . . ."

* * *

In the 1700 to 1810 volume of *Laws of the Commonwealth* concerning arrest, it is stated that:

> No freeholder living in the Province for two years who has 50 acres of land in fee simple, seated, and 12 acres cleared, or hath a dwelling house worth fifty pounds, shall be arrested in any civil action, but the original process against freeholders shall be a *Writ* of *Summons* under the seal of a Justice of the Court of Common Pleas directed to the Sheriff.

In cases where persons brought an action for injury to their good names, etc., they were described as "good, true, faithful and pious subjects of the Commonwealth." When a physical attack was made, the wording was ominous: "with force of arms, with nives, barrel staves, hatchets. . . ." From the number of assault and battery charges in court records, there was more "righteous wrath" and standing up for rights in those early times. Fines were collected for strange amounts and for strange infractions; a justice was fined one cent for assault in 1798, and the fine for a "hog thief" was one penny. Jury duty was taken very seriously and members of the grand jury were fined eight dollars for nonappearance unless excused for good reason. In 1798 the Greene County "Gaoler" was fined for the misdemeanor of using the "Gaol" for a stable.

Whenever there was some special matter of local concern to be investigated and a decision made, a jury of twelve "good and true" men, usually citizens of the neighborhood involved, and called "peacemakers," was appointed by the court. One of the principal duties of such a group was to check out proposed millsites as there was great danger from flooding and damage to nearby land if sites were not carefully chosen and approved.

Late Greene County Clerk "Bill" Meighn told the writer that the conduct of county business at the courthouse was influenced for many years by weather and travel conditions. On good days when the mud or snow was minimal and travel easy, the county treasurer was kept busy paying all those who had come to town with their claims. Often settlers who lived near the boundaries of the county only made it in to town two or three times a year and then they came with a group of neighbors.

Quarter sessions court records show the following items on which the treasurer paid out during 1789 in Washington: wolves and squirrels as reported by the constables (panther heads brought as high as twelve dollars some years), jury and election expenses, allowance for "lost money" chiefly by merchants transporting goods, waste land payments, and fees for "western" lands.

There was some inclination to the New England type of

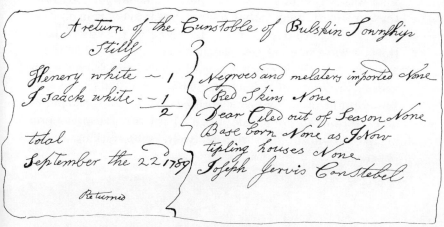

Constable's return, 1789. Fayette County Quarter Sessions Court records.

town meeting. On June 13, 1812, a public "Town Meeting" was announced at the courthouse in Washington to discuss the matter of raising local taxes; at a February 13, 1822, meeting of citizens at the courthouse, they consulted over procurement of a fire engine. One of the duties in the towns fell to a committee appointed to "see that all cisterns in the business district are filled with water and all business houses supplied with leather buckets for fire use."

* * *

Some of the comments found in Sandford Cox's recollections of the Wabash Valley, published in 1860, apply equally well to Penn's Southwest:

> The early lawyers traveled on horseback, sometimes alone and sometimes in squads before the days of turnpikes, railroads and canals.

> To witness a troop of these early attorneys entering a village as they traveled the circuit, themselves and their horses spattered with mud, and their huge portmanteaus surmounted with overcoat and umbrella, they resembled the forlorn hope of a company of mounted rangers.

> Their long rides on horseback along blind paths and dimly defined roads, crossing unbridged streams, sleeping in the open air as they frequently had to do, and leading colts and driving steers home taken on fees, fully developed their physical and intellectual energies and gave them a vigor and self-reliance possessed by few of our more modern students.

It was a common thing for judges and lawyers to travel thirty to forty miles in one day to appear in court in another county the next day. No wonder some of the early magistrates worked to erect new, smaller counties.

In August 1808 Zadok Cramer, the Pittsburgh bookseller and publisher of the *Navigator* announced publication by subscription of a new work entitled *The Lawyer, or Man as he Ought not to be—a Tale;* price $1 for this 250-page book or free to those who bring in twelve subscriptions to this paper.

During 1813 in June term, Washington County Common Pleas Court considered the certification of Thomas Cunningham as attorney:

> The undersigned having been appointed by the Court on the 15th of June to meet at the house of David Morris for the purpose of examining Thomas Cunningham on the elementary and practical principles of law; in pursuance of his appointment, we have examined Mr. Cunningham whose answers have given us entire satisfaction. We therefore consider him duly qualified to be admitted an Attorney & Counselor at Law at the bar of this Court.
>
> Washington, 16th June 1813   P. DODDRIDGE
> OBADIAH JENNINGS
> H. PURVIANCE

On June 14, Parker Campbell made this statement: "I hereby certify that Thomas S. Cunningham has studied the law with assiduity under my direction for the term of three years. I also certify that he is a person of integrity and good behavior." (Campbell was considered the most distinguished lawyer of his day.)

The name of John Simonson appears in court records and in land transactions throughout Washington and Greene counties for many years. During the process of his certification as an attorney in 1796, Judge Alexander Addison reviewed notes in his "book of rules":

> In addition to our former rules for admission of attorneys we will require from the gentleman under whom the person proposed has studied, a certificate that he has studied the time prescribed . . . and that his moral character is good; and a certificate from the gentlemen appointed to examine him and these certificates to be filed in the prothonotary's office. Students knowing this will be more assiduous in their studies and circumspect in their deportment and the gentlemen from whom these certificates will be required, knowing that they will be presented, will be cautious in giving them to unworthy persons.
>
> Under these circumstances, application having been made for the admission of Mr. Simonson on a Certificate from a Gentleman of the law of known abilities in New Jersey as follows: . . . I am

desired by the court to request from the gentlemen of the bar written answers to the following questions.

1. Whether a certificate for studying three years partly in New Jersey and partly in this state be not explicitly required by the rule.
2. Whether on the principles on which this rule was made, the want of it can be dispensed with except in case of death, unexpected absence, etc.
3. Whether Mr. Simonson's case is within any such exceptions.

Members of the Washington Bar who answered the questions were: H. H. Brackenridge, Thomas Collins, Parker Campbell, G. Henry Keppele, J. Penticost, and James Morrison. They agreed that three years of study was necessary if under age, and two years if over age, with no distinction for having studied in different states. "A certificate was produced for his study in the state of New Jersey which, with the time of study in this state, makes nearly three years, since he was of age, and the unexpected absence of Henry Purviance, the gentleman with whom he studied . . . it being within our knowledge by our own observation or by information from Mr. Purviance that Mr. Simonson has applied himself with diligence and is a man of integrity." John Simonson died suddenly in December 1809 in Steubenville, Ohio, when only thirty-six.

Boyd Crumrine in his *Bench and Bar* wrote of the early voices heard at the old courtroom bar railing. James Ross was admitted in 1784, Alexander Addison in 1787, Joseph Penticost in 1792, and Parker Campbell in 1794. "All distinguished lawyers and really great men in legal learning and personal worth and ability."

The local justices were not required to have legal training. Under the first state constitution of 1776, power was lodged in the Supreme Executive Council and then justices of the peace were commissioned for seven years and could sit as judges in quarter sessions court, but only specially selected justices could hear orphans and common pleas courts. The

David Reddick Esquire Prothonotary of Washington County
    to the Prothonotary of the Supreme Court of Pennsylvania Dr

      To the price of a Circuit Court Docquet for
        Washington County — — — —   } $1.50

      To 2½ days employment of a Clerk in transcribing
        the docquet and also copies of the Circuit Court
        Rules for the use of the Judges and for the printer }   4. ...
        @ 12/

      To a printed Copy of the Rules of said Court with
        a leather cover   }   . 50

                                   $6. ..

Received January 1. 1800 of David Reddick Esquire Prothonotary of
Washington County the above Sum of Six dollars.
    1 January 1800.

                                  Edwd Burd Proy

Received of David Reddick Esquire
1 January 1800 thirty three cents for
a red morocco Labell in gold letters
Circuit court docket Washington

$0. 33/100   J Young

An 1800 item from Washington County Prothonotary files.

second state constitution placed in effect in September 1790 changed the judicial system and divided Pennsylvania into circuit or judicial districts.

* * *

Some of the laws in effect and a few local ordinances which touched the lives of many citizens during the founding years are cited.

Appearance docket "jacket files" for Common Pleas Court of Washington County contain papers dating back to the 1760s and 1770s involving cases for "Ejectment and Quieting Title." The history of these actions, using standard fictitious names, is reviewed in the Pennsylvania Statutes:

> It will be impossible to understand the method of the time-honored action of ejectment without an examination of those ancient, obsolete devices of the English law which, although they are now disregarded, form the support and ground plan of the modern structure.

The matter of ejectment is concerned with obtaining a writ to try the title, with lease, entry, and ouster. This was in effect from about 1500 until Cromwell's time when a new method for trying titles was invented. In 1901 in Pennsylvania, the modern method of compelling the parties to set forth their titles in abstracts or statements was adopted. A typical ejectment action in very abbreviated form is taken from a June term 1788 file:

> Timothy Turnout, a yeoman was attached to answer John Goodright of a plea wherefore with force and arms he entered [premises described] which Thomas Bond devised to said John for a term not yet expired and ejected him from his farm. . . .
>
> JOHN DOE
RICHARD ROE

A very early Pennsylvania law stipulated that all cornfields and grounds kept for enclosures should be well fenced at least *five* feet high with rails or logs and viewers of fences were appointed by the court. In Penn's Southwest, worm fences were to be four and one-half feet high with sufficient stakes and riders, the under rail not more than five inches from the ground and the first four rails four inches apart; post and rail fences were to also be four and one-half feet high.

An act of 1800 stipulated how flour made of rye or Indian corn brought to any port or place for export, should be handled:

> ... shall be packed in casks of good seasoned materials, nailed and branded with the name of the miller or bolter and marked "Rye Flour" or "Kiln-dried Corn Meal" ... hogsheads to be of good seasoned white oak bound and tightened with *sixteen* good and sufficient hoops secured with not less than four nails in each chine hoop, three wooden pegs at upper edge of each upper bilge hoop and staves to be forty-one inches long and diameter of the head to be twenty-seven inches and to contain *800* pounds.

In 1811 this act was amended to state that rye or Indian corn flour could be packed in strong, tight puncheons of seasoned *red* oak with pine heads for molasses.

Lighted lanterns were to be kept burning on bridges all night except when there was moonlight, and there was a five-dollar fine for anyone caught mutilating mile or road signposts or dumping rubbish on the roads in 1812. Free Negroes, mulattoes or Indians were to appear for musters without arms and to be employed as drummers, trumpeters, or "pioneers."

One of the most interesting and revealing areas for courthouse research is wills and estates where it is often possible to establish the character or personality of a person who left no other records. John Gabler's will written in Greene County in 1811 is an example of the respect and trust of some husbands for their wives:

> ... all my property to my trusty and well-beloved wife, Sophia placing full confidence in her justice, parental affection and management, concluding that she will consider it her bounden duty to

276

maintain, bring up, educate and put or bind out to tradesmen of reputable standing, such of our children as may require it. . . .

In the Ohio County, West Virginia, records an agreement made June 9, 1787, is typical of arrangements made to apprentice young people:

Jonathan, son of Elizabeth Hook puts himself to apprentice to Hugh Means, citizen and joiner of Washington, State of Pennsylvania to learn the art, trade or mystery of joinery for nine years and nine months.

He shall faithfully serve his mother and keep his secrets, do no damage to his mother nor see it done by others. He shall not waste his mother's goods, shall not commit fornication nor contract matrimony nor play at dice, cards or other unlawful games . . . he will be paid 8 pounds Pa. currency, a new sute of apparel, a set of bench tools fitting for a journeyman.

When Henry Luse of Greene County died in 1886 he left a very unusual will:

. . . I believe that reason is the only true guide to what is right and that the only way to arrive at a just conclusion on any subject is to thoroughly weigh and consider the evidence on both sides. It is my earnest desire and will that my children be furnished with and permitted to read all kinds of liberal, religious and scientific works, such noble works as those of Thomas Paine, Voltaire, D. M. Bennett, R. G. Ingersoll as well as those of their most able opponents. It is my will that the guardians of my children shall instill into their minds the habit of *thinking* and *reasoning* and believing things to be true because they are reasonable rather than because they are popular. . . .

* * *

In 1787 Pennsylvania enacted a law whereby the president or vice-president in council could cause a town to be laid out complete with both in and out-lots. Out-lots usually involved some acreage and were reserved for the use of the state. As much land as was deemed necessary was set aside for a courthouse, "jaol," and market house. It is interesting to note that from very early times in Europe, to keep or establish a mar-

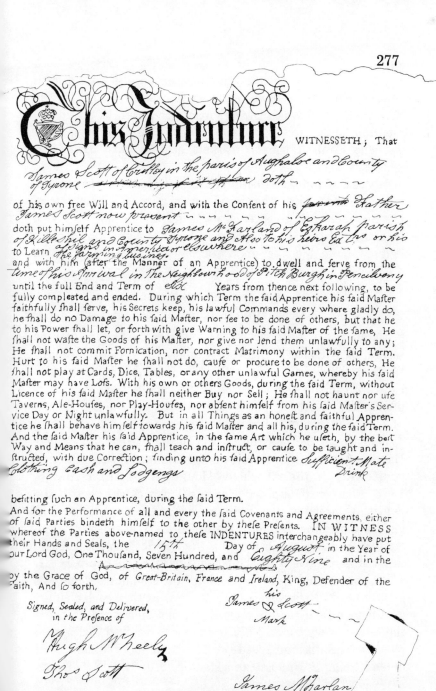

This Indenture

WITNESSETH; That

James Scott of Crilley in the parish of Aughaloe and County of Tyrone ~~~ doth ~ ~ ~ ~

of his own free Will and Accord, and with the Consent of his ~~parents~~ *Father James Scott now present* ~ ~ ~ ~

doth put himself Apprentice to *James McFarland of Eskarah parish of Killeshil and County Tyrone and Also to his heirs Ex Ers or his assigns in America or elsewhere* ~

to Learn *the farming busines*

and with him (after the Manner of an Apprentice) to dwell and serve from the *time of his Arrival in the Neighbourhood of Pitch Burgh in Pencilveny* until the full End and Term of *Six* Years from thence next following, to be fully compleated and ended. During which Term the said Apprentice his said Master faithfully shall serve, his Secrets keep, his lawful Commands every where gladly do, he shall do no Damage to his said Master, nor see to be done of others, but that he to his Power shall let, or forth with give Warning to his said Master of the same, He shall not waste the Goods of his Master, nor give nor lend them unlawfully to any; He shall not commit Fornication, nor contract Matrimony within the said Term. Hurt to his said Master he shall not do, cause or procure to be done of others, He shall not play at Cards, Dice, Tables, or any other unlawful Games, whereby his said Master may have Loss. With his own or others Goods, during the said Term, without Licence of his said Master he shall neither Buy nor Sell; He shall not haunt nor use Taverns, Ale-Houses, nor Play-Houses, nor absent himself from his said Master's Service Day or Night unlawfully. But in all Things as an honest and faithful Apprentice he shall behave himself towards his said Master and all his, during the said Term. And the said Master his said Apprentice, in the same Art which he useth, by the best Way and Means that he can, shall teach and instruct, or cause to be taught and instructed, with due Correction; finding unto his said Apprentice *Sufficient Mate Drink Clothing Cash and Lodgings*

befitting such an Apprentice, during the said Term.
And for the Performance of all and every the said Covenants and Agreements, either of said Parties bindeth himself to the other by these Presents. IN WITNESS whereof the Parties above-named to these INDENTURES interchangeably have put their Hands and Seals, the *15th* Day of *August* in the Year of our Lord God, One Thousand, Seven Hundred, and *Eighty Nine* and in the

by the Grace of God, of Great-Britain, France and Ireland, King, Defender of the Faith, And so forth,

Signed, Sealed, and Delivered,
in the Presence of

Hugh McNeely

Thos Scott

James ⟨his Mark⟩ Scott

James McFarlan

Apprentice contract, 1789, made out in county Tyrone, Ireland. From James McFarland estate file, Washington County Courthouse.

ket house was a privilege and granted by the courts. This carried over into town practice in Penn's Southwest in Brownsville and Washington, particularly; there is no known mention of a market house in Waynesburg although there were no doubt, farmers' markets held in most towns and villages.

Houses of public worship and burial places for public use were included with other public areas at a time when assembly members had to swear to a belief in God and to divine inspiration from the Scriptures. Churches were considered a "great public blessing upon society and burial a Christian duty."

Hannastown and the Western
Declaration of Independence

Hannastown, founded by Robert Hanna shortly after he served as a justice in Bedford County, before formation of Westmoreland on February 26, 1773, is historically significant both locally for its current "dig" and nationally, as producing the "Western Resolves" a year before the Declaration of Independence in Philadelphia.

Greensburg became the county seat in 1787, but Robert Hanna's log tavern northeast of Greensburg, is where the first court west of the Allegheny Mountains was held April 6, 1773. Many had opposed Hanna's Town as the seat of the courts, thinking it too unimproved and crude. When Virginia's Governor Dunmore returned to Williamsburg from western Pennsylvania, he set up the District of West Augusta as a counter move to that of Pennsylvania and February 21, 1775, the Virginia Court opened at Fort Dunmore. There was great conflict between the two systems as they each claimed jurisdiction over the same territory, but their purposes were the same. In March of 1775 both courts resolved that a well-regulated militia composed of gentlemen and yeomen could defend them, as opposed to a standing army which they considered a threat to liberty. It was also in March that a notice appeared in Philadelphia comparing the rights of people in England where for one thing, judges were independent of the crown and the people, and in America, where they were dependent on the crown.

The Pennsylvania Assembly met May 1, 1775, and on the sixth, Governor Dunmore wrote again to London saying that a "certain Patrick Henry and a number of deluded officers" had taken up arms and dispatched letters which excited the people.

The two meetings reported held on May 16, 1775, produced almost identical resolutions which have become famous as forerunners of the Declaration of Independence, and written four days before the well-known Mecklenburg Resolution.

There appears to be no complete list of those who composed the resolves at either meeting; it would be possible to make a tentative listing from names of regular attendants at both courts. Attorneys have remarked about the "dignity of the writing" and it would be safe to assume that Squire Thomas Scott, a 1773 justice in Westmoreland and bar member, and Arthur St. Clair were in attendance at Hannastown. It would be easier to name the Virginia contributors by referring to those who were leaders at the Catfish Council of War in 1777.

While May 16 is the date around which resolution publicity revolves, the official notice as given in Volume II of *American Archives Correspondence, Proceedings*, etc., for May 1775, reads:

At a meeting of the Committee of Westmoreland County, held at the Court-House the 23d of May, 1775, present the Rev. Thomas Smith, Chairman, and fifteen other members of said Committee.

A discussion of Lord Dunmore's seizure of the powder is reviewed as a "determined plan of wicked administration to enslave the Colonies, by first depriving them of the means of

At a Council of War held at Catfish-Camp in the District of West Augusta on Tuesday the 28th day of January Anno Domini 1777

Present

Dorsey Pentecost Co. Lieut
John Cannon Col.
Isaac Cox Lieut Col.
Henry Taylor Major

} Yohogania County

David Shepherd Co. L. Lieut
Silas Hedge Col.
David McClure Lieut Col.
Samuel McCullogh Major

} Ohio County

Zackquill Morgan Co. Lieut
Jno. Evins Major

} Monongahela County

Captains

John Munn	David Owings
David Andrew	Henry Hoagland
John Wall	John Pierce Duvall
Cornelias Thompson	James Brinton
Gabriel Cox	Vinson Chin
Michael Rawlings	James Buckhannon
William Scott	Abner Howell
Joseph Ogle	Charles Orecraft
William Price	John Mitchell
Joseph Tumblenson	John Hoagland
Benjamin Frye	Pearson Virgen
Matthew Richey	William Harrod
Samuel Mason	David Williamson
Jacob Libler	Joseph Gilmsay
Peter Peasonor	Charles Martin
James Rogers	David Davis

} Capt.

Colonel Dorsey Pentecost was unanimously Chosen President of this Council, whereupon Col. Morgan, & Col. Shepherd Conducted him to his Seat

Col. David McClure was unanimously Chosen Clerk

Original list of those present at 1777 Council of War at Catfish Camp.
Washington and Jefferson College Library historical collection.

resistance," followed by the resolves (herewith the five resolves abstracted):

1st. That the dissatisfaction discovered by the people of this Country . . . proceeded . . . from a well grounded alarm, occasioned altogether by the Governour's late conduct, which clearly evinced his steady pursuit of the . . . ministerial plan to enslave us.

2d. . . . his Lordship, since the late unhappy differences between Great Britain and the Colonies have subsisted, hath deprived us of the constitutional mode of application, by refusing to have an Assembly.

3d. That so far from endeavoring or desiring to subvert our ancient, and to erect a new form of Government, we will at the risk of our lives and fortunes, support and defend it, as it existed and was exercised until the year 1763. . . .

4th. That His Majesty's Council, who advised the Proclamation before-mentioned, have not acted as they were bound to do from their station in Government, which ought to have led them to be mediators between the first Magistrate and the people, rather than to join in fixing an unjust and cruel stigma on their fellow-subjects.

5th. That the thanks of the Committee are justly due to the Delegates of the late Continental Congress, and to the Delegates from this Colony particularly, for their prudent, wise, and active conduct, in asserting the liberties of *America;* and that the design of Government which, in some instances, we are informed, has already been carried into execution, to deprive them of all offices, civil and military, tends manifestly to disturb the minds of the people in general; and that we consider every person advising such a measure, or who shall accept of any office or preferment, of which any of the noble asserters of *American* liberty have been deprived, as an enemy to this Country.

—James Davenport, Clerk

Under Proceedings for July the following letter was written from Philadelphia July 25, 1775, "To the Inhabitants of Pennsylvania and Virginia, on the West Side of Laurel Hill":

"Friends and Countrymen: It gives us much concern to find that disturbances have arisen, and still continue among you, concerning the boundaries of our Colonies. In the character in which we now address you, it is unnecessary to inquire into the origin of these unhappy disputes, and it would be improper for us to express our approbation or censure on either side, but as representatives of two of the Colonies, united among many others for the defence of the liberties of *America*, we think it our duty to remove, as far as lies in our power, every obstacle that may prevent her sons from cooperating, as vigorously as they would wish to do, towards the attainment of this great and important end. Influenced solely by this motive, our joint and earnest request to you is, that all animosities which have heretofore subsisted among you as inhabitants of distinct Colonies, may now give place to generous and concurring efforts for the preservation of every thing that can make our common Country dear to us.

"We are fully persuaded that you, as well as we, wish to see your differences terminate in this happy issue. For this desirable purpose we recommend it to you that all bodies of armed men, kept under either Province, be dismissed; that all those on either side, who are in confinement, or under bail, for taking a part in the contest, be discharged, and that until the dispute be decided, every person be permitted to retain his possessions unmolested.

"By observing these directions, the publick tranquillity will be secured without injury to the titles on either side. The period we flatter ourselves, will soon arrive, when this unfortunate dispute which has produced much mischief, and as far as we can learn, no good, will be peacably and constitutionally determined.

"We are your friends and countrymen,

Patrick Henry	John Dickinson
Benjamin Harrison	Benjamin Franklin
Richard Henry Lee	Charles Humphreys
Thomas Jefferson	George Ross
	James Wilson"

Shortly after the Pennsylvania courts met at the Hanna Tavern, a hewed log courthouse was erected. First prothonotary was Arthur St. Clair and Robert Hanna was first presiding justice before the court of common pleas where Hugh Henry Brackenridge made his legal debut. "It was on the Forbes Road to Fort Pitt and the periodic return of the court brought together a hardy, adventurous, frank and open-hearted set of men from the Redstone, Georges Creek, Yough, Monongahela and Catfish Settlements with those from Old Westmoreland."

The burning of Hannastown July 13, 1782, as the last hostile act of the Revolutionary War, is a stirring tale. The town contained about thirty log houses but most of the inhabitants had fled during the early summer to escape the Indians. Those who remained had assembled in the fort and laid plans for carrying on. During the night of the twelfth they took groups of horses at full trot over the plank bridge across the ditch around the fort to make it sound like reinforcements were arriving. Two old drums were found and with a fife, they made music through the night to the sound of the hoofbeats.

The stockaded fort, Robert Hanna's house, and the courthouse escaped destruction, so the records were not destroyed. Robert Hanna made his will April 19, 1785, and it was probated May 2 of the following year:

> ... my land on which is Hanna's Town is to be sold unless it be established as a county town, then it should be laid off in lots to be sold and the proceeds to go to my estate, my wife Elizabeth and my four daughters. ...

The courts removed to the new county seat of Greensburg on January 7, 1787, where another log courthouse was erected on the site of the present court buildings. In 1798 it was replaced by a brick building and in 1856 the county erected a "stone Roman porticoed temple-type" courthouse. The present French-renaissance Westmoreland County Courthouse

284

was completed in January 1908. The bell which hung in the 1798 brick building was cast in Philadelphia in 1813 by George Hedderly in his foundry. The bell has been preserved by the county historical society and bears the legend: "I will sound and resound unto Thy people, Oh Lord, and call them to Thy Word."

Among the well-preserved records housed in the courthouse at Greensburg is the beautifully executed continuance docket showing the first court before William Crawford, Esq., and his justices April 1773. In July term the court met before Robert Hanna as Crawford had been removed "as a Virginia officer." By 1781 both Hanna and Crawford were serving together on the grand jury.

On September 23, 1969, the Westmoreland County Historical Society in league with the county commissioners, purchased the "Hannastown Courthouse Farm" from the family of William Steele and the day the deed was recorded, Jacob L. Grimm, research associate for the Carnegie Museum, with members of the Allegheny Chapter of the Society for Pennsylvania Archaeology, and a determined group of "diggers" started to excavate where Hannastown had once stood. Arrangements were made with the Smithsonian Institution to identify, evaluate, and interpret artifacts as they were found. In the summer of 1970 students

Design for National Air Mail Week May 15-21, 1933, showing the Charles S. Kilpatrick bronze statue of Colonel William Crawford "burned to death at the stake by Indians 1782." Statue on grounds of Connellsville Carnegie Library. From *Courier*.

from the University of Pittsburgh earned credits during a six-week "dig" and excavation continues.

In September 1972 the Westmoreland County Bicentennial Association was incorporated and has gone "all out" to support the rebuilding of Hannastown. Since September 1969 more than 400,000 artifacts have been found, including pieces of Delft ware, Bonin and Morris porcelain, white salt-glazed stoneware, lead bullets, rings, buttons, English and Spanish coins, including pieces of eight, several coins dated in the 1600s, all from 300 square feet of test pits in seven areas of occupation.

From photograph by Bob Donaldson, Greensburg *Tribune-Review*, of 1973 reconstruction of Robert Hanna Tavern at Hannastown, with Charles M. Stotz and Huck Schultz in foreground.

Old Hanna's Town is not what is known as Hannastown today, which used to be Jamison No. 2 Coal Works. The site of Old Hanna's Town is a mile or so southwest, and some four miles northeast of Greensburg, where it can be reached by Routes 119 and 819. The first building erected on the exact side of the original as determined on July 13, 1971, on the anniversary of the burning of the town, is the Robert Hanna log house. Under the supervision of architect Charles M. Stotz working with Carl "Huck" Schultz, the log construction expert, the project calls for the stockade fort which was almost the same size as Fort Duquesne, Foreman's Tavern, and five other log houses, on sites uncovered by the archaeologists.

During a recent visit with "Huck" Schultz at his handsome log and stone home high on Laurel Hill, details of early construction and materials were discussed at length by the man who built Fort Ligonier, the largest totally timber fort in the U.S.A., and other restoration and reproduction buildings in Penn's Southwest. In the rebuilding of the Hanna house, it was decided that they would lay up the logs in one day with a crew of firemen from various parts of the county. The logs, shingles, and hardware were fashioned with the same kind of tools and in the same way as in the eighteenth century. The Greensburg *Tribune-Review* reported:

> It was a bunch of hard-working volunteers, in the tradition of their pioneering forefathers, who gathered to help build Robert Hanna's cabin on July 11, 1973.

The Names and Courthouses
of Washington, Pennsylvania

In the spring of 1771, David Hoge of Cumberland County purchased two large acreages at the location long familiar to traders and frontiersmen as "Catfish Camp." Delaware Chief

Catfish had three different camps where the town of Washington was laid out.

According to Earle Forrest's feature article on Catfish Camp for the 150th anniversary edition of the Washington *Reporter* in 1958, the old chief had his first camp at a large spring at the corner of South Main and Maiden which shows on the 1781 map as "Catfish Spring." After it had been covered over for years and piped under the B&O tracks, when the present Firestone Station site was prepared, the shovel struck the spring and the flow of water was so heavy work had to be suspended while it was drained off.

About the same time that Hoge purchased the Hunter and Reynolds claims (1770-71), William Huston built a log cabin at Catfish Camp at a point in the rear of the Fifth Ward School on East Maiden. The foundation of this cabin, and its springhouse with the lower logs still resting on their stone foundations, was discovered in 1954 when workmen drove a tunnel for a large sewer. Aside from being the home of Washington's first settler, William Huston, the cabin is significant as the stopping place on the night of April 29, 1774, of a group of frontiersmen including George Rogers Clark and Michael Cresap. The murder of Chief Logan's family on April 30 was blamed on Cresap although Clark vindicated him by saying they had left the country on their way back to Redstone Old Fort and had stayed with Huston.

As other settlers began to close in at Catfish's main camp, he moved to another spring about 1788 where South Main, Prospect, and Park avenues converge. The third and last move was to a spring in Shirl's Woods in the Catfish Creek bottom opposite the Chestnut Street Station. It is not known when Chief Catfish and his followers left the section entirely and moved to the Scioto River in Ohio where he died.

Of all the early towns we've tried to trace, Washington had the most trouble deciding what its name would be. After "Catfish Camp" it was called "Dandridge" very briefly, and then named "Bassett Town" for William Bassett, a Hoge relative. When David Hoge finally received permission to lay out the seat of Washington County on his lots "for a Court house and Prison, given gratis" he had the map drawn by surveyor-draftsman David Reddick, who signed it on October 13, 1781. Marginal notes on the original map which is preserved in the municipal building, indicate in addition to the four town squares fronting on Main Street from Pine Alley on the North to Cherry Alley on the South, where Catfish Creek emptied into Chartiers a "Great Plain given by Mr. Hoge for a Commons of about 70 or 80 acres" was located due west of present Spruce and Chestnut streets.

The area chosen for the new town was in the midst of a thicket of black and red hawthorn, wild plums, hazel bushes, scrub oak, and briers. A traveler going through Washington in 1788 wrote: "The town was a street of houses, all new, with stumps of trees in the street; there are some handsome buildings, a courthouse and jail in the center of town." In 1845, William Darby, who had come as a boy with his parents in 1782, remembered picking hazelnuts where the courthouse then and now stands. Boyd Crumrine tells us that David Hoge's log cabin where the first sessions of Washington County courts were held, stood on the northwest corner of Main and Strawberry Alley. The early map shows a log structure on Lot 58 with a tavern on the opposite corner of Strawberry and a stone building kitty-corner.

In one of Ray Knestrick's amazing series of *Observer* articles on "Old Buildings on Main Street" he relates that David Hoge built his log building before the town was laid out in 1781 and sold the property to settler John Dodd whose brother, Charles, was licensed to keep tavern there in April 1781. It was in this log tavern room that the first Washington County Court was held and receipts still exist for payment to Charles Dodd for use of his room to hold court in.

All those who were original lot purchasers in David Hoge's new town received a "ticket" which read:

This will entitle —— to receive a sufficient title, subject to one dollar a year in specie, for a lot marked in the original plan of said town No. —— provided there shall be erected thereon, on or before the thirtieth day of October 1784, a house 18 feet square at least, with a stone or brick chimney therein. [There were 272 lots in the original plan.]

Among the John Hoge Papers is an envelope marked "Important" and it contains a paper written November 27, 1782, by David Hoge, appointing his son, John as his attorney regarding the "Town of Bassett . . . to collect from any who purchased lots or out-lots in the town and to settle with William Forbes or James Wilson, and to dismiss the Power of Attorney given to Daniel Leet in Washington County, October 22, 1781." With this paper is a detailed contract for alterations to the courthouse signed by Andrew Swearingen, John Hoge, Matthew Winton (contractor for the building with Daniel Harris), Samuel Davis, Joshua Hazelrigg, Philip Coe, and William and Elizabeth Hoge.

The log courthouse built in 1787 burned in the winter of 1791 and the Hoges presented a block of four 60 x 240 foot lots to the Washington Academy which had used the top floor of the destroyed courthouse. Crumrine's note regarding the campus area states "on which lot the lime-stone building (present Administration) was located can be told by measuring westward from Lincoln. That building was ready for occupancy in the fall of 1795 for on February 16, 1796 the Trustees asked the Legislature for money to build the wings." Lot No. 102 in the academy block was presented by the Hoges to Martha Washington.

The second courthouse, begun in 1792, was of red brick with a frontage on Monongahela (now Main) Street of fifty feet and a depth of seventy feet. It was two stories with a mansard roof and in 1794 a cupola was constructed on the flat central portion "as high from the roof as the roof was from the ground, and pointed like a church steeple." The Pittsburgh *Gazette* reported that after the second Washington

County Courthouse was built, people thought the cost too high and refused to pay taxes to support it. One thousand pounds was raised to build the first courthouse and jail destroyed by fire in 1791. The vestibule was floored with brick and there were long seats like church pews in the central hall for the public. The courtroom and jail were on the first floor. Earle Forrest reported the cupola was so well constructed that when the courthouse was demolished in 1839 and they planned to crash the cupola to the ground, men in the street with ropes pulled it from its supporting wooden pillars but it fell intact. The weathervane of an arrow mounted by a two-foot diameter gilded ball was found to be pierced with many bullet holes.

Isaiah Steen who had a chair factory on the second floor of the Market House and always had special prices on "the

From photograph of third courthouse, Washington County, taken before 1898 showing wooden Washington statue on cupola dome. Washington *Reporter*, 1958.

most fashionable and elegant Windsor chairs" during court week, was paid eight dollars in 1810 for making the chairs for the Prothonotary's Office.

The July 1817 *Examiner* gave notice of a proposal to build cells for prisoners in the "jaol yard" with stone and labor to be bid by the perch, carpenters' work by the measurement and iron work by the pound. The grand jury specified that the jail walls and ceilings were to be whitewashed twice a year and floors were to be washed once a week. This jail building must have followed quarters in the courthouse but it is not known how long it functioned.

David Shields, town clerk, advertised for laborers to work on the streets of Washington and to return any tools which belonged to the "corporation." Curbstones were to be in place within ten days of May 31, 1811, on the part of Main Street that was being paved.

The third courthouse was built at a cost of $25,000 and the cornerstone was laid in 1840. It was also of red brick with two very high stories and another massive, but well-proportioned cupola on which stood the first wooden statue of George Washington. Crumrine in his *Bench and Bar*, published 1902, commented on the good taste that went into this building as well as the excellent acoustics of the courtroom. This is the courthouse that was sketched by Henry Howe in his view of "the central part of Washington" from the National Road corner at Walnut and Main Street. Shortly after the third courthouse was built, the Washington Brass Band played on the balustrade of the courthouse cupola, and this was no doubt, a regular occurrence.

An agreement was made with James P. Millard to furnish a statue of General Washington for the dome of the new courthouse. On May 6, 1842, after quite an interval of waiting for the statue to be delivered, the commissioners sent a letter to Mr. Millard in which they informed him that because of his failure to furnish the statue on time as agreed, they would decline accepting it.

Mr. Millard did not take the rejection lightly and brought Judge Baird from Pittsburgh to handle his suit for $257. The case was given to the new Washington law firm of Alexander Murdoch and John L. Gow. Murdoch had just been admitted to the bar and this was his first case, with trial set for August 31, 1843. The jury found for the plaintiff for $152 and Mr. Murdoch collected the remainder from the commissioners and won the case.

There seems to be little or no detail concerning the wood used or the carving details but early photographs indicate a large figure. Shortly before construction of the fourth courthouse, there was much grumbling about not enough room, with stacks of old books and records in the cellar; farmers who were in the depths of winter "mud and misery" wondered why they had to help pay for such an elaborate and expensive new courthouse as the commissioners had planned. Sidewalk watchers kept asking, "What will become of the old effigy when the courthouse is torn down?" That problem was solved when the statue was sold to Charles Hallam. "One of the knees had become affected by a kind of necrosis even though the body maintained its erect position overlooking the town for sixty years." Hallam strengthened the legs, gave it a new coat of paint and mounted it on a pedestal in the yard of his home on the corner of Highland and Locust. There are two versions of the last days of wooden George Washington. *Observer-Reporter* columnist Ray Knestrick sent the writer a note about the statue and said, "several years ago it was in an old stable in the Lincoln Street section." The other version is that when the Point Service Station was established on the Hallam corner, the statue was thrown down and covered with fill dirt.

The large iron bell cast by A. Fulton of Pittsburgh which had hung in the bell towers of both the second and third courthouses, was given to the Elm Street School where it rang for years. It was then presented to the city fire department and was eventually hauled to the junkyard from where it was rescued. The three-face clock installed in the third courthouse at a cost of $1,000 was sold to James McCullough, Jr., of Kittanning.

The Market House was considered a part of the "public buildings" and was first located on the Beau Street end of Courthouse Square, which at the time David Reddick drew his map, was on the corner of Ohio and Monongahela. A meeting of citizens of the borough was held on Monday, January 16, 1815, and it was resolved to change the seat of the Market House from the north to the south side of the Public Square for the purpose of erecting a new banking house on the northeast corner. Later a second Market House was constructed under the direction of Dr. Absalom Baird and Judge Alexander Addison on William Seaman's lot on

294

Main Street for $202.96. Market days were Wednesday and Saturday from daylight to 10:00 a.m. and it was strictly understood that no one was to buy any place else in town or they would be fined five dollars.

The fourth and current courthouse was begun in 1898 and dedicated in 1901. The story of this elaborate and expensive Italian Renaissance structure is well known. Unlike its predecessors, the fourth courthouse dome has held two different statues of Washington. The first figure placed in 1900 was made of terra-cotta. The head seemed to become a target for lightning strikes and after brick contractor Charles Curran had repaired it several times with concrete, a bronze replacement was recommended. The monument firm of Simon White & Son had charge of the job. The statue was designed by Chicago sculptor Leon Hermant and cast by the American Art Bronze Factory in Chicago. It stands fourteen feet and it must have been quite an undertaking to erect for it is recalled that it stood on the courthouse lawn for some time but was finally hoisted into place in 1927.

'Good Day, General Greene'

Before it was separated from Washington, the area of present Greene County con-

From Jim Fuller 1969 photo of present bronze statue of Washington on courthouse dome.

sisted of the townships of Morgan, Cumberland, Greene, Franklin, Richhill and a small portion of Finley. When Colonel John Minor, boatbuilder and first settler, was elected to the assembly in 1791, he began his fight to have Greene set apart as a county. During his third term in office his measure passed both branches of the legislature and received Governor Mifflin's approval February 9, 1796. On the same day, the first trustees for the new county were commissioned: David Gray, Stephen Gapen, Isaac Jenkinson, William Meetkirk, and James Seals.

These men were authorized by an act of the General Assembly of Pennsylvania to purchase a tract of not over 500 acres near the center of the county on which they were to lay out a new town. Stephen Gapen and Isaac Jenkinson worked on the plan as both were qualified draftsmen and surveyors. The two hundred town lots were immediately advertised in Pittsburgh and Washington papers as proceeds from their sale were needed to complete the purchase price and to "erect a courthouse and prison." The land consisted of a 158½-acre tract called Eden purchased from Thomas and Eleanor Slater. The county seat was named for General Anthony Wayne, hero of the western frontier, who was anything but "mad" and who also never set foot on the soil of the townsite. Waynesburg is often confused with another Pennsylvania town, Waynesboro, and except for the national publicity accorded its *Rain Day* celebration on July 29, is little known in other parts of the U.S.

Nathaniel Greene, for whom Greene County, Pennsylvania, is named, was born in Warwick County, Rhode Island, May 27, 1742. His formal education was sketchy and of short duration, but through his own efforts, he acquired a fair knowledge of English grammar and other subjects and made some progress in the study of law. After joining the Continental Army, he distinguished himself in 1777 at the Battle of Brandywine, where so many of Penn's Southwest pioneers fought. He was then made commander of the Southern

First map of Waynesburg town lots recorded in
Greene County Deed Book No. 1.

296

troops and showed outstanding ability in restoring confidence in the army. The last engagement in which General Greene took an active part was the defeat of the British at Eutaw Springs which put an end to their power in South Carolina. He was known as "Washington's favorite General" and held his command until the end of the Revolutionary War. On June 19, 1786, at the age of forty-four, he died from the effect of a sunstroke at Savannah, Georgia.

Approaching the town of Waynesburg from any compass point, the erect figure of General Greene atop the classic dome of the courthouse cupola dominates the landscape. One hand doffs his tricorn to one and all as if we had just shouted up to him, "Good Day, General Greene," and the other hand is on his sword in a gesture of alert defense; and we are reminded that the Indians knew well his alertness and called him "the man who never sleeps." Altogether, a pleasant prospect which residents and visitors alike have been viewing for the past one hundred twenty-five years.

There were no suitable buildings in the area loosely described as "Jackson's Fort" so first county court with Judge Alexander Addison of Pittsburgh presiding was held on January 2, 1797, in the log house of Virginia Justice Jacob Cline, who had been dispensing justice and keeping tavern since his arrival in the Muddy Creek settlement. The 1798 tax list describes the dwelling as "24 x 18, 1½-story with 2 windows of 8 lites each" which seems rather limited for either tavern purposes or to accommodate court sessions, until completion of the log courthouse on Greene Street in Waynesburg.

Greene County historian Andrew J. Waychoff hunted as a boy all over the Cline land and knew exactly where the old buildings had stood. He described the present marker location as but a short distance from where Jacob Cline built his second cabin. President Judge Glenn Toothman of the Thirteenth Judicial District, who has taken a great interest in both the restoration and preservation of the present courthouse, carved the rustic sign which marks the gardened roadside site on Route 21 between Carmichaels and Waynesburg.

* * *

In considering western Pennsylvania courthouses, the Pittsburgh restoration architect, Charles Morse Stotz, has written:

> Three eras of courthouse building occurred which were more or less contemporaneous with the style periods of early architecture: the log period before 1800, the Post-Colonial period before 1830 and the Greek Revival between 1830 and 1860. Thus, before 1860 most of the older counties had built three courthouses . . . only a few remain from the period up to 1860 and these are of the Greek Revival period.

When another early Greene historian, L. K. Evans, addressed a Fourth of July gathering at Jefferson in the centennial year 1876, he reviewed the building of the first courthouse: "They then proceeded to erect a log building which is still standing in a remarkably good state of preservation and makes a comfortable dwelling for the family of Charles S.

Drawing of log courthouse on Greene Street from centennial 1796-1896 souvenir medals in the shape of a keystone and a star. Note the rocking arm for raising bucket from the town well. Courtesy Mrs. Lewis's Antique Shop, Waynesburg.

Hickey" (who was married to trustee David Gray's daughter). Then the building was used as a scour house for wool until 1890 when it became a tourist home. Today, after nearly 180 years of service, this same structure, surely one of the few existing original courthouses built in the eighteenth century, still stands on Greene Street, covered with weatherboarding and Johns Manville, posing as a modern store for George Albert's heating and metal work concern.

In the volume of *Laws of Pennsylvania 1790-1802*, a law passed March 21, 1797, stated that qualified electors residing in Franklin Township "shall hold elections at the house now occupied by Thomas Slater in or near Waynesburg, until a courthouse is built." With a good crew, log buildings didn't require much time to erect and on April 2, 1797, by unanimous consent of the court and commissioners, court was moved to Waynesburg where it convened in a log house on Lot 195 between Whiskey Alley and Morgan Street.

In the capsule history of the court and courthouse of Greene County prepared by Judge Toothman, the statement was made that "early records of the construction of the first courthouse on the present site are incomplete and very meagre, but it appears that a brick building of a very modest dimension was first erected around 1800." During many prowling excursions in the stone-lined cellar vault of the Recorder's Office, the writer came upon a worn, calf ledger entitled *Greene County Auditor's Expense Book from 1809* and from a careful reading of dozens of entries, quite a complete picture emerges of activities on Court House Square through 1822.

A rare drawing of the second courthouse by Henry Howe was found in the 1843 volume of Sherman Day's *Recollections of Pennsylvania*. The Irish-born brick-moulder, Robert Milliken made the bricks and acted as chief bricklayer; Milliken lived on Lot 42 at Richhill and Franklin where the Dr. Phoebe Jane Teagarden house stands, but records show the early brickyard was located on the Commons of Waynesburg College.

Notes from the 1809 Ledger

Samuel Kincaid, one of the first of a long list of "Gaolers" was paid $12.50 early in May 1810 for jail repairs. Reed & Paxton were paid $4.75 for stationery and repairs. Joseph Seals, whose house and blacksmith shop were on Lot 77 between Strawberry Alley and High Street, was a tavern keeper in 1797 and active around the courthouse as jurist, road viewer, repairman, and for a while, he served as jailer. There were many entries for the activities of James, Joseph, and William Seals during the period of the ledger. After the death of Joseph Seals, Joseph Gorrell took over in April 1814 as jailer and in November he was paid for leveling the "Gaol Yard" and supplying wood for the stoves. James Seals, Sr., attended to the "prison" and Asa McClelland, the local gun and locksmith located on Lot 118 at the corner of High and Blackberry Alley, repaired a lock for the "Gaol" in October.

Patrick Martin, listed as a Waynesburg lot-holder in 1798, was paid $1.75 for cleaning the courthouse in 1814 and by 1819 he was constable of the township. The early Syphers family makes its appearance in the records when Jacob Syphers was paid $15.75 for the "Courthouse Hall" in June 1815 and was back in August for another $19 in repairs. Martha Davis, Hannah Shoock, and Catherine Renny were some of the women of the community who were regularly paid for "scrubbing" the courthouse. In August, Martha received four dollars for the job, and no doubt, walked to and from home and brought her own lunch!

The public well came in for a lot of attention. In November 1815 before winter set in, William Reese was paid $120 for work on the well and the following January received another $16. Samuel Houlsworth was paid $7.50 for "Gaol blankets" early in 1816 and as he lived out Jefferson way, they probably came from the Clarksville Woolen Mill. William

Seals charged five dollars for prisoner's fetters which he turned out in the family blacksmith shop. There was a Jones & Batson Hat Shop on Lots 80 and 81 at the corner of High and Strawberry Alley and Nathaniel Batson had only to cross the street to cry the sale of unseated lands in front of the courthouse in 1816.

While histories of the county buildings indicate a stone jail was constructed about the same time as the brick courthouse in 1800, we find that in August 1816, considering the many repair items for the jail, either the 1800 building was in a state of collapse, or an entirely new one was erected. At that time former Indian hunter Richard Morris was paid $100 for "Gaol walls" but the material used is not mentioned. Morris lived on Lot 45 at the corner of Blackberry Alley and Franklin in 1799, the same lot occupied at one time by Jonas Smalley, another courthouse "regular" by 1811. By the end of August there was a $50 payment for a "Gaol wall" and in October, Morris was paid $150 for work on the "Gaol Yard." When the *Pennsylvania Gazetteer* of 1832 described Waynesburg, it mentioned the courthouse "of brick and handsome, with a stone jail."

Jonas Smalley who had a carpenter shop on Lot 198 next to the horse mill down on Cumberland and Greene, built the Gallows for six dollars in January 1817 and on April 24 he was paid eight dollars for hanging the "Court House Bell." This first courthouse bell and the stoves were the only items not given to Contractor Bryan when he was permitted to take the materials from the old courthouse during razing in 1850. The bell was recast in 1926 and today strikes the hour and tolls, in the traditional manner, for fifteen minutes before court is in session. In 1971 when the county commissioners entered into a contract with the I. T. Virdin Clock Company of Cincinnati to install a new clock in the courthouse cupola, provision of a striking mechanism that activates the old bell was part of the agreement.

In February 1817 William Seals made a pair of hinges for

the "Gaol door" for $1.25 so the old jail must have been functioning as Morris was still constructing jail walls in August and received a payment of $300 for the final wall in November. We can only guess where all the oil and paint

From Henry Howe's sketch of 1840 view of "Central Part of Waynesburg" in Sherman Day's *Recollections of Pennsylvania.*

ordered from James Robb was used. They either decided to paint the exterior brick or after the plastering was finally finished, they painted all the rooms. George Heisey and Jim McClain, Abijah McClain's oldest boy, hauled it to Waynesburg, probably from McClain's boat landing which was called Newport until it became Rice's Landing. Robb did the painting, starting in June and he was still painting well into the fall months when he received $130. In August, Rees Hill, who was a Revolutionary War veteran and a squire, was paid eleven dollars for "Gaol lath" but there was no entry for plaster expense. Most plaster at this early date was made from the local yellow clay with a little sand and horsehair and little if any lime, so the workmen who slithered it on were probably just paid for labor or repair work.

William Mitchner came in to town from Jefferson to shingle and lath and was paid $72.75. Rafters for the roof came to $35.50 and Thomas Fletcher supplied another $15 worth of nails from his store at Jefferson. After the new jail was completed they must have decided the courthouse needed major repairs after nearly twenty years, so Jonas Smalley was contacted and began to reroof in October. The winter must have been mild or at least dry, as he worked through into January 1818. There was no end to the nail purchases, and Thomas Fletcher delivered another twenty-seven dollars worth on November 24 and Joseph Gorrell did some more leveling in the jail yard, probably at the request of the grand jury whose members were always concerned with the condition of prisoners. Joseph Gorrell, active for many years at the courthouse, was a member of a family identified with trading and soldiering with Colonel Bouquet at the time of the French and Indian War. Gunsmith Asa McClelland was called in again; this time to make a key for the courthouse lock for which he charged one dollar.

Completely validating the Henry Howe sketch of the 1800-1850 courthouse, on December 10, 1817, W. Robb was paid $41.50 for "painting the cupalow." John Work supplied the "Gaol" with six dollars worth of blankets; the weather was changeable that fall and winter as orders for still more blankets alternated with work on the courthouse roof. William Bradshaw supplied "bedding" in April 1818 when Aaron Day was "Gaoler." With the roof repaired, the cupola painted and the bell hung, the finishing touch was a payment of $1.50 to Samuel Jewel (wheelwright) "for turning the ball for the courthouse." Certainly from the careful detail of this ball in Howe's sketch, it must have been gilded and a handsome ornament.

Escape by picking the locks must have been frequent for again in June 1818 James Seals repaired both courthouse and jail locks, and Daniel Devall of Devall's Hill received $76.12 for handling prisoners to the Philadelphia prison. After a jail escape in September 1818, Sheriff Adam Hays was paid for "bringing in Fetty" supplying his handcuffs and guarding him in jail. Aaron Day and Joseph Gorrell were both paid jailer's fees in 1818. Isaac Teagarden who was commissioned Greene County sheriff November 23, 1820, cried the sale of lands from the courthouse steps.

Jonas Smalley was paid another $112 for courthouse roofing for which John D. Work supplied $11 worth of nails and this was followed by a payment of $25 to Jim Robb for "painting the courthouse roof," which probably referred to flashing and metal work as this was the period of chiefly shingled roofs.

Referring to the Howe sketch of the "central part of Waynesburg," author Day described the "courthouse and public offices" so we assume the wings on each side of the main building were used for offices. John Rush and Jonas Smalley paid substantial amounts in July and August for roofing the "office buildings" for which job John Work was paid thirty-three dollars for more nails. "Jaoler" Aaron Day ordered more blankets, Tobias Henry cleaned the public well for two dollars, and Jacob Johnson, who had served under William Crawford as a frontier ranger in 1793, was paid sixty-five dollars for "work on the Gaol House."

The courthouse was heated by wood-burning stoves and James Seals, Esq., who had no foolish pride, continued to be paid for cleaning the courthouse stove pipes. In December it was very cold and Seals supplied a stove for the splendid sum of one dollar; it must have been a jury-rigged affair which barely got them through the winter, for by March of 1819 Adam Hays submitted a bill for twenty-five dollars for a stove and pipe for the courthouse. "Jaoler" Aaron Day scrubbed the building himself in August when Tobias again cleaned the well.

In March 1820 Adam Hays, who was also a council member, was paid twenty-four dollars for ringing the courthouse bell during 1818-19. Adam went on ringing the bell and sup-

From photo by J. S. Young of Washington, ca. 1875, showing man working on Greene County Courthouse statue, iron railing around courthouse yard, and brick store of Sayers and Hoskinson. From Catherine Sayers, Waynesburg.

plied the court with candles, ink pots, and printed stationery through 1820 but by February 1821 he had been replaced by Ephraim Sayers who supplied ink stands, candles, and snuffers.

It may be that by the time Henry Howe sketched the court buildings, such primitive items as the "gallows" and the "public block" had been phased out for they are not visible on the High Street grounds. In March 1821 the "Public Block" was repaired by Smalley and Amos Pyatt helped with repairs in September. The official bell ringer in 1822 was Sheriff Lot Lantz. The old Jacob Lantz farm was located where there is now an industrial park and the local airport but Lantz lived in town where he was a tavern keeper. In March 1822 Peter Hiller called the sale of the state road, Aaron Day supplied a table for the jail for one dollar in November, and we come to the end of the auditor's ledger.

* * *

In November of 1849 the Greene County Grand Jury recommended a new courthouse be built and the prison improved "upon such plans and terms as the commissioners shall deem suitable." Authorities admired the neighboring colonial-style courthouse erected in Fayette County in 1847, and entered into a contract with Samuel and John Bryan to build a replica of the one they had just completed following "the general plan, style and materials" with some variations:

> ... to place a full portico in front of the house, and if cast iron caps can be procured, then the Corinthian capitols are to be adopted, and cellars built. ...

The price of the two-story brick building was set at $16,500 with $6,000 to be paid upon completion, $5,000 in one year, another $5,000 the next year, and the final $500 the third year. There was another feature of the Fayette Courthouse that appealed to Greene and that was the large statue of Lafayette mounted on the cupola. David Blythe, the eccentric artist who was then living in Uniontown, had carved the figure of Lafayette for $125. When the Greene County commissioners asked Blythe to name a figure for a similar statue of Nathaniel Greene, the artist, elated by the praise for his first statue, said he would make one for $300.

This was just too much, so the commissioners told Blythe his price was too high and anyway, "We have some good woodcarvers who will 'do' General Greene for $100." They had in mind redheaded Bradley Mahanna who ran a little woodworking shop on Greene Street not far from the old log courthouse.

When the new courthouse was ready for the cornerstone laying on June 25, 1850, artist Blythe was present with fellow Masons; he stayed at the Bull's Head Inn and made up some locally famous and rather acid doggerel verse which he exchanged with Waynesburg's poet, William Siegfried.

* * *

Working from a sketch made by the German Dominicas Haas whose original trade was pointing and fitting up German clocks brought to this country in the rough to avoid duty, Bradley made the statue

Drawing of General Nathaniel Greene by John F. Pauley for the 1926 wooden statue atop the courthouse cupola.

from poplar plank which Haas probably called "poblar" as it was spelled phonetically in the records of early German sawmill and cabinet men. The statue was carved in Mahanna's log shop and was nine feet high. In the ca. 1875 photograph of the courthouse, there is a ladder up to the dome on the cupola with a man apparently painting or repairing the wooden figure that stood another fifty years, when the December 24, 1925, Waynesburg *Republican* reported:

> The worst fire in the history of Waynesburg! Took the Hotel Downey . . . then a strong west wind blew so the cupola of the Courthouse caught fire, which with the wooden statue of General Greene was soon a burning mass and fell to the ground. . . .

Shortly after arriving in Waynesburg in 1968 the writer became curious about the history of the courthouse statue and was told to see John Pauley on Richhill Street who had made the sketch for the replacement figure. The visit with John Pauley and his sister Geraldine, descendants of generations of publisher-editors of the Waynesburg *Democrat-Messenger*, was interesting in several directions. They told their favorite story about their grandfather, W. T. H. Pauley who had been a printer's devil at thirteen. When he was seventeen he had a yen to talk to Andrew Jackson about some political questions, so he walked from his home in Youngstown, Ohio, to Jackson's home, The Hermitage in Nashville. His knock was answered by a Negro who told young Pauley that Jackson was ill (died in 1845), and could not see him, but the ex-president heard their voices and called down to ask who was there. When he was told that a young lad had walked all the way from Youngstown just to talk to him, Jackson said, "Invite him in and I will come down." Young Pauley was particularly interested in knowing who the next vice-president would be and when he posed the question, Jackson told him it would be James K. Polk. After the visit was over and Pauley had walked back to Youngstown with his preferred bit of news, he was so tired he didn't wake up until late in the morning after election day when people came in to see him and said, "You'd never guess who was elected vice-president," and he surprised them by naming Polk.

In discussing General Greene, John gave some details of the fire and the statue that had not been found in newspaper accounts. During Christmas Eve of the disastrous fire at the Downey House across Washington Street from the courthouse, an ember had lodged under the tail of General Greene's coat and eventually set the figure on fire. When it fell to the ground they were able to save one arm and part of a hand intact and from these pieces, John was able to make a proportioned sketch of the full figure a trifle larger than the original as it was now ten feet high. The original sketch which hung in the commissioners' office could not be found but it was identical to the copy drawn especially for this chapter by John Pauley. As templates they made plasterboard cutouts of the four sides of the figure and took these down to the Acklin Lumber Company in South Waynesburg where they hung on the wall for years.

Mr. Acklin gave the job to his head carpenter, Albert Wise, and with some help from John Pauley, they started to construct the figure from 350 board feet of laminated yellow poplar plank. Another man who worked on the job was Ed Day, who at age eighty, told the writer that he used a foot adz and the process was called "whittling." All of this work was carried on in the Acklin shop which had an eighteen-foot ceiling. "Spike" Ullom, the talented stair-builder of Waynesburg, also worked off and on at Acklin's lumberyard and he became rather jealous when he noted all the town interest in Albert Wise's carving. One day he went down to the shop and sputtered, "Just you wait, one of these days I'll whittle him out a coat, and then you'll see!" "Spike" could build literally anything, especially a fine stairway, but he couldn't read a rule. He is remembered by Waynesburgers as one of the town "sights" half running down the street holding the measurement of a board or a screen door between his outstretched arms. Furman Rinehart recalled that "all the Ulloms were carpenters and were born with hatchets and saws in their hands."

One of the most time consuming details recalled was the carving of the plaited pigtail of the general's colonial hairdo; the thick pigtail attached separately to the back of the head was blown down at one time and disappeared. Also tedious to achieve, were the fingernails and the lapels, buttons, and epaulets on the coat.

When the statue was completed, it weighed 600 pounds and it was no mean job to hoist it by man power to the top of the rebuilt cupola. Ed Day related that before the statue was placed, they loaded it into a truck and took it to Jacktown where they were celebrating the opening of a new road. No one else in the area was able to recall that wooden General Greene made a sort of farewell tour over the hills to present Wind Ridge and back, but several townspeople could recall the scaffolding and careful work with pulleys and cables to take the figure up by stations to the top. When Ed Day was asked if he had ever been inside the cupola, he said, "It was the dirtiest place in God Almighty's world you ever saw in your life." On a Wednesday afternoon, November 17, 1926, with a program arranged by the Greene County Historical Society, the unveiling of the statue took place.

In 1972 when Waynesburg steeplejack Miles Davin renovated the figure, he "sharpened" the seventy-one inch long sword, reset the black walnut eyeballs, and reshaped the copper hat which was made by tin and coppersmith W. A. Helphenstine, who had also covered the dome with copper sheets. One-inch reinforcing rods were inserted from the hips through the bottoms of the feet so the figure should be good for another fifty years.

The large, well-proportioned courtroom on the second floor was renovated and redecorated in 1968 with areas of white with the emblematic blue and gold and touches of gold leaf. The coat of arms of the state was painted on the wall behind the judge's bench. Handsome blue hangings at the many-paned windows with their original bubbly glass and the old mahogany benches and railings combine to make it one of the most beautiful and historic courtrooms in the commonwealth, dedicated "to the people of Greene County whose integrity, individualism and intense pride in their heritage and purpose, have built an edifice of freedom of which the Court and Courthouse are but a symbol."

Sherman Day described the town early in 1840:

> The private dwellings, of which there are about eighty, are many of them of brick or sandstone. No stage-coach runs from the town in any direction. Large droves of cattle pass through towards the eastern markets, the clay roads along this route acting more kindly upon their feet than the stony surface of the national road.

Waynesburg Lot Holders
1796 to 1815

Lot

1-4 Unknown
5 Jacob Burley, house/tavern, 1799
6 Unknown
7 Daniel McFarland, 1799
8-9 Unknown
10, 11, 12 Thomas Laidley, 1799
Samuel Clarke held No. 10 in 1796
13 James Hook, 1799
14 Unknown
15, 16 John Boreman after Daniel McFarland in 1799
17 Daniel McFarland, 1799
18 Unknown
19 John Corbly, 1799
20 Unknown

Lot

21, 22 Jacob Adams, 1799
23 John Corbly, 1799
24 Ephraim Sayers, 1799
25-27 Unknown
28-31 William Meetkerke, 1799
32 Unknown
33 David Dodd, house/tanyard, 1799
34-36 Isaac Jenkinson, 1799
37 Samuel Hill, 1799
38-41 Daniel McFarland, 1799
42 Robert Milligan, brickmaker, 1799
43 Ephraim Sayers, 1799
44 Nathan Hughes, 1799
45 Richard Morris, 1799
Jonas Smalley, 1811

Lot

46-47 Unknown
48 Daniel McFarland, 1799
  Robert Adams, 1800
49-50 Unknown
51 John and Jacob Burley
52 Daniel McFarland
53 Britton Lovett, weaver, 1799
  Isaac Jenkinson, 1800
54 Unknown
55 Jacob Smith, 1799
56 Moses Foster, 1799
57 John Denny, 1799
58 Christian Tarr, 1799
59-61 Unknown
62 Jay Thompson, 1799
63 Daniel McFarland, 1799
64 Anias Conkling, 1799
65 Unknown
66 Thomas Smith, 1799
67 William Hunter, J.P., 1799
68 Unknown
69-70 Daniel McFarland, 1799
71 Thomas Slater, 1799
72 Unknown
73 John Smith, 1799
74 Christian Sellers, 1799
75 William Dolloson, carpenter, 1799
76 Samuel Kincaid, tailor, 1812
77 James Seals, 1799
78 Reason Pumphrey, 1799
79 Ephraim Sayers, 1811
80-81 Jones & Batson Hats, 1799
82 Hugh Wilson, 1799
83 Wm. Crawford Store, 1811
84 Unknown
85 John Simonson, 1799

Lot

86-87 Barnet Rinehart Inn, 1812
88-89 Unknown
90 John Denny, 1799
91 James Wilson, postmaster, 1812
92 Jacob Burley Tavern, 1799
  Joseph Seals, 1812
93-95 Unknown
96 William Hunter, J.P., 1799
97 Wm. Colwell, tailor
98 John Denny, 1799
99 Unknown
100 Daniel McFarland, 1799
101 Isaac Jenkinson, 1799
  Thomas Slater, 1811
102 David Blaine, saddler, 1800
103 John Bradford, 1799
104 Unknown
105 James Eagon, 1799
106 Unknown
107 Stephen Gapen, 1799
108 Richard Phelan, mason, 1799
109 Unknown
110 Asa McClelland, 1811
111 Geo. Remley, joiner, 1799-1812
112 Unknown
113 Daniel Pipes, 1799
114 Unknown
115 Samuel Jewel, wheelwright, 1811
116 Jay Thompson, 1799
117 Unknown
118 Asa McClelland, gunsmith, 1812
119 John Simonson, 1799
120 Robert Adams, shoemaker, 1799

Lot

John Inghram Inn, 1811
121 Parker Campbell, attorney
122 Jay Thompson, 1799
123 Nathaniel Jennings, joiner, 1799
124 Joseph Penticost, 1799
125 Jay Thompson, 1799
   Wm. Seals, blacksmith, 1809
126 Christian Tarr, 1799
127 Robert Cather Inn, 1811
128 John Smith-Wm. Sharrad, carpenter, 1799
129 Samuel Clarke, 1799
   James Eagon, 1811
130 Thomas Slater, 1811
131 Thomas Rinehart, 1799
132 Jacob Hager, potter, 1799
133 Christian Tarr, 1799
   Nicholas Hager, potter, 1803
134-135 Unknown
136 Gabriel Blackeney, Washington storekeeper, 1799
137 Barnet Rinehart, blacksmith, 1799
138 Henry Slater, 1799
139 Reason Pumphrey, 1799
140 Elijah Inghram, blacksmith, 1799
141 Unknown
142 Thomas Kent Tavern, 1799
143 Unknown
144 John Simonson, attorney, 1799
145-146 John Boreman, 1799
147-148 Unknown
149 Samuel Seals Tavern, 1799
150 Isaac Pettit, 1799
151 Isaac Jenkinson, 1799

Lot

152 Henry Fesler, cooper, 1799
153 Robt. Milliken, brickmaker, 1799
154-155 John Boreman, Esq., 1799-1811
156 Boreman residence, 1799
157 John Gapen, 1799
158 Joseph Penticost, 1796
159 Unknown
160 Gabriel Blakeney, 1799
161-163 Unknown
164 Jay Thompson, 1799
165 Gabriel Blakeney, 1799
166 John Simonson, 1799
167 David Hoge, 1799
168 Unknown
169 Philip Ketcham Tavern, 1799
   Nicholas Johnston Est., 1811
170 Unknown
171 Jay Thompson, 1799
172 Gabriel Blakeney, 1799
173 Barnet Rinehart, Sr., 1799
174 Unknown
175 Jas. Workman Horse Mill, 1813
176 Unknown
177 Gabriel Blakeney, 1799
178-179 Unknown
180 Hugh Wilson, 1799
181-182 Unknown
183 William Seaton, judge, 1799
184 Unknown
185 Joseph Penticost, 1796
186 Henry Russell and Jonas Smalley, carpenters, 1799
187 James McGowan, 1799
188 John Simonson, 1799

314

'Give Me Liberty or Give Me Death'

The statue of Patrick Henry stood for forty years on the dome of the bell tower of the old Monongalia County, West Virginia, Courthouse. It was placed on the dome August 20, 1851, and removed some time during 1891.

The man who signed his name to many early deeds in Penn's Southwest as first American governor of Virginia, P. Henry was born in Studley, Hanover County, Virginia, May 29, 1736, of Welsh and Scotch ancestry. He had a classical education, was married at eighteen, and worked at various jobs unrelated to either politics or law until he began the serious study of law and was admitted to the bar in 1760. He was spoken of during the critical years just before the American Revolution as "America's unalterable and unappalled great advocate and friend." In 1778 at the suggestion of George Rogers Clark, Patrick Henry drew up plans for the operation of Clark's expedition to the Northwest. He was especially known for his oratorical eloquence and his great patriotism. He died June 6, 1799.

The idea for the statue was proposed by L. S. Hough according to data in the "Scrapbook of Max Mathers" in the West Virginia Collection at the West Virginia University Library, Morgantown. Generals Greene, Lafayette, and Washington were already firmly in place on the handsome cupolas in their respective counties, so about 1850 Mr. Hough made plans to have Ebenezer Mathers carve a twelve-foot figure of Patrick Henry for the recently built courthouse in Morgantown. Unlike the other figures which were constructed of laminated poplar plank, Mathers carved his figure from a single poplar log and used one knife for the entire operation.

Art critics have noted the "remarkable carrying powers of the statue which make it a good likeness from a distance as well as nearby." It braved the storms and weather in wooden silence for many years until the new and present courthouse was built and the statue relegated to Russ Huston's tin shop on Pleasants Street. It was "forgotten" until some time during World War I when members of the Elizabeth Ludington Hagan Chapter of Daughters of the American Revolution decided to have the statue renovated and presented to the Morgantown High School. James H. McGrew, local banker, financed the repair and painting and they worked with a small replica

From photograph taken in 1973 of Patrick Henry statue in Morgantown High School.

figure which Ebenezer Mathers had carved at the time he did the large figure. In a ceremony on October 25, 1916, the renovated courthouse statue was presented to the high school. Unfortunately, when the school moved into new quarters, the statue was left in a corridor of the old building where it now stands, painted an offwhite and looking rather forlorn.

P. Henry has been described as wearing a black coat and scarlet cape, and with his barrister's powdered wig, if the figure were done in color similar to the Lafayette statue in Uniontown, and placed on a pedestal, this remarkable statue would again assume some of its rightful dimension.

What an interesting dialogue could and probably did take place during their lives among these great men, who stood gazing out of their wooden eyeballs into the blue and green hills of Virginia and Pennsylvania for the last half of the nineteenth century, daring people to forget them and their deeds.

Monsieur, le Marquis de Lafayette

The first courts in Fayette County were held on the site of the present courthouse which was called the "Central Public Grounds," conveyed by Uniontown founder Henry Beeson on March 16, 1784, to the trustees for "six pence." The building was originally used for school purposes and served for the courts until the first courthouse was erected and completed in 1796 at a cost of $1,362.53. It was a two-story brick with the courtroom on the first floor and the grand and petit jury rooms on the second floor. In two years there was a need for more room and two two-story wings were built, flanking the main building.

During court session February 4, 1845, this building was destroyed by fire but all records were saved. Plans were immediately made for a new building and contractor Samuel Bryan came from Philadelphia to do the job. The courts were held in the Presbyterian Church until the second courthouse was built and dedicated in 1847. The design of the eighty-five by fifty-eight foot red brick building was essentially classic and the model for the present courthouse in Waynesburg. The well-proportioned belfry held a town clock and the statue of General Lafayette on the dome. David Blythe, the artist chosen to carve the figure, is referred to as "an eccentric character born in East Liverpool, Ohio, in 1815" who was living in rooms over P. V. Hook's store in Uniontown in 1846. At this time, Blythe was composing satirical verse and painting portraits. (Details of Blythe as an artist can be found in Chapter 20.)

Blythe was paid $125 for the Lafayette figure which is constructed of two-inch pegged poplar plank and dimensioned nine feet tall, three feet wide, and about thirty inches front to back. The fee was collected by subscription and for a model, he worked from a large wood engraving owned by Nathaniel Brownfield of Uniontown, probably engraved during the time of Lafayette's visit to America 1824-25. The carving was done in the old West School house, later used as a Girl Scouts headquarters.

In 1890-92 the present stone Italian Renaissance courthouse was erected at a cost of a quarter million dollars, and the Lafayette statue was placed on the grounds for a number of years until it was realized the figure was deteriorating from exposure to weather, and it was taken inside. After David Gilmour Blythe was "discovered" and had become very

From photo of David Blythe statue of Lafayette in "Two Hundred and Fifty Years of Art in Pa.," Westmoreland County Museum of Art, 1959. "Rare example of folk art," according to museum curator, Paul A. Chew.

collectible as a nineteenth century painter, the faded statue of Lafayette in the courthouse corridor, where it had been gathering dust for years, was also suddenly discovered. It was restored and painted; black coat and boots with red tops, light gray trousers, a peach vest, red buttons, white stock, black tie and red-brown hair. The statue then traveled to art exhibitions all over the country during the 1960s. It became a smash hit at an exhibit in Atlanta, Georgia, where it was viewed with great interest and appreciation by the French ambassador and his wife.

It is possible to have a little chat with the marquis any day in the lobby of the Fayette County Courthouse, where with top hat and cane in hand, he views us all with wooden composure.

* * *

A paragraph or two about the village of New Geneva does not belong with courthouse material, but it does tie in with the figure of Lafayette and the subject of town planning as we have followed the erection of county seats.

Pierre Charles L'Enfant born in Paris in 1754, came to America at the same time as Lafayette as a French army lieutenant, and fought on the side of this country. He was close to both Washington and Lafayette and as a talented, adaptable companion, he was called on to do all sorts of jobs: portraits, sketches, maps, etc. Almost entirely self-taught in architecture, we know him best as the planner and architect of the Federal City and today he is considered to have been the first city planner in the modern sense. Pennsylvania Archives contain an interesting letter from the secretary general of Pennsylvania to L'Enfant dated October 11, 1792:

> To Major L'Enfant at or near Alexandria in Virginia, to inform you of a grant of 20,000 pounds by an Act of Assembly to purchase a lot of ground at the southwest corner of Market Street near Ninth and erect thereon a suitable building for the President of the United States. . . .

When L'Enfant was soldiering in western Pennsylvania, he apparently worked with Albert Gallatin in laying out the plan for New Geneva. First known as Wilson's Port for George Wilson who lived near the mouth of the Georges River, the land was deeded by Wilson to Gallatin shortly after his arrival in 1780. Involved were two tracts, Elk Hills and Three Hills, and more difficult, hilly terrain can hardly be imagined. It must have taken all of the young Frenchman's ingenuity to lay out the formal plan with a "fancy" town square as it is recorded in an early Fayette County deed book.

16

HORSE RACING—RED FOX CHASERS—
PICTURE BARNS—HORSES

THE FIRST ARTICLE in a series of columns by McCready
Houston entitled "Your Brownsville and Mine" appeared in
the Brownsville *Telegraph* on June 14, 1937, and continued
at regular intervals for over thirty-five years until Houston's
death in California in 1973. Born in the "Neck" over his
dentist father's colonial office, McCready Houston wrote
with great flair and flavor of the old days. Like Earle Forrest
of Washington County who regularly made trips deep into
"Old Greene" for stories with atmosphere, he visited early
towns, his ear cocked for tales.

On a trip to Carmichaels many years ago, he talked with
Fremont Flenniken about one of the county's favorite pas-
times, fox hunting, or chasing. Flenniken told about the fox
hunters who came by steamboat from Pittsburgh to the
Rice's Landing wharf where it was his job to pick them up in
a hack and drive them to Carmichaels where they kept their
horses at his father, James Flenniken's stable. A group of
wealthy men who enjoyed hunting would ship their fox hunting mounts and hounds to Carmichaels; at one time there
were twenty-five horses and seventy-nine hounds at the Flenniken stables for two weeks.

In spite of its quiet, rather pious atmosphere, the town of
Jefferson, a few miles inland from Carmichaels, was also a
center for fox hunts and early photographs show hundreds of

local horsemen ready to start off from near the old Presbyterian Church. And there is the legend of Thomas Jefferson
hunting there although the town of Jefferson was named by
Thomas Hughes because of his politics.

The late Ed Huffman of Waynesburg, when in his eighties,
reminisced about the days when he was a great hunter. Sometimes during the best season in October and November when
the weather was still good, they would be out all night with a
big bonfire on a hilltop going from after dark until midnight.
The early people preferred night hunting and would take a
jug of whiskey or cider, turn the dogs loose and let them run
listening for them to pick up the noise or scent of a fox.
Another way was to let the fox hunt all night and just before
daybreak, set out after him. The object, of course, said Mr.
Huffman, was "never to get the fox" and sometimes they
would hunt one fox all winter. This did not always hold for it
is also said that the sport was so popular at one time they had
to import foxes from Missouri. Mr. Huffman gave up fox
hunting about 1918 when the roads made it almost impossible to control a pack of hounds or "keep the fox." Sometimes the hounds would get mixed on a track that crossed
that of their fox and then the intricacies of fox hunting could
be very exciting. Huffman preferred day hunts because he
wanted to see the excitement.

Greene County fox hunts are mostly on foot in recent
years because they are enjoyed greatly by many who cannot
afford to keep both hounds and horses. They were always
quite different from the social hunts of Virginia with a few
exceptions. Across the river at Friendship Hill during the
early years of coal exploration, when the name of J. V.
Thompson loomed large in both coal and banking, Thompson
purchased the old Albert Gallatin estate near New Geneva.
His granddaughter, the late Evelyn Thompson Martin who
raised and rode fine horses, held fox hunts on the grounds of
the estate that were grand affairs with overtones of "Old
Verginny." A few old-timers recall being invited to the Mar-

tin hunts when they gathered in the courtyard of the old mansion and were served lavish breakfasts.

In very recent years, to escape increasing development and ever higher land values and taxes, several Virginia breeders of fine horses, including the famous Lipizzan, have moved their operations to Penn's Southwest. One of the most notable of these horse farms is in Donegal Township, Washington County, on Dutch Fork. During one of the recent Dutch Fork hunts in late October, some fifty riders from surrounding "hunts" followed a course through Donegal and into West Virginia. The hounds were cast at 1:00 p.m. and hunters and hounds were out till nearly five o'clock, running the course. Members of the Dutch Fork Hunt Club assemble until the "Gone Away" call of the hunting horn sends the mounted hunters surging after the hounds, hot on the scent of a fox. As recently reported in a feature article in the *Observer-Reporter:*

> Nowadays the fox in many cases has gone so far away from the drama of the hounds and horsemen that he is no longer a part of the hunt. Shifty old Reynard is being quietly dropped from the ancient pageant of the fox hunt from horseback, to be replaced by a rag soaked in fox scent that is dragged over a course where the hunters want to go, not where a broken-field running fox might lead. No one seems to miss the departure of the fox too much. Everything else remains, all of the tradition and pageantry.

In the spring of the year, the Dutch Fork Hunt Club holds the annual ceremony of "Blessing the Hounds" with local ministers presiding, followed by the traditional sherry. This is followed by the Dutch Fork Hunt Horse Show in June which is run over a course being developed into one of the best in the country. Included in the jumps is one constructed to resemble a railroad crossing with a plywood train complete with sound effects bearing down on horse and rider.

Historically, aristocrats rarely hunted the fox but if they had to, they sought an isolated woods, blocked all the fox holes for several days before the hunt, when the moon was full and the time about midnight. Holes were blocked with a small fagot pushed into the opening with a mound of earth on top. With two crossed sticks, the fox will not come near. Three or four dogs were first released, then a few more. They considered the best season for fox hunting to be January through March when the trees were bare and the fur at its best.

The Rolling Rock Steeple Chase held the last of September at Ligonier at the foot of Laurel Hill in Westmoreland County, with its social overtones, the bagpipe players and races, is better known but is another story.

Purdon's *Pennsylvania Statutes* contain regulations which provide that any fox hunting club or individual owning and hunting an organized pack of twenty or more fox hounds to hunt foxes for sport from August 1 to March 31 is engaged in a legal activity but there is an annual permit fee of $50 for organized packs; in hunts with hounds under permit, individuals are not required to have a license or tab.

Traditional in Greene County and described in considerable detail by early historians is the "Circular Hunt." This hunt developed as a means of combatting bands of wolves which made it virtually impossible for settlers in the "wilds of Virginia and the Fish Creek Hills" near the Pennsylvania border, to raise sheep. In 1834 there is a record of a circular deer hunt and circular fox hunts continued until about 1900 and one of the last was held near Canonsburg February 22, 1901. There is something traditional about fox chasers and Washington's birthday and in Greene County there is an annual Fox Chasers Dance held on February 22. Here is a description of a circular hunt held in the mid-1800s:

> The outline of the circle of the hunt is given . . . the third line to the head of Dunkard Fork of Wheeling Creek and down it to Thomas Courtright, Jacob Nyswanger and Connell's Mill to the mouth of Crabapple Run. The fourth line thence by the road from Durbin's Mill to Samuel Teagarden's and by road to Sargent's Mill.

Two persons superintended each station. Each Captain recruited ten men with one of them able to blow a horn with skill. All signals of the horn passed from right to left from the starting point at Byellsby's [near present Wind Ridge]—a long, well-filled note on the horn by a signal from the starting station at sunrise. At the proper signal all men stationed at one hundred paces from each other would start toward the center of the circle. There were horsemen on each line who rode along the rear of the line and gave notice to the captains whether the men were advancing too fast or too slow. All game taken was considered the common property of the hunt.

The writer attended a recent meeting of the Greene County Red Fox Chasers Association which meets regularly at the fairgrounds in Waynesburg. At one time membership in the group was around 300 but it is somewhat smaller now. President Bill E. Davis owns "the best fox hound in the United States, 'Davis Ozark Sportsman,' a Walker hound" that has won "best of show" and "best of opposite sex" trophies in several states, but having won the national title, can no longer be shown in competition.

Bobtown, near the site of the old Paw Paw Stand in southern Greene County, was named for Bob Maple whose French ancestors came to America with the Huguenots in 1721. In Bobtown near the Maple family, lived a great fox hunter by the name of Clark. When Clark died he requested that he be buried, not in the Clark Graveyard, but "in the woods beyond on top of the creek hill where I so often hunted so that I can hear the hounds run." The sound of fox hounds chasing must be as contagious as the sound of bagpipes to some.

* * *

When Earle Forrest took his grand tour of Greene County in 1952, he stated in an *Observer-Reporter* article about the trip that he had gone primarily to see the famous "picture barn" with the fox hunting scene. When he got to the Armstrong farm near Jefferson, he found that the barn had been torn down in 1950, the same year that the man who painted the scene, had died.

William Stark, known during his years in the Jefferson area as "Bill Stark, roustabout," came to Greene County in 1916. People living in the town who remember Bill said he came from Fayette where he had followed the bakery trade. In the days when bread was still kneaded by hand, he developed a skin poisoning from the scale of dried dough which forced under his fingernails. There were probably other reasons, but the story goes that he left his home and trade and crossed the river to Fredericktown where he worked in a mine until it shut down and then drifted to various farms, working as a handyman.

When Stark reached Jefferson, winter was coming on and he applied for work to Lee Armstrong, a local farmer who raised hunter and racing class horses; Armstrong was also a great fox hunter. Bill Stark was given a place to stay on the Armstrong farm for the winter and it soon became apparent that he had great skill with a bit of chalk or paint as he sketched neighbors who stopped by sometimes on the back of the barn door. He could do a quick crayon portrait in cartoon style that was completely true to life. Soon he was lettering on trucks, painting signs for church suppers and

Drawing from only known photograph of Armstrong "Fox Hunt Barn" mural painted by Bill Stark. Courtesy of Frances Armstrong Murphy and A. E. Moredock for the enlargement.

bazaars, and staying with people in the neighborhood, in the back of barbershops, and extra rooms. He was remembered and liked by everyone, but his taste for liquor was a handicap for any steady job.

His favorite hangouts were the local barbershops and he painted signs which hung in all of them; one of his favorite themes was a sketch of an old dog lying stretched out with the words, "Old Crust Is Dead." He worked for a time at the Jefferson Lumber Company when he boarded with the Folwells and Harry Folwell who had a local service station recalled him as neat and clean but would never discuss his age or his past. He was also a great practical joker, as fox-hunting Dr. Titus found out.

One day at the Armstrong farm, Stark was asked if he would paint a fox hunting scene on the large hay barn. "I'll do it for a quart of good liquor," was the answer, and the bargain was struck. Dr. S. J. Titus who was one of Armstrong's neighbors in Jefferson had a very fine fox hound. When he found out about the proposed painting he wanted his hound to be shown in the fox chase, so he offered Bill a quart of whiskey if he would paint him. As the story goes, after the dog was painted, Titus reneged on his offer. So Bill Stark changed the gate of the dog to a "trotter" knowing it was a sin to have a dog trot while chasing a fox. The doctor came through on his bet and the hound went back to running. Stark had never seen a fox but used the picture of one on a fruit crate label as his model.

In his article about the picture barn, Forrest reported 1916 as the year the scene was painted and it became famous as far away as Montana and California where pictures and articles had appeared in magazines. Letters to state libraries failed to produce any results, or a better photograph than the small Brownie shot lent by Francis Armstrong Murphy for the sketch in this chapter. It has been a strange quest to search for even one other photograph when hundreds of persons over the years stopped to take pictures of the barn, and come up with nothing. Searches in the area and in Fayette County for other examples of the work of this eccentric but talented primitive painter, or some trace of his family, have met the same fate. Bill Stark died in the Greene County Home in 1950 and was buried in the county cemetery.

Recently the writer saw a copy of a painting "The End of the Hunt" by an unknown artist ca. 1780 which hangs in the National Gallery of Art. This painting is very like the one on the Armstrong barn with stake and rider fence, riders on horseback mounting the fence with running dogs, and it was presented by Edgar Garbisch, formerly of Washington, Pennsylvania, and longtime friend of painter Malcolm Parcell.

The late widow of Dr. S. J. Titus of Jefferson told the writer she remembered another "picture barn" near her childhood home in southern Greene County. The barn was owned by a member of the Fox family, who were, appropriately,

Picture barn on National Road, U.S. Route 40, between Scenery Hill and Washington. Painted for Triangle Oil Company, ca. 1940.

fox hunters, and the scene was similar to the one on the Armstrong barn. The writer was unable to find any trace of the barn or a photograph of it.

Another weathered grey barn at the side of the National Road west of Scenery Hill has the rather startling painting of an elephant in harness, done by an unknown artist for the Triangle Oil Company of Washington about thirty years ago.

* * *

Horse racing, both flat track and harness, has a long tradition in Greene and Washington counties. But racing was not well regarded as a pastime in early days. An early *Constable's Law Manual* provided a chapter on horse racing, and in 1820, acts of the assembly prohibited the activity as a "public nuisance" with heavy fines imposed. Any person caught racing on a public road would have his horses seized by the "Overseer of the Poor." Wagering meant a fine of thirty dollars and for putting up a sign for wagering, the fine was twenty dollars. Anyone caught in the town of Washington galloping a horse was fined one dollar and a newspaper notice in 1795 announced:

> Grooms with their horses are requested to retire to an out-lot or the Commons when serving their masters and not on the cross streets where children pass to and from school and are in danger of having their brains dashed out by stud horses.

In spite of all the regulations, Stockton (Stogden) Lane on the road from Jefferson to Carmichaels and Dry Tavern, is where from very early days down to even later than 1870, the long, straight, level stretch of road was used as a race course. Talks with the late Colonel Charles Faddis on his front porch on a summer evening yielded much detail on Stockton's Lane. Colonel Faddis's Moredock family raised and rode fine horses and at least one of their farms was lost in the feverish betting and racing that went on there. Flimsy board stables were erected at intervals and when drovers from other areas brought their horses through to the river at Rice's

Landing, they often camped along the lane waiting for the river to rise or an available boat. There were horses from Virginia, Kentucky, Ohio, and New York and the betting, gambling, boozing, etc., took place in the little woods at the east end of land owned in 1927 by Samuel Cox.

Searight in his volume on *The Old Pike* wrote about when stagecoach driver Jerry McMullen wished to vary the monotony of driving and stage life, he made a trip to Stockton's Lane to see the races "which occurred at regular periods at that place in that day."

John Stockton was a famous horseman who had come in to the Tenmile Country from "Jersey" before 1800 and settled on George and Rachel Newland's "Yellow Banks" on Stockton Lane. There was a famous horsewoman in more recent times, Sudie Hatfield Savolini of Jefferson, who participated in Madison Square Garden horse shows during residence in New York.

In Clarksville where the racetrack must have been at nearby Sandy Plains, races were announced in the "Sporting Intelligence" column of local papers:

> Races to commence on Wednesday, October 25, 1811. First Day's purse is $40; Second Day's $25 with Sweepstakes on the Third Day; free for any running horse except Squire Hughes' "White Stockings"—races run each day according to the established rules of horse racing.
> —Managers John Heaton, John L. Hovus and Asa Stephenson

In 1810 there was a complaint made in a sessions meeting against a group who, on the way to Washington to inspect and view a road, decided it was a good place to run their horses. One man said, "My Bab can beat any of your horses for a quart of cider," and the race was on! At this same period, innkeepers were cautioned to not allow any cockfighting or horse racing on their premises.

In March 1973 Greene County's John O'Hara reported on "Spring Training" at the local fairgrounds, carved out of farmland in 1913 and lying between Routes 21 and 188 south of Waynesburg. Harness racing, especially at the annual county fair, was big among the farm folk until the automobile, and then interest in sulky racing started to wane. Trotters and pacers faded into memory. In 1957 Del Miller introduced the first Arden Downs Stakes (at the present Meadows track in Washington County), which drew top horses on the Grand Circuit and marked the revival of harness racing in the area.

Greene County with its long tradition of horse lore, is now a very popular place. The annual horse show in May when over 300 of the country's finest horses assemble, is like everything in the area, unpretentious. Young riders wear well-tailored habits with little velvet caps, correct stocks, and their mounts well-groomed and spirited—three-pacers, five-pacers with their tails swishing color in the sunlight. Open bleachers painted red for sitting and gray for feet were muddy with dried clay and it didn't seem to matter if you sat on dry mud. With a southern, mountain drawl a woman next to the writer said about the rather muddy track, "Oh, they can jump in any kind of weather, snow, rain or anything." Excellent Negro riders hinted at the nearness of the Mason-Dixon line. In 1975 the fairgrounds' half-mile oval is surfaced with pulverized limestone and is popular as a year-round facility for training horses which compete on nationally known raceways, especially at the Meadows where racing is an all-year sport.

Early newspapers carried ads for stallions every spring: Jolly Chester, Shillelah, Irish Gray, Young Shakespeare, etc., and recently discovered and "preserved" by recorder of deeds Olga Woodward in Washington County, is the early *Stallion Register*.

Swapping horses was a favorite practice on the frontier and nearly every town in Penn's Southwest had a "Horse Traders' Alley." The Greene County Historical Society has a fine, early ca. 1860 photograph of the "Horse Market" in Waynesburg from the collection of Albert Moredock. When the Jacktown Fair was first held in Wind Ridge, traders came from all over and used a town lot as a campground. It was well recognized that people in Greene County knew just about all there was to know about horses. The Jacktown Fair is known locally as the oldest continuously operated fair in the country. The women of the community were determined to get rid of the rough horse traders camp in their midst, so they had the lot ploughed one year before fair time and planted it to Chinese sugar cane which thrived so that they set up an operation for cane grinding and sugar making.

* * *

The Orndorff Belgian Horse Farm is located on Smith Creek Road south of Waynesburg and the lovely May morning the writer drove to the farm from Brownsville, the seventy-eight year old founder, Charles Orndorff, had just come out of the long horse barn where the stallions are kept in completely enclosed stalls. "Sure, I'll show you one. I'll get my prize winner out."

He unclipped a snap and chain and swinging open the slatted gates, led a very gentle, huge Belgian out and down through the barn. He was a gleaming, dark chestnut with a curly blond mane and a long white Roman nose. Of all the horses he has raised, Mr. Orndorff said this one had the best disposition. For statistics, he was six years old and weighed 2,400 pounds; had sired some wonderful colts and won every ribbon in the United States and Canada for three years running. He mentioned another horse that had been immense, weighing 2,700 pounds.

The farm is very cheerful with most buildings painted yellow with orange trim and as we sat on the clean, well-painted porch, Charlie Orndorff talked horses and auctioneering. In 1924 he bought his first registered Belgian stallion in Illinois and "got into it big about thirty years ago." At one time he had the largest herd in the country and has won more "Firsts" than anyone, with both grand champions at the Harrisburg show.

Orndorff breeds for good feet, legs, and backs and describes his horses as more refined than those raised in Belgium where they are used for cart animals and so are more squatty. Their colors run from dark chestnut to blonds and the group of dams and colts on a hillside looked from a distance, like palominos. He brought out a photograph of himself standing in front of a semicircle of fifteen huge Belgian horses. That day he expected a new stallion from western Iowa, the first horse he has ever bought without going to see it first. We talked about Clydesdales and Mr. Orndorff said he does not care for the breed as the great amount of hair on their lower legs gets full of mud and freezes in the winter.

When we talked about his activities as a stock auctioneer, he laughed and said his wife tells him he "talks down in his guts when he isn't selling" and then he switched to the booming rhythm of an auction call and there was no doubt about his having a tremendous voice. Lamenting the lack of mental arithmetic taught in today's schools, he said he couldn't operate without it. "If you sell by the head you have to know in an instant, the weight and the value—young people today can't figure." This very lively, well-spoken gentleman who is pushing eighty still cries sales at Waynesburg, Uniontown, and one other place, and it is pleasant to know that his granddaughter works with him and is carrying on the breeding and raising of Belgian horses in Greene County. Nearly seventy head have gone to Canada for both show and breeding and many are used by the Amish in eastern Pennsylvania.

17

TWO PREPOSTEROUS SUPPOSITIONS
THAT MAY BE TRUE

George Rexworthy
Son of George III of England

HOWARD LECKEY began his chapter on the Rex family of
Greene County with this statement:

> The story that George Rex was a son of George III, King of
> England, by a morganatic marriage with the beautiful Quakeress,
> Hannah Lightfoot, is a lot of balderdash, just as the statement
> that he wrote with his own hand in his family Bible, that he was
> born in England . . . he did not write, he made his mark.

Data on early settler, George Rex(worthy) in the original
notebook files of Leckey now in the Greene County Historical Society Library, is less contentious than his published
statement:

> George Rex was born near London in 1750, came to America at
> twenty-one years of age, supposedly the son of the beautiful
> Quakeress Hannah Lightfoot and George III who had a morgan-
> atic marriage in Curzon Chapel in Mayfair.

> I have the estate paper of George Rex in 1821 in which he direct-
> ed his friend, Thomas Fletcher of Jefferson to buy a Bible for
> each of his children and in each Bible was his own history of his
> life and family [Leckey does not say whether he ever saw one of
> these Bibles].

He settled on the William Harrod "Drawl" where he erected an Episcopal Church long ago. The Rex property passed to the Thistlewait family in 1907.

In the Leckey-Swainson correspondence of the 1940s, Leckey remarked about the very fine two-story log house on the Rex property which he felt was the original "Kentucky Meeting Cabin" on Warm Springs Run built by William Harrod many years before the property was sold to George Rex and taken down ca. 1932.

Another local historian, Boyd Crumrine, tackled the matter of the lineage of George Rex from a more personal standpoint as he was descended from the marriage of George's daughter, Elizabeth and John Bower of Fredericktown. Crumrine gives data which came from his mother, Margaret Bower Crumrine's Bible account of the family and again, we do not know if this was one of the George Rex Bibles, but it seems likely that it was.

Crumrine says the name "Worthy" was not part of the family name but was a distinctive appellation to denote that George was of noble descent, supposedly the illegitimate son of George III who was induced to come to America where he was kept out of the way and where he received a yearly

Original log portion of George Rex's first home near Jefferson from 1932 photograph in *George Rex Genealogy*. Described in 1798 direct tax list as "2-story log dwelling 20 x 17, 2 windows of 12 lites each."

stipend or pension from England. A careful and competent historian, Crumrine considered the naturalization papers made out in Lancaster County December 8, 1777, as the most important evidence for the link with George III as the name used was clearly "George Rexworthy." The writer found a summons dated January 1, 1800, in Greene County records, naming "George Rexworthy, otherwise called George Rex" which shows that the complete name was used over the years. Also the fact that this paper was written by English-born John Boreman may indicate he was familiar with and supported the story.

The Rex data from the Crumrine family files relates that George was intensely Loyalist at the time of the American Revolution and kept a large, white ox set apart for a barbecue to celebrate the end of what he considered a "rebellion." After first locating in New York State, early in the Revolution he was driven out by "American cowboys of that day" and put on board a ship for return to England, but George had other ideas and had himself landed at Philadelphia where he arranged to meet his wife and three small daughters. "In the dead of winter, by themselves, these four floated in a canoe down the Susquehanna from New York to Harrisburg to meet George. From there they settled on the Juniata." In 1795 George Rex and his family arrived in Tenmile Country and purchased the Harrod's Drawl, then in Cumberland Township.

George Rex was always very reticent about speaking of his own family and descendants had varying versions of what he did say. His grandson, George Rex of Jefferson considered by Boyd Crumrine to have been a very intelligent man, died ca. 1900, and always believed in the paternity tradition.

There is an 1882 letter in the Crumrine Papers from Samuel Bower concerning his grandfather's stone house in Fredericktown and he also wrote "when George III was Prince of Wales he acted as Godfather to George Rexworthy and gave

The Commonwealth of Pennſylvania, to the Sheriff of Greene County, Greeting :

WE command you, _that you Summon_ *George Rexworthy,* _otherwise called George Rea_

late of your County *Yeoman* _if he_ *he* _be found in your Bailiwick,_ _to that he_ _be and appear before our Judges at Waynesburgh, at our County Court of Common Pleas, there to be held the_ *fifth* _Monday of_ *March* _next, to anſwer_ *Valentine Hunter and Elizabeth his wife of a plea of Trespass on the case &c.*

AND have you then and there this Writ. WITNESS the Honourable Alexander Addiſon, Eſquire, Preſident of our ſaid Court at Waynesburgh, the _firſt_ _Day of_ *January* _in the Year of our Lord One Thouſand_ *eight* _Hundred._

John Boreman
Proth.

Summons from Greene County Common Pleas Court records of 1800
signed by John Boreman, prothonotary.

him money to come to America where he dropped the name
of Worthy."

Scott Bower who lives in the stone house begun by Fredericktown mason and gunsmith David Blair in the late 1700s
and added to by John Bower in 1806, lent the writer his
copy of the rare *George Rex Genealogy* published by Leda
Ferrell Rex in 1933. The author is chiefly concerned with her
line from George, eldest son of the founder and his wife,
Margaret Kepler. She quotes from an oath subscribed and
sworn to at Ogden, Utah, July 17, 1929, by the daughter of
son George, Sarah Jane Rex Kelly Beggs when she was
eighty-nine years old:

> I, Sarah Jane Rex-Kelly-Beggs being of sound mind . . . do hereby
> make the following statement for the information and benefit of
> all whom it may concern, that according to my best knowledge
> and belief, I have known by common conversation within my
> father's household and family history of the Rex family from the
> years of my childhood (b. July 17, 1840) that I am a direct
> descendant of Prince George William Frederick, who was later
> crowned George III of England and Hannah Lightfoot, "the fair
> Quakeress" and of George Rex and Margaret Kepler, and of
> George Rex and Jane Black, and of William Winters Rex and
> Mary Ann Mesler.

"The story as I have always known it," writes Leda Rex,
"is that for reasons of state, Hannah Lightfoot and her son
George were brought to America accompanied by a colony of
people among whom were relatives who located in New York
State. She was well provided for with cattle, horses, servants,
material necessities and luxuries such as silver plate which has
been treasured and handed down in the Rex family." In the
Greene County administration of George Rex' estate in 1821
the inventory included a lot of pewter and an unusual item of
"two salvers" which may have been silver.

Records have been produced, according to the Rex volume, showing the legal marriage of the prince and Hannah
and they were very happy together until interference from

the Royal Marriage Act which provided that a marriage of minors without consent of the regent and council was void. As this book states, if George III was born in 1738 and the Jefferson tombstone date for George Rex is 1750, there is obviously something wrong with the idea of marriage at age twelve. The only possibility seems to be that the date of birth for George Rex may have been falsified for "state reasons."

Anne Rex Vale wrote to the author of the *Rex Genealogy* and said she had heard her father, Benjamin Rex talk many times of "Grandfather George Rex I" receiving a pension from George III to the day of his death, which would have been only a year after the death of George III who reigned from 1760 to 1820. Both Hannah and George had red hair and this feature came down for generations in the Greene County Rex family. A marked resemblance to Queen Victoria was also noted. A Chicago member of the family said she found it very difficult to get the older members to talk of their origin. "They would say, 'Let sleeping disgrace lie' and only recently have some of my cousins and I begun to really investigate the matter."

Another family version states that George III married Hannah quite legally two years before he was persuaded by his ministers into a marriage with Charlotte, princess of Mecklenburg. This would have been in 1759 when George was twenty-one but would not work out with a birth date of 1750 for their son. This version gives three children for George and Hannah, one married to an East Indian officer, the second died insane, and the third, George Rex, came to America in his twenties. "I don't know much about him save that he was a pronounced Tory, never mentioned his parentage, had a small income and brought with him some Church of England prayer books and silver marked G.R." There may be a point of contradiction here as we know George Rex instructed Thomas Fletcher to buy a dozen English prayer books for his children.

In 1960 J. C. Long wrote a history of George III published

by Little-Brown which reinforces some of the earlier family statements. Long wrote that a "marriage mill" was conducted in the Mayfair and Curzon Street chapels where clandestine marriages were performed. There was a persistent rumor that George had had an affair with a beautiful Quaker girl, but no concrete proof was found. She was the first to have her name associated with that of George, but there were other romances in his life.

The *Public Advertiser* for September 7, 1770, dealt with a scandalous affair of a brother of George with a commoner and another publication cited threatened to publish "The History and Adventures of Miss Lightfoot." That there was a Hannah Lightfoot and that she disappeared under mysterious circumstances is thoroughly established in documents in possession of the Society of Friends in London. She was a member of the Westminster Monthly Meeting and assisted an uncle in his shop near St. James's Palace. After 1754, Hannah who had been a regular attendant at meetings, no longer appeared and her mother said she had been married but would not tell where she was. It was said she married Isaac Axford in the Curzon Chapel and in April 1757 the will of Robert Pearne left a trust fund to Mrs. Hannah Axford, formerly Hannah Lightfoot. A member of the Rex family tried to learn more of the portrait of Mrs. Axford by Sir Joshua Reynolds which hangs in the gallery of Knole Castle, the Axford seat at Sevenoaks, England, but no further information was found.

It has also been mentioned that George III was devoted to the Quaker persuasion all his life and would have been one except for the coronation oath he was required to take. By 1756 he had an affair with Elizabeth Spencer Pembroke, wife of the earl of Pembroke and did not marry Charlotte until 1761.

For Howard Leckey to have made the statement that George Rex could not write his name is a little ridiculous when his associates and the various items in his estate are considered. The fact that he had nearly $1,000 in cash which was found in the house at his death and held notes on many people would indicate that he very possibly acted as the neighborhood banker. One of his executors was Hugh Barclay, a founder of the Greene Academy in Carmichaels and trustee of the Episcopal Church there and he was also Benjamin Rex' father-in-law. Hugh Barclay was born in Philadelphia in 1763 and his estate papers disclosed that he wore satin breeches and had silver buckles on his shoes. His wife was Ann Darrah whose grandfather had been a Philadelphia merchant and whose summer place was used by George Washington as headquarters during the Revolutionary War. Charles, the twelfth child of George and Margaret Rex, was said to have been very aristocratic in demeanor and played the violin well. Charles married Mary Hickman and left many Greene County descendants.

George Rex(worthy) made his will in April 1817 but it was not probated until May 1821:

> ... to be buried at the north side of my daughter Margaret under a properly carved tombstone ... my friend Thomas Fletcher to purchase 12 quarto Bibles of good print and paper for not to exceed $4 each and 12 books of Common Prayer according to the rights of the Episcopal Church, for my children and grandchild.

An unrelated but amusing George III anecdote appeared in a little volume, *Gauging Epitomized*, published by Benjamin Workman in Philadelphia in 1788:

> After the Revolutionary War, George ordered Thanksgiving to be kept throughout the Kingdom. A Scotch nobleman asked him "For what are we to give thanks? That Your Majesty has lost thirteen of the best provinces?" "No," said the King. "Is it then that Your Majesty has lost 100,000 lives in the contest?" "No, no." "Is it that we have lost hundreds of millions in money for the defeat of Your Majesty's arms?" "No such thing," pleasantly replied the King. "It is to give thanks that it is no worse!"

The Book of Mormon

*(As taken from an historical novel
written by Solomon Spaulding
of the village of Amity, Pennsylvania)*

Alfred Creigh published his *History of Washington County*
in 1870 and in the chapter on Amwell Township, he dwells in

Drawing from photograph of log and frame Amity Tavern taken
shortly before removal. Courtesy of Washington and Jefferson College,
collection of photographs.

some detail on Reverend Solomon Spaulding and the Book of
Mormon. Creigh made this statement: "The Village of Amity
in all coming time will be regarded as the Mecca of Mormonism."

Amity was founded about 1790 by Daniel Dodd, Esq.,
who laid out the town on his land and whose brother, the
Reverend Thaddeus Dodd, preached in the early hewed log
Presbyterian Church. "Both before and after preaching, the
male part of the congregation used to resort to the tavern to

warm themselves, and tavern keeper Solomon Spaulding would read aloud portions of a book he had written."

After the writer's fourth great-grandfather William Seaman died at the old tavern in Amity in 1814, his widow turned the tavern-keeping over to Spaulding and his wife who had just come to town. While the writing was done in Ohio before Spaulding came to western Pennsylvania and people there had been familiar with it, apparently the reading of the novel at the Amity tavern gave rise to the story that Mormonism originated there, which is rather an extreme view, given the facts.

Spaulding was a graduate of Dartmouth College and was known as an antiquarian, having traveled widely to examine Indian mounds and American antiquities for the purpose of tracing the aborigines to their original source, a portion of one of the "lost tribes of ancient Israel." Forced by ill health into retirement in Ohio, while investigating ancient tribes and customs, he wrote a romance based on fiction although it left the impression that it had been found in one of the mounds and Spaulding had deciphered the hieroglyphics.

Creigh quotes from the testimonial letter of seventy-nine year old Joseph Miller who had known Solomon Spaulding:

> Mr. Spaulding kept a tavern and although we understood he had been a preacher, his health failed and he ceased to preach. He had in his possession some sheets of foolscap on which he had written a novel called "Manuscript Found," written to pass the time when he was unwell and portions of which he read to amuse us in the evening in the tavern. Afterward, he thought he would publish it to help support his family.

> Some time since, a copy of the book of Mormon came into my hands and my son read to me from it. I recollected hearing several of the passages when Mr. Spaulding read from his pages, there were a number of passages from his manuscript in the Book of Mormon. I write this that it may prevent people from being led into Mormonism, that most seductive delusion of the devil.

Creigh had also been in correspondence with Spaulding's widow, than a Mrs. Davidson who wrote a letter which originally appeared in a religious magazine published in Carthage, Missouri, in 1839:

> As the Book of Mormon has excited much attention I deem it a duty which I owe to the public to state what I know touching its origin. That it claims to a divine origin is wholly unfounded. . . .
>
> Rev. Spaulding was distinguished for a lively imagination and a great fondness for history. When we were married we first resided at Cherry Valley, New York and from that place we moved to New Salem, Ohio where he failed in health and could not labor actively.
>
> There are numerous mounds and forts in the town, supposed by many to be the dilapidated dwellings and fortifications of an extinct race. These ancient relics arrested the attention of the new settlers, and became objects of research and numerous implements showing great skill in the arts, were found.
>
> Mr. Spaulding being an educated man and fond of history, took a lively interest in all this and in order to beguile the hours of retirement, conceived the idea of an historical sketch of this long lost race. In writing he imitated the style of the Old Testament in keeping with the antiquities. His sole object was to amuse himself and his neighbors; this was about 1812. There was great interest from the neighbors in the story, claiming to have been written by one of the lost nations and recovered from the earth.

The Spauldings then moved to Pittsburgh where he contacted a newspaper editor by the name of Patterson and showed him his manuscript. Mr. Patterson asked to borrow it to read and kept it a long time during which he and Spaulding could never seem to agree on how the book should be printed, so it never was. Mrs. Davidson's letter continues:

> Sidney Rigdon who has figured so largely in the history of the Mormons, worked in the Patterson Printing office at this time and it was well known that he had access to the Spaulding manuscript. After the book material was finally returned to my husband, we moved to Amity where he died in 1816. I kept the manuscript after his death and it is at the home of my daughter in Massachusetts where I now reside.

Alfred Creigh had this to say about the Rigdon involvement:

The manuscript was left with Mr. Patterson for two or three years and in the meantime a journeyman printer, Sidney Rigdon had copied the entire manuscript, and hearing of Joseph Smith, Jr's digging operations for money through "black magic" or communing with the dead, he decided he would turn some profit for himself. He arranged an interview with Joseph Smith, they revised the manuscript somewhat and instead of finding money, in the course of time they found "curious plates" which, when translated turned out to be the "Golden Bible" or Book of Mormon. Many members of the Smith family were involved and all acted as witnesses to the finding of the plates of gold, saying they had handled them themselves and they were of curious workmanship.

Such is the account of the most stupendous imposture which has been perpetrated for many centuries . . . at which the religious world stands amazed.

After the Book of Mormon was published, people in New Salem who read it immediately recognized the historical part as being identical to the area of Spaulding's writing in which they had been so deeply interested. They were highly incensed at the piracy and held a meeting in New Salem where they chose a Dr. Hurlbut to go to Amity in 1834 to compare the original with the Mormon Bible. Spaulding's widow closed her letter with these remarks:

This historical romance with the addition of a few pious expressions and extracts from the Sacred Scriptures has been construed into a new Bible and palmed off upon a company of poor deluded fanatics as "divine." Nothing could grieve my husband more, were he living, than the use which has been made of his work.

The original manuscript of Spaulding was given to the library of Oberlin College in Ohio.

After the Mormons were formally organized, local newspapers carried small notices of their westward migration and the view usually expressed was that they were glad to see them go out of their communities. A news item from Carthage, Missouri, in 1843 indicated people in the area were "so sick and tired of the Mormons in their midst that they want them to move on." In another news item, undated but about this time:

> Twenty-eight years ago Joe Smith and Harris, his first convert, applied to the Editor of the Rochester *Journal* to print his Book of Mormon which he had found in the cleft of a rock, but which was such jibberish we could not read it. Joe was a tavern idler in the Village of Palmyra and Harris, a substantial farmer, offered to pay for the printing.

A wide reading of newspaper and magazine reaction indicated no support and little sympathetic feeling toward the group. Typical reaction appeared in the March 1858 issue of *Frank Leslie's Magazine:*

> In a preceding number we gave the early history of Mormonism, closing the account with the arrival of the "saints" at Salt Lake City. Our purpose now is to present as clearly as possible the character of the delusion as it develops itself in the social life of these deluded people.
>
> ... the very existence of the fanaticism depends on the will of Brigham Young ... that he is unscrupulous ... displays itself in his open defiance of the authorities of the U.S. Young was born June 1, 1801 in Wittenham, Vermont and joined the Mormons in 1832; he was with Joe Smith and was President in 1836. When Joe Smith was killed in 1844 the apostles were scattered and in the confusion which followed, Sidney Rigdon to whom by right according to Mormon Law, the Presidency belonged, assumed his authority and began to prophesy, endow and institute mysteries in imitation of Smith, but he was ousted by Brigham.

Illustration from March 1858 *Frank Leslie's Magazine* entitled: It is common for an Elder on his return from a foreign mission to bring back two new wives. From Mabel and Ross Crawford collection.

The Washington *Reporter* carried a small news item in the December 13, 1871, issue:

Middle-aged men remember visiting Solomon Spaulding's grave in the old Amity Churchyard, noting the style of the inscription, and now this headstone is crumbling. We assembled the bits and determined the date of death was 1816. He was an educated minister and an invalid who spent three years writing a book which was completed in 1813. Amity, New York also claims the grave of Spaulding. We solicit contributions of 10¢ and upward to a new grave stone.

The "new stone" is one of the sights in Amity as it stands at the roadside in the graveyard near the site of the tavern.

18

THE FUNNIES

SOME OF THE situations, misspellings and remarks found while searching early records were so hilarious it seemed a shame to pass over them laughing alone, so the writer decided to extract a few of the more entertaining, which may not have been so "funny" back when—but are pretty amusing today.

From Pennsylvania's *Colonial Records* is a letter written in 1758 by Colonel Adam Stephen concerning the general area of Laurel Hill:

> There is nothing that would have a greater effect on the rocks in the path than essence of fat beef mixt with rum! Please send us three or four cross cut saws to separate the numberless damn'd petryfyd old logs, hard as iron, break our axes to pieces. There is not a Dear in this neighborhood—.

The Pittsburgh *Gazette* carried this notice in August 1792:

> Phelim Coole wishes it known that his wife, Bridget Coole has run away. She is a tight, neat body and has lost one leg. She was last seen riding behind the Priest of the Parish through Fermony [sounds like this was copied from an Irish paper in Fermanagh] and as we was never married, I will pay no debt that she contracts. She lisps with one tooth and is always talking about fairies, and is of no use but to her owner.

In an 1871 issue of *Josh Billings Farmers Allminax* the following verse appeared:

347

Teach us when tew wean lambs,
When tew pay our debts,
How tew set a hen,
With eleganse and precision.

On November 10, 1834, the following letter was sent from Millersburgh [*sic*], Ohio, to William Waugh, Esq., at Washington:

Dear Sir: I wond you to git my money of Aston before the furst of March nax with out fale. I in tenet to lay in goods to keep Store in Claysvill Washington County and I can not due with out et; and plese to let John Wilson now that I wond all the mony that is coming on his Docket to me; not to faver now man as I must haf my money and not to disapind me I intent to haf my goods in Claysvill on the furst day of April from new york City. Thare is the plase that I lost my cretit and you will se that I will due well thare gif my best respect to J. Dagg, thomas Hoge, William Hoge and John Grason

CHRISTIAN WEIRICH

During October term 1797 in common pleas court, the following case was considered:

The Sheriff of Greene County wishes Richard Swan to answer to the charge that he bit off a piece of John Moore's ear thereby damaging the peace and dignity of the Commonwealth.

Indian Trader George Croghan's heavy Irish brogue and quaint spelling come through in several of his letters to Colonel Henry Bouquet:

February 1753 . . . I am surprised to think that the Gentelmen of Philadelphia are so litle acquainted with ye back parts of this province and that it couldn't be above 140 miles on a streat line and I ashure you from where the Alegania Road croses ye Lawrel Hill, Wanango where John Cure is now building a fort, lays due North. I wish with all my Hart some gentelman who is an Artist in Philadelphia and whos account [map] wold be depended on whould have ye curiosety to take a journay in those parts, whos return I dear say wold give a ginrel satisfaction to ye whole Province.

May 1754 ... Half King wants to meet imeadetly with ye chiefs of ye Ohio Indians at Monohongela to know what ye English intends to do as the Shannas are in desprett condition for want of amonisions ... great numbers of people are setling beyond the blue hills.

Carmichaels had an early literary society which must have been a hoax as it was called the "Stopfun Association." One of their resolutions was that the duration of man's existence should be determined by a fixed period, say seventy years. Meetings were held at the Literary Society Hall and officers included: Most Worthy Promulator, Chief Scriblarious of the Rolls, Guide to the Inner Oraculum, Boss of the Portals, Preparatory Hoodwinker.

Among papers in a Greene County estate file was this note:

Madam: You'll please to take the small white powder at night going to bed in syrup. Next morning take the Purgh, drink fowl Broath during the Operation.

When the Bull's Head Tavern was moved from High Street in Waynesburg to make way for the Downey House, it was taken to Meades Hill which took its name from the following incident:

Two men had been to the tavern, one by the name of Meade, and they were walking up the town flight of stairs where someone had left a stepladder at the top. Meade went up the steps and continued on up the ladder and off the top. He called back to his companion, "Watch out, there's a hell of a step-off here."

Albert Gallatin published an open letter to the people of Westmoreland County in the *Gazette*, stating that half the population of that county was German, and for some reason, Germans were not being elected to office or allowed to serve, if elected. (Gallatin had a personal experience along this line.) In a later issue the following letter appeared:

Take notice everybody that I, John Fling will stand a poll and run for the Assembly next Tuesday. I expect every sensible man will vote for me. I am more fit for an Assemblyman than any of the other 9,999 candidates. I can cypher very well. . . . Sam Swingletree can write speeches for me. Oh, such laws and speeches as I could make! I would make a canal from the lakes into the Ohio and drown the Indians; I would catch all the wolves, kill all the crows, poison all the rats. I would do everything! I need not tell where I live—everybody knows me. . . .

his
JOHN X FLING
mark

Myles Haiden a prominent Tenmile settler ran the following notice in the Washington *Telegraphe* in October 1795:

. . . one Ralph Smith of Morgan Township some years ago called me a *convict* and said it in such terms as his good breeding would afford. I hereby request that Mr. Smith wash and shave and inquire of James Gillespie on Buffalo Creek and Robert Carrel, two gentlemen who sailed with me from Londonderry on August 14, 1768 and landed at New-castle October 3. . . .

John McKee, who laid out the town of McKeesport on the Monongahela above Pittsburgh, inserted this notice in November 1795:

. . . inform the public with pleasure that in spite of all the people who said John McKee could not found a town, he now has a patent for the ground on which he laid out the town. . . .

The following retraction was taken so seriously it was recorded in an early deed book:

This is to certify that I, Jacob Crow, the subscriber did some time ago advertise John Hanley to have taken a black mare away from me clandestinely and I do now with sorrow and reluctance state the advertising to have been false and groundless, done this 3rd day of April 1778.

The following incident took place while a group of men repaired the local schoolhouse, and it was reported during a session at the meetinghouse in 1802:

. . . being cold, we sent out for whiskey and James—took two drams out of a coffee pot and soon after fell asleep. He was taken to a house and put to bed with some appearance of the conduct common to an intoxicated person, until 9 p.m. We testify that one-half gallon whiskey was brought to the school house and the seven or eight men who were there to work, partook of it. In defense of James, we say he went over the fence without help and appeared to drink sparingly out of the pipe of the coffee pot.

The incident was discussed in detail at several more sessions but no judgment was made. Later, at a prayer meeting of this same congregation, it was noted that the minister's wife "was said to have had some difficulty rising to her feet at the time of prayer."

The Wheeling *Repository* in 1807 was an entertaining newspaper. Among various columns, marriages were listed under the heading of "Matches—Such as They Are" and one item reported Esau Bicknell aged sixty married a blooming Susannah Rogers, aged sixteen.

An interesting will, amusing in its detail, was made by Michael Koutz of Morgan Township, Greene County, previously of Baltimore County, Maryland.

January 18, 1823 . . . to my wife Mary my citchen dresser chest that contains her clothes, with the piece of flannel therein, 1 piece of black cloth of 28 yards for the immeditly use of my younger boys . . . one barrel of brandy for her use absolutely, and all beds, beding and feathers on hand. Son Jacob shall have two years free rent if he takes good care of the property. If not, they shall put it immediately under rent until they git it in repair, then sell it. My daughter Elizabeth to have one bed cost $4, 1 bed tick, bolster and piller ticks of flax chain filled with wool with 21 lbs. of new feathers, 1 under tick, 2 new tow linen sheets. . . . My widow to se to learning of my six youngest children. . . .

Westmoreland County records an intriguing will made in January 1824 by Jacob Kline of Franklin Township whose wife was either a very large woman or kept a store:

. . . to my wife, Hanna and my three sons, John, Michael and Jacob and my daughters . . . every year each of my sons and daughters is to deliver to my wife, 4 lbs. of coffee, 7 lbs. of sugar,

1 lb. of tea, ½ lb. of pepper, ½ lb. of allspice, 50 lbs. of dried pork, 3 pecks of salt and sufficient flour, bran and buck-wheat....

This letter to "Mr. John Hogue, neer Washington" was written by Joshua Yardley from Burgettstown July 20, 1824:

I want you to send me the plan of your hous as soon as you can as I do want to begin to fraim soon. I have goot the most of the stuf. Plees to draw the plan so that I shall make no me Stak of wood. I wood be glad if you could git the wether bording be for long so I cold be dressing them in wet wether. Thar was nothing said about the selar windows. Plees to tell the Sis and wether for glass and how many. Mr. Hogue if you could send me $10 it would oblige me much as I want sum tools and meet and I shood be glad to see you if I had the Plank I could work in wet wether and git the hous closed in sooner.

A West Virginia deed contains an unbelievable name:

Benjamin Johnstone, Sr. as "next friend" unto Genral Washington Johnstone, his son, both of Ohio County but formerly Yohogania County, sold 1,040 acres in 1785 for the advancement, schooling, edication and bringing up the said Ginral Washington Johnstone, for the sum of 385 pounds 10 shillings, the land on the Ohio River near Muckmore's Run.

A file of early family letters was lent to the writer by a Waynesburg resident who had not been able to burn them even though they were marked "Destroy." Written during the 1840s they are remarkable for their information, sentiments and sometimes, spelling.

October 17, 1841—Waynesburg ... there was a tremendous temperance revival here since I left home and all the men, women and children signed the pledge, Doc Hawkins, H. Hook, Jim Lindsy and all the rest. I think we will go to Ohio in the Spring ... as we are tired of this damned rascally Town and if you have any notion of settling here give it up at once for of all places for a young man to live and do business, this is the very worst ... we are bound to leave these diggings next spring. We are sitting up here in the room, suffering for some liquor but dam the drop we get, so much for Temperance. Tell me about all the girls in the Buckeye diggins and if there is any right handsome and wealthy, tell her of me and I'll come and marry her, for I cant get a wife here that suits me. . . .

In March 1846 there was a letter from Rolla, Missouri:

The river is now open . . . we want to sell our land and invest in one place in the West and put sheep on it. This is good country to make a livin inn if a man was setled hear and had a small capitle but the great majority of the people are in moderate or poor circumstances. . . . I have some whisky to sell yet. . . . I have not any pursin in this cuntry that I care anything about—I have often thought as there is but you and me that feels interrested in each others wellfare what is the reason we cant locate both in one country and enjoy each others company while we both live in this world? Sell that property in Jifferson if you can. . . .

Later in 1846 letter from Missouri:

. . . had some whisky in the ware hous at Millers and some at Galeny. Miller started to orleans with a load and took the meat with him and the boat sunk but he had it inshured. I am living most of my time in Hannable buying and selling a little bacon. Don't make any verry expensive improvements on the hill farm these hard times. The men that salted beefe in this country this season will loose money. Porke here last fall was from $2.50 to $3.00 cwt. and now bacon by the quantity is from 3 to 3½ cents. I want you to come to the West this fall and see the country and if you dont see plenty of plases that you like beter than you do green county I will give it up. I remain your sincere friend till Death. . . .

In the spring of 1846 the following letter came from Hannibal:

. . . there are wonderful opportunities for sheep as they can graze on the prairies for nothing . . . made a speech at a Surcular Hunt that was mutch talked of. Come out here as I cant bear the idea of being a survent for the people inn green county. There are five families from Green that are near neighbors.

A letter was written from Cinsonatey [*sic*] April 17, 1845:

Sur: It is unnesary to give you a long preliminary about our dificulties at Pits burg, in short, there was not any of us lost nor any of our things all though they come very nerit. We was compeled to stay there three days before we could git a boat to start. We are on the Yeutacon Whitch . . . we have seven preachers on board and have two sermonds every day.

A Hannibal letter written in November 1842:

We landed safe in this country without any axident, the water was very low and it took us a good while to get hear. The mosury river is not large and verry dificult to navigat with boats—the water has bin so high that all the chanels are fild up and changed. We went over to Pike County near the missipy and I bought 24 cattle and two very fine horses and took them to Saint Lewis and shipt them to orleans. I want you to take care of everything in our room and pay all the attention to your study that you can this winter. Collect all the money you can but don't trade that property in Jifferson for sadles as they will not do to bring here. Have had very good health and less coughing since I left Waynesburg.

A letter dated July 17, 1845, was sent from Rolla:

Deer Sur: We got a severe weting and took the chills and got sick . . . applied to a Whig Canetucky Doctor who came to see me three times and cured me right up. Mr. Coly, a good oald babtist and me went up to Galeny this spring and took 1,300 pounds of bacon and 70 head of sheep. We went on a steam boat and was only gon a few days—a collyer in Pallmyra was up and bought some of our penn Sylvany sheep. I have soald some of the whisky of a fair profit. Now my dear friend, I hope it is not necessary to say anything about our things in that room as they are the last remembrans of our mother, aunt and sisters and this is what makes me prise them so hi. I do a great many little thanky jobs for the people hear sutch as riting for them and making calculations. I must stop or I cant rop it all inn.

There was no year on a letter written on "fryday September 3 Suckers Tavern 15 miles above philadelphy":

I hav gist com up from philadelphy after you left me and swopt for 20 head of fat catle and hav bin twisting all throw the country and it does seem impossable to sell catle and hav been inn Delaware as low as Willmountan and hav yet 26 catle. I have had the horrors ever sens you left me. I am verry tyard of staying here.

We cant git no plase but what is full of catle . . . so many Drovers swaping their stock for fat, yours in haste—

On November 6, 1846:

Left Waynesburg and arrived Washington, Pa., 25¢ for supper and $2 for passage to Wheeling and wated for a boat, shipped the 7th for Cinsonaty, paid $5 for passage and had a Dutch convertible seat which was a pleasant place to sleep. Great many good looking ladies on board, arrived Cinc. Monday the 9th on board the *Pike*. This is a grait place for business. Left for St. Louis on the *Colorado* paid $6 for passage and arrived the 15th, put up at the *Planters House*. The 16th took passage for Pittsburg, paid $13 for self and Joe my black boy.

From Waynesburg January 13, 1844:

. . . nothin new nor strange inn this Dry Viledg and hav bin uneasy about you on account of the severe cold you had. I want you to sell as mutch of that land as you can as it is expense and not any income. I would like to try it one summer in the West if I did not take more than $500 to begin with. With that amount I could be respected and soon be a head of the mess and my spirits is broake down of trying to do anything in this country. Mr. A— wants to rent the room we now have, he is getting very good at appearance but I think he has a great room to improve in heart.

A letter from Missouri August 25, 1842:

. . . the girls in this part of the country are fine and healthy, they can run as fast, jump or swim or dive as deap as anny you ever saw in your life and if you will come hear you shall have your choyse of them. I have only picked too for you, I'll tell you their names. The one is Long Polly and the other is Slim Sally—their Daddy's are as rich as a Pig and I think this is a good chance. . . . Money is verry scarse heare. Land can be bought for cash from 3 to 10 dollars per acre, well improved farms with brick houses and barnes from 160 to 300 acres. If I cant show you some of the Best bar gans you ever saw then tell me for wonce that I deceive you and if you come and tell me so I will ceep you all winter for nothing. Sheap can be bought from 50 to 75 cents per shear as large as enny we ever drove and as fat as butter—horses is high and hard to be bought. hogs is verry low, less than one dollar per hundred . . . coffee from 9 to 10¢ per lb., butter 8¢ and sugar 6¢.

Between you and me it is the dearest time for money I ever sean. If you have any indianna scrip an can buy it I will tak some of it, I think it can be bought for one half of what it sells in madison. Come and it shant cost you anny thing this winter. I have plenty of corn and we can eat cakes together. . . . I feel there is nothing but respect and friendship between us. I want you to fetch an send me a Rifle Gun plain stock, bras thimels and musel peas runing from 180 to 200 waing from 8 to 10 lbs., a new one or a good one. If you cant read the within, fetch it here and I will read it for you!

On the back of the above letter was an item cut from a newspaper that appears to be a bit of local humor about the old W&W, the Washington and Waynesburg narrow-gauge railroad:

If we don't get to go to Aunt Sally's during the Maple Sugar Run by reason of the Narrow Gauge failing to get a grade round "that walnut tree" someone must send us a cake of sugar made on a shingle.

The last "Waynie" train was run in 1929 and many humorous stories were told about the narrow-gauge railroad between Waynesburg and Washington. A time table of January 1, 1919, gives the distance between the two points as 28.16 miles and there were twenty-one stations; a stop was made at practically every curve! Originally there were 174 curves which gave rise to a poem:

It wiggles in and wiggles out;
It leaves the passenger still in doubt
Whether the man who built the track
Was going in or going back.

19

POTTERS AND THE MAGIC
OF GREENSBORO STONEWARE
AND GALLATIN-KRAMER GLASS

IF POTTERY is traced from the very first to be produced in
Penn's Southwest, the various utensils of the Monongahela
Valley Indians must be at least mentioned. "Prexie" Stewart
in a 1969 interview said Indian pottery made here was never
molded or turned, but was paddled into shape. In the thousands of shards unearthed by area archaeologists and currently being assembled into their original forms, there is little
evidence of incised designs. Most of the pottery is plain, or
cord marked as cord is pressed into the clay to make a pattern with basket characteristics.

Some of the urn and pedestal-based shapes from the Adena
period which have been found fairly intact, are quite subtle
in their proportions, and the thin, fragile quality of the clay
is surprisingly sophisticated.

The earliest Indian pottery is supposed to have been grit
tempered but most of the shards found have been tempered
with pulverized shell. Some pottery such as containers used
for cooking, was fired but it was not known just how this was
done until the summer of 1975 when the Donley Indian
Village Site in Greene County was opened for a short few
weeks before strip-mining operations commenced. The site
had been known for many years as an Indian village and
burial place, but the owner of the property did not wish to

see the area violated and did not disclose its location until the surface was sold for mining purposes.

Here, in one of the largest village sites so far discovered in Greene County, diggers found a round pit completely lined with material similar to common red brick with fragments of broken pottery within. It was assumed that this was an early kiln for pottery and unique in the area.

A school history of West Virginia ca. 1900 locates "possibly the first pottery west of the Alleghenies" at Morgantown ca. 1785 and the first potter there was Master Foulk, followed by John W. Thompson; some of their ware is exhibited at the Smithsonian. In 1788 in the estate papers of Leonard Boyer of Ohio County (now West Virginia) a recorded bill of sale to merchant William McKinley of West Liberty includes a "spindle for potter's use." These early potters made their own molds for buttons, clay pipes, dishes, food jars, etc., and their molding tools were of pear and apple wood, similar to those used today in river glasshouses such as Blenko on the Ohio River.

The Wheeling *Repository* in September 1808 ran ads for S. R. Bakewell & Company to merchants and all persons descending the Ohio who could be supplied with "excellent quality stoneware" on reasonable terms on credit or for cash, at Charlestown, six miles below Steubenville. In the spring of 1814 the Bakewell Company advertised in the Washington *Reporter* for two journeymen potters to learn the stoneware business, for both summer and winter employment. The year 1814 marked the beginning of steamboat traffic on the Mississippi and greatly expanded markets in the Middle West for

all kinds of stoneware; it was also the founding year for the Greensboro stoneware industry.

The 1946 centennial history of Point Marion on the Monongahela River states that no dates are available as to when the pottery *industry* commenced, even though the generally accepted date appears to be 1814, with the formation of the Greensboro Manufacturing Company.

A careful search of existing records reveals considerable pottery activity before 1800. Coarse redware was produced in small folk potteries in most towns shortly after their founding, as there was a brisk demand for tavern and household ware which did not require high firing. Not all redware was early; the Ruth Craig collection of red, unglazed pitchers in the Stewart pottery exhibit at Waynesburg College has some very graceful, well-proportioned shapes and simple but effective designs. Dr. Stewart called this "decadent pottery" because it was unglazed, but the designs are in glaze and therefore, a darker red than the vessels, and the total effect is very pleasing. The sketch of a redware pitcher is from the "late classical period" 1890-1900 and probably made by Hamilton and Jones. The coffee jar of red unglazed ware is from the Hamilton Pottery.

Whiteley Township in Greene County was originally called "Whiteclay" for the outcroppings on both Big and Little Whiteley creeks which became the valuable beds of potters' clays used in the manufacture of stoneware from clay deposits in the meanders of the Monongahela River related to the glacial periods of the great ice age. Waychoff reported early potter's shops in Greene somewhere adjacent to the "Salt Hole near Swan's" and near the Bailey Bridge on the Waynesburg Road:

> Under this land for miles about is a large deposit of fine clay. The potteries at Greensboro for many years got their supply of clay

from the hills back of New Geneva and when it became scarce
there, a reward of $100 was offered for the discovery of clay on
the west side of the river.

Before clay beds were discovered east of Mapletown near
Greensboro, workers hauled wagonloads across the *Mon* during times of shallow water, from the original banks near New
Geneva.
The Hamiltons, beginning with James Hamilton in 1852,
who were associated with the production of stoneware in
Greensboro, came from Fayette County where Franklin Ellis
reported early pottery activity. Christian Tarr in Jefferson
Township, a potter himself, may have also been active as a
sort of pottery entrepreneur before 1800. Official records
show these entries for Tarr:

> 1798 Direct Tax list, Union Township, Fayette County—John
> Slack, tenant in Christian Tarr's 2-story 16 x 30 foot brick house
> with nine 12-pane windows, a 12 x 16 brick kitchen with three
> 12-pane windows and a 1½-story 16 x 30 log stable. (An impres-
> sive group for the period.)

> Christian Tarr in a 2-story 16 x 24 brick house with eight 12-pane
> windows, a 12 x 13 brick kitchen with one 12-pane window and a
> 1-story 20 x 26 log *potter's shop* with two windows of 20 panes.

Tarr probably made the bricks for his buildings as records for
some of the early potteries include items of brick molds.
Apparently headquartered in Fayette, Tarr purchased three
lots in Waynesburg in 1799 and established Nicholas Hager,
potter, on Lot 133 at the corner of Whiskey Alley and High
Street. In 1803 Hager purchased the lot on which there was a
fourteen by sixteen-foot cabin, no doubt the potter's shop.
Tarr's other lots were No. 126 which will be remembered as
the corner lot across from the courthouse square on which
the Bull's Head Tavern and later, the Downey House, stood,
and lot No. 58 where a small one-story brick, one of Waynesburg's original houses, still stands facing Franklin Street. In
1820 Waynesburg attorney Andrew Buchanan owned a lot
with a potter's shop. In the town of Washington, "Henry

Tarr, potter" was one of the signers of the Whiskey Oath in 1794 and in 1796 he was taxed for a lot with two houses, one probably his potter's shop.

Other Fayette County potters whose identification is taken from tax lists, were:

Georges Township, 1816—William McClane, clay potter
Bridgeport Boro, 1817—Jacob Bowman had a potter's shop, Cephas Gregg, Merchant and Potter on Water Street, John Riley, Potter and Robert Rogers, Potter

In September 1824 there was a sheriff's sale at the suit of the Brownsville Bank which included Lot No. 26 where a twenty-four foot square shop contained a potter's kiln, next to Jesse Townsend. Thomas Collins of Uniontown (1803-1873) was another potter who learned his trade in Greensboro. Both William McCormick and John Slonaker, first citizens of Connellsville, had potteries. Robert Barton, Uniontown merchant, kept a ledger for the years 1845-50 and sold quantities of earthenware, some or all of which was made by Garrett Greenland who also paid for his milling at the Barton Mill with pottery.

Very early pottery activity in Fredericktown led to the naming of "Pottery Alley." When John Bower (1772-1836) received his patent for "Apple Bottom" from gun and blacksmith David Blair in 1801, he began very shortly to make some sort of pottery. He is listed as a potter in business with his sons, Jonah and Benjamin Bower, in 1810-11. What we know today as "moonlighting" must have been carried on at a furious pace by the Bower men as records over a period of years show they were active as tavern keepers, blacksmiths, boatbuilders, potters, distillers, and keepers of the early town library. Other potters who worked in the Bower Pottery were Eli Gapen, youngest son of early settler, Zacchariah Gapen, Jacob Wise of the Fredericktown founder family, and John Rowe (John Hupp's wife was Anne Rowe). They made redware and also a well-fired drain tile, hexagonal in shape and about three inches in diameter which was produced in 1824 according to stamped and dated sections.

The *1859 Directory of the Monongahela and Youghiogheny Valleys* published by George Thurston in Pittsburgh listed a stoneware manufactory at Fredericktown which turned out 30,000 gallons annually, with a large saltworks nearby for the salt glazes. Polk Donaghoo was the proprietor and the potters were C. A. Woods and Nicholas Debolt. Several members of the pioneer Debolt family were potters, and at one time in New Geneva, George and Henry Atchison and later John Debolt had a potters' shop at the corner of Old and Country streets. Ware from the Donaghoo Pottery also known as A. P. Donaghoo & Beal, and as Donaghoo & Hill of Fredericktown at one period, was similar to Greensboro stoneware but not as elaborately decorated. The Washington County Historical Society has a large stoneware pitcher with closed lip which the pottery made for innkeeper Edward Burson with lettering and borders in the traditional cobalt-oxide glaze.

The 1820 census of manufacturing for Washington County, gives an account of the rather limited early pottery activity there:

Somerset Township—Pottery reported by S. K. with one mill and one kiln, made earthenware of all kinds, a one man operation with yearly sales of $300 but demand not very good.

Nottingham Township—Pottery using clay and lead with two men and one boy employed, one mill, one kiln and three turning machines producing coarse earthenware of all kinds with yearly sales of $1,000 but demand not as good as formerly. Reported by Manager T. S.

In more recent years, the Canonsburg Pottery on Chartiers Creek operated from about 1900 and still produces fine tableware and miscellaneous pottery items.

Thomas B. Lincoln's ledger shows that he was making pottery as early as 1828 near Carmichaels, although another early Muddy Creek ledger mentions John Baners making earthenware in 1798; he paid for his milling at John Heaton's mill by making a "watering pott and earthenware." Carrying on the play on "famous names in Penn's Southwest" we find Abraham Lincoln making trips to the early Lincoln Pottery near Carmichaels for chamber pots more frequently than anyone else in the area. Howard Leckey in his unpublished volume nine states that the Carmichaels Lincoln family was descended from the same common ancestor, Mordecai Lincoln, as President Abraham Lincoln. Both John and Jonathan Barrymore (locally spelled Bearmore) took washbowls and crocks over several years.

Neri Hart of Carmichaels locates an early pottery where the old Glades Church parking lot is laid out but neither he nor Dr. Stewart identified this as the Lincoln Pottery. Some of the redware from the Glades Church location is in the Waynesburg College collection. The bank back of the landmark brick Harper house on Route 88 is where they dug clay to make the dummies for the kilns.

Merchant Tom Lincoln's ledger for the years 1822-30 contains this entry: "August 19, 1828—Began to burn the first kiln of ware." From that date on there were many sales of earthenware which included pots, pitchers, wash "boles," chamber pots, dishes, ink stands, gallon jugs and crocks. Contrary to the statement about the "first kiln of ware" Lincoln sold items of pottery to Isaac Hunt in 1823 and in July 1828 Hunt "made a peare of overalls and spun some wool in exchange for sundry earthin' ware." In November 1828, George Oldshoe came to work in the pottery and took credit with fish, tea and shingling the pottery shop. There were numerous purchases of lead, manganese, and straw for packing the crockery. In November 1830, potter John Mariatta boarded with the Lincolns at three dollars a month but he had to "find half the fewel," glaze, and do all the work in the pottery for which he received half of the finished ware.

There are a few items in the Lincoln ledger which point to operation of a paper mill about the same time the pottery

364

was begun. August 29, 1825, William Walker came to "work in the Paper Mill" and on November 3 the entry indicates he cut twenty-five reams of paper and also some "strip wrapping." He tended "both engines for two days at $1 a day" and also worked nights for one dollar, so for a while it was a twenty-four hour operation. In February 1826 Walker cut reams of paper, strip wrapping, and rags and this activity continued through December of that year, coupled with tending the engines day and night. Neither the pottery nor the paper mill activities at Carmichaels are mentioned in area histories, including the ambitious bicentennial booklet produced by the Carmichaels community in 1967.

The pottery activity at New Geneva as researched by the students at California State College does not cover the earliest periods of limited output of ware, but commences with the operations of Alexander Conrad in 1872, various members of the Williams family, the Eberharts, Leander B. Dilliner, and Arthur Robbins; the most recent date for Robbins pottery as given in 1915. A small grey stoneware jar called a "Jigoo" from the Paul R. Stewart collection, was made at the Alexander Conrad Pottery. While the grape vine has been a favorite motif for many kinds of decoration, it is unusual on Greensboro-New Geneva ware.

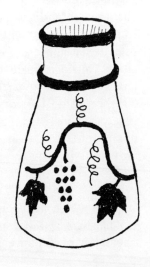

Franklin Ellis reported the small establishment of James Enix south of Friendship Hill in Springhill Township "where a good article is made, but little capital invested. He does all the turning himself with eight kilns burned annually for an output of 12,000 gallons of ware." Earliest dates for "James D. Eneix" are 1874-76 and some of the designs on jugs and crocks from this pottery are unique as compared with

those of Greensboro. The sunburst design shown is on James Eneix grey and blue two-gallon jug from Paul R. Stewart collection.

Stenciled design in cobalt on a four-gallon jug made by A. Conrad in Paul R. Stewart collection is shown.

Isaac Hewitt began to make pottery about 1870 at Rice's Landing using some very handsome stenciled designs. Because of the smaller operation there are fewer of the Hewitt jugs and crocks and they bring high prices at sales and country auctions.

On May 20, 1803, a public auction was held in New Geneva to dispose of lots held by Albert Gallatin in Greensboro and the pioneer potters Alexander and James Vance were the purchasers. The *1859 Thurston Directory* described the two Greensboro potteries as employing thirty hands, exclusive of woodchoppers, clay diggers, and haulers and they turned out 225,000 gallons yearly:

Attached to the pottery of James Hamilton, begun in 1852, is a manufactory for pumps known as "Hamilton's Patent Improved Stone Pumps." Business has been carried on only part of the year but they plan to increase to $20 to $25 thousand a year. They also manufacture stone tubes for water pipes which stand a pressure of many pounds. Mr. Hamilton also manufactures chemical ware as good as any of English make, his establishment for this being the only one west of the mountains.

J.E. ENEIX & CO.

They make brick from stone clay and mammoth 40-50 gallon jars are made with ease. There are but two men in the country who can turn such work and both are at the Hamilton Pottery.

* * *

The production of salt was closely associated with pottery making and the drilling of a salt well was a tedious, laborious, and expensive operation. At the time of the War of 1812, salt was both scarce and high priced, and there were not too many "licks" where brackish water oozed through rock fissures, where wells could be located. William Johnson described his effort to perforate the rock near the mouth of the Loyalhanna to a depth of 450 feet where he struck a fountain impregnated with salt.

Furnaces were erected, pans assembled, and he was able to make about thirty bushels of salt per day. "Very soon the solitary, silent banks of this river were bustling as well after well was sunk. So much was produced that the price of salt went down to a dollar per barrel."

Wells or perforations are from 300 to 600 feet deep and two and one-half to three inches in diameter. They were made with common stone chisels attached to poles held by men who forcibly struck the chisels against the bottom. Two men would usually work for more than a year at this process. When water of the required strength and quantity was obtained, the well was tubed to exclude freshwater and a pump inserted, first worked by horse power, but later by a small steam engine.

The water was first boiled in large, square sheet-iron pans until it attained a strength just short of crystallization; it was then transferred to large cisterns in which the sediment was deposited. Purified, it was put into large kettles placed in the rear of the pans in which it soon became crystallized. Spear after spear of the most delicate structure and fantastic shapes darted into shape and suddenly there was a kettle of salt. Sufficient water was drawn from one well to supply three to five pans, making from fifteen to twenty barrels of salt a day.

About thirty gallons was evaporated to every bushel of salt. Coal used as a fuel, was often thrown from the mouth of the pit adjacent to the salt hole into chutes and by gravity to the furnaces.

* * *

Before Alexander Vance moved from Fayette County he erected a large three-story sixty by sixty-foot steam flour mill in anticipation of the Chesapeake and Ohio Canal extending to New Geneva on the Monongahela. When this development did not take place, Vance moved to Greensboro and we find him listed as a "single potter" with seven lots, one house, and two cabins in 1805. This listing may have been the beginning of the stoneware industry in Greensboro although April 1814 marks the date for the purchase of lots from Emmanuel Hoover by the Greensburgh (later changed to Greensboro) Manufacturing Company. Trustees of the new company were Vance, C. A. Mestrezat, and Enoch South. Alexander and James Vance's sister, Mary, had married Daniel Boughner, a potter and shortly after founding of the pottery, the Vances moved to Ohio, leaving their brother-in-law in charge. Alexander Vance was taxed for one house, two lots, and a quantity of "poundstone" in 1816 but in September 1819, Daniel Boughner purchased the Vance pottery for $3,450 and it became known as the Boughner Pottery.

Boughner floral spray, very Japanese in feeling, incised design, from Stewart collection.

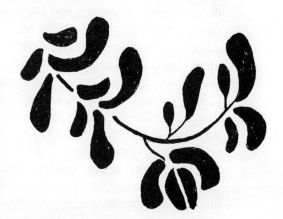

During the first years of the Vance and Boughner operation, they used a dark clay dug on the west side of the river which produced the redware, a porous biscuit pottery

partially or entirely covered with brown or black slip. In her Greensboro pottery articles in the Greene County Historical Society quarterly, Doris Hawk reports that the fine grey and blue stoneware was not produced until discovery of the stiff, white clay, found first near New Geneva and later on the west side of the river. Daniel Boughner was followed in 1859 by A. V. and William Boughner who ran the pottery for the next ten years. The Boughners made some of the first flat roofing tile which can be seen on a few outbuildings today in and around Greensboro.

The history of stoneware manufacture in the New Geneva-Greensboro area has been subjected to much scrutiny and research in recent years. One of the first and most able historians, Doris Hawk of Greensboro, became interested in pottery many years ago and has contributed most of the data used by more recent lecturers and writers. Mrs. Hawk breaks down the stoneware into categories of basic and unique forms. In the latter group are found piggy banks, pumps, dog figures similar to Staffordshire, meat tenderizers, gravestones, unusual baking dishes, water coolers, doll heads, umbrella stands, covered butter dishes, spittoons, grease lamps,

and cake molds. The basic forms such as jugs and canning jars had a symmetrical axis of revolution.

Doll's head shown is from California State College collection. The Greensboro gravestone in grey stoneware with cobalt lettering is from the Greene County Historical Society Museum, Waynesburg, and the grey and blue handled ten-gallon jug is from the Stewart collection.

Mrs. Hawk describes pottery making:

> ... in early pottery, the clay was ground in a "pug mill" which was a bowl-shaped vessel with a shaft with protruding knives. A horse hitched to a beam walked around in a circle, revolving the knives, thus grinding the clay and mixing it with water to the right consistency.

> Young boys who were apprenticed at an early age, made balls of clay for the potter who threw a clay ball on his wheel and shaped it by hand. As the wheel turned, he held one hand on the inside and the other held a cedar rib which smoothed and shaped the outside of the pottery. The pieces dried for twenty-four hours before handles were put in place.

John Rumble was one of the early potters at the Hamilton plant and his descendant as a very old man in Jefferson in 1970 told the writer of his experiences working as a "clay boy" and how expert they became in judging just how much clay to make a ball for a twenty-, thirty- or even fifty-gallon jug.

> After another day or two of drying, depending on the warmth of the drying room, the kind of ware, etc., the dried pieces were packed in firing kilns with chucks, jug collars and stilts between to prevent sticking, and fired for forty-eight to seventy-two hours. Salt glaze, put on while the ware baked in hot kilns, was difficult to apply. Standing on scaffolds built

around the kiln and wearing extra clothes to protect them from the intense heat, the laborers threw the salt through holes into the kiln.

Upon removal from the kilns and after cooling, the decorations were applied. The best of the grey stoneware was decorated with blue, usually festoons in the Dutch tulip pattern. Most of the brown decoration on tan ware carried out the same motifs. Colors were applied free-hand with a brush made of deer tail hairs, with a quill used for the finer detail. [Finger painting was also employed as the decorators, usually women, dipped a finger into the cobalt glaze and applied certain designs.] After stenciled patterns came into use, artists lost interest in the free-hand designs.

In 1836, Uriah Hunt published a small book by Edward Hazen of Philadelphia entitled *Panorama of Professions and Trades, or Everyman's Book* for the Eastern District of Pennsylvania. In reviewing the various trades, the chapter on "Stoneware" gives this additional bit about the decorations: "Paper patterns were applied in some way to the wet stoneware and later rubbed off with water."

There is an Oriental quality to the free-hand work, especially what appears to be finger-painting, and most of the numbers marking the size of jugs and crocks. Some of the finest Greensboro ware is remarkably like the best Japanese and chinese pottery and stoneware familiar to the writer in early Seattle and San Francisco Oriental shops.

Sketch shows very fine decoration of stenciled eagle combined with free-hand borders from James

Hamilton's Eagle Pottery; owned by David Brocklebank of Pittsburgh.

The finished product was loaded onto large wooden barges called "ware-boats" or "pottery arks" for the trip to delivery points. The larger potteries leased fleets of barges that carried the ware by river to southern and Middle West towns. The barges were pushed out into the river by long poles until the flow of water carried them along. Charlie Williams who floated down the river as far as Cincinnati, was one of the last men to run a ware-boat. Sometimes they were able to get a "ride" from a packet boat whose captain would toss them a rope and tow the barge as far as his destination.

Now that Greensboro and other river stoneware has become one of the higher priced and most sought after items at any town or country auction in Penn's Southwest, families who remember their cellars and springhouses filled with stoneware canning jars and pickling crocks, resort to digging in the refuse piles on their old farms for discarded crockery.

Gallatin-Kramer Glass

"Old Glassworks" downriver from Greensboro was the location of the "new" Gallatin-Kramer Glass Company after the initial glassmaking at New Geneva. On May 10, 1797,

John Badollet whom Albert Gallatin had persuaded to leave Switzerland for America, wrote from Greensboro to Gallatin in Philadelphia:

> Since signing my letter, we three (Badollet, Bourdillon and Cazenova) unanimously have begun an affair which is no less an undertaking than a *glass works.* (There are) six Germans containing all the necessary workmen we are trying to deal with and we have a well grounded hope of success. Such an undertaking considered in either a public or private point of view ought to supersede every other . . . we will attend to it with the utmost of our abilities and by report, inform you of the success.

After Congress adjourned on September 20, Gallatin returned to New Geneva and drew an article of agreement for a partnership of himself, his brother-in-law James W. Nicholson, Louis Bourdillon, John Badollet, and Charles A. Cazenova on the one part, and the five glassmakers, George Kramer, Adolphus Everhart, Ludowitz Reitz, Christian Kramer, and George Reppert on the other part, to erect and operate a glass house for six years. The Gallatin group put up the capital and the land, the Kramer group their knowledge of glassmaking and skill as blowers. The glassmakers were to receive regular pay and from their share of the profits, to pay their full share of the invested capital. Baltzer Kramer had blown glass for both Stiegel and Amelung and later became a full partner in the New Geneva works. The first glass was blown in January 1798 in a small four-pot furnace on Georges Creek, just outside the Village of New Geneva. The first building was forty by forty feet with one wall of stone and the other three frame. The four pots soon grew to eighteen and wood was used to melt the glass sand, until the discovery of an outcrop of coal at Greensboro when they moved across the river, and opened at "Old Glassworks."

Conflicts developed among the partners, but operations continued at a profit for the term of the agreement. Gallatin's friend, Mussard, managed the glassworks after 1799 until the agreement expired in 1803. Baltzer Kramer died about 1813 and by 1816 the seven partners netted an annual profit of $8,000 on a capital investment of $40,000. Ten years later, Albert Gallatin was still interested in the glassworks and the Gallatin-Kramer glass they produced was considered superior to Pittsburgh glass for many years. After 1830 the works was operated by B. F. Black & Company who produced window glass and it was finally destroyed by fire in 1847.

After being involved for many years in the affairs of Albert Gallatin & Company as a partner of Gallatin's, John Badollet moved to Vincennes. When he sold his Greensboro property the price paid was 1,600 gallons of whiskey to be paid in four installments within one year.

Gallatin-Kramer glass has become very valuable and much sought after by collectors. One of the Westmoreland County Museum of Art catalogs lists a few of the articles made by the company:

Calabash liquor bottles of green window glass, some swirled Milk Pans of window glass, free-blown, folded-in

Many other types of bottles, flasks, and milk bowls were produced and may be seen in the fine collections at the Oglebay Museum in Wheeling, the Greene County Historical Society Museum out of Waynesburg, and other Penn's Southwest collections.

Greensboro glass lilies, or morning glory flowers are an interesting by-product of the Old Glassworks of Gallatin-Kramer. In the Beallsville office of Dr. Milton Manning is a painting by his son, Jim, of these flowers which were made ca. 1805-10 by the glassblowers at the end of their workday if they had a little molten glass left; not enough for a utensil, but enough for them to blow a few lilies.

Louise Syphers Cline of Dry Tavern has told the writer how she and other youngsters used to comb the river and creek banks for odd bits of metal and objects they could trade for glass from the river barges that hawked glass in the manner of the pottery arks. She recalled both first quality and seconds and for pennies they could buy such pieces as Spanish lace and thumbprint pattern tumblers, small compotes of blue opalene river glass, cranberry vases with sprays of flowers engraved on the glass, cloudy blue-green bowls. It is not known whether Gallatin-Kramer produced colors other than the pale greens of their window glass, for which they were especially famous.

As part of the heritage of southeastern Greene County, residents of Greensboro have taken over the old two-story stone schoolhouse in town for a Monon center called the River Museum where they will commemorate the traditions of glass and pottery making and boating.

Greensboro glass lilies.

20

PAINTERS BOTH THEN
AND NOW IN PENN'S SOUTHWEST

THE SPECIAL 1776 ISSUE (in 1976) of *Time* in its section
on art contains this statement:

> ... there is another tradition in American art that has been too
> little appreciated. That is the tradition of the simple journeymen
> artists who make their living by painting likenesses for pleasantly
> prosperous people. . . . Like peddlers, they come to the door and
> inquire whether the master or mistress wants a portrait painted.
> Their range is the range of their (travel or perhaps their horse)
> and their reputation passes by word of mouth in the town squares
> or local taverns.
>
> . . . their heritage comes from sign painters for taverns rather than
> salon painters for courts.

During the year 1818, Isaiah Steen, chair maker, of the
town of Washington advertised in the *Reporter* that he carried a line of artists' supplies as well as "Portraits, Signs and
Ornamental Painting done" and a collection of "one hundred
paintings of the highest military characters of our Country."
It is said that Windsor chairs were not made in quantity in
America until after the Revolutionary War; Isaiah Steen commenced his Windsor chair making in 1796 with "twelve of
the most fashionable patterns." It was his son, John Steen,
who probably began at a very early age to decorate his
father's furniture and paint signs for local taverns.

Biographies of James Audubon tell of his meeting a wandering artist, young John Steen, in Natchez where Steen gave

375

him a few lessons in oils in 1822. During his travels in the swampy areas of the south, John Steen contracted a "pulmonary complaint" which caused his death at his father's home in Washington on June 29, 1825, when he was only twenty-three. The official notice described him as an "artist of genius and taste, who by fourteen was executing portraits with great accuracy and dispatch. He had visited many parts of the U.S. and wished to go to Italy to study."

Steen's plans to travel to Europe to study and paint followed those of most of America's early major painters who received more acclaim and success there than in their native land. Robert Fulton, before his association with steamboats, was known as a "miniature painter" and after settling his family on a Washington County farm, went to England to become a pupil of Benjamin West, historical painter to George III. West's Quaker family also had ties in the Monongahela Valley and at least one Washington family claims the silhouettes of their ancestors were made by West during a visit.

In October 1818 a nameless artist traveling with the Wax Museum displayed at Mary McCammant's tavern advertised "profiles taken during the day for 25¢." On May 18, 1818, George Harrison, miniature and portrait painter, moved from Beau Street to the McClure Building near the college in Washington. He painted likenesses for three dollars and also did store and tavern signs, window plates on tin or glass and had a few "elegant tavern signs" already painted, for sale at half price. In February 1820, Harrison ran a notice in the *Telegraphe* that he planned to leave Washington in April, but had a number of tavern signs already painted and would do miniature and portrait painting at his residence near the college.

Much later, in October 1869, Washington County undertaker John Lowe entered in his ledger that William Atlen had ordered an "oyster sign" made for which he paid Lowe with a half can of oysters and crackers to go with them. John Lowe also made many entries for "fixing paintings" for customers. At regular intervals during 1873 he was busy "putting up paintings" at the seminary and filling orders for gilt and walnut frames for Henry Schoenthal.

In the Washington County Circuit Court docket, September term 1803, it was ruled that "Isaac Jenkinson, artist" should make a draught of certain lands in dispute, indicating that some who were certified surveyors were also considered to be "artists."

Mrs. Margaret Best, who did a portrait of early attorney Parker Campbell ca. 1800, was noted in the *Reporter* in June 1832:

> Mrs. Best of Cross Creek Village was in town at the residence of Samuel Marshall making miniature portraits for one dollar.

Among the more famous of the early local painters was David Gilmour Blythe, born May 9, 1815, in East Liverpool, Ohio, to John and Susan Blythe who had come to this country from Scotland. As an artist, Blythe was almost entirely self-taught. Very early he showed an aptitude for drawing and astounded adults with his charcoal drawing of a cobbler on the door of a building near his home. When he was fifteen, he left East Liverpool and went to Pittsburgh to learn the wood-carver's trade in the shop of Joseph Woodwell. Here he did cabinet work and finish detail and designed and carved shop signs.

Blythe probably had his first glimpse of European paintings in the gallery opened by J. J. Gillespie in 1832, one of the oldest art establishments in America. Dealer Gillespie displayed some of the first paintings from foreign schools to be seen west of the Alleghenies. His studio became a meeting place for all the artists and it was also the headquarters for many prominent painters who came to Pittsburgh on portrait commissions. Thomas Sully is said to have stopped at Gillespie's while he painted nine portraits of Pittsburghers.

About 1834, David Blythe visited New Orleans and not long afterward went to New York and enlisted in the navy as a ship's carpenter. He was so employed from 1837 to 1840 when he returned to Pittsburgh and worked as a cartoonist, itinerant portrait painter in the countryside, and did genre paintings of life in the city, for which he is, perhaps, most famous. In the winter of 1846-47 he moved to Uniontown and the following year on September 30, 1848, he married Julia Keffer who contracted typhoid fever and died within a year. Blythe never completely recovered from the shock of her death. He continued to travel about as an itinerant painter and also did a number of oil portraits for Uniontown residents. During an early period of his life, it is the writer's feeling that Blythe may have made the charming and skillful charcoal portrait of Elizabeth Seaton (Dulany) at age fifteen or sixteen, reproduced in this chapter. The fifteen by twenty-inch portrait so tinted with age that it appears to be a watercolor, hangs in the old brick home of her late granddaughter, Mrs. Maud (S. J.) Titus of Jefferson. So that it could be reproduced in this book, the Titus family allowed Myers Crayne to remove the picture from its walnut frame and take it to Greensboro where photographer descendant of early Kramer glassblowers, Deb Kramer, took this fine photograph. It is obvious that the artist was an accomplished draftsman who did not miss a detail of Miss Seaton's costume and coiffure and who knew so well the cardinal rule in art classes, how to fill the paper.

In the early years of the 1800s painted panoramas were a popular forerunner of today's movies. In 1818, Mrs. McCammant advertised the exhibition of a panoramic view of "Life in Rome" at her tavern. During his years in Uniontown, David Blythe painted a very ambitious and spectacular panorama, showing historical events and the natural scenery he had sketched on his wanderings through Albemarle County, Virginia, and up through the Ligonier Valley of Pennsylvania. It was called a panorama of the Allegheny Mountains painted on seven by fifteen-foot sections of canvass, sewn together to

Charcoal portrait of Elizabeth Seaton Dulany painted by an unknown itinerant
rtist when she was fifteen or sixteen years of age, ca. 1835-40. From original in Titus
ome, Jefferson, Pennsylvania.

make a 300-foot strip, which Blythe exhibited by unwinding it from revolving rollers.

The painted scenes exhibited in major cities of the area, included:

Monticello with Charlottesville in the distance

The Potomac winding through the rocky gap at Harpers Ferry

The Natural Bridge in Virginia

Washington's 1754 route on his expedition against the French

The American Army at Fort Necessity

Braddock's encampment and the burial of General Braddock

Washington and Gist in consultation

Arthur St. Clair in front of his log house, Ligonier Valley

Fishing at Ohiopyle Falls

Uniontown from Pine Knob

A snow and a stagecoach scene

White Rocks where Polly Williams was killed in 1810

The rocks where Jumonville was killed in 1754.

Unfortunately, this venture was unsuccessful and after exhibits in Baltimore, Pittsburgh, East Liverpool, Cincinnati, Cumberland, Maryland, and Winchester, Virginia, in 1851 the immense painting was cut up and sold piece by piece for theatre backdrops and scenery. It seems incredible that not one of the panels escaped eventual destruction.

After a few years in East Liverpool ca. 1850 where there are a number of Blythe paintings, he returned to Pittsburgh. There was a brief interval during the Civil War when Blythe followed the Thirteenth Pennsylvania Regiment as an artist and produced many sketches of army life as well as paintings of military and political events. He planned to paint another panorama using this material, but his health failed while he lived in a small attic room on Third Avenue in Pittsburgh. He died May 15, 1865, in Passavent Hospital there.

In the Fayette County issue of *Tableland Trails* quarterly, published in spring 1955, there is a rundown of his work. Over fifty of his portraits and their owners were known; thirty more portraits were known but the owners were unknown. Some sixty genre paintings were located, ten of them in the Duquesne Club in Pittsburgh. Many are owned by area residents, and some are in the Brooklyn Museum, Museum of Fine Arts in Boston, various New York City galleries, and the Carnegie collection in Pittsburgh.

Local legend tells that Blythe was related to the Rice family of Rice's Landing and members of this family are said to own a chest which was handsomely carved and painted by David Blythe. There is also an amusing story about F. H. Rice, a Yankee shoe merchant who told Blythe how he would drive through the mountains and exchange his merchandise for country produce. One day he fell asleep and his wagon overturned and spilled apples, onions, butter, and a live turkey on top of him. Blythe, with his flair for comedy and sarcasm, made a painting of the episode and called it "Rice's Landing" to the mirth of all his fellow boarders at Uniontown's Seaton House.

* * *

There are a few scattered references in local papers to the "noted glass sign painter, George Faddis" but very few facts about his life and how he started to draw and paint are known. The writer was able to locate only one example of his work which is hardly a fair sampling, although it does show his excellent draftsmanship. George Rex Faddis was born April 7, 1850, in Greene County and was a brother of the late Colonel Charles Faddis's father. His pencil drawing of the Monongahela House in Rice's Landing must have been done when the Faddis family ran the hotel and carried on a commission business in the lower level of the building.

Front-porch conversations with Colonel Faddis disclosed all that is known about this very talented painter, who early in his life rode the riverboats from Pittsburgh and river ports to New Orleans and did barroom decorations along the way, as well as scenes in the steamboat saloons. When P. T. Barnum ran an ad in the New York *Times* shortly after he founded the circus in 1871, George Faddis answered the ad. Details are not known, but a friendship developed and Faddis was commissioned to paint many of the early Barnum circus posters and was given a free pass to their shows. He painted all the way down the Mississippi and was one of the best swimmers on that river, so it is tragic that his early death came about by drowning. One day while on a riverboat, a small craft nearby capsized. George dove in to the river, rescued the passengers, but as he swam back to his own boat, he drowned, on April 16, 1883.

Present members of the Faddis family have inherited some of George's talent; Jane and Charles Faddis's son, George, is an accomplished painter and art instructor, and George's son, Robert Faddis, teaches art in the Waynesburg schools and

Traced sketch of George Faddis's pencil drawing of the Monongahela House Rice's Landing about 1875, built by Thomas Hughes, Jr., and his son-in-law, Ja Lucas. The lower level was used as a forwarding commission house where mercha brought their goods twice a year from Baltimore and Cumberland by six-horse tea over the mountains. Loaned by George Faddis, grandnephew.

designs and makes replicas of early Pennsylvania rifles and powder horns, with their intricate metal work and engraving. Another local painter descended from the Bowell family of iron foundry fame, is Nellie Ammons, retired teacher who lives in Rice's Landing and paints covered bridges and local scenes, using a gay palette and a modified Grandma Moses style.

* * *

Early in the spring of 1968 when the writer drove from her home in Berkeley, California, to Penn's Southwest to spend the summer researching material for a book (*this* book) she didn't dream that by that fall she would be living on the historic Parkinson farm near Prosperity, which had been the last home of the well-known illustrator, model, and diorama maker, Lindsey Evans Parcell. The widow of Evans Parcell had died in the spring and the farm with the 1830 farmhouse filled with Parcell furniture, keepsakes, drawings and some paintings, and experimental model buildings was for sale. The family did not wish to have a public sale of household items and the writer and her family were able to purchase the house and contents.

Information for the biographical sketch and project data has come from the Parcell personal files and scrapbooks in the old Greek Revival farmhouse, restored and renamed by the writer, Old Springhouse Farm.

A few years after the turn of this century, the youngsters in Claysville used to flock to the home of a young lad who made his own playthings. They liked to visit handy little Evans Parcell who had a knack for building miniature oil wells, battleships, and model Indian villages.

Evans Parcell graduated from Washington and Jefferson College as an engineer and after studying painting at the Carnegie Institute in Pittsburgh and a period at the Art Students League in New York, he became one of the most sought after magazine illustrators of the 1920s. Then, in 1930 his studio on Main Street in Washington with all his paintings and some personal belongings was destroyed in a fire. Many people puzzled over his decision to give up illustration and turn to dioramas. To forget the catastrophe, Evans and his wife Estelle Prigg Parcell, took a trip to Florida and on the way home they visited a museum in Charleston, South Carolina, which featured an exhibit in miniature. It caught Evans's artistic eye and struck an emotional chord from the past. "This is what I have really wanted to do ever since I was a child," he told his wife.

As soon as they reached Little Washington, Evans went to work on his first model, the old farmhouse which typified the rural construction he had seen from western New York to the Carolinas, but most typical of southwestern Pennsylvania. The sketches and notes which went into that first creation became characteristic procedure for Parcell dioramas. Later he was able to draw upon his research into local history which had begun with his child's play among model Indian villages.

A combination of mechanical ability and art is necessary in constructing dioramas, and Parcell used the tools of all trades in his work. This included a surgeon's scalpel, sculptor's chisel, painter's brush, and implements of the dental and mason's trade. He built special saws and lathes to do special work and it took nearly fifty motors to run the unusual machines, many of his own design, which turned his workshop into a magical production line.

The July 1925 issue of *Contact*, the Westinghouse magazine, had a cover by L. Evans Parcell, slightly reminiscent of early Norman Rockwell *Post* covers. The next record of paintings in the Parcell files were page proofs of ads for Follansbee Forge Steel of Pittsburgh which appeared in the *Saturday Evening Post* in March, April, and June 1927. These are powerful drawings of a steelworker in various poses in ads reading:

FORGING ADDS STRENGTH—Very graphically this painting by L. Evans Parcell conveys the Spirit of the process whereby "perfection is forged in and defects forged out"—the Spirit of the Follansbee Forge.

In January 1933 while working on the construction of the miniature mountain farm, Parcell said:

> My natural interest in pioneer America led me to specialize in illustrations of rural life. For years I had studied, photographed and drawn buildings, furnishings and all manner of man-made objects common to earlier American times. When I had some free time about a year ago, I began making models of trees from plant and tree roots. Gradually I conceived the idea of reconstructing on a small scale, a diminution of an American farm scene with old trees round about. I felt the necessity of preserving an image of an integral part of the American scene during the last hundred years.

Following his impulse to work in the third dimension rather than flat illustration which had never satisfied him, Parcell built a pioneer log house with clapboard addition to a scale of seven-eights of an inch to the foot. The springhouse and corncrib, the farm wagon, the sled with hickory runners, plows, and saws were designed and fabricated in the same spirit that inspired the originals. They were not copies reduced in size, but were fashioned to work. His method of assembling hundreds of objects as they occur in natural use, combined with the beauty of design and craftsmanship which is manifested in the most minute detail of the whole, and the refreshing absence of the theatrical, creates reality. So wrote Penelope Redd in a November 1933 feature article in the Pittsburgh *Sun-Telegraph*.

The November 1931 issue of Washington & Jefferson College's Alpha Chapter of Phi Gamma Delta *The Wiji Fiji* has a photo of the McMillan log cabin built in 1780 by the Reverend John McMillan in Canonsburg, "the first college building west of the Allegheny Mountains, which is to be preserved for posterity by the fraternity."

> It is only 15 feet 3 inches square and the crevices between the logs once filled with clay, now have cement stoppings. The cabin

was moved and entrusted to Phi Gamma Delta in 1907. . . .
Benno Jannsen of Pittsburgh is working on the plans for the
canopy which were drawn by Brother Evans Parcell '14.

In November 1932, *Antiques Magazine* in New York wrote
Evans regarding the photographs and notes on his model
farmhouse and asked him to state the scale for a possible
feature story.

In September 1935 Evans received a letter from the advertising manager of Kaufmann's in Pittsburgh, sent to the Dun-
can Avenue address:

> Since seeing your old farm model, I have been busy formulating
> plans for showing it. I wish you would stop in as soon as possible,
> as I would like to go over this with you and settle up a few
> details.
>
> Recently we showed a Doll House built for Colleen Moore which
> is touring the country and which met with a great deal of interest.

In January 1937 a committee wrote to Mr. E. Parcell,
Supt. Museum Extension Project, WPA., Philadelphia:

> The much regretted fact that you are leaving us places us in the
> position of being supervised by . . . whose inability to cooperate
> with qualified technicians in their respective professions, would
> be contrary to the efficiency of this project. We wish to thank
> you for your splendid cooperation and helpful suggestions in solv-
> ing many technical problems.

In 1938 Parcell made the Louisville University campus
model to one-thirty-second inch scale. He worked on this
model nearly full time for five months and then built the
seven by ten-foot model of the Colby College campus in
Waterville, Maine. He also made a model of his alma mater,
the Washington & Jefferson campus.

December 1941 brought a letter to Parcell at East Beau
Street from the Industrial Division of the Pittsburgh Chamber
of Commerce:

> There will be another meeting of the Camouflage Group in the
> Conference Room of the Chamber on Thursday evening, Decem-

ber 11. In view of what has occurred [Pearl Harbor on the 7th] it is essential that immediate steps be given to camouflage protection for industrial plants and by pooling ideas, it is hoped that a start can be made on assembling suitable models to show what can be done.

In June 1941 there was a bill from the Mayflower Storage Company for moving the Parcell household goods from Pittsburgh to the old Clokey farm near Eighty-Four. Until their move to Prosperity in 1956, Evans and Estelle Parcell worked on a restoration of the ca. 1812 stone Clokey farmhouse and surrounding grounds.

In 1947 there was a plan to set up an exhibit in the lobby of the Union Trust Building in Pittsburgh during Pennsylvania Week and Parcell's diorama of Fort Duquesne was to be part of it. "We are agreeable to the idea and think it would be all to the good for you. How about it?" In November of 1947, Director Franklin Holbrook of the Western Pennsylvania Historical Society advised Evans:

> At last we have been told that the Fort Pitt Chapter of the D.A.R. has definitely given up all idea of purchasing your diorama of Fort Duquesne, as you have probably suspected . . . now there seems to be some possibility that the Society might purchase it, if you are willing to let it go for considerably less than the original price. How would an offer of five hundred dollars strike you?

In December Parcell received a check with a note saying the money had come from funds bequeathed to the society by the late Anna Moody Browne "and it is to serve as a memorial to her. Mr. Stotz was authorized to seek your advice in the matter of providing a suitable plate for it. . . ." Later that year the ladies of the Board of the Block House at the Point asked for a photograph of the diorama of the site of old Fort Duquesne to reproduce on a color postcard.

The Fort Ligonier Memorial Foundation was organized in November 1946 without even the assurance that the accepted location of the fort was correct. In March 1950 "Charlie" Stotz wrote Evans:

> I presented your material and bid to the Fort Ligonier Memorial Foundation last Wednesday night. They are very much interested and I believe we can get action soon. No model work can be done until the ground is surveyed and this is to get under way soon. Will keep you advised—

In October 1954 Stotz sent Parcell a copy of the booklet *The Story of Fort Ligonier* and wrote: "In the two weeks I had to write and organize material for the booklet, there was no time to get a better picture of the model but this can be corrected in subsequent editions." A fine photograph of the Parcell model of Fort Ligonier was included in *Drums in the Forest*, a collaborative effort of Alfred P. James and Charles Stotz published in 1958. At his own request, there is no mention of Parcell's name on the model. A modest, retiring person, Evans Parcell was always reluctant to accept praise for his remarkable gifts and accomplishments.

During 1950 Evans was asked to make a painting of the coat of arms of Phi Gamma Delta, the thirteenth oldest Greek letter fraternity in America which was founded at historic Jefferson College at Canonsburg, May 1, 1848.

In 1953 there was a project for three dioramas of the old Pennsylvania portage railroad for the Penn Traffic Company in Johnstown. There were many more projects and exhibits over the years and in June 1956 the well-known writer, Stefan Lorant, wrote to Parcell from Lenox, Massachusetts:

> It was so good to see you and talk. I was very impressed by your drawings and do hope you will be able to do the sketches we talked about, especially the one about the Pack Horse Train and the other, the Clearing in the Wilderness. Of course, if you find time to do the Ambush of the Indians at Fort Pitt during the Pontiac Uprising, I would appreciate it. I am making up my book. . . .

In 1958, the last year of Evans Parcell's life, he painted a series of six masthead panels for the sesquicentennial issue of

Charcoal drawing of L. Evans Parcell by his brother, Malcolm Parcell.
Photograph by George Melvin of Claysville.

the Washington *Reporter* and general manager Jim Lyon wrote:

> Enclosed is our check to cover your quoted price. . . . Needless to say, your paintings were the highlight of the entire 240-page production. . . . We are deeply grateful to you for your price consideration as we know you devoted many hours of research in addition to the actual painting. We are indeed proud to have had the opportunity to include your work in the biggest newspaper we have ever published.

Besides the various historical projects, Parcell invented a number of mechanical devices over the years for wheel truing, mixing faucets, electric furnaces, and a product that would utilize the waste from glass dumps. He was considered a leading authority on western Pennsylvania forts and Indian lore. His ingenuity in contriving miniatures of many forms seemed limitless; in one campus diorama he used over one thousand small trees made from the dried, upturned roots of ragweed. Railroad tracks were simulated by using strips of celluloid run through a sewing machine and his oak leaves were painstakingly cut from brown kraft paper and glued to branches.

* * *

The New York *Tribune* for May 7, 1922, reported on the debut of an interesting young painter at Macbeth Galleries, with eight paintings, his second showing in New York. About Malcolm Stephens Parcell the critics said, "It is a great talent, not fully formed. The delicate draftsmanship and his decorative taste will lift him above convention, but he tends to be a little thin and sweet."

In the words of William Gill in a 1959 feature in the Pittsburgh *Press*, Malcolm Parcell had "rocketed to prominence in the international art world by winning the Saltus Gold Medal at the National Academy of Design exhibit in New York when he was only twenty-three." The prizewinning portrait was "Louine" which portrayed the "delicate aloofness" of its subject, Helen Louine Gallagher, schoolteacher in Little

Washington who was Parcell's favorite model and who became Mrs. Parcell in 1937.

Parcell's work was exhibited in 1923 at the Gillespie Galleries on Wood Street in Pittsburgh and was sold out immediately. More than just a recorder of fact, Parcell was described as making a "poetic gesture" in nearly every painting. By age twenty-five he was considered a prodigy and through all the years since that time, he has maintained a rigid self-discipline which means that every morning after breakfast he heads across the grounds of his rambling Elizabethan home with the heavy shake roof to the modern A-frame studio with fat, black Mutsie, another favorite model, at his heels. It is a privilege to visit this sky-lighted, well-ordered room with its drawers of brushes, its romantic balcony, built by Malcolm, and the workbench where he now constructs his own varied and interesting frames unless he locates a choice old one at an auction and then he paints a picture to suit the frame. There are a few of his "mythological fantasies" hanging in the studio and in the house, as he has been painting these for years as a sort of foil for his exacting portrait work and the carefully composed paintings of landscapes and historical buildings.

Many articles about Malcolm Parcell and his paintings appeared in English and French magazines which commented on the great variety of his subject matter. "His decoration reflects American customs and manners very pictorially; he is given to pageantry." The inclination to pageantry or theatre, is evident in Malcolm Parcell's own costume as he appears in the frame of his dull red Dutch-doorway in subdued woodsey-toned corduroy, or Pendleton muted tweeds with his own particularly vibrant red in tie or socks, and a felt skullcap ingeniously cut from one of Helen's old hats. The piercing dark eyes and neatly trimmed white hair and beard give an appearance which has been described as "Edwardian."

The *Carnegie Magazine* for January 1935 tells of a portrait of Malcolm in the collection of G. David Thompson and comments on this period of his painting when he "painted as an escape into the unknown with such curious Gothic pieces as 'The Gravediggers' and 'The Corner House.' " Before it was dispersed, ca. 1959, the Thompson collection included a group of sketches Parcell had made of historic buildings in Brownsville during the early 1930s.

Malcolm Parcell tells the story about his sketches of "historic St. Peter's Catholic Church" in Brownsville which drew so much comment he felt they were responsible for the restoration of the old stone church, built by Irish stonemasons in the style of an Irish parish church and dedicated in 1849. In the restoration (1936), the stained-glass windows of historic American scenes were made by George Sotter with whom Malcolm had studied at Carnegie Tech's School of Fine Arts. Historical paintings by Malcolm Parcell include the old stone Trinity gateway described by New York architect Bertram Goodhue as "the finest example of a rural gateway in the U.S.," a combined landscape-portrait of Sally Simpson, pioneer woman who dealt in herbs and made oak and hickory splint baskets in a log cabin on Malcolm's farm, and early barns and tollhouses along the National Road.

Today anyone who wishes his portrait painted must come to the A-frame studio for sittings as Mal-

Pen and ink sketch of the artist, by artist, Malcolm Parcell.

colm Parcell rarely leaves his beloved Moon Lorn except for short drives out in the Scout to see a springtime hillside of trilliums, or down to the Greene County Historical Society to check on his brother Evans's miniature farm scene, soon to be displayed in the museum there.

* * *

John Howard Iams, painter, was born April 10, 1899, in West Bethlehem Township in the farm home of his Baptist minister father, Demas Garber Iams and his wife, Anne Dunn, both Washington County natives. He was a descendant of pioneer Greene and Washington settlers who built many of the water and grist mills of the area. During the 1760s and 70s, his second great-grandfather, Isaac Dunn, operated a packtrain from Greene County into Virginia, so that much of his knowledge of pioneer activities was firsthand.

In order to be able to attend Carnegie Institute where he was enrolled in 1919, Howard worked as a carpenter with his older brother, Elisha, who was a building contractor before he retired to become one of the area's most accomplished researchers and historians. The Elisha Iams collection of genealogical data is now at Citizens Library in Washington, Pennsylvania. Later, Iams studied at the Art Students League in New York with his artist friends and neighbors, the Parcell brothers. These three gifted painters, for whom their native Washington County held such fascination both pictorially and historically, gave up any thought of abdicating and after a few years in New York, all returned to paint the scenes and subjects of their native Pennsylvania countryside.

Howard Iams had his first show in 1926 and his first major oil painting was "The Pack Train" painted under the auspices of the Public Works of Art Project. It shows a string of horses following a trail over the hills, laden with a shipment of whiskey from Pittsburgh. These trains consisted of as many as twenty or more horses and six men and it took about three weeks to pack out from near Pittsburgh to Philadelphia. Howard Iams was a great student of area history and the

1791-94 Whiskey Insurrection interested him especially; he considered it as important historically as the Boston Tea Party. In his own words, during an interview in 1934:

> Whiskey was the medium of exchange when money was scarce and seldom seen on the frontier. It cost twenty-five cents a gallon to produce and fifty cents a gallon to transport to Philadelphia where it sold for a dollar, whereas in Pittsburgh it just barely brought the cost price of twenty-five cents. It meant starvation to the pioneers when the tax of twenty-five cents was placed on each gallon, and they naturally revolted.

> It is my aim to make a pictorial history of the Whiskey Insurrection, probably a dozen or more paintings. I am now planning to paint the old Bradford house in Washington, as Bradford was a leader in the movement. Then I want to paint General Neville's house on Bower Hill between Little Washington and Pittsburgh, which was burned during the insurrection. I am also making a map of the roads in those days.

> Several of the old landmarks still have parts remaining and there are old people living who have positive knowledge about them, but they will soon be gone and then definite knowledge will be lost.

Described as "tall and gangling" and "thin and gaunt" with light hair, Howard worked with his brother Elisha when both were involved in research programs for the WPA in Washington County. They collaborated in the organization founded by Elisha called the Upper Ohio Valley Association for which Howard was the artist. He loved old houses and knew the history and exact location of the fifty-odd he sketched or painted, driving around the countryside in a rented car, working from old survey maps.

Howard Iams was mentioned in dispatches from Washington, D.C., according to a Pittsburgh *Press* feature on his work May 13, 1934. His oil of the LeMoyne House, after being hung with the PWAP show at the Corcoran Gallery was described as a "genuinely distinguished piece of work" by Edward Bruce, head of the national project. President Franklin Roosevelt selected it to be hung in the White House offices.

In 1973 the stone LeMoyne House built in 1812 by the French physician John J. LeMoyne who came to America during the French Revolution, was added to the *National Register of Historic Places;* it was presented to the Washington County Historical Society by the last resident-member of the family, Madeleine LeMoyne Reed in 1943.

About 1939, Howard Iams married Margaret Lewis, a native of Washington County and they moved to Camp Hill where Howard worked as a draftsman and illustrator for a major oil company in Harrisburg until he was transferred to Marion, Ohio, where his widow still lives. Before 1940, Iams had his work exhibited at the Art Institute in Chicago, the National Academy of Design in New York City, and at the Corcoran and National Gallery of Art in Washington.

Elsie Iams, historian of the North Tenmile Baptist Church and widow of Howard Iams's cousin, Bayard, recalled when they were married in 1935, they drove to New Geneva with

ALBERT GALLATIN MANSION

Sketch of Gallatin home by J. Howard Iams for later wood-block and oil painting. From Washington and Jefferson College Library.

Howard so that he could make a drawing of the home of Whiskey Rebellion leader, Albert Gallatin. She remembered him walking all around the building before deciding on the best position. The resulting sketch was used for one of his wood-block series which he sold by the set.

He had a fondness for rural scenes and the huge, virgin sycamore trees that grew along Tenmile and the various creeks in his childhood. He painted a small oil and a larger pastel of the 1820 Silas Clark homestead near Marianna where Elsie Iams now lives and where Howard was born. The simplicity and the clear, delicate colors of his palette evoke a feeling of nostalgia for old times and old places. Elsie Iams's daughter, Mary, attended a recent antique show in New York City and was surprised to see a painting that looked very familiar—painted by her uncle of the valley where he was born. The painting brought a very good price and recalled the statement once made by Malcolm Parcell to some local people, that Howard's work was better known in Paris than in America.

When the Pittsburgh *Bulletin* ran its column on Howard Iams in 1937 at the time of the Gillespie Galleries' show of his whiskey series, it commented that it was "one of the most ambitious and original efforts of any regional artist." The show consisted of three of his four large oils, ten of fifteen pastels, and seventeen of his twenty-one wood-block prints. During these years he had an early Gulf Oil show in Pittsburgh where he exhibited his subtle paintings "Spring Rain" and "Morning Fog." The "Japanese delicacy" of these works and also his "Trees" caused comment. In May 1964 Howard Iams died in Marion, Ohio.

21

NOTABLE WOMEN

PUBLIC SENTIMENT proclaims this to be the Golden Age of woman—let her choose her own vocations—if her tastes and capabilities are for masculine employments, why should the befogged customs of the past raise a hue and cry?

In one of her recent columns in a Washington paper, Marcia McKenna Biddle commented on the above quote, written not in 1975 for the "women's lib" movement but by Mary Fonner Hanmer in 1896 for the Greene County *Woman's Centennial Paper*, published and written entirely by Waynesburg women to raise money to beautify the parks.

Women may not have been liberated nearly a century ago, but the thoughts they expressed were largely those of today's woman. In another of the *Centennial* articles, Mary Temple Bayard even took on General Greene:

I suppose there could be no ranker heresy than to in any way decry General Greene, the patron saint of our county. And yet, at the risk of being executed in the public square, under the very shadow of his imposing image, I want to claim free speech and add an item that has been left out of the platform orations. Surely there has been enough gush over his bravery to turn his wooden head 'tother side front, but there has not been a biographer with the courage to call him a coward. Physical courage we know he had in plenty, but there is a moral courage in which he seems to have been lacking.

Would we not today call a man a coward who would not allow his wife to confess to the world her discovery that her head was not filled with cotton or sawdust, as he had been making her believe it was? Well, that is just what General Greene did when he prevented his wife from acknowledging herself the inventor of the first cotton gin. To her second husband is due the credit for her ever having braved the ridicule, and claimed her invention. Up to this time we have excused all domestic tyrants who at the expense of the brains of their women folk have made names for themselves. Katherine Greene could have claimed the invention of the cotton gin and brought no discredit thereby upon her great husband.

* * *

Maria Harvey—Miss Harvey, born in Philadelphia in 1792, rode horseback with her family over the Allegheny Mountains to Greene County ca. 1802, and lived on the Harvey family farm in Richhill Township until she was about eighteen and began to think about a career for herself. Her grandniece, Miss Sarah Dinsmore of Waynesburg, has given the writer many family anecdotes about this rather remarkable woman who became the first woman pharmacist west of the Alleghenies and who was thoroughly capable of earning her own living in a number of ways when most women remained sheltered within the home.

In a group of family letters is one written August 29, 1811, from eastern Pennsylvania to Maria from her brother, William Harvey, who made an important railroad survey through Penn's Southwest in 1828. William counseled his sister to collect their mother and brothers and to "calm down and ask them if they want you to continue to live with them or go away. Read and study the third chapter of James, and *check your tongue!*" Heeding her brother's advice, Maria sold her interest in the farm for $300 and moved to Waynesburg. She built a small house on the corner where the Abner Tharp house stands and opened a millinery shop where she taught young girls how to make hats and bonnets. She used a bleaching process in preparing the straw for the bonnets which endangered her life and she had to give up this endeavor.

William Harvey continued to write and Maria was concerned with matters at home on the farm. In January 1812 a letter came from Buck County:

> Strange, surely say you, that William wanders from place to place so much. . . . Your bedstead pattern I have procured for you. Against each of the forms of the post is written its length and proportion . . . as to a road run through our farm for a mile, you should stop the opening for six or nine months and I will put a stop to it running through our fields. I think it very strange that people are so opposed to our welfare and interest. I believe I could write to you for twenty-four hours and still not get at all the *heart* of the subject.

There was no pharmacy in Waynesburg at this time and Miss Harvey's fertile brain conceived the idea of starting one. So, encouraged by her male doctor friends, she rode horseback to Philadelphia for supplies and set up the town's first drugstore. She ran the business for over thirty years with a record of never incorrectly filling a prescription or selling whiskey unless she knew it was required for medicinal purposes. Her disposition was bright and sunny and over the years she also managed a small hotel, conducted the post office, and taught a select school. When she retired she had amassed quite a fortune for the times and had also assisted her nieces and nephews to study at the new Waynesburg College. She died in 1884 and is still remembered for her twice a year horseback trips by herself over the mountains.

* * *

Sarah Jane Price Parker Ackley—in honor of this woman who typified "The Pioneer Mother" her great-granddaughter, Lucille Carroll, erected a monument with a bronze plaque near her homestead in Greene County. Sarah Jane Price was born near Little Egg Harbor, New Jersey, on September 4, 1754. When she was twenty she married John Parker, Revolutionary soldier who was killed in the Battle of Brandywine in 1777, leaving Sarah with a son, John Parker, Jr. In 1779 in Philadelphia, Sarah Jane married a second time, to a man who was also wounded at Brandywine, Daniel Ackley, born

April 30, 1747. They had six children born to them in Luzerne County but young Sarah died in infancy.

Daniel Ackley had explored in the Ohio Valley as early as 1765 when he was out with the Virginia militia; there are numerous legends about how the Ackleys and the Teagardens swapped and traded land on Owens Run where Daniel's family settled in Richhill Township after his death in 1794. Sarah Jane decided her destiny lay out in the wilderness where Daniel had explored, and where some of John Parker's family had settled. Selling her possessions and gathering her children, with two other families, they started out in a covered wagon in 1816. Sarah Jane took up a tract of several hundred acres on Wheeling Creek, and with the help of her sons, built a double cabin of hewed logs. While the boys labored, Sarah superintended and until Daniel, Jr., built the house where Lucille Carroll now lives, Sarah is said to have moved about on her land and built several other log houses.

She was a charter member of the first Methodist Church established in the region and in summer when the horses had been working all week, Sarah Jane walked four miles to the "Valley Meeting House" to attend all of the preaching services conducted by the circuit rider. A week before her death, she had walked a half mile to have dinner with her favorite granddaughter and when complimented on the fact that she had never been ill and bid fair to live out a century, she said: "Oh, I know better than to expect that. Look at the veins in my hands, my work is done. The journey is over and I am ready to rest." On the following Friday morning in June 1851, she fell asleep. "The splendid courage and strict honesty, the helping hand and wise counsel of this woman made an impression upon the whole community which is still felt, though sixty years have passed since she left us."

* * *

Ann Quail Moreland Hoge (second wife and widow of John Hoge, surveyor and proprietor of Washington)—Because of a letter written by Ann Hoge September 13, 1867, in some bitterness over the hard labor of her younger years, we have a vivid picture of a pioneer woman:

> To William M'A., William and Alexander Quail—Gentlemen:
>
> I take the liberty of addressing a few lines to you. . . . We came into this country in 1812, I believe. Father purchased a farm and we went on it in the fall. In the spring Robert went to Pittsburgh to acquire a knowledge in the carpenter business, the other boys went to hard work on the farm. The farm was much out of order and it took a great amount of hard labour to put it in good repair. Produce was very low and it took a great amount of it to make a little money, so we began to work and economize. Jenny soon married, then Mother and I had to breast the work.
>
> We worked hard; milked from six to ten cows and fed the same amount of calves, churned, made cheese and butter, cooked, scrubbed, washed and baked and no little baking it took for so many working men, entertained our friends and attended to all the household business.
>
> Then I pulled flax and spread it down to water, lifted it, dried and made handfulls for the breaker, scutched some, hackled it, spun and got linen made for the family and shirts and pants for the work hands to help to pay them their wages. Then I knit and sewed and made the men's wearing apparel.
>
> Then sugar making was not the least of the hard work. One spring Mother and I stirred on the kitchen hearth, *one thousand pounds*—James weighed it.
>
> Then came the building of a barn. Men quarrying stone, hauling stone, men taking out timber, hauling timber, masons and their attendants and carpenters for a long time. In all that time we had no help but Susan Hagerty for four and Elizabeth Ferguson for two weeks. All the sweat, strength and labour that was wrung out of Mother and me was centered in that farm. There were times when our wardrobe became so low that we could hardly appear decent.

In connection with the general subject of women, it is interesting to note that John Hoge who had a very large library and attended auctions whenever he was in town, was listed in a "Vendue" in January 1794 as having purchased *Rights of Women* and *Briggs' Cookery*.

* * *

Lydia Boggs Shepherd Cruger—Lydia Boggs of Wheeling witnessed the siege of Fort Henry as a girl and later became influential in having the National Pike swing by her door. Columnist James Mullooly in his "Westsylvania Corner" of the Washington *Observer-Reporter* wrote a column on Lydia, calling her the "Perle Mesta of her time" who had come to Wheeling as a child in 1774 when her father, Captain Boggs, staked a claim to a piece of riverfront acreage. She grew up on the frontier and even made an escape from Shawnee Indian captors who had scalped one of her brothers and burned their cabin to the ground. During this period she met young Moses Shepherd whose father, Colonel David Shepherd, commanded at Fort Henry built on the site of Fort Shepherd. Lydia and Moses Shepherd, after their marriage, inherited a large fortune from his father and Lydia took care of the accounts for the sawmill, tannery, distillery, and tavern. After they built the Georgian stone mansion they called Shepherd Hall (now a Shrine headquarters), Lydia became noted as a hostess to most of the major figures of the day, including a number of presidents. It is said that Lafayette stopped there in 1825 and danced a minuet with Lydia Shepherd in the elegant grand ballroom on the second floor. Henry Clay had his own special bedroom and stopped often on his way from Lexington to the capital.

After Thomas Jefferson authorized the building of the National or Cumberland Road, Shepherd secured the contract for building all the bridges between the Pennsylvania line and Wheeling. The Washington County Historical Society has a fine collection of papers pertaining to the activities of Moses Shepherd and other National Road figures. At this time the Shepherds spent their winters in the capital so that they could be close to Congress; both Lydia and her husband were politically oriented and were very much a part of the Washington scene. Colonel Shepherd died during the cholera epidemic of 1832 and Lydia then married a New York congressman, General David Cruger. She outlived him by many years and at the age of one hundred or more kept abreast of the times by reading newspapers and was keenly interested in events of the Civil War. She died in 1867 at 102 years and had a temperament and the physical stamina to have been a leader in a women's movement in any century.

* * *

Sally Simpson—The biography of this woman, who was known both as an herb doctor and a basket maker, was assembled by Donald Burnham, president of Westinghouse from an area history, when he purchased Malcolm Parcell's portrait in 1964.

Sally Simpson, who lived alone on the dividing ridge between Greene and Washington near Prosperity, was a character so unique and of such rare personality that "we write so as to preserve the fast fading memories of her in our local history [in 1918]." She had an education that would have fitted her for almost any station in life; above average height and weight and with great executive ability, she taught school in her younger days and then took up a piece of vacant land on Hame String Run (Malcolm Parcell's farm) where, with her own hands she constructed her log house and surrounded herself with a library of the best books of the day and lived her strange life.

She made baskets and put splint bottoms in homemade chairs; she cut the saplings from the forest surrounding her home and prepared them herself. Besides supplying the local demand for baskets she often hired someone to take a wagonload of various sizes, and perched on the seat with the driver, she would start for some of the trading marts along the Monongahela and Ohio where she would barter for calicoes, crocks, cloth, etc., which she would then sell to her neighbors. Her baskets were skillfully and honestly made and today there are two of them which Eben Blatchely purchased from her and have been in constant service for more than fifty years.

She was a skillful Thompsonian doctor and her library

included his formula for compounding the herbs and roots whereby he cured many people in the early days. Thompson's Sixth Formula known to druggists as No. 6 was used by Sally to heal many of her neighbors before there were many doctors in the area. She raised her chickens in her house and when a hen had set on the eggs until they were "pipped" she would place them in her ample bosom until they were all hatched so the hen would not step on them.

* * *

Elizabeth Tanner—There was another well-known basket maker who lived west of Burnsville who was featured in a 1914 story in the Washington *Reporter*. At that time she was eighty-seven and living on the old Tanner farm "the most remarkable woman in S.W. Pennsylvania." Born in North Carolina December 10, 1826, she had come with her parents over the mountains to Greene County when she was eight years old. After she married in 1848 and raised twelve children, she reminisced, "Many a day I would split one hundred rails from the stump; cut down the tree, trim it and split out the rails." Many of her baskets are still in use, and like Sally Simpson, she mended chairs. In 1914 she was still playing the violin as she had since she was a little girl and the old airs were "The Irish Washerwoman," "Pop Goes the Weasel," and "Fisher's Handspike."

* * *

Phoebe Jane Teagarden, M.D.—"Doctor Jane," as she was known in Waynesburg where she practiced medicine for forty years, is remembered pitter-pattering briskly down the street, her long black skirt and petticoats rustling, on her way to deliver a new baby. She often wrote columns for the *Republican* and the following paragraphs are from the August 1920 "Woman Citizen":

> In the winter of 1879-80 when a student in the Woman's Medical College at Philadelphia, I first met and heard Miss Susan B. Anthony, who came to lecture . . . in a love of a black velvet bonnet, handsome silks and gracefully stepped to the platform. At that

time Waynesburg College was being financed by nearly every teacher, student and woman in Greene County and I asked Miss Anthony if she would come and give a benefit lecture for the college. . . .

On the evening of May 7, 1880 I met Miss Anthony at the W&W station on arrival of the evening train; the sunset revealed the beautiful Tenmile Valley at its best as we came to my home where she was to be a guest. I recall how she talked with my father who had all his life been a universal suffragist and she didn't spare her criticism of my lukewarm interest in equal suffrage, saying, "Oh, you probably get the same pay for the same medicine and service as men doctors do, but your sister gets forty dollars and a man gets seventy for less work in your Union School."

* * *

Lucille Ackley Evans Carroll—The writer has been visiting Lucille in her big white farmhouse at the site of the Ackley Covered Bridge since 1942 and it is always a treat to drive down the creek opposite the place called Burdette. This particular trip was made on a frosty-chill December Sunday afternoon and the turquoise painted metal roof loomed ahead through the lavender-brown of bare branches as the car moved across the short metal bridge over Owens Run and up to the back porch where there were strands of tinsel and Christmas red on the railing and bushes. Lucille answered the bell in robe and pajamas as is her custom on her one free day from the office when she stays in bed till noon and then relaxes by not dressing as she moves about her lovely old rooms and into the formal living room where she may sit down to the grand piano and play some of her own compositions for you.

On such days we have talked over the period of early Thomas Ryerson at Wind Ridge and the log blockhouse still standing at Ryerson's Station, and one of Lucille's favorite subjects—the many unusually intelligent, refined and capable women who lived in the West Finley hills. Lucille recalled that in her group they judged people as acceptable by whether or not her mother called on them. One of her mother's favorite friends was Callie Boyd who lived on Templeton's Fork and was a fine musician; she had a small ebony spinet on which she played for Mrs. Ackley.

Lucille's mother had insisted that her children be exposed to the theatre, concerts, good libraries, and the advantages of Pittsburgh so they moved from the country to town when they were all quite young. Lucille married a man who set up and operated steel plants and after their marriage, the Evanses moved to New England and lived in Portland, Maine, Worcester, Massachusetts, and Bridgeport, Connecticut. They were always in touch with good music and theatre in New York and today in the summer the old Ackley homestead overflows on some weekends with New York friends of Ackley nephews who marvel at the quality of "early Americana" along the byways of Greene County.

After Mr. Evans's death, Lucille and her mother returned to the old house in 1937 and began to restore it. A beautiful and capable woman, Lucille plunged into local activities, both social and business. Since that time she has successfully managed the operation of a fleet of huge school buses over the narrow, steep roads of Greene in the snows of winter, run a garage, pioneered laundromats in the Graysville community for women isolated in the hills without running water, acted as postmaster at West Finley, justice of the peace and notary, and the moving force in the Henry Ford bridge acquisition and the naming of Ryerson State Park. Today she still drives in to Graysville six days a week to her office next to the post office and puts in a full day. When the writer asked for one of her songs, she sent the lyrics to "Morning" which she composed for a local singer:

Out of the night comes the new-born day
Pushing the cover of dark away.
Winging and singing—laughing, so gay
Speeding the morning on its way.

Out of my heart comes this love so true
Tenderly wending its way to you.
To hold you my dear one, forever so near
Morning is breaking at last, night has gone out with the
    past,
My Dear.

* * *

There has been a long tradition of fine music and singing
schools in Penn's Southwest. Some of the finest singing has
been in the Upper and Lower Tenmile churches where there
seems always to have been unusual musical talent. Several
years ago a group of McGuffey High School girls called the
Pentachords presented a mini-musical called *Persons, Places
and Things.* It was written and the music composed by
Edythe Anderson of Claysville, with the assistance and accompaniment of Marjorie Fischer of Prosperity. In spite of
their busy teaching schedules, Edythe and Marjorie assembled
all of the clever verses which Marjorie then typed for the
writer after she had seen the highly entertaining "show."
There were ten separate acts, each based on an historical
event or place, set to music.

  I. Little Washington, Pennsylvania

 II. Towns and Places:

> There are places of mutual interest,
> Not far from this very place.
> There are names that stick right with us,
> There are memories we can't erase.
> There are little towns and villages,
> With names that may sound queer.
> Like Amity, Prosperity, Good Intent and Speers,
> Windy Gap or Pleasant Grove, Gabby Heights or
> Baker's Station. Lagonda, Pancake, Buffalo
> Village, Old Concord or Dunn's Station.
> Plumsock, Sparta, Tenmile and Enon, East and
> West Finley, Claysville and Beham.

There are many more that come to mind,
That we could name, if we had the time.
Things that happened, but belong to us today.
Places that are famous, we pass them every day.

III. An Old Covered Bridge

IV. The Little Crematory on the Hill:
There's a little red brick building
At the top of Redstone Road
Where Francis LeMoyne was buried, long ago.
There's a sign there, and it tells us
That the hill was once called 'Gallows'
But here's some history I'm sure you'd like to
know.

It's just the little crematory on the hill.
It's all so quiet and so very, very still.
But the cars go whizzin' by,
No one stops to wonder why,
It's just a little crematory on the hill.

Way back in eighteen hundred twenty-three or so,
They hung poor Billy Crawford there, he had to
go.
And the fife and drums were playing,
His body gently swaying,
From the highest tree there was upon the hill.
The horse and cart that brought him up the hill
Has long been gone, so quiet and so still.
And the people marched behind him, everyone
was sad.
It was the greatest, saddest day they ever had.

That was long before the red bricks and the stone
Laid Francis LeMoyne to rest and peace, he was
at home.

It was the first one of its kind,
In this country you could find.
This little crematory here upon the hill.

That was nothing to do with butter or with
cream.
No dairy ever stood there, it would seem.
No cheese, no curd, no whey,
Ever found the time of day,
In this little crematory on the hill.
Its function was merely to fill a vase,
With whatever was found left in the place.
This little crematory on the hill.

V. Chief Catfish:
When our ancestors came from East and South,
To settle and stake their claim.
They were met by a friendly Indian,
Chief Cat Fish was his name.
His tribe camped here in Washington
They hunted night and day.
He would look at you straight in the eyes,
And this is what he'd say.

Me—Catfish, me—Friend.
Let us smoke our pipe of peace with you.
You can plant your corn and taters, and your
tobacco, too.
This friendly tribe of Indians will never let harm
come to you,
Or you, or you, or you, or you, or you.

If it had not been for Chief Catfish
We might not be here today.
It was his friendly attitude, helped our ancestors
on their way.

This town was then called Catfish Camp, a name
    now seldom heard.
Then Bassett Town, later Washington,
Long after these friendly words were heard.

VI. McGuffey—the little one-room schoolhouse:
    It's a long, long way back to the schools of yester-
        day,
    Where one teacher taught all grades, in one big
        room.
    Where the plumbing—it was missing,
    But the pot-bellied stove—it was there.
    Now here's a little story, we would like for you to
        share.
    There's a little one-room school house,
    That we pass by every day.
    With its doors and windows broken,
    And the insides stuffed with hay.
    The old bell up in the steeple, that is missing to-
        day,
    Ringing out a cheerful greeting, at the starting of
        each day.
    Then the children would assemble,
    From the country, here and there.
    They'd pledge allegiance to our flag,
    And start the day with prayer.
    In the little one-room school house,
    Where they spent most of their day,
    Where the teacher was loved and respected,
    In that good old-fashioned way.
    They learned their A, B, C's,
    They learned to spell and read and write,
    But best of all they learned—
    The difference between wrong and right.
    Where authority was respected, human kindness
        not neglected.

Everyone learned what he was meant to know,
In this little one-room school house,
But that was long, very long ago.

VII. Washington and Jefferson (Liberation or Confusion):
"Washington and Jefferson"—who hasn't heard
the name!
But Washington and Jefferson will never be the
same.
It's now become a Co-ed, which all sounds very
well,
But is it liberation or confusion, only time will
tell.

There's a college in our town,
Where both boys and girls are found.
The future of our country, one might say.
Everything they say and do, has a strong effect on
you.
They're so erudite, persistent and blazé.
Not so very long ago, it was the boys who "ran
the show."
It was masculine way down to the very core.
But now that the girls are here, and the feminine
touch appears,
Is it liberation, or confusion? We would like to
know.
Has a man's domain been invaded?
Have the females merely stirred things up?
Will our country really benefit, one might say?
Can he concentrate more fully? Will his Latin and
Greek improve?
Will his philosophy, psychology, theology, anthro-
pology,
Ecology, and all other "ologies" really be on the
move?

Well, if Eve could stir up Adam, to such a dish of
applesauce,
Who knows what good may really come from all
this holocaust.
So, W&J, we salute you, whichever way you go.
But is it liberation, or confusion?
We would like to know.

VIII. Railroads—the Waynie, the Pennsylvania, the B&O

IX. Necessity—the mother of invention

X. Little Washington—with audience joining in the singing.

22

THE LACOCK WALKING EXPEDITIONS

THE CONNELLSVILLE *Daily Courier* carried the following news item March 28, 1932:

> The reconstruction and dedication of Fort Necessity as a national shrine on July 3 and 4, memorializing George Washington, has drawn the attention of historians anew to the historic spots in Fayette County . . . none are more qualified by original research and investigation than Professor John Kennedy Lacock, conceded to be the greatest authority on Braddock's Road.
>
> Professor Lacock, A.B., A.M., a graduate of Washington and Jefferson College, and of Harvard University is a native of Washington County where he was born in 1871. . . . During the summers of 1908 and 1909 he conducted "on foot" expeditions over the old Braddock Road with a view to relocating and preserving to posterity this historic highway. . . . This summer he is conducting a party of one hundred over the road and plans to finish the trip in order to be present at Fort Necessity July 4.

The first efforts to relocate the old Braddock Road were made in 1907 by Mr. Lacock in company with the man under whom he taught at Harvard, Professor Albert Bushnell Hart, professor emeritus of government at Harvard, and in 1932, historian of the George Washington Bicentennial Commission. These two men drove over the old National Road from Cumberland to Wheeling, and also made a preliminary survey of the early Indian trail from Pittsburgh to Fort Le Boeuf taken by Washington and Gist in 1753. This first route of Washington was the only one of all his journeys that had

413

never been accurately traced and the various encampments located. They worked in part from the Gist diaries at the Harvard Library.

In this year of the Bicentennial of the Nation we recall some of the events of the 1932 George Washington Bicentennial which brought to the surface many hidden or forgotten facts about Washington's experiences in Penn's Southwest. While Fort Necessity was accepted as the place where Washington fought his first battle, Professor Lacock advanced the argument that his first battle was really at Jumonville on May 28, 1754, before the July 3 battle at Necessity. Quoting from Francis Parkman who wrote "this obscure skirmish at Jumonville began the war that set the world afire," Lacock went on to consider that an actual "battle" was fought, although there was controversy over the number of troops involved and the time, which was less than twenty minutes, in order to qualify as a battle. In 1932 an unpublished Washington letter was found which appeared to confirm the Jumonville encounter as the first battle.

As part of Professor Lacock's contribution to the 200th Washington anniversary, he acquired title to about four acres of land encompassing the original Jumonville site, from a native German settler, Samuel Rosenik, who owned the surrounding farm. This place, described as "Washington's Rocks" about fifty rods from the Braddock Road on Laurel Hill and the ledge where the action took place, is an area twenty feet high and two hundred feet long. Mr. Rosenik had become such a patriotic American that he told Professor Lacock if no other group was going to commemorate the spot he considered sacred, he planned to erect a flagpole there at his own expense. The place was eventually marked and a park established.

McClelland Leonard, outstanding authority on Fayette County history, described Jumonville as "hidden in the forest for 178 years" until Professor Lacock began his investigations. When John Lacock died in the summer of 1937 from injuries received in a fall at Jumonville, he had just concluded a series of articles on the historic routes which were published in the Connellsville *Courier*. He had completed his latest effort to establish the various encampment sites which were later marked by the D.A.R.

In 1908 and 1909 Lacock conducted foot expeditions over the Braddock Road with parties of interested persons and photographers, noting the remaining traces of the original road and encampments. In 1910 and the following two summers, he conducted foot expeditions over the Forbes Road from Bedford to Pittsburgh, after he had been contacted at Harvard by Westmoreland County historian John Boucher. Accompanying him in 1912 were Drs. Henry W. Temple of Washington and George P. Donehoo, former state librarian, and other college men, including Professor Andrew J. Waychoff of Waynesburg. As a result of these walks, the Department of Internal Affairs at Harrisburg made a map of the warrantee surveys of original land patents along the line of the road from the Maryland line to Fort Necessity. The course of the road was indicated so that it would henceforth be possible to hike or travel the entire distance more or less on target. Recently, in a conversation with Miss Catherine Zimmerli of Hopwood, the writer learned that the depressions of the original Braddock Road and some of the old pine trees, which emigrants tapped for tar for their wagon axles, are located on her farm near Jumonville.

A group from the Phalanx Fraternity of the Connellsville YMCA volunteered and cleared over three miles of the road, one rod wide, across Laurel Hill in 1932 when the Walking Expedition of that year followed this schedule:

Tuesday, June 21—Cumberland, Maryland—starting point
Wednesday, June 22—Cumberland to Frostburg, Maryland
Thursday, June 23—Frostburg to Grantsville
Friday, June 24—Grantsville, Maryland, to Somerfield, Pennsylvania

Saturday, June 25—Somerfield to Fort Necessity

Sunday, June 26—Rest at Camp Washington

Monday, June 27—Fort Necessity to Mount Braddock (Gist's)

Tuesday, June 28—Mount Braddock to Mount Pleasant

Wednesday, June 29—Mount Pleasant to (Old) Madison, Pennsylvania

Thursday, June 30—Madison to McKeesport

Friday, July 1—McKeesport to Braddock

Saturday, July 2—Braddock to Pittsburgh.

On Sunday they rested again at Camp Washington and on Monday, July 4, celebrated at Fort Necessity.

23

PAPERMAKING AND WATERMARKS

PAPERMAKING was first introduced in the American colonies in the late seventeenth century according to paper authority Dard Hunter in his 1943 classic book on the subject, *Papermaking*. It was late in the eighteenth century before paper was made in Penn's Southwest at the Redstone Paper Mill on Redstone Creek in Fayette County.

It is interesting to consider a few of the aspects of how early paper was made and to review the rather meager information about watermarks. Because so much of the data in this book is from old papers, soiled, torn, stained, and often beautifully watermarked, the writer became fascinated with the wide range of designs and decided to trace and preserve in sketches as many of them as possible.

Early newspapers constantly carried "Wanted—Rags" ads, as early papers, including newsprint, had a high rag content. A beater or stomper was used to reduce the rags to fiber and it is reported that in some of the early mills, both flour and paper, were produced with the same millstones. There is a basic difference between "laid" paper, where the paper pulp is laid on wires in a mold, and "wove" paper which is what is used today. Wire plays a major part in watermarks also as the designs or emblems were held in place by fine wire. This is why there is always some variation in the marks made in the same mill at the same time; the wires shift and also after a certain amount of usage, the designs have to be repaired, and not always as expertly as the original. Some of the fine writing papers of today use the simulated antique lines laid by what is called a "dandy roll."

In the making of early paper, mention is made of the drying lofts of old mills where paper was hung over ropes made of woven horse or cow hair, coated with beeswax. Also, the wet paper was laid on felt and squeezed dry with large screws. In this area, round wooden poles were used for the loft drying. Paper sized with glue did not absorb the ink as did less carefully made paper and it was found that paper took ink better after being stored for some time. Some paper was polished with an agate or stone, and often paper made in the winter was tinted by the muddy stream water used.

The *Genealogy of the Sharpless Family* traces this Quaker family from the birth of Jonathan Sharpless on October 17, 1767, in Delaware County, Pennsylvania. Jonathan married Edith Nichols, an overseer in the Redstone Quaker Meeting, and their daughter, Elizabeth, married Samuel Jackson's son, Jesse; the two families were closely associated by both business and family ties.

In his *History of Fayette County*, Franklin Ellis reports that the young bachelor blacksmith and mechanic Jonathan Sharpless made a trip to visit his brother-in-law, Solomon Phillips, in Washington County in 1791. While in Redstone Country, he met a fellow Quaker, Samuel Jackson, who had a sizeable gristmill at the mouth of Redstone Creek. Soon the two men decided to pool their resources and build a paper mill. Sharpless went back to Delaware County and worked as a blacksmith for two years until he had saved $1,500 and then returned to Redstone. Others report that Samuel Jackson provided the capital for the mill and Sharpless the mechanical ability. The mill building was forty by seventy-five feet with a half-story cellar on the creek side and the large iron screws for squeezing the moisture out of the pulp, made of five-inch rod and four and one-half feet long, were tediously shaped by hand in the Sharpless blacksmith shop.

In July 1818, Samuel Jackson died at age sixty-nine and beginning with that year, assessment rolls for Washington Township give some mill background:

Alexander Dearman	Paper man
Chatsworthy Givens	Paper maker
David Harland	Paper maker
Jackson & Sharpless	Paper Mill val. $8,000 on 96 a.
	Grist Mill val. 1,000
	Saw Mill val. 500.

In 1819 the death of Samuel, Sr., is reflected in the listing of Samuel, Jr., and John Jackson as heirs, and Jesse Jackson as the manager of the paper mill. In the period 1820-23, Samuel's widow, Rebecca Jackson is given as "Manager" and by 1823 the glass factory is listed with the paper mill as a family operation, although founded much earlier, and Rebecca moved to Perryopolis. By 1830, William Sharpless managed the paper mill and the saw and grist mills. In 1832 there are no Jackson names on the tax rolls and by 1842 the paper mill had been destroyed by fire.

Dard Hunter reports there are no rules for distinguishing the paper of one century or one country from another. Deception was practiced in the use of watermarks by copiers, and watermarks cannot be used for exact dating because of their variations. It is also almost hopeless to classify watermarks with mills.

Hunter considers the various watermarks as forming an "encyclopedia of design" and there is historical importance in their subject matter; the earliest were thought to be symbols which conveyed special meanings. The post horn first appeared in 1670 when the post office was first established in England, however, some designs representing "hunting horns" were dated earlier. Another of the early designs was the dove and branch. Only the finer grades of writing paper bore these marks of identification.

There are four categories of watermark designs according

to Mr. Hunter and we have been able to find examples from all of them in area collections.

1. Crosses, ovals, circles, triangles, stars, etc.
2. Man and his parts—head, hands, feet; works of man—ships, anchors, staffs (plow)
3. Flowers, trees, grain, fruit
4. Legendary animals such as the unicorn, which took the most dexterity to make

Symbolic designs were replaced by emblematic, especially in Pennsylvania where workers were responsible for most unusual designs. The shield and crown device, adopted by the Dutch from the French, shows the influence of both countries; also the clover or trefoil and the fleur-de-lis or iris design. Early users of the popular dove and olive branch were Thomas Wilcox, the Gilpin Mill ca. 1789, and Thomas Amies in 1805; the Amies name is found on many early papers in this area. The copy of the Declaration in the Library of Congress is on paper watermarked "J. Honig" well-known papermakers of Zaandyk, Holland. We have reproduced the elaborate and beautiful beehive watermark of J. Honig.

Fayette County Common Pleas Court, bail bond, Jonathan Riggs and John Dille, November 29, 1787.

Fluer-de-lis design shows wire holding it in place in paper mold.

Washington County estate paper of Hardman Horn, April 9, 1812.

Washington County, estate of Christopher Horn sale paper, January 1810. Papermakers probably Jackson and Sharpless.

Washington County Common Pleas Court, judgment bond, October term 1813, *John Roberts* v. *George Morgan.*

Probably from Jackson and Sharpless Redstone Paper Mill.

Left: Washington County Common Pleas Court, June term 1793, *Lucy Wright* v. *Charles Call. Right:* Washington County Common Pleas Court, May term 1800, *executors of George Washington* v. *Alexander Addison and Matthew Ritchie.*

Note slight variations in horn design and lettering; both probably from Sharpless paper mill.

Hampshire County court records August 9, 1761, estate inventory of Richard Heazill.

Washington County, Pennsylvania April term 1807, Common Pleas Court *William Seaman* v. *John Hughes, the younger.*

Fayette County Common Pleas Court,
December term 1785.

Washington County,
Pennsylvania, Common
Pleas Court, May term
1799, patent of William
Vaughn, insolvent debtor.

Also found on earlier
Hampshire County records
with C. & I. Honig as pa-
permaker.

Very fine quality paper from Washington County
Common Pleas Court, October term 1787, bond of
James Galbraith and James Ross v. *Thomas Straw-
bridge.*

Washington County Common Pleas Court miscellaneous records; receipt from John Ross to Michael Jones, 1781.

Also on 1783 receipt from Henry Enoch to Michael Jones and Reuben Pribble.

Bail bond from Fayette County Common Pleas Court, December term 1784.

Compare with design of same subject with figure of Britannia, the fence (denoting the empire), and rampant lion in the 1781 Washington County records at top left.

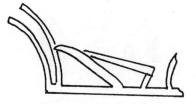

Hampshire County, Virginia, 1795 inventory of
Michael Harness, Sr. Appraiser, D. Welton.

Only watermark found with a
date; Martha and Matthias Marsh
appraisement. From West Virginia
University Library.

Left: Hampshire County, Virginia, court records, September term 1785. *Right:*
Fayette County court records, April 28, 1786, petition of Jacob Downer of Union-
town, insolvent debtor in "jaol."
Interesting variation in same design from same papermaker.

This watermark found in Hampshire County, Virginia, court records at West Virginia University Library, Morgantown, on Solomon Hedges bond, 1761, to George III for £1000, on 1769 George Parker paper, and on Jacob Shively estate sale bill for May 26, 1760.

Hampshire County, 1736, Jonathan Seaman to John Woodson, bond for £40, Pennsylvania money, both of Orange County, Virginia, "yeomen in the 10th year of our Sovereign Lord, George II." Witnessed by Morgan Morgan, first permanent white settler in West Virginia.

Washington County Common Pleas Court, June term 1786; *Archibald Steel* v. *Henry Heath.*

This design with slight variations also found on 1760-70 Hampshire County, Virginia, records.

Fayette County Common Pleas Court, September term 1784, *Thomas Gaddis for John Calhoun* v. *Wm. Henshaw and Jacob Springer.*

Fayette County Common Pleas Court, June term 1784, *John Irwin for David Irwin* v. *Andrew Grime* for wheat.

This design found in 1761 Hampshire County, Virginia, court records.

Note change from Maltese to Christian cross.

Fayette County Common Pleas Court, June 12, 1773, note of Samuel Miller.

428

Fayette County Common Pleas Court, June term 1785, Brackenridge case involving Hugh MacAnelly, John McKown, John Wilkins, Stephen Hall, Henry Swindler, Philip Pierce, John Simpson, and Samuel Kincaid—capias debt £5,000 Continental currency.

Most elaborate watermark found on any papers.

INDEX

438

Crooks, Richard, 92
Crooks, Thomas, 43
Cross Creek Village, 244, 377
Crow, Jacob, 350
Crow Massacre, 157
Crozier, Robert, 68
Cruger, Gen. David, 403
Cruger, Lydia Boggs Shepherd, 240, 402, 403
Crumrine, Boyd, 103, 139, 146, 172, 245, 272, 288, 289, 291, 334, 335
Crumrine, Daniel, 105, 106
Crumrine, Margaret Bower, 334
Crumrine Papers, 103, 105, 245, 335
Culbertson, Samuel, 66
Culpeper (family), 10
Cult of the Dead, 73, 76, 77
Cumberland, Md., 24, 128, 380, 382, 413, 415
Cumberland County, Pa., 66, 69, 250, 251, 286
Cumberland Road, 45, 71, 102, 111, 402
Cumberland Township (Greene), 175, 183, 194, 234, 335
Cunningham, Thomas, 271
Cunningham and Dill, 148 map, 202
Cure, John, 348
Curran, Charles, 294
Currin, Barney, 22
Curzon Chapel, 333, 339
Cusutha's (Guyasutha), 143, 144

Dagg, J., 348
Dailey, James, 146
Dandridge, 287
Darby, William, 288
Darlington, William M., 121

Darlington Library (University of Pittsburgh), 77, 122, 146
Darrah, Ann, 340
Dartmouth College, 342
Daubing Frolic, 266
Daughters of the American Revolution (Fort Pitt Chapter), 387
Daughters of the American Revolution (E. L. Hagan Chapter), 315
D.A.R. marker, 415
Davenport, James, 281
Davidson, Mrs., 342
Davidson, John, 22
Davidson, Joseph, 227, 228
Davidson, Thomas, 233
Davidson, William, 233
Davidson ferries, 227
Davin, Miles, 310
Davis, ——, 14
Davis, Azariah, 233
Davis, James, 233
Davis, David, 280 illus.
Davis, Martha, 300
Davis, Samuel, 289
Davis, William E. ("Bill"), 233, 324
Davison, George, 45 illus.
Davistown, Pa., 255, 258
Day, Aaron, 303, 304, 305, 306
Day, Ed, 309, 310
Day, Sherman, 121, 299, 311
Dearborn, Mich., 242
Dearman, Alexander, 419
Death, John, 91
Debolt, John, 362
Debolt, Nicholas, 362
Decker, Jacob, 69
Decker, John, 69
Decker, Moses, 69

McFarlane, Samuel, 223
McGee, ——, 225 illus.
McGiffin, Thomas, Esq., 102, 241
McGowan, James, 313
McGrew, James H., 315
McGuffey, William Holmes, 247
McGuffey buildings, 242
McGuffey Eclectic Readers, 247
McGuffey High School, 407
McGuffey schoolhouse, 410
McGuire, John, 22
McGuire, Samuel, 162, 164, 165, 168, 169
McHenry, Joseph, 155 illus.
McIntyre, John, 238, 239
McIntyre, William, 233
McKee, John, 350
McKeesport, Pa., 350, 416
McKelvy, William, 185
Mackey, Burl, 71
McKibbon, Thomas, 148 map
McKinley, William, 358
McKown, James, 155 illus.
McKown, John, 428
McLain, D., 190
McMahan, James, Esq., 39
McMechen, James, 58
McMillan, Rev. John, 267, 385
McMillan log cabin, 385
McMullen, Jerry, 329
McNath, James, 104 illus.
McNeely, Hugh, 277 illus.
McSherry, Keady, 99
Mad River, 180
Madison, James, 246
Madison, Pa., 416
Madison Square Garden, 329
Mahanna, Bradley, 307, 308
Maloney, ——, 14
Manning, James, 373
Manning, Milton, M.D., 373

Manuscript Found (novel), 342
Maple, Robert, 324
Mapletown, Pa., 360
Maria Forge, 107
Marianna, Pa., 396
Mariatta, John, 363
Marietta, Ohio, 62, 72, 250
Marion, Ohio, 395, 396
Market houses, 100 illus., 101, 278, 290, 293
Marmie, Peter, 183, 219
Marsh, Martha and Matthias, 425
Marshall, ——, 14
Marshall, Moses, 232
Marshall, Samuel, 377
Marshall, William, 148 map
Marshel, Col. James, 63
Marten, Charles, 280 illus.
Martin, ——, 65
Martin, Colonel, 12
Martin, Evelyn Thompson, 321
Martin, John, 91
Martin, Mary Walton, 167
Martin, Patrick, 300
Martin, American purple, 260
Maryland, 2, 13, 16, 26, 27, 44, 59, 97, 102, 118, 119, 121, 122, 126, 127, 177, 192 illus., 227, 248, 251
Maryland Archives, 127
Maryland Legislature, 122, 128
Mason, Charles, 28, 59
Mason, George, 146
Mason, John, 88
Mason-Dixon line, 28, 63, 70, 71, 183, 244, 255, 330
Masonic Lodge, 159
Masons, Order of, 307
Masontown, Pa., 88
Massasoit, 5
Mathers, Ebenezer, 314, 315
Mathers, Max, scrapbook, 314

472